I Believe in Church Growth

By the same author:

BORN INTO BATTLE
BODY BUILDING EXERCISES FOR THE LOCAL CHURCH

I Believe in Church Growth

by

EDDIE GIBBS

WILLIAM B. EERDMANS PUBLISHING COMPANY
GRAND RAPIDS, MICHIGAN

Printed in the United States of America.

First published 1981 by Hodder and Stoughton, London.
First American edition published 1982 through special arrangement with Hodder and Stoughton by Wm. B. Eerdmans Publishing Co., 255 Jefferson Ave. S.E., Grand Rapids, Michigan 49503.

Library of Congress Cataloging in Publication Data

Gibbs, Eddie.
I believe in church growth.

Bibliography: p. 454
1. Church growth. I. Title.
BV652.25.G48 1982 254'.5 81-22047
ISBN 0-8028-1921-4 AACR2

Acknowledgements

THIS BOOK WOULD never have appeared without the encouragement and practical help of a large number of people. I would therefore like to express my appreciation to Edward England who encouraged me to write it in the first place; to Tom Houston and the Bible Society who allowed me time away from a hectic office; to Dr Peter Wagner and other members of the faculty of the School of World Mission, Fuller Theological Seminary who stimulated my thinking and to whom this volume is presented in partial fulfilment of the D. Min. course requirements; to Peter Brierley, Ian Bunting and Fred Evans who read the first draft and gave me many valuable comments; to Lynda Barley of the Bible's Society's research department who helped me with the statistics; to my three daughters Rachel, Helen and Linda who tried to 'play very quietly' while dad marshalled his thoughts; to Honor Gilbert for reading the proofs; and to my son Stephen, and wife Renee who helped with the typing.

I would also like to thank Roy Pointer, the Bible Society church growth consultant, for bearing an extra work-load while I was preoccupied with this task. Lastly, but by no means least, I record my gratitude to all of the church leaders up and down the country who have attended the Bible Society basic church growth courses, who have provided so much material from their experience which they have permitted me to use in the following chapters.

To my wife Renee

Col. 2:19

Under Christ's control the whole body is nourished and held together by its joints and ligaments, and it grows as God wants it to grow.

(GNB)

Notes on Referencing system

As an aid to easy reference I have avoided page footnotes and end of chapter lists by following each quotation with the name of the author, the date of the publication and the page number. The titles of the books mentioned can be found at the end of the book in the Bibliography, listed alphabetically according to the author.

Contents

List of Figures

Editor's Preface

When has any book like *I Believe in Church Growth* been put out by an Englishman? It is not only an imaginative and illuminating new book, but almost a new *genre*. For a long time the churches in the West have been accustomed to think in terms of survival, not of growth. Battered by the disastrous results of the scientific controversies at the end of the last century, depressed by two world wars and the emerging secularism, all the denominations of mainline Christianity have been in retreat for years. Growth? Unthinkable!

Yet in the rest of the world it is not so. There are far more Christians in the world than there have ever been. Church growth is taking place (sometimes, as in South America and Africa, at a startling pace) in most parts of the world. The deadest areas are those traditionally associated with Christian culture, namely Western Europe: here the faith is in decline in most countries. But take Korea, Russia or China, Colombia or Uganda, or many parts of the United States, and a totally different picture emerges. The Church grows in size, vitality and sacrifice. Numbers are not the most important thing: qualities of character, service to others, confidence in the gospel, appropriate styles of leadership – these are some of the notable features. And in this book Eddie Gibbs, whose own background is far from the middle-class Anglicanism commonly found among English writers on religion, and whose experience is widely based in Europe and, much more important, in Latin America, gives a fascinating diagnosis of the Church's disease in the West and offers some prescriptions. If every clergyman were merely to read the chapter on 'Leadership and Relationships' this book would have been eminently worth while.

I commend *I Believe in Church Growth* with enthusiasm. It is quite different from the other books in the *I Believe* series, and could prove one of the most significant. Like Eddie Gibbs, I too believe in church growth, and have seen it happen in England and in many other countries. This book explains some of the principles which seem to underlie that growth, and makes it apparent that there is no part of the world where this might not happen – if we are prepared to pay the price.

MICHAEL GREEN

Prologue

As THE FAMILY service got under way the church was crowded wall-to-wall with people. Children were being coaxed out of the pews and seated in the chancel to make room for more adults. The sidesmen invited the people gathered in the porch to occupy the seats they had hurriedly arranged down the aisles. This was a relatively new problem for this West Midlands Anglican Church. 'How are we to cope with the growing crowds of young marrieds?' the vicar wondered. And he is not alone in his dilemma. During the last few months I have witnessed the same phenomenon in a Baptist church in Kent, a Methodist church in the north-west, and Anglican churches in Surrey and Merseyside. There are increasing signs of growth in many suburban churches in England which collectively are just beginning to turn the overall tide of Protestant churchgoing.

Come with me across the Atlantic to the West Coast of the United States. On the south-eastern outskirts of Los Angeles is the new housing development of Yorba Linda. The assembly hall of the Canyon High School is filled three times each Sunday with several thousand new Christians. The church, which has no premises of its own, is just four years old. The minister, John Wimber, who has the body build and voice-tone of Burl Ives, conducts the evening service from behind a synthesizer. As part of his 'backing group' there is a drummer and trombone player. Their easy-going leadership style and music tempo fits the congregation which largely consists of young people under the age of twenty-five. The minister, who baptises by immersion, jokes that he has baptised so many during the past few weeks that his skin has become permanently wrinkled. Now he has delegated his baptising to members of his congregation who perform the ceremony in their back-yard pools. Many of the converts are from the drug counter-culture. The church has no formal membership, but people are made to feel that they belong. He pauses in his sermon to say, 'Hi, there. Glad you made it,' to one person who has just sauntered to the front row looking for a seat. Part of the attraction of the church is that it has a strong doctrine of restoration as well as salvation. This is a church where you can fail and still come back. At the conclusion of the service groups gather around individuals who indicated that they wanted prayer. That night bodies, lives and relationships were healed. Physical healings take place and the pastor has the medical reports which testify to the fact.

This book is written for the growing number of ministers and lay Christians who long for fresh spiritual vitality and numerical growth to be experienced by their churches. For those totally new to church growth concepts it will probably be most helpful to read right through from the beginning. You will then become aware that the two opening chapters are different in emphasis from the bulk of the book. They are more theological and theoretical, providing a basis for the practical concerns covered in the following eight chapters.

I Believe in Church Growth is intended to serve as a practical handbook. For this reason each chapter is complete in itself, so the reader who is familiar with the broad field of church growth can select those sections which deal with the specific concerns which he has at the time of reading. Many practical suggestions are made in the course of each chapter which may be difficult to absorb and apply at one reading, so the volume is also intended to serve as a reference work, to which one can return to spark further ideas.

CHAPTER ONE

God's People and the Nations

1 A change of climate

THIS CENTURY HAS witnessed numerical church growth on an unprecedented scale according to a number of recent reports. In 1970 Bishop Stephen Neill challenged the widely held view that the Christian percentage of the world population has already begun to decrease and will continue to grow less till the end of the century, asserting to the contrary that the percentage of Christians has been slowly increasing since the beginning of the century (Neill 1970: 78, 79).

Detailed country by country surveys conducted by the Missions Advanced Research and Communications Centre as part of the Lausanne Committee for World Evangelisation programme have more than substantiated Bishop Neill's claim. Dr Ralph Winter reported that 'while non-Christians in Africa and Asia have more than doubled since 1900 and will more than triple by the year 2000, the number of Christians in Africa and Asia was in 1974 thirteen times what it was in 1900 and by 2000 it will be thirty-four times as large' (Evangelical Mission Quarterly Jan 1974: 12). According to the 1979 estimate of the MARC Centre, at a conservative estimate the churches are experiencing a daily net gain of 63,000 members and 1,600 new churches open each week around the world. In Africa alone 6,052,800 new Christians were added to the Church in the year 1978 (Information Service Lausanne Committee for World Evangelisation June 1979).

One of the most dramatic examples of Asian church growth is to be found in South Korea. Dr Joon Gon Kim reports that nineteen per cent of his country's population of 37 million are known Protestants. He also declares that sixty per cent of the soldiers are now professing Christians. On the final night of the four-day World Evangelisation Crusade held in Seoul, August 12–15, 1980, a crowd of 2.7 million gathered in the Yoido Plaza, a converted aerodrome! The Christians of South Korea are currently planning to send 10,000 of their number as missionaries to other parts of Asia! (ISL May 1980).

The Church in Indonesia has an annual growth rate of ten per cent, with an estimated two million people having been added to the Church in the last decade, mostly in the islands of Sumatra, Java and Kalimantan. Other growth spots include Nagaland in North India (now sixty six per cent Christian), Burma, Sarawak, the Philippines and Singapore.

In Latin America, where the population is nominally Catholic, but with church attendance below ten per cent, the Protestant churches have made enormous gains this century. In 1900 there are estimated to have been about 50,000 Protestants, the majority of whom were migrants from Northern Europe. In the early 70s the Protestant community numbered around twenty million (Wagner 1973:25), and today they are estimated to have passed the fifty million mark. Alongside this Protestant growth there is widespread evidence of Catholic renewal with a variety of emphases.

Dr Donald Anderson McGavran, one-time missionary in India and now Dean Emeritus of the School of World Mission, Fuller Seminary, Pasadena, USA, was among the first to urge the missionary agencies to believe that there was a receptive climate to the gospel in many areas of the world. Twenty years ago in his book *How Churches Grow* he wrote about 'a change of climate like the end of an ice age'. He maintained in the face of his unconvinced critics, that 'the chill wind of suspicion of the Christian faith has abated. The glaciers of an anti-Christian nationalism have retreated. The sun of faith has risen higher in the heavens. Explain it in whatever metaphor you will, churches can multiply.' (McGavran 1959:2).

He was aware of the preoccupation of western missionary agencies with social issues, providing life support systems for ailing national churches which they had brought into being, promoting ecumenism and exporting patterns of church organisation suited to slow growth. The fact that the great majority of the world's missionary personnel came from Europe and the United States, where either rapid church growth was largely unknown or numerical decline was accepted as the irreversible norm, meant that missionaries were either content with meagre results or perpetuated a maintenance attitude. He considered that their presuppositions blinded them to the growth potential around them, and caused them to hold back from supplying essential resources needed to reap a spiritual harvest.

This overriding concern has continued to burn through his speaking and writing over the years. Six years after writing *How Churches Grow* his appeal appeared in the influential *International Review of Missions* periodical. There he challenged the 'seed-sowing' concept of missions, that 'the objective and measurable growth of churches must neither be expected nor counted as a measure of effectiveness'. He argued for a narrow definition of mission, emphasising the goal of church planting, in place of one which 'attempts to take in everything that the Church and the Christian faith ought to do'. For McGavran 'the whole gospel for all mankind means little, unless it is preceded by stupendous church-planting. There can be little hope of sustained signs of the Kingdom in the world without the influence of a sufficient number of sons and daughters of the Kingdom. . . . What the fantastically mounting population of this world needs is fantastically multiplying churches. . . .' (IRM Oct 1965:451–461).

It was not until three years later that McGavran's outspoken article was challenged in the July number of *International Review of Missions*, which was dedicated entirely to the subject. Most of the articles were hostile to his position, but McGavran in his reply remained unrepentant. He declared that he was surprised at the depth and thrust of the anti-church growth sentiment in several of them, and hoped that when they saw their combined and enthusiastic opposition to the growth of Christ's Church, they themselves would be surprised and possibly dismayed. He ended his article with the observation that the preparatory documents for the 'Renewal in Mission' section of the Fourth Assembly of the World Council of Churches said precisely nothing about presenting the gospel to the two billion who now owe Jesus no allegiance (IRM July 1968:335–343).

2 Church growth and mission

At the heart of McGavran's position is the profound conviction that God wants lost people found. He believes that the Bible teaches that it makes an eternal difference whether a man believes in Jesus Christ as God and Saviour and becomes his disciple and a responsible member of his Church (IRM June 1968:337).

This concern reappears in his most comprehensive volume on church growth entitled *Understanding Church Growth*, which was published in 1970. There he concedes that 'Mission defined as "God's programme for man" is obviously many-sided. Each aspect of it can be called mission. Has God assigned any priority among these myriad good activities?. . . We believe He has. His will in these matters can be learned from His revelation and is mandatory for Christians' (McGavran 1970:31). 'The Finding God wants humankind brought into a redemptive relationship to Jesus Christ, where, baptised in His Name, they become part of His Household' (1970:32).

Dr McGavran, now in his mid-eighties, has become the sprightly patriarch as well as the sparring prophet of the church growth movement. Advancing years have in no way drained his enthusiasm. He still travels the world to add to his encyclopaedic knowledge and to test the church growth principles he has propounded.

Dr McGavran's combative style reflects the polarisation which existed in the mission debate in the 50s through to the early 70s. Then evangelicals were attacking what they considered to be the syncretism and universalism of the liberals, while the liberals accused the evangelicals of preaching a truncated gospel of personal salvation to the exclusion of social justice as an essential element of the Good News.

At the present time these important issues are far from being resolved. Yet a significant shift has taken place. The polarisation has given way to cross-pollination as the former combatants learn to listen to one another and as radical voices emerge within the various camps. Playing a significant role in this experience are those non-western churches which are both witnessing rapid church growth and at the same time proclaiming a gospel message which speaks with striking relevance to their situation.

Many radical Christians would remain unimpressed by the statistics with which we began this chapter. They are more concerned with the content and quality of the commitment rather than the numbers involved. This is a legitimate concern. Enrolment as church members cannot uncritically be equated with a genuine, life-transforming turning to Christ. It is a legitimate question to ask. What are they turning from and what are they turning to? On the other hand quality must not be set against quantity, for God has sent his Church into the world to make disciples. He longs for more Christians as well as better Christians. Numbers are not simply numbers; they stand for people, and each digit represents an individual of intrinsic worth and dignity, for people are made in the image of God.

In the early days of the formulation of church growth thinking there was an over-emphasis on the numerical growth of the empirical church. This stress represented an over-reaction to the non-growth presuppositions of many influential voices at the time. In the past decade there has been a growing concern among those identified with the church growth movement to come to terms with the quality of individual commitment and nominality within the existing church. These opening two chapters attempt to provide a theological contribution in that area.

Another criticism of the church growth emphasis must also be taken seriously into account. Sometimes church growth has been represented as the totality of mission. This may arise out of an extremely negative attitude to the world by some evangelicals, which results in mission being regarded as a rescue operation, saving individuals from a doomed cosmos sliding into chaos. Alternatively, it is argued that for society to be transformed the overwhelming priority must be given to evangelism until there are sufficient Christians to be able to influence their situation. This position is argued by Dr McGavran in his *International Review of Missions* article in 1965. However, it must be conceded that such results do not follow automatically. Church growth can result in decanting people from the world to seek an alternative sub-culture in isolation, rather than equipping the saints to act as yeast, salt and light in the world.

When church growth is regarded as the sum totality of mission it results in a preoccupation with the empirical church to the exclusion of the world. In contrast to this ecclesiastical narrowing of mission the Scriptures represent mission as being from God and directed to the whole world and every area of life. The contribution of the church growth emphasis is to draw attention to the centrality of the Church in God's cosmic plan, while its critics emphasise that God's concern is for the whole of his creation (Eph. 1:20–23; Col. 1:19–20). This being so, the Church must avoid an attitude of self-preoccupation, whether that be manifested by self-preservation or expansionism. The focus of our attention is not therefore the Church, but Christ and his world.

Orlando E. Costas, a Latin American Baptist theologian, has offered one of the most perceptive criticisms of church growth emphases from among the evangelical ranks. He writes:

> When church growth theorists affirm that the aim of evangelism is the multiplication of churches, they are advocating a theology that makes the Church the end of God's mission. Granted that the gospel is community-oriented. The question is whether the community is the objective or a result (a necessary and imperative one) of the communication of the gospel. Or to put it in other terms, whether the community is an ultimate or a penultimate goal of God's mission.
>
> Isn't the gospel the good news of the kingdom? Who is the centre of the kingdom – Christ or the Church? Who is the object of the kingdom – the community or the King? What is the aim of the kingdom – the exercise of Christ's righteous, peaceful, and loving reign in heaven and on earth in a restored and transformed universe, or the gathering of a community to Him? (Costas 1974:135).

These pertinent questions underline the fact that for the Church's witness to be authentic it must point beyond itself. Conscious of its weakness and source of life, the Church points to Christ who is Redeemer and Lord, and aware of its incompleteness it points forward to the Kingdom which, although already present in a provisional and fragmentary form, will one day come in completeness, power and manifest glory.

In order to appreciate the biblical expectations of growth, we turn now to a detailed examination of the witness of the people of God among the peoples of the world and in the following chapter consider the role of the Church as a sign and servant of the Kingdom which God is bringing into being.

3 God's concern for his entire creation (Gen. 1–11)
The Dutch missionary theologian, J. H. Bavinck, writes that, 'At first sight the Old Testament appears to offer little basis for the idea of missions. This part of the Bible speaks of bloody wars and the annihilation of various heathen peoples; it appears to have very little room for mercy, nor does it seem ready to grant the blessings of the gospel to the heathen' (Bavinck 1961:11). Yet on closer reading we discover a more promising scenario.

The scene is set for mission in the Old Testament doctrine of creation. The Bible is unique among ancient records in making this the starting-point for the history of a nation. The entire world, including all its inhabitants, is regarded as belonging to God, for he created it in the beginning and continually sustains it (Gen. 1–2; Pss 24; 33:13; 47:2). His watchful eye is upon the world so that nothing escapes his notice. He exercises a universal jurisdiction, which means that not only Israel, but all the nations, are accountable to him. 'God is not localised in His interests and activities; He is the God of the nations. No one escapes his provisions, though nations may grossly misuse such. None evades His moral government. He is present in a certain sense everywhere, even though He has chosen to limit his unique disclosures to and through a particular people. Thus universality and particularism are not mutually exclusive' (Peters 1972:108).

In the section 'A covenant to embrace all nations' we will explore in detail the relationship of God to his creation as it begins to unfold in the stories of Adam and Eve and Noah and his family.

4 Abraham: a blessing to the nations
Scripture explains the origin of the people of God not in terms of natural causes, but as a consequence of divine initiative. God calls an individual, Abram, out of Ur of

the Chaldees. From the outset the people of God are the people of the word. They are those who hear and obey the command of God and place their confidence in his promises. The faith of Abram gave him a new identity signalled by the new name of Abraham, which God bestowed on him. This faith and that of the Patriarchs in general is not expressed as a response to specific laws, but in following where God directs. It is being prepared to step out without knowing beforehand the destination; to leave a life of settled security for one of pilgrimage, not really belonging anywhere, and constantly encountering new situations (Heb. 11:8–10).

The most emphatic indication of God's intention for the nations of the world is to be found in his promise to the aged and childless couple Abram and Sarai. He reassured them with these words: 'I will give you many descendants, and they will become a great nation. I will bless you and make your name famous, so that you will be a blessing.

> I will bless those who bless you,
> But I will curse those who curse you.
> And through you I will bless all the nations.' (Gen. 12:2–3)

The Good News Bible provides a footnote which gives as an alternative translation of the last phrase: 'All nations will ask me to bless them as I have blessed you.' The Old Testament scholar Gerhard von Rad comments that, 'The question has been raised at vs 2b and 3b whether the meaning is only that Abraham is to become a formula for blessing, that his blessing is to become far and wide proverbial' (cf. Gen. 48:16). Against this weakened understanding he maintains that 'the accepted interpretation must therefore remain: It is like "a command to history". Abraham is assigned the role of a mediator of blessing in God's saving plan, for "all the families of the earth" ' (von Rad 1961:155).

Such a far-flung, if unspecified, promise emphasises from the outset that God is not calling a people to himself to the exclusion of the nations but for the sake of all nations – that they might share in the blessing. The substance of this blessing does not become clear until the New Testament (Acts 3:25; Rom. 4:12; Gal. 3:8–16). His role is described in the new name which God gave him, 'Abraham', which sounds like the Hebrew for 'ancestor of many nations' (Gen. 17:5).

Abraham stands as a spiritual prototype. He hears the call of God to leave Babylonia and venture out in faith not knowing where that might lead him (Gen. 12:1; Heb. 11:8). His attitude of trust and confidence in God serves as a model of the kind of response that God seeks from man in every age. It is this which puts him in a right relationship to God. Man is justified by his faith not by his works (Rom. 4:9), yet that faith must be shown to be genuine by our practical response (Jas. 2:21, 23). In exercising faith Abraham was prepared to commit everything.

The Old Testament establishes Abraham as a reference point to remind Israel that her very existence has its historical roots in the call of God. His covenant with Abraham gave birth to the nation (Ex. 2:24; Lev. 26:42; 2 Kings 13:23; Ps. 105:9). Yet such a guarantee of God's continuing commitment to his people was open to manipulation and mis-application by the unscrupulous. At the time of Israel's defeat and exile experience, there were those left in the land who took advantage of the situation to annex abandoned properties on the ground that they were the inheritors of the promises given to Abraham (Ezek. 33:24)! The promises of God can all too easily be severed from their contexts and made to mean what people want them to mean to serve their own purposes.

Through succeeding centuries Abraham presents a constant challenge to the people of God. He confronts their complacency and serves as a reminder of the saving initiative of God. Our Lord challenged those who presumed to say, 'We have Abraham as our father,' by telling them that God was able to make descendants for Abraham even from the stones scattered around them. (Matt. 3:9). Later in response to the faith displayed by the centurion Jesus challenged the Jewish bystanders, 'I tell you, I have never found anyone in Israel with faith like this. I assure you that many will come from the east and the west and sit down with Abraham, Isaac, and Jacob at the feast in the Kingdom of Heaven. But those who should be in the Kingdom will be thrown out into the darkness. . . .' (Matt. 8:10–12).

St Paul also speaks to the racially mixed churches in Rome and Galatia reminding them that they share a common ancestor in Abraham, who is the spiritual father of all who believe (Rom. 4:11). 'You should realise then, that the real descendants of Abraham are the people who have faith' (Gal. 3:7).

So the promise made many years before to Abraham finds its fulfilment not simply in the emergence of the nation of Israel, but in the Church of Jesus Christ. His life of faith in God shows how mankind can enter the Kingdom and be incorporated into the Church of Jesus Christ. It also underlines the fact that life and growth can occur in seemingly impossible circumstances, for Abram and Sarai were well past the years of normal parenthood when they were given offspring. They were not simply encouraged to think in terms of an intimate family circle to comfort them in old age, but to see far into the future to a phenomenal expansion. God helped Abram comprehend something of the immensity of his purposes by pointing him to the stars in the sky, speaking in terms of the sand on the seashore, assuring him, 'You will have as many descendants as that.' (Gen. 15:5; 22:17; 32:12; 2 Sam. 17:11; 1 Kings 4:20). When we here in urban Britain look up, we more often see clouds and look down to see concrete. But behind the clouds are the myriads of stars, and under the concrete (and indeed within the concrete!) are the countless grains of sand of God's unbreakable promise regarding the expansion of his Church.

5 A covenant to embrace all nations

The term 'covenant' means an agreement or solemn pact. Here we are concerned with the covenants (for more than one are mentioned in Scripture) that God makes with humankind. Such agreements are not the result of negotiation between equal partners, but are the expressions of God's gracious initiatives. They are neither merited nor manufactured by man. They are given by God.

5.1 The covenant with Adam and Eve

Some scholars, particularly within the Reformed tradition, see the first covenant obligation in the Adam and Eve story, where these persons, made 'in the image and likeness of God', are first blessed by him and then commanded to 'have many children, so that your descendants will live all over the earth and bring it under control'. God tells them, 'I am putting you in charge of the fish, the birds, and all the wild animals. I have provided all kinds of grain and all kinds of fruit for you to eat' (Gen. 1:28). This is the classic covenant form: the granting of a blessing 'which bestows not only a gift but a function' (Kidner 1967:52), leading to the acceptance of responsibilities and the assurance of provision. This command to propagate and to take charge is given to man as God's vassal. It is, therefore, not simply a cultural mandate, but a covenant mandate (Conn 1976:2, 3), to extend the conditions which prevailed in Eden throughout God's entire creation.

5.2 The covenant with Noah

The first occurrence of the term 'covenant' is to be found in Genesis 6:18, where God makes Noah and his family the sole exceptions to his purpose of destroying mankind through the Flood. He is spared because he is found to be a righteous man, that is, a man who stood in right relationship to God in response to his covenant obligations (von Rad 1961:116). God warns him of his intentions and instructs him to construct a boat according to his specifications in which he and his family and representative livestock will be able to survive. 'Everything on the earth will die, but I will make a *covenant* with you. Go into the boat with your wife. . . .' Here the covenant concept is essentially linked with God's saving intention. Noah 'goes into the ark not as a mere survivor, but as the bearer of God's promise for a new age' (Kidner 1967:89).

The full extent of the covenant blessings, beyond the initial act of preservation, is not spelt out until the flood waters have subsided and the occupants are free to roam on dry land again (Gen. 9:9–17). This covenant is *universal*, embracing 'all living beings', which includes animals as well as humans. It is *permanent*, applying not only to Noah and his generation, but to his descendants. Therefore it is termed an 'everlasting covenant'. Furthermore, it is *ratified by a sign* for all to see – the rainbow in the skies – which will serve as a reminder not only to man but also to God, of his promise never again to destroy all living beings by flood waters. The glory of the rainbow against the gloom of the clouds shines as a token of God's grace (Kidner 1967:102).

The Adamic and the Noachic covenants, which are both universal in their scope, provide the broad basis against which God's narrower, elective covenants should be seen. Through them God's gracious will is assured to all humankind.

Some have seen in the sign of the bow in the sky a picture of God having put aside his bow of war (von Rad 1961:130). The same word is used for both in Hebrew as in English. God will still exercise forbearance in the face of human violence, guaranteeing the continuance of the stability of the natural order, although the repeated occurrence of floods, earthquakes and famines at the local and regional level still serves to warn us against complacency and defiance towards God. 'The *natural* orders, fixed by God's word, mysteriously guarantee a world in which in His own time God's *historical* saving activity will begin' (von Rad 1961:130). In the experience of Noah, as in the outworking of future covenants, we see that God's selectivity is with a view to universal benefit.

5.3 The covenant with Abraham

This important development can be dealt with briefly at this point because we have already considered how God called this man to be his 'friend' (Is. 41:8; 2 Chron. 20:7; Jas. 2:23) as a prototype of the life of faith. Here we simply pause to mention some of the main points specifically relating to the covenant which God made with him.

As on previous occasions, the covenant is made through God's gracious initiative. For Abraham the circumstances are awesome, as he watches a flaming torch passing through the dismembered animals which God had ordered him to prepare (Gen. 15). Once again the covenant is described as 'everlasting' (Gen. 17:7). And his election is not exclusive, but extensive; it is with the blessing of all nations in view. There is also ratification by a sign, not this time displayed by God, but administered by man in the form of circumcision (Gen. 17:11). In other contemporary cultures where circumcision was practised, it was as a puberty rite marking manhood. Here it has a distinctive meaning which is indicated by its early administration when the male child was only eight days old (Gen. 17:11, 12). It signifies purification and separation for God from the time of birth and within the context of the family of God.

5.4 The covenant with Moses

This covenant is superimposed on the Abrahamic pact to prepare the people of God to meet an entirely new situation. From being a people, or kinship group, they are now to become a nation alongside other nations. Israel is about to become 'a political entity and begins to take a place in the history books' (Goldingay 1975:6). The radical change of status from slavery to nationhood was only made possible by divine initiative, securing the release of Israel from the oppression of the Egyptians through a series of miraculous interventions.

As a small emergent nation, occupying militarily indefensible territory between the powerful pincer arms of Egypt and Babylon, she could not hope to survive without the protection of Yahweh her God. She was not only vulnerable to attack from outside her borders, but to moral and spiritual subversion from within generated by the Canaanite enclaves which survived the conquest. In anticipation of the complex legislation required by Israel's promotion to nationhood, the covenant with Moses 'itemises her commitment' (Goldingay 1975:7) with detailed ethical, social and cultic requirements.

While the Mosaic covenant set Israel apart from the nations, it by no means excluded them from its benefits. There are specific provisions laid down for non-Israelites to become members of God's people. The qualification for membership is not birth, but willingness to commit oneself. From the time of the Exodus from Egypt foreigners formed part of the company (Exod. 12:38; Num. 11:4). The subsequent narrative continues to provide instances of an openness to others. This is seen in the case of the Midianite priest (Exod. 18:11, 12), Caleb the Edomite (Num. 13, 14), Rahab the harlot (Josh. 2:1–11, 6:25), the Gibeonites (Josh. 9:9, 10) and the surrender and willing allegiance of the inhabitants of Shechem (Josh. 24).

Let us now pause to summarise the main features of the covenant relationship.

In the first place the covenant represents *an intensely personal relationship*. The God of Israel was one who calls by name. 'It is in the realm of the personal, which is the highest we know . . . only a person can send' (Davidson 1969:23). This was the experience of Moses at the burning bush (Exod. 3:4–10). God called him by name, 'Moses. Moses!' He identified himself as the God of his ancestors, Abraham, Isaac and Jacob. He makes Moses realise he is fully aware of the appalling conditions which his people are enduring in Egypt, and that he intends to do something about it. His first move is to send Moses to appeal to Pharaoh, King of Egypt. But when the initial approach by Moses and Aaron, his spokesman, prove to be of no avail God then reveals to his servant Moses that he intends to take matters into his own hands (Exod. 6:2–10).

Secondly, the covenant represents *a redemptive relationship*. Redemption signifies deliverance from bondage and propitiation for sin by the payment of a price. God's people in Egypt were preserved from the destroying angel by the offering of a passover lamb and the smearing of its blood on their door posts and lintels. This Passover sacrifice remained at the heart of the elaborate sacrificial system which was subsequently initiated, serving as an annual reminder of God's mercy. In the Jewish sacrificial system the price paid to secure forgiveness of sins was the shed blood of the innocent victim represented by the animal or bird offered in sacrifice. This price is not paid by the man offering the animal, but by God who gave the life which was to be sacrificed. In Hebrew thinking the life of the animal was considered to be in the blood, and God was the giver of life. Redemption, therefore, speaks of what God does for man to secure his release from the punishment, bondage and guilt of sin. How great is the full cost of man's redemption is not clearly revealed until God's redemptive plan is finally fulfilled in the sending of his only Son to give his life as a ransom (i.e. redemption price) for many (Mark 10:45; Eph. 1:7; Rom. 3:24; Heb. 9:15; 1 Cor. 6:19f; 7:22f).

Thirdly, the covenant describes *a responsible relationship* initiated by God, establishing a mutual pact, in which man is held accountable before God for his actions. It is a call to an ongoing relationship as adopted children who are required to live a distinctive life-style to show to the world what God intends for his people, and requires of them. His people are called to be holy because he is holy (Lev. 19:2; 1 Pet. 1:15; Heb. 12:14). The covenant relationship demands an unreserved allegiance to God and obedience to his commands. It emphasises that covenant privileges carry covenant obligations.

Fourthly, the covenant makes possible *an extendable relationship*. J. H. Bavinck, the Dutch missiologist, makes clear it is precisely this covenant relationship that opens up the possibilities for mission. 'If Jehovah is the God of Israel because He has made a covenant with Israel, it is conceivable that other nations will also some day be included in that covenant. For Israel has no individual and peculiar claim upon God; its privileged position is due solely to God's electing grace. Israel is not better than other nations, it simply bears greater honour and greater responsibility. And its distinction consists precisely in the fact that it may and shall be the means by which other nations shall one day receive the salvation of Israel's God' (Bavinck 1961:14). This glorious prospect is eventually realised through the operation of the new covenant which we now move on to consider.

5.5 The new covenant

As God's people repeatedly fail to live up to the demands of the covenant relationship and sense the inadequacy of the sacrificial system to cover their failings, for there was no offering which could secure forgiveness for wilful disobedience, so they come to realise that God's demands can only be met in his strength. Their own is demonstrably inadequate. So God speaks to his wayward people through the prophet Jeremiah, promising a new covenant. There will be a continuity with the old in terms of his promises and requirements, yet there is also a fundamental difference. The Lord declares, 'It will not be like the old covenant that I made with their ancestors when I took them by the hand and led them out of Egypt. Although I was like a husband to them, they did not keep that covenant. The new covenant that I will make with the people of Israel will be this: I will put my law within them and write it on their hearts. I will be their God, and they will be my people. None of them will have to teach his fellow-countryman to know the Lord, because all will know me, from the least to the greatest. I will forgive their sins and I will no longer remember their wrongs. I, the Lord, have spoken' (Jer. 31:31–34).

The essential distinction lies in the fact that the new covenant will not be one of external requirements and restraints, but of an inward motivation and constraint, for the law will be written on their hearts.

When the people of God are truly renewed they will become the servant of the Lord, embodying the new covenant, then the Lord will be able to fulfil his wider purposes through them. 'Through you I will make a *covenant with all peoples*; through you I will bring light to the nations.' (Is. 42:6). The phrase italicised is literally 'covenant of people', which has led some interpreters to restrict the description to Israel. However, the Good News Bible rendering is justified in that the same word 'people' is used in the singular in the previous verse with reference to the entire population of the earth – 'He (God) fashioned the earth and all that lives there; He gave life and breath to all its *people*.' Furthermore, the second half of verse 6 provides as a poetic parallel to 'covenant of people', 'a light to the nations'. Ulrich Simon in his commentary on this verse writes that the Servant 'is wholly dedicated to God and in that sense He *is* the embodiment of the covenant which He also mediates. The relationship sheds all legalistic limitations and is restated in terms of transcendent promise and of human need. It concerns itself not with external data, as in a court of law where judgement is given *about* cases, but conveys a direct personal union between God and man' (Simon 1953:87).

The same phrase 'covenant of people' occurs a second time in Isaiah. In chapter 49, verse 8, God declares, 'I will guard and protect you and through you make a *covenant with all peoples*'.

The covenant idea testifies to God's consistent desire to establish an intimate relationship with his people. In the Old Testament the main thrust relates to his special commitment to Israel, and their persistent unresponsiveness constantly frustrates his wider purposes. All that we can detect are occasional hints and prods which only become explicit in the New Testament.

The Epistle to the Hebrews twice refers to the prophecy of the New Covenant in Jeremiah, chapter 31. The author sees its fulfilment in the coming of Christ, who inaugurates the New Covenant by becoming both the Great High Priest and the all-sufficient sacrifice for sins (Heb. 8:7–13; 10; 15ff; 4:14ff; 7:23ff; 9:25ff). This is not simply the fanciful exegesis of a Judeo-Christian apologist, for Christ himself, in offering the cup of his disciples during the Last Supper, declared, 'Drink this all of you, . . . this is my blood which seals God's covenant, my blood poured out for many for the forgiveness of sins' (Matt. 26:27, 28; see also Mark 14:24; Luke 22:20; 1 Cor. 11:25). The Lukan and Pauline versions explicitly state that the cup represents God's '*new covenant*', and some versions of the other Gospel accounts include the adjective '*new*'.

The coming of the Holy Spirit on the disciples individually and corporately provides that new relationship anticipated by the prophets. In the Upper Room the Lord reassured his followers he would not leave them orphaned, but would send another Comforter, who would dwell among them and teach them (John 14:17). He abides with them both to witness *to* them of the Lord's living presence and to witness *through* them to reveal the nature and power of God to the world (Acts 1:8). In addition to operating through his followers that same Spirit is at work in the world to 'convince (convict) the world concerning sin and righteousness and judgement' (John 16:8).

Thus the New Covenant holds out the prospect of mission which is startlingly realised through the witness of the disciples and the thousands throughout the Mediterranean world who responded to their testimony. There is a further faint echo of Jeremiah's prophecy in Paul's words to the Corinthian believers whose radically changed lives read like an open letter from Christ himself (2 Cor. 3:1–3).

This covenant relationship also serves as a constant reminder to the Church that she herself is subject to him. She has no monopoly on God, and she has no magical power with which to manipulate him. Her task is to bear faithful witness to a covenant relationship which she has neither earned nor deserved. Her witness is at best partial and approximate. In drawing people to herself she points beyond herself to a covenant-keeping God who grieves over, struggles with and yet delights in his people. A growing Church must be continually experiencing correction, reformation and renewal.

6 The Temple: a house of prayer for all nations

King Solomon's prayer on the occasion of the consecration of the Temple in Jerusalem reveals that he regarded it as far more than a national shrine. He envisages it becoming a place of international pilgrimage. As foreigners hear of the great things which God will do for his people, so they will want to come and worship. Solomon beseeches God to hear the prayers of these pagan pilgrims 'so that all the peoples of the world may know you and obey you, as your people Israel do. Then they will know that this Temple I have built is the place where you are worshipped' (1 Kings 8:43).

The prophets Isaiah and Micah take up this theme, foretelling the day when the Temple will become the centre on which the nations will converge in their search for the one, true and living God.

In days to come
  the mountain where the Temple stands
  will be the highest one of all,

towering above all the hills.
Many nations will come streaming to it,
and their people will say,
Let us go up the hill of the Lord,
to the Temple of Israel's God.
He will teach us what he wants us to do;
we will walk in the paths he has chosen.
For the Lord's teaching comes from Jerusalem;
from Zion he speaks to his people.
(Is. 2:2, 3 and Mic. 4.2)

Yet Israel must not thereby think that God's presence in her midst secured automatic immunity from enemy attack or conquest. If God's people persisted in a rebellious attitude then his glory would depart from the Temple and his protection would be removed. This is in fact what happened. As a consequence of Israel's idolatry and social injustices she was defeated by the Assyrians and the Temple was looted by Nebuchadnezzar in 587 BC and destroyed soon after.

When the Jewish exiles began to return in 537 under Cyrus the Temple site was reconsecrated and the repairs started. The rebuilding was completed in the period between 520 and 510 BC. Years later Herod made substantial alterations and additions to this modest structure. He began work in 19 BC, but his building programme was hardly finished before the Romans destroyed it completely as a reprisal to a Jewish insurrection in AD 70.

Our Lord, on visiting the Temple, was grieved at the way religion had been commercialised. As he overthrew the tables of the money-changers he recalled the words of Isaiah, 'My Temple shall be called a house of prayer for the people of all nations' (Is. 56:7). Instead of that prophecy being fulfilled they had turned it into a hideout for thieves (Mark 11:17). Consequently he warned his disciples that it would be completely destroyed during their generation.

However, the destruction of the sacred edifice did not

signify the removal of the possibility of a meeting-place between God and man. Jesus transferred the Temple concept from a place to his own person. He became the new Temple – that is the focal meeting-place where people could experience the mercy and grace of God (Matt. 27:51). Thus, when he died on the cross, 'the curtain of the temple was torn in two from top to bottom' (Luke 23:45). The direction of the tear demonstrated that it was an act of God which opened the holy of holies to every believer as they put their trust in Christ who was High Priest and Sacrifice as well as Temple. In this radical form the Temple became truly universalised. Furthermore every believer is described as 'temple of God', that is the place where he dwells by the Holy Spirit (1 Cor. 3:16, 17; 6:16), and believers collectively grow together to become a sacred temple dedicated to the Lord (Eph. 2:21). When John the Divine is granted a vision of heaven he observes that there is no temple to be found there. 'I did not see a temple in the city, because its temple is the Lord God Almighty and the Lamb' (Rev. 21:22).

The vision of the Old Testament prophets finds its fulfilment not in the nations streaming to the Temple on Jerusalem's Mount Zion, but in their being drawn to Christ himself through the witness of the people he indwells.

At the same time we must recognise that these expressions of God's universal rule and call to the nations to acknowledge him represent the songs of pilgrims and Temple worshippers and not evangelists. 'Such expressions are not missionary preaching in the strict sense of the word. It is quite possible that such utterances were not heard by a single pagan' (Bavinck 1961:16).

Viewed from the vantage point of the New Testament dispensation the Psalms teach us that mission is rooted in and inspired by the worship of the community. True praise provides a clearer vision of the world and its need. This safeguards us from the danger of seeing mission in terms of human activism and the extension of our ecclesiastical institutions. The raison d'être of mission is nothing less than the universal rule of God. This same perspective is drawn by Matthew in his version of the Great Commission. The command to go and make disciples of *all nations* occurs as a consequence of the ascended Christ having been given *all authority* in heaven and earth (Matt. 28:19). This places church growth firmly within a Kingdom context.

7 A glorified people attracting the nations

The Old Testament emphasis is not on Israel moving out in mission, but on the nations spontaneously converging on Jerusalem. They are attracted by the evidence of the God of Israel uniquely and gloriously present in the midst of his people. So they come to pay homage to a foreign deity, not compelled by conquest but convinced by the covenant God has established with Israel and extends to the world.

Pilgrims en route for Zion will encourage others to join their ranks: 'Those from one city will say to those from another, "We are going to worship the Lord Almighty and pray for His blessing. Come with us" ' (Zech. 8:21). The response will be widespread including 'many peoples and powerful nations'. Wherever Jews are to be found they will become the centre of attention surrounded by those seeking to share their destiny because the news has been spread abroad that God is with them (Zech. 8:23; see also Hab. 2:14; Zech. 8:22, 23: Mal. 1:11).

'Arise, Jerusalem, and shine like the sun; the glory of the Lord is shining on you! Other nations will be covered by darkness, but on you the light of the Lord will shine; the brightness of His presence will be with you. Nations will be drawn to your light, and kings to the dawning of your new day' (Isa. 60:1–3).

Israel is called by God to be a witnessing people. The form of her witness is not so much a missionary force as a magnetic presence. Her quality of life was intended to demonstrate to the surrounding nations that God was in her midst. As a consequence they would be attracted to Jerusalem where the throne of God was located to enjoy his presence and offer him sacrifice and service. '. . . As far as is known, Judaism was never a missionary force in the sense that organised efforts were made by the Jews as a whole to win others. We have no evidence that Jews were sent to Palestine with the express purpose of winning converts to Judaism, or that Jews of Palestine felt any personal responsibility for this work. It was left to the individuals who made contact with non-Jews in the lands to which they were scattered to make converts or not as they felt inclined' (Rowley 1950:92).

The clearest challenge to Israel to be open to the possibility of other nations responding to God's law appear in the stories of Ruth, Jonah and Daniel. The first of these shows how a foreign Moabite woman becomes a member of one of the most respected families in Israel, thereby becoming the great-grandmother of King David. The book of Jonah describes the begrudging responses of a prophet of Israel to the Lord's command to warn Nineveh, capital of Assyria, of God's impending judgement. He cannot come to terms with God's intention to have mercy on the implacable enemy of Israel. The prophet's intolerance is in stark contrast to God's patience. Jonah chose to sulk outside the city, longing for God's judgement to fall, rather than proclaim the message of God's love to the repentant Ninevites (Jonah 4:2). He is more concerned about a castor oil plant which perished, thus denying him shade, than with the fate of the 120,000 people in the city who were so confused they didn't know their right hand from their left. The isolated and resentful Jonah is held up to Israel as a mirror image of their exclusiveness.

The third story describes how Daniel and his friends were transported to Babylon during the time of the exile. It tells how they face the challenge to their way of life presented by their conquerors. Yet God enables them to remain faithful. Furthermore, he gives them insights beyond those possessed by the greatest minds of that renowned civilisation. The message is clear. Provided Israel remains faithful to the Lord, she has nothing to fear and much to give. She holds the key to unlock the meaning of history.

It is evident from our Lord's condemnation of the leaders of the law and Pharisees who sailed the seas and crossed whole countries to win one convert (Matt. 23:15) that some zealous individuals did feel inclined to propagate their religion. But those were exceptions. In the main, Gentiles were left to take the initiative if they felt attracted to Judaism. Those Gentiles who attached themselves to the Synagogues of the Jews were technically known as 'god-fearers'. It was this group which was frequently ready to respond to Paul's preaching as he visited synagogues throughout Asia and Macedonia to proclaim and argue the gospel during his missionary journeys.

Before Israel could become a light to the nations she had to experience a genuine conversion herself. Jeremiah describes her as unfaithful Israel needing to turn back to God. When she demonstrated a genuine repentance then she would know the mercy of God and his law would be written in their hearts. 'When that time comes, Jerusalem will be called "The Throne of the Lord", and all nations will gather there to worship me.' (Jer. 3:17; 31:31–34). As the details of this expectation unfold it becomes clear that this spontaneous coming will not be within the normal course of history, but will be a direct result of the coming of the Messiah and the outpouring of the Holy Spirit (Joel 2:28).

In the New Testament we find that this stress on the centripetal movement of magnetism is not entirely displaced by the centrifugal movement of mission. The New Testament church is described in a number of places as an *attracting* fellowship. The Lord prayed for his disciples just prior to his arrest and crucifixion, 'May they be one, so that the world will believe that you sent me. I gave them the same glory you gave me, so that they may be one, just as you and I are one: I in them and you in me, so that they may be completely one, in order that the world may know that you sent me and that you love them as you love me' (John 17:21–23). The unity of which the Lord speaks is not a regimented uniformity but a supernatural harmony, orchestrated by God through his Spirit at work within them. The word 'glory' refers to the manifest presence of God among his people.

Christ assured his followers that his death on the cross would itself have enormous drawing-power. It brought about the overthrow of the 'ruler of this world' so that Satan would not be able to restrain those whom the Spirit moved to respond to the gospel. 'When I am lifted up from the earth, I will draw everyone to me' (John 12:32).

The church in Jerusalem so manifested the presence of God through miracles and wonders that everyone was filled with awe, and their depth of commitment and degree of practical concern made such an impression that they enjoyed the good will of all the people. They could not simply be ignored. 'And every day the Lord added to their group those who were being saved' (see Acts 2:43–47). This response did not simply occur as a result of their evangelistic zeal, but through the fact that they were such an effective advertisement to the value of knowing God.

Writing in old age John reflects on the nature of the invitation which the Church issued. 'What we have seen and heard we announce to you also, so that you will join with us in the fellowship that we have with the Father and with His son Jesus Christ. We write this in order that our joy may be complete' (1 John 1:3). The Church has no hesitancy in inviting others to join them because what they enjoyed was worth sharing. To deny others would be to deprive them of blessing.

There can be no spiritually significant church growth without church renewal. Our Lord warned that not all growth is valuable or even desirable. Weeds which have every appearance of being wheat will grow up alongside the genuine wheat, but would bear no fruit and would ultimately be separated for burning (Matt. 13:24–30; 36–43). A fig tree with foliage but no fruit was cursed by Christ (Luke 13:6–9). True growth is not so much the result of activism and popularity, as an evidence of a unique quality of personal and corporate life, which comes into being because God is with his people.

8 The servant of the Lord: a light to the nations

The servant appears in Isaiah, chapters 40–55, where he is mentioned eighteen times. Scholars have argued at length over his identity. In the earlier references it seems to be the nation as a whole who is referred to. This is quite explicit in Is. 41:8.

But you, Israel my servant,
you are the people I have chosen,
the descendants of Abraham, my friend.

The context underlines the fact that servanthood was a privilege, they were chosen by God for the role and could count on his protection. He had been at work behind the scenes to create the conditions for Israel to return to Israel from exile. Cyrus, the Persian emperor, had, without realising it, been God's instrument to help God's servant Israel (45:4) by overthrowing their Babylonian captors (41:2, 25). If Cyrus could not be expected to realise the significance of current events, Israel had no excuse. She had failed to learn the lessons of the exile, which had come upon her on account of her disobedience, neither did she apparently see the hand of God to secure their return, which prompted God to exclaim,

Is anyone more blind than my servant,
more deaf than the messenger I send?
Israel, you have seen so much,
but what has it meant to you?
You have ears to hear with,

but what have you really heard?
(42:19, 20)

God does not abandon his servant Israel. He calls upon her to bear witness to him as the one true God, who in contrast to man-made idols, lives and speaks. He predicts what is to happen and provides insight into the significance of events (43:10; 44:6–8). Their obstinacy in refusing to listen to God's voice meant that they were both defeated militarily and depleted in numbers.

If only you had listened to my commands!
Then blessings would have flowed for you
like a stream that never goes dry!
Victory would have come to you
like the waves that roll on the shore.
Your descendants would be as numerous as grains of sand,
and I would have made sure they were never destroyed.
(48:18–19)

But God gives her another chance.

Go out from Babylon, go free!
Shout the news gladly; make it known everywhere:
The Lord has saved his servant Israel!'
(48:20)

He restores her to her land (48:2) and calls upon her to bear her witness to him as the one true God.

Within the concept of the servant as the personification of the nation begins to emerge an individual servant who embodies Israel's mission, and surpasses her in the fulfilment of that mission (Rowley 1950:119). The first glimpse occurs in chapter 42:1–4, where the servant of the Lord is described as filled with the Spirit and with the assurance that he will succeed in his mission to bring justice to every nation. His approach to achieve this end will be a gentle one. He will speak in a quiet and restrained manner, he supports the bruised and broken plant, and blows into flame the dying spark.

The servant has a two-fold task, which is described in chapter 49:1–6. Firstly, he is appointed to bring back his scattered people (v. 5). Yet in this he is frustrated by their unresponsiveness (v. 4). His second assignment is of a much wider nature.

I have a greater task for you, my servant.
Not only will you restore to greatness
the people of Israel who have survived,
but I will also make you a light to the nations –
so that all the world may be saved.

(49:6)

However, this will not be accomplished without suffering. He will be rejected by men, despised and brutally ill-treated so that people will not bear to look at him. They will turn their backs believing he is finished (50:6–7; 52:14; 53:2, 3).

Yet the suffering of the servant will attract world-wide attention.

'But now many nations will marvel at him,
and kings will be speechless with amazement.
They will see and understand
something they had never known.'
The people reply,
'Who would have believed what we now report?
Who could have seen the Lord's hand in this?'

(52:15–53:1)

When its significance is explained to them they will be overwhelmed, it will seem utterly incredible. In the first place *he was an innocent victim*. His God-inflicted suffering was undeserved. The pain he bore was the punishment which those who tortured and killed him should have borne.

But he endured the suffering that should have been ours,
the pain that we should have borne.
All the while we thought that his suffering
was punishment sent by God.
All of us were like sheep that were lost,
each of us going his own way.
But the Lord made the punishment fall on him,
the punishment all of us deserved.

(53:4, 6)

In the second place *the punishment inflicted upon him was for their healing.*

We are healed by the punishment he suffered,
made whole by the blows he received.

(v. 5b)

It secured their forgiveness (vv. 10, 11).

In the third place he was a *voluntary victim*. He made no attempt to resist, v. 7, 8, and prayed for sinners that they might be forgiven. In the fourth place he will *survive the suffering of death*. He will see his descendants (v. 10). After a life of suffering he will again have joy (v. 11). In the fifth place he will know that it has *all been worth while*. He will see his offspring and be given a place of honour.

These prophecies find their remarkable fulfilment in the self-giving ministry of Christ. He forged the essential link between the concepts of Messiahship and Suffering Servant which had not occurred to his contemporaries. The growth of the people of God was not to come about through military conquest but along the costly pathway of crucifixion which would lead to resurrection. The Lord viewed his own cross not in terms of extinction, but germination. He declared, 'a grain of wheat remains no more than a single grain unless it is dropped into the ground and dies. If it does die, then it produces many grains' (John 12:24). This was not only true for him in his unique act of redemption, but it was an abiding principle by which his followers were called to live (John 12:25; Luke 9:23). There can be no sustained growth until we have learned to die daily. We cannot preach the cross effectively unless we are carrying it.

Whereas in the prophet Isaiah the concept of the Servant starts with the nation and then narrows to an individual, in the New Testament the unique servant enlists and empowers his followers in his servanthood. 'As the Father has sent me even so send I you.' And when Paul in the introductory paragraph of so many of his letters to the churches describes himself as a servant of Jesus Christ, he is not describing a servile position, but one of highest honour. Those who have leadership positions in the Church of Jesus Christ do not lord it over the followers, but act as towel-bearing servants (John 13).

9 Summary

In this chapter we have briefly reviewed the relationship of the people of God to the nations of the world. This presents us with a consistent picture, namely that it is God's declared purpose that his people will grow in numbers not simply through biological growth (i.e. by children of Christian parents becoming church members), but as they exert a powerful spiritual influence upon the world.

God's call and promise to an *individual* (Abraham) results in a *family*. The family diversifies into a group of tribes – a *people* sharing a common kinship. The people become institutionalised as a *nation* ruled by a king. As a consequence of Israel's persistent disobedience God permits the kingdom to be overthrown, and the nation driven into exile is reduced to a *remnant*. But in the providence of God that remnant is not intended as a survival from the past but as a stump from which future growth can develop. The remnant therefore becomes a *religious community* – the servant of the Lord – membership of which is not confined to any ethnic, geographical or political groupings, but is open to all who are committed to the word of God (in Old Testament terms, 'the torah', his law). 'Here is the birth of the confessing church.' (Goldingay 1975:2, 19).

We learn that church growth is on God's agenda, not simply through a few isolated 'missionary texts' but through the long strands of teaching which extend back from the New Testament through the previous centuries of divine revelation recorded in the Old Testament. If such growth appears on God's agenda then it should also appear on ours!

At the same time, we must heed the warnings of Old Testament scholars not to read back into the period the concerns of the New Testament for the mission of the people of God to all nations. There is little or no evidence of their awareness of such a calling. Israel's consciousness of her election led to an exclusiveness which blinded her to her spiritual responsibilities to the nations. In place of a concern for mission we find the constant drive for preservation and prosperity. Here are warning notes for the Church to heed today, otherwise our concern for church growth will be wrongly motivated.

One further element must be underscored lest it escape our attention. The divine intention for, and possibility of, mission emerges most clearly in the worship of the people of God and as they hear the challenge of the prophetic word. Mission has its starting-point not in ideas and plans, but in praise offered to God and in learning to listen intently to him. It is the praying rather than the talkative church which is most likely to be effectively engaged in mission. We will return more than once to this vital, yet frequently neglected, point.

CHAPTER TWO

Church and Kingdom

THE FOUR GOSPELS represent different versions of the life of our Lord. Although they draw on common material, they each write from a distinct viewpoint with a particular readership in mind. In Matthew we are aware of a Jew writing for Jews. Mark, on the other hand, was written, according to a number of early traditions, for Gentiles, probably located in Rome. Luke's two-part work of Gospel and Acts is dedicated to one man, Theophilus, who was clearly a Gentile, who seems to be receiving Christian instruction at the time. John's Gospel may have been written with both Jews and Gentiles in mind. If the readership cannot be described with certainty there is no doubt as to its purpose. John carefully selected miracles for a reason. 'These have been written in order that you may believe that Jesus is the Messiah, the Son of God, and that through your faith in him you may have life' (John 20:31).

1 A basis for belief

Each of the Gospels was written with a clear evangelistic purpose, to introduce enquirers to the authentic and essential facts of the gospel and as a basis of instruction for those who were preparing for baptism.

Michael Green draws attention to the fact that the Gospels represent an entirely new literary form, which was neither history, nor biography, but a highly selective weaving together of fragments using preaching and teaching 'arranged in order to show what sort of person Jesus was, to give the evidence on which the disciples had followed him and had adjudged him the Messiah and Son of God, and by the strongest possible implication, challenge the readers to make the same act of faith in Christ as they themselves had done.' (Green 1970:229, 230).

In a more recent book he suggests that the gospel was also made available as widespread and cheaply as possible by a novel process. The gospel was bound in a compact book form rather than produced as a bulky scroll, with paper made from cheap papyrus rather than the very expensive vellum (i.e. treated skins) (Green 1979:125). These also made for easier reference with page turning being easier than unwinding a scroll to find your place. The early Christians may therefore be credited with the invention of the forerunner of the popular paperback!

There has been a great deal of argument as to what a new enquirer needs to know before or immediately upon making a decision to follow Christ for that decision to be meaningful. As we have seen, the Gospels were written to meet that need, so by examining carefully their contents we will gain an overall impression of the range of information which the early Christians deemed to be necessary for an adequate on-going commitment to be made. In the great majority of cases this teaching would be communicated orally, for Gospels were in short supply and many converts were illiterate. As a general rule those who could read had to make their own copy. Having to write it out was a good way to absorb the contents.

By switching from concentration on a few 'proof texts' in evangelism to a more balanced and comprehensive approach adopted by one of the four Gospels we might see better short and long-term results in our evangelism. They give a clear picture of the identity of Christ, show the radical all-or-nothing nature of commitment to him, describe the life of discipleship as a corporate not individualistic activity, spell out the cost involved, and show

how our present experience relates to the Kingdom of God, which is both present and yet still to come.

The first three Gospels each place a heavy emphasis on the 'Kingdom'. Matthew, to suit Jewish susceptibility, prefers to speak of the 'Kingdom of Heaven' rather than the 'Kingdom of God', because Jews were reluctant to utter the divine name. He refers to the Kingdom fifty-two times, while Mark uses it nineteen times, Luke forty-four times and John only four.

The lack of Kingdom emphasis in John is probably explained by the fact that he is writing more in retrospect and possibly to play down false expectations in the contemporary Jewish understanding of the Kingdom. The 'Kingdom of God' is only mentioned twice (3:1, 5) because it 'calls to mind that apocalyptic Judaism which John seems for the most part to avoid. Perhaps this general avoidance suggests his criticism of that Judaism which was content to await the miraculous vindication of Israel in the Kingdom of God and to ignore the necessity for inward conversion and rebirth' (Barrett 1960:173). If John, apart from the important reference in Chapter 3, which we shall consider later, avoids the term Kingdom of God, he does on the other hand lay more stress than the other three Gospels on Jesus as King of Israel (Barrett 1960:346). The Gospels therefore lay a heavy emphasis on the gospel of the Kingdom and the Kingship of Jesus.

In our consideration of the Old Testament role of the people of God among the nations of the world we saw that Israel attracted people to herself as she pointed beyond herself. It was as she manifested the reality of God in her midst through her life of obedience to his commands and faith in his promises that she succeeded in fulfilling her God-given mission as a witness to the nations. In their response the nations were not coming to Israel as such, but to God who dwelt in Israel. The same emphasis appears when we turn to consider the relationship of the Church to the Kingdom of God. Here, once again we see the Church as a magnetic presence, but now also fulfilling a missionary role in actually going to the nations. But her witness is still to point beyond herself. She points upwards to the Lord who is the head of the Church and forwards to the Kingdom, which, although inaugurated, is still to be consummated.

2 Neglect of a Kingdom emphasis in church growth thinking

The writings of Donald McGavran do not make clear the relationship he sees between the Church and the Kingdom. At several points he seems to use the terms interchangeably. Church planting becomes synonymous with Kingdom building. Mission is not simply self-proliferation, for the Church is not the Kingdom. As Rene Padilla cautions, 'To speak of the kingdom of God is to speak of the purpose of God, of which the empirical church is little more than a pale reflection' (Padilla 1975:43). The failure of church growth thinking, at least in its early formulations, to differentiate between Church and Kingdom has led to a great deal of misunderstanding and criticism. It has resulted in Christian mission being caricatured as denominational aggrandisement, or a plan for survival for western-based churches and their related mission agencies. Church growth thinking has been slow to come to terms with the problem of nominality within existing churches, and has consequently given the impression that mission is simply making more and more people to become like ourselves. It has not sufficiently emphasised that the Church itself is in the process of becoming and through its disobedience can present a distorted or even completely erroneous picture of the Christian life. In recent years this aspect has been corrected to a large extent through the response of Third World Christian thinkers and the radical discipleship movement which is emerging among younger Christians in the more affluent nations.

The criticisms of McGavran come thick and fast in the July 1968 issue of the *International Review of Missions*. Matthew P. John from the Syrian Orthodox Church draws attention to the fact that the denominational churches cannot simply be equated with the Church of Jesus Christ, '. . . it is not at all clear that the multiplication of churches is the chief aim of the Christian mission. The consistent use of the plural "churches" implies a distance from an essential dimension of the meaning of church in the Bible. It may be meaningless to talk of an invisible church except in the context of a visible one, but it is also relevant to remember that the visible church or churches share in the ambiguities of human existence and can become demonic like other human institutions' (IRM July 1968:280). And again, 'Dr McGavran's proposals about classifying societies for the purpose of seeing what particular technique is to be applied to them to turn the raw material into churches, treats them as less than human and justifies the non-Christian critics of mission who describe it as a form of imperialism and domination' (IRM July 1968:281).

While multiplying Christians may result in a more just society, it does not necessarily follow. If Christians see their spiritual vocation in life simply in terms of making other Christians, many areas of life can be conveniently overlooked. Their light may shine with the narrowness of a laser beam rather than provide the illumination of a beacon.

When people are being added to the Church it is legitimate to examine what they are being converted to. Jordan Bishop, a Roman Catholic missionary, on the basis of his Latin American experience, reflects that thousands of Indians were forcibly baptised during the time of the Spanish conquest of Latin America and, today, Protestant converts are made through the material advancement their allegiance offers. He concludes that 'the authenticity of conversion to Christ (freed, one should add, not only from economic but also from sociological and psychological pressure) is more important than the number of men converted or churches planted.' (IRM July 1968: 287).

The Anglican professor J. G. Davies also takes McGavran to task for not distinguishing the Church from the churches. 'When he speaks of planting the Church, he can only mean the planting of denominations. This immediately reduces such a definition of mission to well nigh an absurdity, as it would mean the increase of Methodists, Lutherans, etc. Can it seriously be maintained that this is God's purpose for the world? . . . Is this not to reduce the living God of radical monotheism to a tribal deity?' (IRM July 1968: 291). Davies writes these words against a background of English church life where many churches 'are groups of inward-looking people, introverted to such a degree that their ecclesiastical interests are primary' . . . they are 'frequently judgemental, non-acceptive, conservative and backward looking. To many people their religious practices belong to a dream world which has no point of contact with the real world. Their structures, devised in a bygone day, have petrified and institutional loyalty seems to command more respect than faithfulness to God' (IRM July 1968:292).

He concludes, 'To define the goal of mission as church growth is to indulge in an ecclesiastical narrowing of the concept of the Kingdom of God. The Church is an instrument of the kingdom, or should be; it may also be conceived as the first-fruits of the kingdom; but it is not to be identified with the kingdom, which is what we are doing if we rest content with church growth as our objective' (IRM July 1968:293).

These extended quotations illustrate the heart of the concern and the depth of feeling of church growth critics. The nub of the matter is the relationship between the Church of Christ and the Kingdom of God. More specifically, what is the relationship between the *growth* of the Church and the *coming* of the Kingdom?

The Kingdom In Recent Thinking

Biblical scholars have understood the 'Kingdom' in a variety of ways. Those who regard the kingdom as entirely 'future' or 'present' have emphasised one or other aspect of the biblical evidence, while ignoring or explaining away other strands of teaching. We will summarise their views under three general headings:

1. *The Kingdom considered as lying entirely in the future.* This view was propounded at the end of the last century by Johannes Weiss as a result of the rediscovery of many documents of the apocalyptic type which threw fresh light on Jewish expectations regarding the Kingdom in New Testament times. It was Albert Schweitzer's book, *The Quest of the Historical Jesus* which brought them to the notice of English readers, and his famous name added support for this futurist understanding of the Kingdom. Relying heavily on Matthew's material Schweitzer argued that Jesus envisaged that the Kingdom would come within his own lifetime. His ethical teaching was therefore an 'ethic of the interval' which could remain in operation for a brief span of time as an interim measure. Schweitzer portrays Jesus as the Apoclyptic Messiah fired with Jewish expectation going to Jerusalem to be crowned as King either by popular acclaim or by violent action. The failure of the Kingdom to materialise at that point resulted in Jesus dying in despair and disillusionment. From Schweitzer's reconstruction of the events it is difficult to understand why Jesus understood in his terms should have been subsequently followed – especially by Schweitzer himself!

2. *The Kingdom considered as an accomplished fact realised in the coming of Christ.* This understanding of the Kingdom as fully present is the view of Professor C. H. Dodd, who describes his theory in terms of 'realised eschatology' – that is, the End Times are with us now. He uses the word 'realised' in opposition to those who look for the Kingdom in an 'anticipatory' sense. In his original formulation he emphasised the Kingdom as a transcendent order, which while being beyond time and space, had yet broken into history in the mission of Jesus. He emphasises the many strands of evidence in the Gospels to the Kingdom as a present reality, while explaining

the future references as a re-setting by the Church of Jesus' original teaching in terms of the Apocalyptic expectations of the day, as a way of coping with the nonfulfilment of Kingdom expectations. More recently Professor Dodd has modified his position, admitting that he awaits a consummation of the Kingdom beyond history.

In company with C. H. Dodd are many liberals who understand the Kingdom in humanistic terms. Among them we may mention Ritschl who regarded it as a sort of Utopia; an organisation of humanity through action inspired by love. Harnack regarded the apocalyptic element in the Kingdom as only a time-conditioned husk. For him the kernel of the message was the Fatherhood of God, the brotherhood of man and the ethic of love. Such an understanding is also popular among many theologians identified with the Ecumenical Movement and propounding 'Theologies of Liberation'.

3. *The Kingdom considered as partly present but mostly future*. This is perhaps the most popular position among contemporary New Testament scholars as it seems best to explain the totality of the New Testament teaching on the subject. Rudolf Otto used the phrase, 'anticipated eschatology'. For him the fact that the Kingdom has drawn near means that it has already come in an inaugural sense – but there is yet more to come. For C. H. Graig it is like the coming of dawn before the sunrise. For J. Jeremias the Kingdom is eschatology. Others speak of the Church as a sign or even a sacrament of the Kingdom. The emphasis of T. W. Manson and G. Eldon Ladd on the other hand is on the present reality of the Kingdom in the heart of the believer. It is the eternal fact of God's kingship, manifested on earth at present in the community of individuals who accept it, and having a future consummation at the end of time.

Having briefly outlined the main positions taken by New Testament scholars we now turn to examine the biblical material on the theme of the Kingdom.

3 The gospel of the Kingdom

From the outset the Gospels establish the relationship between the coming of the Kingdom and the appearance of the Christ. John the Baptist, as the last in the long line of Old Testament Prophets, called upon the nation to repent to prepare for the Kingdom whose coming was imminent (Matt. 3:2). When his public voice was silenced through imprisonment, Jesus established the continuity of his ministry with that of John. Like him, he calls the nation to turn away from their sins because the Kingdom of heaven is near (Matt. 4:23; 9:35). This is the new element which Jesus introduced. Whereas for John the Kingdom came as a threat to a people who were unprepared, for Jesus it represented good news to those who felt unworthy or excluded.

'The transition from "the days of John the Baptist" (Matt. 11:12) to Jesus' independent career was signalled by the priority of "the reign of God" over "the wrath about to come". . . . The call to baptism bore immediately on the restoration of Israel and the concomitant salvation of the nations. The key to the difference is the motif "free gift", with which Jesus charged the expression "the reign of God". This is why his proclamation came eventually to be known as "gospel" or "news of salvation" ' (Meyer 1979:130).

As the Gospel narrative unfolds we are quickly made aware that the good news signifies more than rescue from divine wrath. It is the establishing of God's Kingly rule, which entails both God's provision for his people and requirements from them.

The inauguration of the Kingdom is an act of God and not the result of human achievement. However, its coming is not automatic; it requires a response from man. For this reason the message of the Kingdom has to be both proclaimed as fact and promise. Christ himself came *preaching* the Good News of the Kingdom, describing its nature and calling for a response. His silent presence was not sufficient of itself. The Kingdom needed explaining and people needed exhorting. If presence was inadequate by itself as a strategy to extend the Kingdom in the ministry of Christ, it is even more deficient when left to his stumbling followers.

This need for proclamation is expressed with sensitivity in section three of the World Council of Churches Conference on World Mission and Evangelism Report (Melbourne May 12–24, 1980) *The Church Witnesses to the Kingdom*, in the following paragraph:

> The proclamation of the Word of God is one such witness, distinct and indispensable. The story of God in Christ is the heart of all evangelism, and this story has to be told, for the life of the present Church never fully reveals the love and holiness and power of God in Christ. The telling of the story is an inescapable mandate for the whole Church; word accompanies deed as the kingdom throws its light ahead of its arrival and men and women seek to live in that light (1:3).

In fact Christ explicitly commanded his disciples to proclaim the Kingdom. He sent out the Twelve to the towns and villages of Israel with this charge, 'Go and preach, "The Kingdom of heaven is near!" ' (Matt. 10:7). Subsequently, with the sending out of the Seventy, they were to announce, 'The Kingdom of God has come near you' (Luke 10:9).

Seeing the extent of the need and the readiness of the response, Jesus calls upon his followers to pray to the owner of the harvest that he will send out workers to gather in his harvest (Matt. 9:37; Luke 9.2). Elton Trueblood comments, 'when Christ said the labourers were few, He and those to whom He spoke were surrounded by large numbers of priests and semi-professional religious men. The priests in Jerusalem were so numerous that they had to take turns in performing Temple ceremonies. The dearth was of persons who could give the only kind of witness that counts with those looking for help, the kind that is couched in the first person singular' (Trueblood 1961:51). The Kingdom must be announced by 'insiders' and not simply treated as a subject for speculation.

Within hours of his death Jesus sets forth a world-embracing scenario. 'And this Good News about the Kingdom will be preached through all the world for a witness to all mankind; and then the end will come' (Matt. 24:14). This leaves no doubt as to the universal and abiding significance of the Kingdom concept. Gospel preaching will be seriously deficient if this dimension is omitted. The Kingdom gives content and purpose to the act of commitment. It represents a radical and all-embracing transfer of allegiance. It is therefore essential for the Christian witness to understand to what 'the Kingdom' refers in Scripture.

4 The Old Testament expectation of the Kingdom

When John the Baptist and then Jesus spoke of the 'Kingdom of God' or the 'Kingdom of Heaven' they were not introducing a novel concept which needed explaining from scratch. On the contrary, the idea of the Kingdom had a long history in the life of Israel, and the coming of Christ coincided with a feverish wave of expectancy within the nation. They longed for deliverance from Roman oppression, and were encouraged to think that they would not have much longer to wait as the prophetic voice was heard once more in the land after centuries of silence. As the crowds listened to Christ's unconventional preaching and observed his miracles they acknowledged him as sent from God. After Jesus feeds the Five Thousand the crowd respond by declaring, 'Surely this is the Prophet who was to come into the world!' As they advance on him Jesus realises that they are about to seize him to make him King (John 6:15).

Similarly, when he enters Jerusalem crowded with pilgrims and with a politically charged atmosphere, they prepared a royal route and cry out, 'Praise God! God bless him who comes in the name of the Lord! God bless the coming kingdom of King David, our father! Praise God!' (Mark 11:10). Matthew in his version makes clear that this was no mistaken identification. The event was staged to fulfil Zechariah's prophecy of the Messianic King riding into Jerusalem (Matt. 21:5). However, the crowd missed the symbolism of his riding on a donkey in humility rather than a horse as military conqueror.

Chief among the political activists were the zealots, who were the Jewish first-century freedom fighters. Their motivation was not simply political or patriotic, but religious. By their guerrilla activities they hoped to generate a revolt against Rome, thereby hastening the coming of the Kingdom. In the New Testament we read of the insurrection under Judas and Theudas (Acts 5:36, 37), and a further revolt under an unidentified Egyptian (Acts 21:38). The eventual destruction of Jerusalem was brought about by the Romans to crush the rebellion of Bar Kokhba who was styled by the Akiba, the most famous rabbi of the time, as the Messiah (Ladd 1974:62).

Israel's expectation of the Kingdom was not confined to the political activists and zealots. It was also shared by the pious saints, referred to as 'the quiet in the land'. Other groups such as the Essene sect had withdrawn completely from society to await the eschatological consummation of the Kingdom. They expected the angels to come down and join battle with them – 'the sons of light' – against their enemies – 'the sons of darkness' – and to give them victory over all other peoples (Ladd 1974:62).

Within the New Testament we find reference to pious individuals who were awaiting the redemption of Israel through the mission of a Messiah who would be King David's greater son. Such longings find expression in the Song of Mary (Luke 1:46:55), the prophecy of Zechariah (Luke 1:68–79), among Andrew, Simon Peter, Philip and Nathaniel as disciples of John the Baptist, who were encouraged by their self-effacing master to transfer their allegiance to Christ (John 1:29–50), by spiritually discerning Pharisees such as Nicodemus (John 3), and in the case of Joseph of Arimathea, a member of the Jerusalem Council, who 'was waiting for the coming of the Kingdom of God' (Luke 23:50, 51).

So Christ ministered in Israel to those who had preconceived notions about the coming Kingdom. His many references to the Kingdom recorded in the Gospels must be seen in the light of this context.

Although the Old Testament nowhere expressly mentions the Kingdom of God, the world is represented as existing under his cosmic rule (Ps. 24:1; 93:1; 95:3). His sovereignty is not confined to the created order but includes political powers. As the King of the Nations (Jer. 10:7; Ps. 47:3; 99:2), he exerts his sovereign power by guiding their fortunes and acting in judgement. Certain individuals and peoples become instruments of his justice and anger. Thus, in a number of ways through the Psalms and Prophets the Old Testament continually reminds us that God is King (Snyder 1977:14). While for the prophets the envisioned universal rule of God is an eschatological event, for the Psalmist the enthronement of Yahweh is 'a present reality experienced in the cultic ceremony' (Klappert 1976: Vol. II, 372–389).

For the prophets the new age of the Kingdom represented an era of peace, prosperity and justice for Israel brought about by radical economic and social changes (Mic. 4:1–5; Zech. 9:10; Is. 2:4; 9:7; 42:3 and 65:21ff). It would also transform the created order, resulting in geological changes bringing about a favourable climate and fertility of the soil, so that Israel surpassed her early reputation of being a land of 'milk and honey' (Is. 11:6–9; 32:14–20; 38:1f; Zech. 14:3f; Amos 9:13). Conflict in nature would be resolved, with the lion lying down with the lamb. Humanity would also be renewed, both physically with the disappearance of sickness, and the diminution of the power of death; and spiritually with men being given a 'new heart' through the Spirit coming upon all flesh and spreading a universal knowledge of God (Jer. 23:5f; 31:31; Ezek. 36:24–28; Zech. 8:20–23; Joel 2:28). As we noted in the previous chapter, the nation of Israel occupied a central place in the realisation of this hope, serving as the gathering-point of the nations (Is. 24:23; Zech. 14:9; Obad. 21). She would not achieve this position of prominence through conquest but through example and inspiration.

While the coming of the Kingdom is clearly and consistently portrayed as an act of God and not the result of human striving and achievement, it does manifest itself in concrete terms in *this* world. As the Latin American theologian Jose Miguez Bonino has well commented, there is no question of 'two histories'. 'Yahweh's sovereign act does not appear in history as an abstract act or an interpretation but as announcement and command. . . . Every attempt to separate the political from the religious areas in the Old Testament is completely artificial' (Bonino 1975:134).

Against such a background we can begin to appreciate the expectations of our Lord's followers as they emerge in the Gospel narrative. 'It involves the whole notion of the rule of God over his people, and particularly the vindication of that rule and people in glory at the end of history. That was the Kingdom which the Jews awaited' (Bright 1953:18). After being so intimately with Christ and hearing his parables of the Kingdom and private commentary interpreting those stories, his disciples still expected the Kingdom to come in the material and nationalistic terms of the Old Testament (Acts 1:6). To what extent were they in line with Jesus' teaching?

5 *The New Testament realisation of the Kingdom*

Our Lord emphasises the continuity with the past when he inaugurates his public ministry with the announcement, 'The right time has come,and the Kingdom of God is near! Turn away from your sins and believe the Good News' (Mark 1:15). 'The two Testaments are organically linked to each other. The relationship between them is neither one of upward development nor of contrast; it is one of beginning and completion, of hope and fulfilment. And the bond that binds them together is the dynamic concept of the rule of God. There is indeed a "new thing" in the New Testament . . . it has introduced a tremendously significant change of tense. In referring to the Kingdom the Old Testament spoke in such terms as "Behold, the days are coming". But in the New Testament we encounter a change: the tense is a resounding present indicative – the Kingdom is *here*!' (Bright 1953:196, 197).

For Jesus the Kingdom of God represented an approaching new order of things. This new order was no distant hope but already operative . . . God's final saving act was already operative in Israel: now is the new creation, time of the new wine and the new cloak (Mark 2:21f)! The fields are 'white' (John 4:35), the harvest 'great' (Matt. 9:37)! Now is the wedding, the espousal of Israel! 'Can the wedding guests mourn?' (Mark 2:20). The young man dead through sin 'is alive again' (Luke 15:24, 32), 'so it is right to be glad' (Meyer 1979:131). The reign of God has already come upon you (Matt. 12:28).

But in what sense can the Kingdom be understood to have arrived in the person and ministry of Jesus? Part of the mystery is unravelled by our appreciating the differences in the concept of 'time' within the Bible and our modern western understanding. For us time is measurable; it is a quantity concept. For the Hebrews, on the other hand, it was a quality measure. They thought in terms of a right or wrong time, rather than long or short duration. Ecclesiastes 3:1–8 well illustrates their way of thinking, 'There is a time for everything, a time for every occupation under heaven: a time for giving birth, dying, planting, killing, healing, knocking down, building, etc.' 'For the Hebrew, to know the time was not a matter of knowing the date, it was a matter of knowing what kind of time it might be. Was it a time for tears or a time for laughter, a time for war or a time for peace? To misjudge the time in which one lived might prove to be disastrous' (Nolan 1976:74). Recent studies in anthropology have enriched our theological understanding by cautioning us from reading back into the Biblical text presupposition from our own culture.

The task of the prophet was therefore supremely to interpret 'the times'. So when our Lord spoke about the Kingdom of Heaven being at hand, he was referring to its being qualitatively present. His public ministry inaugurates this new 'quality time', and his ascension to the throne of power and sending of the Spirit upon his disciples represents its coming in power. The Kingdom of God as a new dimension of living opens up to those who turn away from their sins, symbolising a radical break with the past. For them it begins to be present as an 'insiders' experience. At the same time, for those who have not arrived at, or hold back from such a step of faith, the Kingdom is not yet.

Our Lord came to inaugurate the Kingdom. As he began his ministry it was present in his person. He represented the dawn of a new age which would never be overcome by darkness. His amazing words and miraculous deeds were signs of the coming Kingdom. As his disciples were identified with him in his ministry and experienced the healing powers of the new age operating through them, so they became partakers of the Kingdom. Wherever they went represented a frontier of the Kingdom (Luke 10:1). To the Pharisees who were blind to the evidence before their eyes and were postponing their hopes to the future our Lord responded, 'No one will say, "Look, here it is!" or, "There it is!" because the Kingdom of God is within you' (Luke 17:21). The Greek word *entos* translated here as 'within' should more accurately be rendered 'among' you or 'in your midst' (Nolan 1976:46). The point Jesus was making was that it was all around them and they hadn't noticed!

In the Acts and Epistles Christians are regarded as

experiencing the Kingdom as a present reality. It is evidenced in the lives of believers who serve Christ in 'Righteousness, peace, and joy which the Holy Spirit gives' (Rom. 14:17). By virtue of the saving work of Christ, Paul describes the Christians in Colossae as having been rescued from the power of darkness and 'brought' (past tense) into the Kingdom of his dear Son (Col. 1:13). The church in Thessalonica is urged to live the kind of life that pleases God, who calls them (now, not one day) 'to share in his own Kingdom and glory' (1 Thess. 2:12). While John the Divine describes himself to the seven churches in Asia as 'your partner in patiently enduring the suffering that comes to those who belong to his Kingdom' (Rev. 1:9).

Alongside this emphasis of the Kingdom as a present reality to be experienced and enjoyed, there is an equally strong strand of teaching which speaks of the Kingdom as in the future to be anticipated and longed for. This second strand, like the first, runs through the entire New Testament. It is associated with the final curtain descending on present world history, when Jesus will descend from heaven in power to destroy his enemies and restore the entire creation. This coming of the Kingdom will be a time of separation (Matt. 25:34; Luke 13:28) and judgement (Matt. 8:12; 2 Tim. 4:1). It will also be a time of rejoicing and feasting in the Messianic banquet (Matt. 26:29; Luke 22:28–30).

The Kingdom is at the same time a heavenly as well as an earthly reality. Our Lord left this earthly scene to occupy his throne and to sit at the Father's table. For the believer the Kingdom as a heavenly reality is no more than one generation away. Jesus said to the penitent thief, 'Today you will be with me in paradise' (Luke 23:42). Paul expresses his assurance to Timothy, 'the Lord will rescue me from all evil and take me safely into his heavenly Kingdom' (2 Tim. 4:18).

The coming of Christ was therefore to inaugurate the

Kingdom in a provisional form. Its final consummation still lies in the future.

This future emphasis of the Kingdom is most strongly present in the Apocalyptic books of the Bible. In the Old Testament the eschatological expectation is elevated to a transcendental level (Dan. 7:13f, 27), while the book of Revelation represents the Kingdom as final consummation (Rev. 11:15; 12:10). The coming glorious age coexists with the present evil age. In other words, 'The Age to Come has overlapped with This Age' (Ladd 1974:42) which results in intermingling and close combat. Thus in his embodiment of the Kingdom Jesus confronts demonic powers which openly manifest their opposition. We therefore find ourselves living in disputed territory. 'The Kingdom has come, but is not yet perfected (Mark 9:1; 13:26); The enemy is stricken, but not yet destroyed' (Stauffer 1975:125).

We have noted the cultural problem in coming to terms with the Biblical understanding of time. There is one further related problem which we must now briefly consider, namely our temporal distance from the events described in the New Testament. In the Gospels there is a powerful sense of imminence regarding the Kingdom. Then it seemed that the consummation would follow soon on the heels of its inauguration. Indeed it would come within the lifetime of Christ's hearers (Matt. 24:34; Mark 9:1). Whatever the intended meaning of those words, there is strong evidence in the New Testament that many of the early Christians expected the Lord's return at any moment.

The German theologian, Wolfhart Pannenberg, emphasises this impact of the future on the present in Jesus' teaching. God's Kingdom does not lie in the distant future but is imminent. Thus, the present is not independent from that future. Rather does the future have an imperative claim upon the present, alerting all men to the urgency and exclusiveness of seeking first the Kingdom of God. As this message is proclaimed and accepted,

God's rule is present and we can even now glimpse the future glory' (Pannenberg 1975:54). The Kingdom is not and cannot be relegated to an appendix which follows the turning of the last page of world history.

This is an attitude of life which the twentieth-century Church urgently needs to recapture. We must avoid the temptation to project time-spans from the past into the future. We need to 'feel' time as well as measure it. 'The *eschaton* is a future event but, to the extent that our lives are determined and qualified by it, it is also a contemporary event, an event that can be seen in the signs of the times' (Nolan 1976:76). 'Now' is not a panic word, but one which conveys the idea of both opportunity and urgency. It is not a command from God to advance on all fronts, but is a strategic arrow word identifying and emphasising what he wants done.

6 The signs of the Kingdom

The signs of the Kingdom are clear pointers to the coming Kingdom. The sign contains sufficient of the content of the thing signified to be more than a symbol. But the sign acts as shield as well as pointer. It shows enough to reveal the nature and genuineness of the reality, but not so much as to overwhelm. Thus the sign can be ignored or disputed.

The clearest most powerful 'sign' of the Kingdom is the presence of Christ himself. In much recent talk about the Kingdom Jesus' centrality has been overlooked, or refuge has been taken in the concept of his anonymous presence which does not square well with the New Testament Kingdom emphasis. This led to the vague talk about the Kingdom which aroused McGavran's protest in the *International Review of Missions*. Jesus stands at the centre of the Kingdom message. The Kingdom of God is equally described as the Kingdom of his dear Son or the Kingdom of Christ (Eph. 5:5; Rev. 11:15). The verdict passed on men in the final judgement will be determined by the attitude they adopted to Christ during their lifetime (Matt. 10:32 cf. Luke 12:8). The unrepentent cities will be condemned because they did not turn from their sins despite his mighty works (Matt. 11:21; Luke 10:13). Christ himself will appear as the judge of all men to separate the sheep from the goats (Matt. 25:31). He will discern between those who say 'Lord, Lord' as an empty profession from those who yielded their lives to the service of God (Matt. 7:23; Luke 13:27). He will plead before the Father the cause of those who confess him (Matt. 10:32; Luke 12:8). The presence of the Kingdom in the person of Jesus faces the individual with a clear-cut decision (Matt. 5:30; 15:8f; Mark 9:43–48, Luke 9:62).

The signs of the presence of God are various. It is to be seen in the *healing* ministry of Christ (Matt. 4:23; 9:35; Luke 9:11) and of his disciples who healed in his name (Luke 9:2; 10:9). These healing acts follow directly on from his teaching about the Kingdom. Yet these signs in themselves emphasise the provisional nature of the Kingdom, because all of those who were healed in the New Testament subsequently became sick and died. In the subsequent experience of the Church in exercising this ministry there have been many instances of failure, partial, delayed and temporary healing, reminding us that we live with the tension of the 'now' and the 'not yet' of the Kingdom.

Tom Smail, writing from a charismatic perspective, maintains a healthy balance. 'Within that tension of the already given and the still to come all Christians have to live – including charismatic Christians. God gives enough evidence of Christ risen to call to faith, but not enough to compel to acceptance . . . In the realm of healing much happens to authenticate Christ's present will and power to heal the otherwise incurable, and yet, often distressingly, enough fails to happen to serve to remind us that we are not yet at the last day, and to leave the mystery of the "not yet" all around us' (Smail 1975:124).

Closely linked with healing is the *casting out of demons*. This ministry was also exercised by Christ and his disciples. Deliverance provided proof that the Kingdom of God had already come (Matt. 12:28; Luke 11:20). This was especially significant for a society in which demonic possession was so prevalent and feared.

Such miracles constitute more than signs and wonders. They are 'mighty works' demonstrating the powers of the Kingdom in operation. They show that 'Satan has met his match (Luke 10:18; Mark 3:27); the cosmic end-struggle has begun' (Bright 1953:218).

Instances of *dead people brought back to life* (Matt. 10:8; Luke 9:2; John 11:44) were also a sign of the life in abundance which Christ came to bestow (John 10:10).

When Jesus began his ministry he made his manifesto the prophecy of Is. 61:1–2 which he selected and read in the synagogue at Nazareth (Luke 4:18, 19):

The Spirit of the Lord is upon me,
because he has chosen me to bring
  good news to the poor.
He has sent me to proclaim liberty to the
  captives
and recovery of sight to the blind;
to set free the oppressed
  and announce that the time has come
  when the Lord will save his people.

Such promises were meant to be fulfilled in the life of Israel in the provisions of the year of Jubilee scheduled for every forty-nine years. However, there is no evidence for that provision of the law ever being implemented. If this is indeed the case the significance of Jesus' words to the congregation as he gave back the scroll, 'This passage of scripture has come true today, as you heard it being read' (Luke 4:21) is even more poignant. Jesus liberated not through a programme of political activism, but simply through his spoken word. His word conveyed power and achieved results as it had from the time of creation itself.

Western commentators have frequently 'spiritualised' this prophecy in the sense of individualising and internalising its application. The 'poor' become the spiritually impoverished, the 'captives' those who are enslaved to sin, the 'blind' those who are unaware of their spiritual plight. On the other hand, there are those who turn this prophecy into a programme for political and economic emancipation: the poor are the exploited proletariate, the captives are the prisoners of conscience and the recovery of sight to the blind is achieved through 'awareness building' (or to use the Spanish loan-word which has gained popularity of recent years, through *concientización*), so that the exploited recognise the factors which have contributed to their plight and come to realise that their situation is not inevitable. The victims can become victors by taking power forcibly in their own hands.

Neither of these interpretations does full justice to the text. There can be no separating of the vertical from the horizontal dimensions of reconciliation. The preaching of the Good News brings reconciliation with God and makes reconciliation possible with our neighbour. Repentance includes turning away from social as well as personal sins. Salvation is not simply individualist and other-worldly. It means God's saving grace working through individuals and communities of people who know him as Saviour and Lord to influence a wider society. But I fail to see how we can talk about the 'redeeming of structures' without an effective Christian presence. This is not to say that there are not many people of good will who are working conscientiously for a more humane society, but such efforts inevitably succumb to the demonic. They are like the newly swept house of which our Lord spoke which was then taken over by more spirits than before (Matt. 12:43–45).

7 *The characteristics of the Kingdom*

Life in the Kingdom presented a challenge to the status quo. Where the gospel of Christ is faithfully proclaimed it is always subversive. It undermines the power-seeker, the affluent materialist and the self-righteous. It comes with equal challenge to the religious as to the irreligious. Many wealthy people will be prevented by their love of money from entering into the Kingdom. Although entrance is free we have to lay aside everything to enter through the narrow gate, so that it costs us everything. The Kingdom of Heaven belongs to the poor who have nothing to bring in with them. The 'poor' in Scripture does not simply refer to those living at or beneath subsistence level – it 'can be extended to cover all the oppressed, all those who are dependent upon the mercy of others. And this too is why the word can even be extended to all those who rely entirely upon the mercy of God – the poor in spirit' (Matt. 5:3) (Nolan 1976).

Whatever our position in society, the Kingdom makes an absolute demand; we either seek it first or not at all (Matt. 6:33). Having accepted the prior claim of the Kingdom, we then discover the generosity of God. We no longer have to worry about what we eat or drink or wear, for we will know his provision. However this is only a practicality within the economy of the Kingdom, where God's will reigns. For the adequacy of God's provision is dependent on our corporate responsibility, including our stewardship of resources and equitable distribution. Individual saints may testify to God's supernatural provision, but their experience cannot be universalised. Among the millions who die each year through malnutrition there are many children of the Kingdom. For we still live with the tension of the 'now' and 'not yet' of the Kingdom. This is allowed to happen not only because of the sin in the world, but also because of sin in the Church. To quote a Christian Aid slogan, because we refuse 'to live more simply that others may simply live'.

The parable of the servants in Matt. 25 and Luke 19 emphasises the point that to whom God gives generously he expects to exercise their stewardship effectively. They are each held accountable for their actions.

Poverty – the recognition that we possess nothing to buy privilege with God, and *prosperity* – which results from our readiness to receive from God, are both characteristics of the Kingdom.

A third characteristic of the Kingdom is an attitude of *forgiveness* which pervades all our relationships. It comes about as a result of our gratitude to God for his wiping out of a colossal debt that we could never have paid back (Matt. 18:22ff). We are able to forgive because we know what it is to be forgiven, and the love of God shed abroad in our heart gives us a new capacity to do so.

Fourthly, the Kingdom is shown through *willing obedience to the law of God* (Matt. 5:19, 20). This is not the keeping of the letter by escaping through the loopholes which we have opened up through clever casuistry. This is a joyful response to the spirit of the law, as we see its deeper meaning and wider application. For 'every teacher of the law who becomes a disciple in the Kingdom of Heaven is like the owner of a house who takes new and old things out of his storeroom' (Matt. 13:52). The new does not cause us to discard the old, but to see its contemporary worth.

Fifthly, the Kingdom is characterised by *suffering*. This comes inevitably to those who belong to the Kingdom precisely because it is 'not of this world' and presents such a challenge which arouses hostility. 'Happy are those who are persecuted because they do what God requires; the Kingdom of Heaven belongs to them!' (Matt. 5:10), Jesus assures the children of the Kingdom. Such was the experience of the believers through subsequent years (2 Thess. 1:5; Rev. 1:9). The faithful Church has been described as the suffering form of the Kingdom of God (Snyder 1977:30).

8 Entering the Kingdom

It is difficult for the twentieth-century, non-Jewish reader of the Gospels to appreciate just how radical Jesus appeared to his contemporaries, and especially to the religious establishment, who held such a powerful position in Jewish life. He completely disregarded strictly enforced social conventions and religious restrictions in order to contact the outcasts of society. He was not afraid to be seen deep in conversation with a Samaritan woman who he knew was cohabiting with another man after having gone through five husbands. He accepted the devotion of a prostitute who anointed his feet with costly perfume, and he dined out on a number of occasions with tax collectors and sinners, who represented the social outcasts – the 'untouchables' of the day.

Within an eastern culture, table-fellowship and the sharing of a meal is regarded as a particularly intimate form of association. The fact that Jesus was prepared to act in such a fashion, and to be *seen* doing it, communicated as powerfully as any pronouncement, both to his friends at the table and his enemies at the window (Matt. 11:19; Luke 15:2; Mark 2:15ff; Matt. 9:10; Luke 5:29). For a man who claimed and was popularly acknowledged to be a man of God, such behaviour was extraordinary to say the least.

His actions were deliberately intended to demonstrate the present reality and radical nature of the Kingdom. In contrast to contemporary society which denied social misfits and those deemed 'irreligious' their civil rights and spiritual privileges, such people are especially welcomed into the Reign of God. 'By accepting them as friends and equals Jesus had taken away their shame, humiliation and guilt. By showing them that they mattered to Him as people He gave them a sense of dignity and released them from their captivity. The physical contact which He must have had with them when reclining at table (compare John 13:25) and which He obviously never dreamed of disallowing (Luke 7:28, 39) must have made them feel clean and acceptable' (Nolan 1976:39).

Such socialising had significance not just at the time but for the future, for table-fellowship was, in Jesus' thinking, an anticipation of that great feast which will mark the consummation of the Kingdom. Those in company with Jesus, therefore, occupied seats which represented a future inheritance as well as present fulfilment.

Jesus pressed home the truth that the Kingdom breaks through all social and religious barriers not only by his startling personal actions which sent shock-waves through society, but also by a story with a sting in its tail. To that representative of the religious élite who by his bland statement, 'How happy are those who will sit down at the feast in the Kingdom of God!,' revealed that he counted on a reserved seat, our Lord told the parable of the Great Feast. In the story, those invited to attend made excuses; a response which so infuriated the host that he ordered his servant to 'Hurry out to the streets and alleys of the town, and bring back the poor, the crippled, the blind, and the lame. . . .' 'I tell you all that none of those men who were invited will taste the dinner' (Luke 14:15–24). The implication is clear. Those who were rejecting Christ's ministry were thereby refusing their invitation and relinquishing their place.

However, Jesus' free association with the poor and despised should not be interpreted to indicate their automatic admission into the Kingdom by virtue of their downtrodden position in society. In addressing them he utters no words of condemnation as he does in the case of the scribes and Pharisees, yet he nevertheless looks for a life-changing response from them. Having assured the woman caught in the act of adultery of forgiveness, he tells her, 'do not sin again' (John 8:11). It is after Zacchaeus has stood up and said to God, 'Listen, sir! I will give half my belongings to the poor, and if I have cheated anyone, I will pay him back four times as much', that Jesus exclaims, 'Salvation has come to this house today . . .' (Luke 19:8, 9). Of the two thieves crucified with Jesus, it is only to the one who expresses his penitence that Jesus responds, 'I promise you that today you will be in Paradise with me' (Luke 23:39–43).

Entry into the Kingom is not automatic. It is not a

consequence of heredity. Neither is it a reward for human effort. Indeed Jesus warned that those who came with an attitude of exclusive nationalism or spiritual complacency were in danger of being thrown out (Matt. 8:11, 12). He used the display of faith by a Roman officer who was a pagan 'outsider' as an occasion to rebuke the 'insiders'.

The key to entry into the Kingdom is the acceptance of Jesus as Saviour and Lord. It firstly demands a genuine repentance and baptism to signify cleansing from sin and death to the old way of life and resurrection to the new. It is not simply a matter of formal profession but of whole-hearted, life-yielding response (Matt. 7:21).

Peter was given the keys of the Kingdom when he came to the point of confessing Jesus as the 'Messiah, the Son of the living God' (Matt. 16:19). But his profession was deficient at the time in that he failed to recognise the necessity of suffering.

Entering the Kingdom is by invitation only, and that invitation must be given top priority. Other commitments must be held over (Matt. 22:1–4).

For some people, they stumble across the Kingdom without looking for it, like discovering a hidden treasure while turning over the soil in the field (Matt. 13:44). For others, they enter the Kingdom after an intense search, like the pearl merchant who sells his entire assets to buy one pearl which was everything (Matt. 13:45).

Membership of the Kingdom is non-transferable. No one can shift responsibility on to others or trade off their resources. The five foolish virgins with no oil for the lamps could neither buy nor borrow from those who had supplied their own lamps. Life in the Kingdom is one of constant readiness (Matt. 25:1–13). There are no gate-crashers; it cannot be taken by storm.

To enter the Kingdom of Heaven one had to come as a little child, who had no rights before the law, had an instinctive attitude of trust towards his parent, and was at a stage in life when he was teachable and flexible (Matt. 18:1).

This same point was made to Nicodemus who came to consult with Jesus cautiously and privately under cover of darkness. The Lord told him plainly that entering the Kingdom demanded a new start. He had to be born of water – that is, new life after the burial of baptism – and of the Spirit. Kingdom membership was only possible through an act of God. The work of the Spirit cannot be predicted or controlled by the religious profession! (John 3:1–13).

9 Growth of the Kingdom

As we noted previously, 'Kingdom' is a dynamic concept which might better be rendered 'Kingly rule or government'. Its growth, therefore, does not come about by territorial gains, but by individuals and groups submitting their wills to that of their Heavenly King. While entry into the Kingdom has an essential personal and individual element, it also has profound and extensive community ramifications. Individuals make their response not as one man islands, but within a framework of family, group, community and national involvements. Dr McGavran has drawn attention to the corporate dimension of conversion in describing 'people movements' to Christ, which we will be considering later in greater detail (see pp. 115–120).

At this point I simply want to underline the fact that Scripture demonstrates clearly that it is God's intention that the Kingdom should grow and not merely remain static, shrink or disappear altogether by seeping into society.

For the growth of the Kingdom man plays a secondary role as sower and husbandman of the seed; it is God who provides the seed and makes the plant grow.

The manifestation of the Kingdom often starts with *small and seemingly insignificant beginnings*. It is like the tiny mustard seed which grows into a sizeable bush that provides sufficient shade for the birds to come and shelter in its branches (Matt. 13:31; Mark 4:30; Luke 13:18, 19). At first people may be tempted to discount it.

The opponents of Jesus were unimpressed by his followers. 'If he really had a divine mission, ran the objection, he would not be surrounded by this rag-tag band, but by the best and the brightest. . . . Appealing for faith and confidence, the parable invites the hearer to see in Jesus' followers the seed of the vast communion of the saved . . . out of this unprepossessing band of disciples is destined to come the restored people, not only the lost sheep of Israel's house, but the nations, as well' (Meyer 1979:164).

The spread of the Kingdom might be *unobtrusive* like yeast in the dough (Matt. 13:33) which causes the whole mixture to rise, or like salt rubbed into the meat to preserve and flavour it (Luke 14:34). On the other hand the Kingdom might appear like a *blaze of lights* from a city located on high ground which can be seen from miles around (Matt. 5:14).

Although the Kingdom may have its origins in small beginnings in the majority of places, it is none the less capable of surprising growth. The seed planted in the good soil produced thirty, sixty and even a hundred times the original sowing. Even by the standards of modern high-intensity farming this is a remarkable yield (Mark 4:3–8).

John Kessler writing in the *International Review of Missions* in qualified support of Dr McGavran comments, 'The parables of the mustard seed and of the leaven (Matt. 13:31–35) give an implied warning of the dangers attending numerical growth, but at the same time they confirm that such growth is characteristic of the Kingdom of God' (IRM July 1968:299);

Other imagery, apart from husbandry, is also used to illustrate the growth of the Kingdom. It is represented as a net full of fish (Matt. 13:47, 48); as a banquet in which all the places must be occupied (Luke 14:21–24).

10 The mystery of the Kingdom

This phrase is used by Jesus in a number of places: Mark 4:11; Matt. 13:11; Luke 8:10, to introduce his 'parables of the Kingdom' and to explain why he used that oblique teaching form. To penetrate the 'mystery' demanded a level of spiritual discernment and faith commitment to Christ. 'Through faith in Jesus the disciples were able to understand what to others was hidden' (Snyder 1977:15). The point is that the majority of Jews expected the Kingdom to come in a *manifest* form arising from their understanding of the Old Testament prophecies and their experience of political subjugation under the Romans. In contrast to this manifestation the Kingdom has come in Jesus as a *mystery*. Eldon Ladd explains this mystery in the following terms; 'Before the day of harvest, before the end of the age, God has entered into history in the person of Christ to work among men, to bring to them the life and blessings of His Kingdom' (Ladd 1959:64), and again, 'The mystery of the Kingdom is this: that the Kingdom which will one day change the entire external order has entered into This age in advance to bring the blessings of God's Kingdom to men and women without transforming the old order. The old age is going on, yet men may already enjoy the powers of The Age to Come' (Ladd 1959:67).

The term 'mystery' is taken up in the letters of the New Testament where we read of 'the mystery of the gospel' (Eph. 6:19), 'the mystery of Christ' (Col. 4:3) and 'the mystery of godliness' (1 Tim. 3:16). These phrases see the unveiling of the divine mystery in the death and resurrection of Christ which brings about the possibility of reconciliation and new life in anticipation of the consummation of the Kingdom at the end of the Age. This 'mystery' of reconciliation has a horizontal as well as a vertical dimension. The terms of salvation are equally applicable to all men everywhere. William Barclay points out that, 'Paul's great contribution to the Christian faith was that he took Christ to the Gentiles and destroyed for ever the idea that God's love and mercy were the property of any one people or any one nation' (Barclay 1975:126) (See also Eph. 3:5; 8; Col. 1:26, 27). Such a possibility is presented as a 'mystery' because to the Jewish mind it would seem beyond the bounds of belief. Although the immediate context in the Pauline letters is the Jewish Gentile division, it also applies to any multi-racial situation in which groups harbour a sense of superiority or wish to retain a position of exclusiveness.

11 The Church and the Kingdom

Theologians across the centuries have struggled to express the relationship of the Church to the Kingdom. Augustine identified the two completely, and this identification has been maintained in traditional Catholic doctrine. In recent years *Lumen Gentium* has described the Church as 'the initial budding forth of the Kingdom'. Within Protestantism such an identification has been carried over in a modified form from the time of Martin Luther in the concept of the 'invisible church'. This distinction is made in recognition of the fact that not only is the Church in the world but the world is in the Church; that wheat and tares grow alongside each other until the harvest (Matt. 13:24–30, 36–43).

Other theologians, for a variety of reasons, draw a sharp distinction between the Church and the Kingdom. Alfred Loisy has expressed this in a phrase which has become classic, 'Jesus foretold the Kingdom of God, but it was the Church that came.' He regards the Church as a humanly devised institution to cope with the fact of the non-appearance of the Kingdom after the ascension of Christ.

Another group who make a complete separation between Church and Kingdom are the Dispensationalists. For them the Church was given by God in response to the rejection by Israel of her Messiah in the person of Jesus. In this scheme, the Kingdom is still future, to be inaugurated at the return of Christ with the Jewish people at its centre.

A third group, among them some Latin American liberation theologians, make the radical distinction between the Church and the Kingdom, because they feel that the institutional Church has become so corrupted and compromised that her only option is to die so that God can raise up a new people to serve his purposes in the world.

Here we see a shift of focus from that of identifying the Kingdom with the Church to one which sees its realisation in the world. The world is regarded as the Kingdom in the state of becoming.

In our concern for church growth it is imperative that we discern the relationship between the growth of the Church and the realisation of the Kingdom. Too close an identification will blind us to the shortcomings of the institutional Church, so that church growth becomes denominational aggrandisement. As soon as our focus of attention moves from Christ to the Church we move towards ecclesiastical deification and our evangelism is in great danger of degenerating into proselytism.

On the other hand to disassociate the Church from the Kingdom breaks the nerve-cord of hope and destroys the community of commitment to Christ as Saviour and Lord.

'Christ points the Church toward the Kingdom of God that is beyond the Church. To the degree that the Church follows his pointing and heeds his reminder, the Kingdom of God will manifest itself through the Church' (Pannenberg 1975:77).

'But note that this is quite different from attributing to the Church in its established structures the dignity of being the Kingdom of Christ. The rule of Christ is effected wherever man becomes aware of the coming Kingom of God and lives in accord with that awareness. . . . Precisely because the Church mistakes herself for the present form of the Kingdom, God's rule has often had to manifest itself in the secular world outside, and frequently against, the Church' (Pannenberg 1975:78).

The New Testament provides strong evidence that the Church occupies a central place in God's redemptive purpose for the world. We have already noted that entering the Kingdom entails a personal, saving relationship with Christ. When Peter made his profession of faith at Caesarea Philippi, Jesus declared that this was the rock foundation on which he would build his Church, which realisation provided the keys of the Kingdom (Matt. 16:17–19).

At the time of his ascension, how does Jesus respond to the question put to him by his disciples, 'Lord, will you at this time give the Kingdom back to Israel?' The way they phrase the question reveals the fact they are thinking in the old materialistic and nationalistic terms. His response is to impress upon them that the time is not now, that only God knows when it will be, and in the meantime they are to concentrate on the number-one task of world-wide witness for which the Holy Spirit would equip them (Acts 1:8). This is in line with his earlier command. When Jesus appeared after his resurrection to his disciples in Galilee, he told them, 'I have been given all authority in heaven and on earth.' In other words, has assumed the throne of the Kingdom. The consequences for his followers are clear. He commands them, 'Go, then, to all peoples everywhere and make them my disciples. . .' (Matt. 28:18–20).

When Philip is preaching in Samaria and the residents believe his 'message about the good news of the Kingdom of God and about Jesus Christ', their immediate response is to be baptised in his name (Acts 8:12). Paul, in presenting the gospel to Jews during his missionary journeys, equated his message about the identity and saving work of Christ with the Kingdom (Acts 19:8; 20:25; 28:23; 28:31). In his letter to the Colossians Paul describes Aristarchus, Mark and Justus, his companions in evangelism and church planting, as those who 'work with me for the Kingdom of God' (Col. 4:11).

Finally, the Epistle to the Ephesians, looking forward to the consummation of the Kingdom, with Christ ruling above all heavenly rulers, sees him given 'to the Church as supreme Lord over all things. The Church is Christ's body, the completion of him who himself completes all things everywhere' (Eph. 1:23).

12 Summary

Yes, the Kingdom is a much broader concept than the Church. God's activity is in no way restricted to the Church. His arena is the world he came to save. Outside the Church are to be found signs of the Kingdom in the form of his image, recognisable, though sadly disfigured, in the lives of all men. These traces not only witness to a sad history, but also hint of glorious possibilities. God, by his unpredictable and uncontainable Spirit, is guiding the destinies of nations and individuals who do not know him, or deny his very existence. Without such works of grace the world would rush even more rapidly towards the abyss. But such divine activity does not obviate the urgent need for witness. It makes it all the more opportune.

I believe that there may be many true children of the Kingdom outside of the institutional churches. Some have dissociated themselves because the churches have turned them off through their disobedience and indifference. Others are isolated individuals with no church within miles to link up to. Still others throw themselves on the mercy of God without being able to name the name of Christ because they have never been told about him. But such responses are inadequate, being less than the best that God intended, and has provided for.

While evangelism may not represent the totality of mission, it rests at its heart. 'How can they hear if the message is not proclaimed?' (Rom. 10:14). Having looked at the broader canvas of mission in these first two chapters, we now focus our attention without apology on the need for 'church growth'. In using this phrase I identify with the popular definition offered by Dr Peter Wagner of the School of World Mission, Fuller Seminary. 'Church growth means all that is involved in bringing men and women who do not have a personal relationship to

Jesus Christ into fellowship with him and into responsible church membership' (Wagner 1976:12). This narrowing of focus does not mean that we are laying to one side the issues raised in these two chapters as now dispensed with. On the contrary, they form the foundation blocks to all that follows, and serve as a constant reminder of the need to ensure that we are building on the right foundation and that the materials with which we build have spiritual survival capability (1 Cor. 3:12). The emphasis of the book from now on is of a pragmatic nature, but I hope it is a sanctified pragmatism applied to operating within and shaping the contemporary manifestations of the Church of Christ. We recognise that the Church is a divinely constituted organism and not merely a human institution; that its task is to point beyond itself and not to indulge in self-glorification; that to be truly the Church it must submit to the Lordship of Christ and live its daily life in dependence on the presence and resources of the Holy Spirit; and that it must be incarnated in the world Christ came to redeem, in which he is already present, and for which he has prepared a transformed future. When such growing churches manifest the marks of the Kingdom of righteousness, peace and joy (Rom. 14:7) both in their own lives and in engagement with the world, then we will be able to pray less wistfully and more hopefully 'thy kingdom come, thy will be done on earth, as it is in heaven.'

CHAPTER THREE

Gospel and Culture

EFFECTIVE COMMUNICATION OF the gospel depends not only upon a thorough understanding of the content of the message, but also on an ability to relate that message to the contemporary situation. Most Christian communicators have been more message than receptor oriented. They have not been sufficiently sensitive to the fact that the message received may differ substantially from that which they imagined they had delivered. When it comes to evangelising, Michael Green reminds us, 'Evangelism is never proclamation in a vacuum; but always to people, and the message must be given in terms that make sense to them' (Green 1970:115).

In the communication process we are more heavily and extensively influenced by our culture in the interpretations that we give to all that we see and hear than we often realise. Communication 'includes not only language but all symbol systems, such as use of time, space, gestures, and rituals' (Hiebert 1976:121), each of which are used in culturally determined ways. Consequently, if we are to achieve greater effectiveness in our ability to communicate, we must increase our understanding of the impact of culture.

If this is true of communication in general, it is even more relevant when thinking in terms of the communication of the gospel. The good news of Jesus was originally conveyed within an ancient culture very different from that of twentieth-century western man. As a first stage in the communication process we therefore need to see that message in its original context in order to discern the timeless truth which God was seeking to communicate within that situation. As a second stage, that timeless truth has to be applied to the contemporary situation in such a way as to make the hearer feel the force of its original impact, without either diluting or distorting its intention.

In the case of a Christian communicator seeking to convey the essence of the gospel and establish a church in a culture other than his own, the communication process becomes still more complex. Having lived with a cultural expression of the gospel adapted to his own context, he then has to divest the message of that cultural adaptation and to seek to introduce the gospel in a form which is culturally appropriate to the community with which he is then seeking to communicate. This is the nature of the missionary gift, namely the ability to operate in a cross-cultural context.

The task of evangelism which begins with how one speaks the gospel in meaningful terms extends, as soon as converts result, to what kind of Christian community can most authentically express the new life of the gospel within that cultural context.

These are some of the complex issues which will be our concern in this chapter. It is the author's conviction that this subject is highly relevant not just to the overseas missionary situation, but to many sectors of society in this country which as yet have remained unreached and resistant to the traditional approaches of the institutional churches.

During his time as Bishop of Woolwich, responsible for an area stretching from the inner-city boroughs of South London to the Surrey commuter belt, David Sheppard conducted a survey of 150 parishes to show the electoral roll members of the Church of England as a percentage of the total population. The results, based on the revised figures of 1972, were as follows:

Surrey	9%
Blackheath and Dulwich	4%
Outer suburban	3.25%
Inner suburban	1.8%
Working class	0.9%

(Sheppard 1974:45)

This pattern is also repeated in an unpublished survey conducted by Richard Whatmore on Church of England parishes in Brighton and Hove. His research showed that the electoral roll membership per percentage of population was 5.6% for upper middle-class areas, falling to 0.9% in working-class parishes consisting mainly of council housing.

Such statistics clearly show that the Church of England has a more widespread appeal in middle-class than in artisan areas. Many people still regard it as the Tory party at prayer. But have the Free Churches succeeded where the Church of England has failed? Regrettably the answer is 'No'. They too failed to make any significant impact, and many struggling churches have either been forced to close or to relocate in the suburbs following the migration pattern of their members.

Bishop David Sheppard raises the question, 'If it can be shown that visible response to the Church is on a totally different scale in working-class areas from middle-class areas, who can we blame?' He identifies four possibilities:

1 *Working-class people* – presumably for being harder-hearted than others.
2 *God* – for not sending revival to those areas of society.
3 *The Church* – for not learning how to be an effective vehicle of the gospel.
4 *Society* – for what it has done to those who are trapped by the forces of the big city.

(Sheppard 1974:42)

Few would deny that the answer to the bishop's question lies with alternatives 3 and 4. Although the Church was slow off the mark following the population migration and concentration in the expanding towns during the Industrial Revolution, her failure has not been for want of trying. The root of the problem is located in the culturally inappropriate methods which were adopted and, in the case of the Church of England, with her parish system which was an inappropriate structure for a densely populated area.

Not only have the churches significantly failed to appeal to those within artisan cultures, they have also been unsuccessful in attracting those of other races from among the West Indian and Asian communities. As the majority of the latter are either Moslem, Sikh or Hindu, it is understandable that the Church has encountered severe problems in trying to communicate her message, either with a view to attracting them into their fellowship or to see the significance of the gospel of Jesus Christ within their own cultural context.

The same problem did not exist, however, in the case of the West Indian communities, as the majority of these were members of churches in their home countries, but lapsed on migrating to Britain. The churches here failed to establish contact, provide a warm welcome, or adjust their ways of doing things so that West Indians could feel at home. As a consequence the majority of black Christians during the 1960s decided to go it alone and formed themselves into separate churches, such as the New Testament Church of God. These churches grew rapidly during the 1960s and early 1970s until today it is estimated that twenty per cent of the total black population is associated with one or other of the black churches. Recent evidence, however, suggests that this rapid growth surge may now have begun to subside.

1 Defining culture

When we speak of 'culture' we are not thinking about high-brow music, or good table manners. We understand the term as defined by anthropologists. Paul G. Hiebert offers the following definition of culture 'as the integrated system of learned patterns of behaviour, ideas and products characteristic of a society' (Hiebert 1976:25). For Dr Eugene Nida 'culture' is 'all nonmaterial traits which are passed on from one generation to another. They are both transmittable and accumulative, and they are cultural in the sense that they are transmitted by the society, not by the genes' (Nida 1954:28).

The Willowbank Report – Gospel and Culture helpfully expands Dr Eugene Nida's definition to show its comprehensive coverage of all aspects of life. 'Culture is an *integrated system of beliefs* (about God or reality or ultimate meanings), of *values* (about what is true, good, beautiful and normative), of *customs* (how to behave, relate to others, talk, pray, dress, work, trade, farm, eat, etc.), and of *institutions* which express these beliefs, values and customs (government, law courts, temples or churches, family, school, hospitals, factories, shops unions, clubs, etc.), which bind a society together and give it a sense of identity, dignity, security, and continuity. (Willowbank Report 1978:7).

2 Christ in relation to culture

When the gospel is proclaimed and the Church begins to emerge there is an inevitable interaction with the cultural milieu which surrounds and permeates this activity. We need, therefore, to understand the relationship of gospel to culture in general terms, and then go on to examine in detail its engagement with the specific culture in which we are involved.

H. R. Niebuhr has shown the range of thinking with regard to the relationship between Christ and culture adopted by theologians at various times (Niebuhr 1951). He categorises five views:

2.1 Christ against culture

This is the radical position which sets the Church against the world. When the individual turns to Christ he rejects the world, for the world 'is in the power of the evil one'. Support for such a position can be found in the Gospel and Epistles of John. The 'world is under judgement' (John 12:31), it is a place of tribulation for believers, which has to be 'overcome' by the Lord (John 16:33). His Kingdom does not belong to this world (John 18:36). Believers are not to love the world, and one day it will pass away (1 John 2:15, 17). The 'Christ against culture' position was adopted by Tertullian in the fourth century and Tolstoy in recent times. It is represented by the thinking of Anabaptists and many fundamentalist and Pentecostal groups, who regard the Church as a rescue post from the world.

Charles Kraft exposes three fallacies in this approach: (i) 'it equates the concept "culture" with only the negative use of the Greek word *kosmos* in the New Testament.' He points out that when John uses that term in a negative sense it is with 'specific reference not to the whole of culture, but to a particular *use* of that culture by the forces of evil.'

(ii) 'it assumes that it is possible by "running" to escape from one's culture. However, this is to misunderstand the nature of culture as something external to us. Culture is within as well as surrounding us.'

(iii) 'it assumes that since Satan is able to use culture to his ends, all of culture is evil. As we shall see shortly, the Scriptures employ "kosmos" in a positive as well as a negative sense' (Kraft 1979: 105, 106)

2.2 Christ of culture

In this view Christ is regarded as the inspirer and perfecter of culture. The best ingredients of each culture are selected which most express his character and purposes for mankind. This was the position held by many of the

Gnostics, Abelard, Ritschl and those who express syncretistic sentiments within the ecumenical movement.

Some would turn the argument around and claim that the concept of deity is the product of that culture, being no more than an idealisation and personalisation of cultural elements, without any objective existence. In the case of the Judaeo-Christian concept of deity this can be strongly challenged on the grounds of the historical basis of divine revelation. For the Christian this revelation comes to fullness in the incarnation of Christ. While the Scriptures speak within particular cultural contexts they present a constant challenge to the concepts of deity and morality which are generated by the cultures addressed to God. He is in no sense the idealised self-image to be possessed and manipulated. His immanence does not displace his transcendence. He dwells in the unapproachable light of the *shekinah* glory, and his thoughts are not our thoughts or our ways his ways (Is. 55:8).

2.3 Christ above culture

This is the position of Justin Martyr, Clement of Alexandria and Thomas Aquinas, who see Christ as 'the fulfilment of cultural aspirations and the restorer of the institutions of true society. Yet there is in him something that neither arises out of culture nor contributes directly to it. He is discontinuous as well as continuous with social life and its culture' (Niebuhr 1951:42). Christians who adopt this conceptual framework recognise that within culture there are laws additional to those expressed by Jesus Christ which are also from God. They must therefore seek to achieve a synthesis of those God-imposed requirements rendering 'to Caesar the things that are Caesar's and to God the things that are God's' (Matt. 22:21).

2.4 Christ and culture in paradox

This view accepts the 'Christ above culture' position, but fails to achieve a workable synthesis. It therefore places them in a paradoxical relationship and leaves the believer to live with the tension of relating to the world. This dualistic position can be detected in the writings of the apostle Paul, a view endorsed by Luther, where the Christian is described as 'under law, and yet not under law but grace; he is a sinner, and yet righteous, he believes as a doubter; he has assurance of Salvation, yet walks the knife-edge of insecurity. In Christ all things have become new, and yet everything remains as it was from the beginning. . .' (Niebuhr 1951:156, 157).

In its negative assessment of human effort it is akin to the 'Christ against culture' position, yet differs in response to that situation. Recognising that man cannot escape, it leaves him to cope with the paradox and frustration, content to walk by faith, not by sight, believing that one day all things will become new and be reconciled in Christ.

2.5 Christ the transformer of culture

This represents a more positive attitude towards culture than 2, 3 and 4, although it is more critical than the second position listed here. While culture remains under the judgement of God it is also subject to his saving rule. This view is sometimes seen as represented in the Gospel of John. In support of this view are the positive responses of John to the world. 'God so loved the world that he gave his son' (John 3:16). John regards him as Saviour of the world and records Jesus' declaration to be the light of the world (John 8:12). Augustine, John Wesley and F. D. Maurice have identified with this emphasis. For them culture is there to be converted rather than replaced by something entirely new. 'Culture, therefore, is seen as corrupted but convertible, usable, perhaps even redeemable by God's grace and power' (Kraft 1979:113).

To Nida's original five categories we venture to offer a sixth.

2.6 Christ above but working through culture
This is the alternative accepted by Kraft. He argues 'though God exists totally outside of culture, while humans exist totally within culture, God chooses the cultural milieu in which humans are immersed as the arena for his interaction with people' (Kraft 1979:114). Such an approach represents a deliberate self-limiting on the part of God in order to speak in understandable terms and with perceived relevance on the part of the hearer. He acts redemptively with regard to culture, which includes judgement on some elements, but also affirmation in other areas, and a transformation of the whole. We will trace in this chapter the significance of the 'Christ above but working through culture' model in terms of God's revelation and the Church's communication task and structural adaptations.

From the beginning man, made in the image of God, was entrusted with a cultural mandate to exercise authority over his environment (Gen. 1:26–30). He was placed 'in charge' and his descendants were 'to live all over the earth and bring it under their control'. 'Those divine commands are the origin of human culture. For basic to culture are our control of nature (that is, of our environment) and our development of forms of social organisation' (Willowbank Report 1978:7).

This cultural mandate was not rescinded by the fall of man, it simply became more complex and energy-draining. Since the fall all that man does involves an exertion 'against the odds' and all his efforts are marred by imperfection and disfigured by selfishness. Yet despite the image of God within man being tragically disfigured it is, for all that, still discernible. Subsequent to the fall man continues to be regarded as made in the image of God (Gen. 9:6; James 3:9). He has not become the image of Satan. He is required by God to fulfil a social mandate by exercising stewardship of the earth (Gen. 8:21–9:17). Because cultural achievement – i.e. building cities, raising livestock, producing music and manufacturing all kinds of tools (Gen. 4:17–22) – is through fallen man, those innovations which should express the positive, beautiful, creative skills bestowed by God can so easily be turned to evil ends. Thus cities built to provide security and express community become the location of violence and alienation; land and livestock which provide independence, nourishment and security are grabbed by greedy exploiters; musical instruments which were intended to express harmony, reflect moods and increase sensitivity, are used to deafen, dehumanise and manipulate; tools which were fashioned to create objects of utility and beauty are used to make instruments of torture and destruction. Like the broom in the Sorcerer's Apprentice they got out of hand. Every culture displays confusion and contradictions. In some aspects they bear evidence of the hand of God safeguarding human dignity and expressing creativity. Yet intermingled are elements which threaten the disintegration of the whole fabric.

Despite the mixed benefits, man cannot dispense with culture. For culture helps to explain and evaluate the realities of life. It provides the stability of psychological reinforcement. It establishes a commonality of understanding on which to build a community. It weaves the societal framework which serves as a bridge to the next generation, preserving continuity, and a wall against encroachment and disintegration.

No one lives outside a cultural context. We are all to a great extent the product of our culture. As we have noted, there are good and bad, strong and weak elements in each culture. The cultural framework in which we have been raised and within which we have been taught to operate provides both security and significance within its frontiers. But beyond those frontiers are alien cultures which impinge on our own for good or ill. Sometimes the relationship is one of *co-existence* – two cultures exist side by side but in separate compartments. At other times they may exist in *competition*, each endeavouring to gain influence in a third area. Yet again, they may give rise to *conflict*, with one seeking to dominate the other either through conquest or infiltration. At other times they serve to enrich each other through the mutual benefit of *cross-fertilisation*. These options indicate something of the complexity of relationships between cultures.

Eugene Nida argues that humans are 'culture-shaped and culture-transmitting beings' (Nida 1954:28). Each transmits culture down to the next generation and out through his network of relationships. He cannot help but notice the presence of other cultures when they come into contact with his own, because their influences are all-pervasive. Having become aware of the difference, his deep-seated bias is to consider his own as not only different but preferable. He is prone to regard his own pattern of belief and behaviour as normative and all others as deviant. 'To view other people's ways of life in terms of our own cultural glasses is called ethnocentrism' (Keesing and Keesing 1971:21–quoted by Kraft 1979:48).

In the early days of the development of anthropology it was the fashion to place culture on an evolutionary ladder ranging from primitive to developed. The fact that Western cultures were placed by the anthropologists on the uppermost rungs reflects their ethnocentric perspective! This evolutionary model has subsequently been replaced by a relativistic one; this maintains that 'an observer should be careful to evaluate a culture first in terms of its own values, goals, and focuses before venturing to compare it (either positively or negatively) with any other culture' (Kraft 1979:49). Patterns of behaviour which appear strange or even wrong from the standpoint of the outside observer interpreting what he seems in terms of his own cultural frame of reference, may, when understood in their broader cultural setting, be perfectly reasonable and even commendable. This is easier said that done. But to highlight the problem helps us to identify and confess our bias. It requires special gifts of insight and patience to move from a mono-cultural to a cross-cultural perspective.

The fact that cultures differ from each other for historical and environmental reasons is understandable. The next question arises. Is it desirable? With increased control over nature, mass media communication systems and rapid long-distance travel, should we expect to arise and seek to hasten a cultural integration? Will cultures so intermingle as to produce a composite and cohesive super-culture or conversely will their interaction produce contradictions and confusions which will bring about cultural disintegration? Or will they cross-pollinate to their mutual enrichment? This is an important question for the future expectations embedded in the mission of the Church. We shall return to it later in the chapter.

3 Culture and biblical revelation

The biblical perspective of divine revelation is of God who speaks at specific times addressing himself to particular situations. He uses language and imagery which communicate most precisely the truths he wishes to convey to a specific audience, be that audience a solitary individual, a group, a nation or a number of nations. 'He reveals Himself in a receptor-orientated fashion' (Kraft 1979:169). Though God is totally free of culture he chooses to clothe his message in cultural form so that people will immediately see its relevance and feel its impact. By the way it is expressed it becomes a word from God to *them*, at their level of understanding, indigenous and applicable to their times and struggles.

Kraft, in Part IV of his book *Christianity in Culture* entitled 'The Dynamics of Revelation' introduces a new perspective to the debate on the inspiration of Scripture among evangelicals. He sees the Bible as containing a section of classic case studies of the ways God deals with mankind in a variety of situations across a considerable period of time. As such, it emphasises that God's revelatory activity is a dynamic process rather than a static product. The completion of the canon of Scripture by the early Church does not signify that they thought the Lord had stopped speaking or that he had nothing fresh to say. The purpose of Scripture is to act as a 'yardstick' and 'tether' by which to assess any claim to contemporary revelation, and to regulate its interpretation. The Holy Spirit continues to operate in revealing the mind of Christ to his Church. 'But the nature of his teaching ministry has changed. We believe that his work of "inspiration" is done in the sense that the canon of Scripture is closed, but that his work of "illumination" continues both in every conversion (e.g. 2 Cor. 4:6) and in the life of the Christian and the Church' (Willowbank Report 1978:9). He speaks in the life situation as well as through the sacred page. He guides our actions according to his revealed character and purposes which are reliably recorded in Scripture. God's redemptive plan is complete in the work of Christ. Nothing can be added to the Scriptural record.

Yet God still speaks by his Spirit to throw fresh light on his word so that we might see its relevance to the contemporary world, and he speaks to his servants to guide them through the perplexities of life. Though he may say things to them that have no exact parallels in Scripture, his word does not contradict Scripture, neither does it have the same normative quality. It is a specific word for a particular situation.

The Bible is no academic tome with an esoteric appeal to those with scholarly minds who can handle abstract concepts. It is a record of events, with interpretative comments woven into the narrative. Kraft records that 'even the most theological portions (e.g. Romans) participate in the "eventness" of the facts that they were written as letters from specific persons to specific persons to meet specific needs' (Kraft 1979:128). Some Bible students have been inspired to feel the immediacy of the communications by the exercise of rewriting one of Paul's letters as though it was addressed to them, paraphrasing in their own words.

Following the approach of Greek logic, many western

educated communicators adopt a deductive approach, arguing from the general to the particular. The Bible takes the opposite approach; it moves from the particular to the general, using the inductive method.

'Many of the problems we have in church are caused by the fact that ministers tend to speak Greek and most people understand only Hebrew. Greek is the language that lends itself to the communication of abstract concepts. Hebrew is a "picture" language. In Hebrew the speaker draws pictures the listener can visualise in his mind' (Schaller 1973:124).

The narrative content and picture-language commentary make for powerful communication. No wonder the Bible has such a universal appeal, and its potential impact so alarms political and ideological leaders antagonistic to its message that its production and distribution is severely restricted in half the world. While many people may be switched off by the complexity of an argument, they can enter into the experience of another person. They, thereby, learn by existential identification what they would never have learned if the only approved approach was by objective, abstract analysis. The Bible regarded as a divinely inspired selection of classic case studies provides an understanding of inspiration which couples 'truth with impact' (Kraft 1979:213).

Our emphasis on the culture-conditioning of revelation poses some problems which must be squarely faced.

Firstly *it must not lead us into a relativist position regarding Scripture as but one of many revelations of God.* It occupies a unique and normative position by which to judge the statements of other sacred writings, be they from other religions or Christian devotional classics.

Lesslie Newbigin expressed the problem in terms of two dogmatic systems. 'According to one dogma, world history is in some sense a coherent whole, and it is therefore possible to affirm that certain events have a unique significance for the entire story. According to the other dogma, there are no events which have such unique significance and therefore no universally valid affirmation can be made about the meaning of history as a whole' (Newbigin 1978:174). The acceptance of the former dogma rather than the second depends on a faith commitment to Christ as Lord and an acceptance of the unique salvation history which has significance for the whole of mankind.

However, such acceptance does not extend to a recognition 'that the cultural forms of the semitic world have authority over all other cultural forms' (Newbigin 1978). Paul firmly resists the strenuous efforts of the Judaisers to demand cultural conformity from the Gentile converts (Gal. 2:11–14).

Newbigin cities the evidence of not one but a variety of Christologies in the New Testament reflecting 'the attempts of that community to say who Jesus is in terms of the different cultures within which they bore witness to him.' The *variety* of Christologies actually to be found in the New Testament is part of the fundamental witness to the nature of the gospel; it points to the *destination* of the gospel in all the cultures of mankind. The *unity* of the New Testament, the fact that it contains not every Christology, but only those which were judged to be faithful to the original testimony, reflect the *origin* of the gospel in the one unique person of Jesus (Newbigin 1978:176).

Secondly *the fact that God's personal self-disclosure in the Bible was given in terms of the hearers' own culture inevitably means that misunderstanding may arise and points be missed when read by people of another culture who are unfamiliar with the cultural milieu of the Bible.* If questions are put to the text which the particular passage was not written to answer then wrong conclusions can easily be drawn. This is a problem with which Bible translators constantly have to battle. They recognise that it is inadequate and sometimes completely misleading to translate the text word for word, or phrase by phrase from the Hebrew, Aramaic and Greek into their mother tongue. Their task is to so translate the text that it speaks with the original intention and force as it did to those originally addressed. In order to achieve this they may from time to time have to change the form in order to preserve the meaning. This translation principle is called the 'dynamic equivalence' as distinct from the 'formal correspondence' method.

Dr Eugene Nida has a fund of examples to illustrate the need for 'dynamic equivalent' translations. 'One cannot say to the Zanaki people along the shores of the sprawling Lake Victoria, "Behold I stand at the door and knock" (Rev. 3:20). This would mean that Christ was declaring himself to be a thief, for in Zanaki land thieves generally make it a practice to knock on the door of a hut which they hope to burglarise, and if they hear any movement inside, they dash off into the dark. An honest man will come to the house and call the name of the person inside, and in this way identify himself by his voice. Accordingly, in the Zanaki translation it is necessary to say, "Behold, I stand at the door and call" ' (Nida 1952:46).

The translation problem is even more difficult when faced with presenting Jesus as the 'Good Shepherd' (Ps. 23 and John 10) in parts of Africa where the care of sheep is relegated to children or the mentally subnormal. It is the care of cattle which is regarded as man's work. Therefore, simply to represent Jesus as the Good Shepherd without any explanatory note would convey entirely the wrong impression.

We are immediately made aware of the problem in translating biblical material which relates readily to our culture into a language and culture where there is no such correspondence of meaning as in the illustrations cited above. But we too are open to misunderstanding where cultural variants go undetected between the Bible and ourselves. For instance, we can easily miss the point made by our Lord when he set a child in the midst of the crowd and declared to the surrounding throng that if they wished to enter the Kingdom of Heaven they would have to become as a little child (Matt. 18:4). He was not here primarily teaching the need for simplicity and trust, though this is within the range of permissible interpretations according to Kraft's 'tether model'. His main point, which his immediate audience would not fail to grasp, was that the 'little child' had not yet reached the age of the 'bar Mitzvah' ceremony, or 'coming-of-age', which within the Jewish culture meant that the 'little child' had no rights before the Law of God. He was in fact obliquely and tellingly challenging the self-righteousness of the scribes and Pharisees.

Such illustrations lead to a third problem: *Does the culture conditioning of God's self-revelation mean that the Bible cannot be understood by ordinary people without the help of theologically trained interpreters?* The foregoing illustrations emphasise some problems of interpretation across culture, however much of the teaching of Scripture is plain and obvious. Understanding it does not require a great intellectual capacity or specialist training. Enlightenment comes through spiritual perception which results from the work of the Holy Spirit in the individual's life (1 Cor. 2:10–13). 'The reader interprets the text as if it had been written in his own language, culture and time. . . . For God intended his word for ordinary people; it is not to be regarded as the preserve of scholars; the central truths of salvation are plain for all to see; Scripture is "useful for teaching the truth, rebuking error, correcting faults, and giving instruction for right living" (2 Tim. 3:16); and the Holy Spirit has been given to be our teacher' (Willowbank Report 1978:10).

One does not need hermaneutical skills to appreciate the significance and personal challenge presented by the great truths of salvation. If a point is missed because it is too deeply embedded in its cultural setting in one place, it stands out prominently and unequivocally in another. In many places the cultural context of the original account may bear sufficient likeness to our own to enable us to interpret what transpires without much difficulty. The exhortations of Scripture which relate to personal qualities and Christian virtues require little adaptation when transposed from one culture to another. The command to 'love one's neighbour', for example, is a cultural universal. Furthermore, despite the diversities of cultures there remains a great deal of commonality. It is chiefly in the realms of social customs and economic arrangements that we must have specialist knowledge of the context to enable us to interpret the passage accurately.

Yet, notwithstanding the problems generated by a culturally conditioned revelation, it has enormous value. 'Because of their specificity to the cultural agreements of the original hearers, these materials communicated with maximum impact to them. This is a major part of the genius of God and of his Word – that it speaks specifically to people where they are and in terms of the culture in which they are immersed. At the same time this fact enormously complicates the task of the person immersed in another culture who seeks to interpret the Scripture' (Kraft 1979:134).

4 Culture and contemporary communication

In the preceding section we emphasised the fact that revelation in Scripture is 'receptor-orientated', not in the sense of affirming the hearers by telling them only what they want to hear, but by speaking specifically to their situation so that they cannot miss what they need to hear. In both Old and New Testament people are addressed through concepts which are already familiar to them. The Old Testament alluded to 'leviathan' the Babylonian sea-monster. It takes up the concept of 'covenant' already familiar in the ancient world. In the scriptural usage of that term there is both continuity and discontinuity with that wider understanding. The Old Testament also alludes to a three-tier universe. Within the New Testament concepts from the Old Testament are taken up and spiritualised, for example 'messiah', 'Son of Man' and 'Kingdom of Heaven'. The teaching and life-style of John the Baptist identifies him with the prophetic tradition in Israel. Our Lord's ministry was styled along the lines of the rabbinic model, with the itinerant teacher followed by a group of disciples who learned by listening, questioning and working under supervision. Yet at the same time there was discontinuity, for Jesus taught 'not as the scribes', for unlike them his message was self-authenticating. He did not flinch from declaring 'I say to you' and then made astounding claims about himself.

As soon as the Church spread from Jewish into Gentile cultures further adaptation was required. Michael Green writes, 'Once Christianity took root in Hellenistic soil, it became necessary to do a tremendous work of translation. Not only words, but ideas had to be put into other dress. Without such a task of translation, the message would have been heard, perhaps, but not assimilated' (Green 1970:115). The terms Logos (Word), Lord, Kingdom, Adoption were meaningful to pagan ears, so the person of Christ and the nature of his mission is expressed in those concepts.

As for initiatory rites, while circumcision was peculiar to Judaism in the Roman world, baptism was widely practised. 'For in the first century water initiation rites were used to induct people into a number of different groups. Among these were Judaism (for proselytes) and the Greek mystery religions as well as the Church' (Kraft 1979:68). The one form is given a new meaning in its Christian context in which the initiate is identified with the death and resurrection of Jesus Christ.

When our Lord calls Peter, Andrew, James and John to follow him he invites them to learn to become fishers of men. He speaks to them in terms of their employment. He does not use this kind of language in calling Matthew the tax-collector. Paul describes himself as a 'bond-slave' of Jesus Christ in the opening sentence of many of his letters. This was a title with which many of his readers who were Christians in slavery would readily identify, and would be a concept which all would understand.

These represent just some illustrations of 'receptor-orientated' communication to be found in Scripture.

While in the north of England I was told the following story which provides an amusing illustration of the same principle brilliantly applied by two small boys who had never heard of the terminology! The two boys lived in Hull, a low-lying coastal town. The highest point was reckoned to be the flyover. One of the boys had been away to the Lake District for his holidays where he had seen mountains for the first time in his life. In returning to Hull he attempted to describe to his friend what a mountain was like. 'You know t'flyover?' he asked, 'Well, a mountain is a million times bigger than that, and covered wi' muck!'

In the communication process the one who speaks and the one who hears each formulate their ideas within their own frame of reference. Each frame of reference is constructed largely through cultural influences. Broadly speaking there are four possible approaches (see Fig. 1):

4.1 Alternative approaches

4.1.1 *Isolation*. This describes the process of non-communication. The speaker expresses his message in terms of his own perceptions and within his own frame of reference without making any attempt to relate what he wants to say with what the other person is likely to hear. His hearers completely fail to comprehend because the message is couched in unfamiliar vocabulary and does not make contact with any of their felt needs. His speaking is no more meaningful than the conversation of adults as portrayed in the televised version of the Charlie Brown cartoons. These adults never actually appear on the screen and their speech is represented as no more than an incoherent buzz of verbal static, because adults are irrelevant to the world of Charlie Brown, Lucie, Linus, Snoopy and Woodstock.

4.1.2 *Extraction*. This describes the classroom (and frequently also the pulpit) approach to communication. The

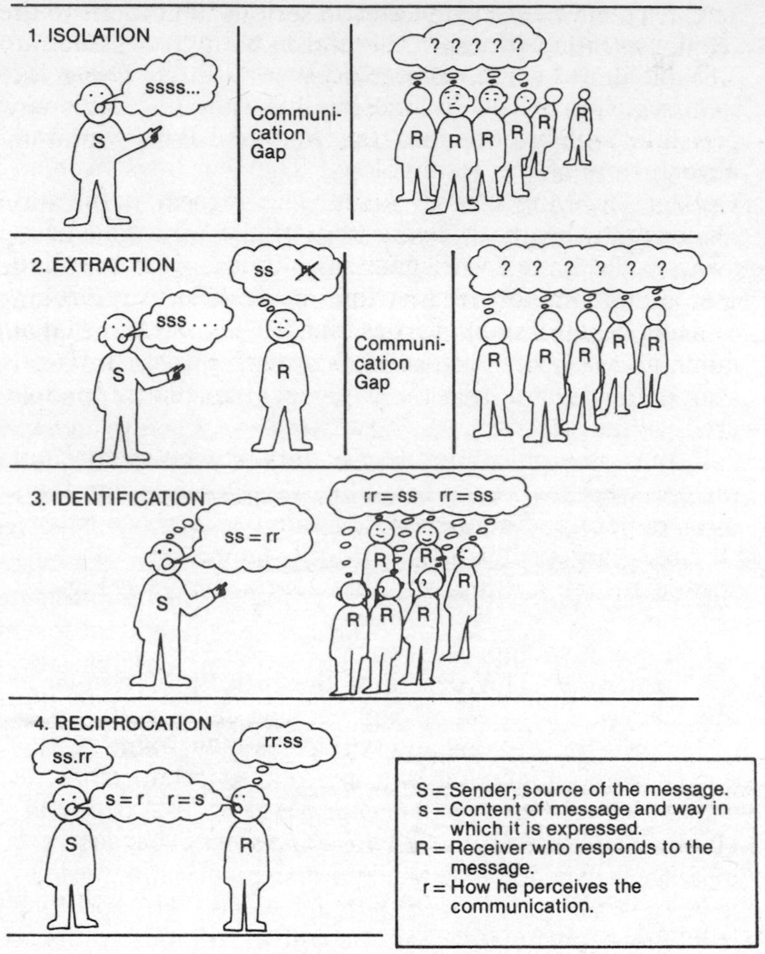

Fig. 1
Attempts at cross-cultural communication.

teacher (or preacher) establishes the lines of communication by educating the pupils (or congregation) into his terminology and concepts. In so doing he extracts his audience from their 'frame of reference'.

Such a method introduces two serious inhibitions to the communication process. The person being processed into the speaker's frame of reference may in so doing lose contact with his own, so that he cannot relate his new knowledge to his life situation; neither can he communicate it to others.

'Extraction' applies to the form of the communication as well as to the content. A Bible translator in one of the Andean republics recounted the following story to the author. The particular tribe among whom he was working couched their teaching in story form, and the main story-line was always the same – the events were set in the context of a journey, for they were a nomadic people. He noticed that when local church leaders had been away for Bible School training, they ceased to tell stories in their preaching. They had been trained at college to preach Western-style sermons based on abstract thinking arranged in linear form. As a consequence they were 'extracted' from their culture and failed to communicate to their own people. He decided to adopt a different approach and to try and teach the Bible through story-telling. He soon realised that the Bible was full of journeys! What better way to describe God's dealing with Israel in the Old Testament, than with the stories of Abraham, the Exodus and the Exile. In the Gospels Jesus is for ever on the move. The Acts is a non-stop travelogue. Paul's letter to Philemon tells how he has urged Onesimus to stop running and return to the scene of his crime and seek reconciliation with his master.

4.1.3 *Identification*. In this communication process the speaker explores his hearers' frame of reference, seeking to identify areas of common ground between them. He then couches his message in terms with which his hearers will be familiar, seeking to move from the known to the unknown. Thus Paul in Athens uses language and concepts with which the Stoics in his audience can identify and before the Sanhedrin, the Jewish supreme court in

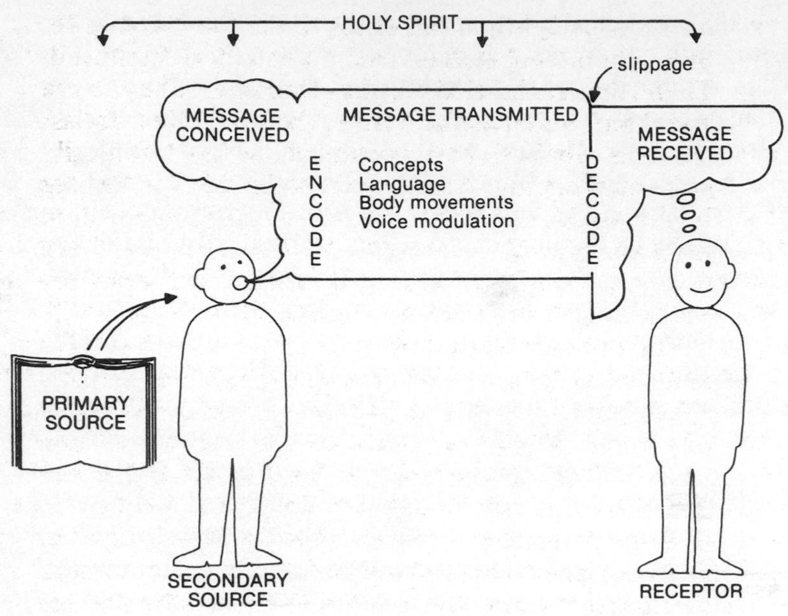

Fig. 2
The communication process

Jerusalem, he establishes common ground with the Pharisees among the council members.

Don and Carol Richardson, in the account of their work among the Sawi tribespeople in Irian Jaya, vividly illustrate the importance of this approach. When he had gained a smattering of language, so Don began to describe the ministry of Jesus to save this animistic, headhunting people from evil.

> Only once did my presentation win a ringing response from them.
>
> I was describing Judas Iscariot's betrayal of the Son of God . . . at the climax of the story Maum whistled a birdcall of admiration. Kani and several

> others touched their fingertips to their chests in awe. Still others chuckled. At first I sat there confused. Then the realisation broke through. They were acclaiming Judas as the hero of the story! Yes, Judas, the one whom I had portrayed as the satanically motivated enemy of truth and goodness! . . . nothing I said would erase that gleam of savage enjoyment from their eyes . . . I saw now that the Sawi were not only cruel, but honoured cruelty . . . treachery was idealised as a virtue, as a goal of life.
>
> The only protection from treachery was to receive a 'tarop' or 'peace child' from the neighbouring tribe which posed the threat. This infant was given up by one family to go and live with the other tribe. The peace child was the 'culturally built-in antidote to the Sawi idealisation of violence.'
>
> When I stopped to think about it, I realised you and your ancestors are not the only ones who found that peace required a peace child, Don later told his hearers.
>
> 'Myao Kodon, the Spirit whose message I bear, has declared the same thing – true peace can never come without a peace child! Never!. . .'
>
> Mahan looked at me and asked, 'Is he the one you've been telling us about? Yesus?'
>
> 'He's the very one!' I replied.
>
> 'But you said a friend betrayed him – if Yesus was a tarop it was very wrong to betray Him.' (Richardson 1974:177–214).

Communication had begun at the point where Don Richardson had succeeded in relating his message to the Sawi frame of reference.

This story vividly illustrates the complexity of the communication process especially when there is a wide linguistic and cultural chasm to cross as in the case of a twentieth-century westerner communicating with animistic head-hunters in a remote island of Indonesia. However, not all of these barriers automatically disappear when the communication event occurs between people of similar cultural backgrounds.

4.1.4 *Reciprocation*. Most attempts at identification in terms of verbal communication and life-style are at best only partially successful. The act of identification is a bridge-building operation to establish contact and to develop a depth of understanding. To accomplish this effectively requires the cross-cultural missionary gift. St Paul had such a gift and so was able when working with Gentiles to live like a Gentile (1 Cor. 9:21). Many attempts at identification appear as unconvincing efforts at imitation from the standpoint of the host culture.

In a mature relationship imitation is replaced by reciprocation, in which the parties frankly recognise their differences while resisting the temptation to think that 'because my ways are different from yours they are therefore better'. The reciprocal relationship embodies two-way communication, with each open to be influenced by the other. Through such cross-cultural pollination the ideas of each are challenged, affirmed, enriched or modified.

4.2 The communication process

The human sciences of anthropology, psychology and sociology have thrown much fresh light on the complexity of the communication process in recent years. Much of this insight has a valuable application to the communicating of the gospel. The Christian communicator is never the primary source of his message in the sense that he is not the originator of that which he is seeking to convey. His *primary source* is the written word of God through which the Spirit of God speaks to him. The prophet and apostle fulfil the role of *secondary sources* when they speak in God's name prefacing their message with an introductory 'Thus says the Lord. . .'. To a lesser extent the preacher and the witness stand in the same relationship to their message, as they declare what has been revealed to them or that which they have personally witnessed. A degree of interaction between themselves and their source is required for them to act in this capacity. What they are seeking to share with others must have become true for them. The communicator who has not interacted with his material and is merely passing on what he has read or been told functions as a *tertiary source*. He is often more of a blockage to communication than a channel. One has to get behind him to appreciate the significance and 'impact' of the message.

In the process of transmission the message does not have an independent existence. It is encapsulated in the mind of the speaker or presenter who sends a complex pattern of signals which enable the receptor to build up his perception of the message in his own mind. In the ideal communication event the result is that the receptor's understanding corresponds exactly with the intention of the communicator, but this is seldom fully achieved. In most instances the communicator must settle for an approximation within acceptable limits (see Fig. 2). This state of affairs causes no surprise when it is recognised that 'what is understood is at least as dependent on how the receptor perceives the message as on how the communicator presents it' (Kraft 1979:148).

The transmission of a message inevitably involves first that the message be encoded by the communicator and then that it be decoded or 'translated' by the receptor. It is in this complex procedure that 'slippage' occurs. The extent to which this is likely to occur is compounded when there is a wide cultural gap between those involved in the verbal exchange.

David Hesselgrave identifies seven elements which are at work in the encoding and decoding communication process. These are:

1 *World views* – ways of perceiving the world.
2 *Cognitive processes* – ways of thinking; our thought processes.

3 *Linguistic forms* – ways of expressing ideas. Different languages reflect in their complexity elements in the culture which are of particular importance.
4 *Behavioural patterns* – ways of acting which carry significance and social acceptance.
5 *Social structure* – ways of interacting between various social groupings and the sexes.
6 *Media influence* – ways of channelling the message to avoid misunderstanding and heighten the probability of acceptance.
7 *Motivational resources* – ways of deciding. Some societies place emphasis on the individual's responsibility in deciding. In others, decision-making is a community concern, either within the family, tribe or peer group. Some precipitate a decision-making process by putting the matter to the vote, while others are content to keep talking until they arrive at a consensus. (Hesselgrove 1978:120).

Each of the components in this complex communication grid is culturally shaped. Where there is a mismatch between cultures, then there is a high probability of 'static' interference and distortion, unless one or the other has the training and perception to be able to remove his own culture grid and adopt the other's in order to begin to transpose the message.

One does not have to be a missionary in a remote situation to become aware of the communication barriers. Many Christians experience them whenever they attempt to communicate their faith to their non-Christian friends. The longer they have been Christians and the more they have been preoccupied with their Christian activities, the more difficult it becomes to relate their beliefs to the perceived needs of their friends. The new convert, on the other hand, has no such problems because his pre-Christian experience is still fresh in his mind and he communicates his faith in an everyday language because he has not yet learned a new jargon. When the communication event takes place outside a common socio-economic framework and age-band then other components in the communication grid begin to 'scramble' the message. Within western society this is the case when middle-class people communicate with artisans, teenagers with the over forties, urbanites with rural dwellers, and especially between various ethnic groups.

The communicator 'encodes' his message by the concepts he uses, the language he employes, and the communication format he adopts, whether that be monologue, dialogue, question-posing, or a dramatic presentation, prose, poetry or song.

That encoding process will also include what Abercrombie describes as '*paralinguistic phenomena*'. 'Paralinguistic phenomena are non-linguistic elements in conversation. They occur alongside spoken language, interact with it, and produce, together with it, a total system of communication. They are not necessarily continuously simultaneous with spoken words. They may also be interspersed among them or precede them, or follow them; but they are always integrated into a conversation considered as a complete linguistic interaction' (Abercrombie:65). They include sounds such as 'tut tut', 'phew', 'ugh', 'shshsh', 'ahem'; gestures (shrugs, nods, winks, hand and arm movements); posture (sitting, standing, leaning forward and back, crossing and uncrossing legs) and facial expressions (smiles, frowns). They are expressed in voice control. The *ways* in which we say things convey as much as *what* we say. This is reflected in how loudly we speak, texture of voice, use of pauses, etc. Eye contact is also an important element. 'In the mutual look the participants express their involvement with one another. The longer the periods of eye contact, the greater the level of this mutual involvement, other things being equal. But in any situation there is a limit to the amount of mutual involvement that may be tolerated, and too much mutual looking may arouse anxiety' (Argyle and Kendon 1972:39). When the preacher looks at the ceiling before long his congregation look at their shoes and then their watches!

Yet another element in 'paralinguistic phenomena' is the distance between those engaging in face-to-face interaction. These vary between cultures and in accordance with the nature of the communication in the scale: intimate, casual, social, public or frozen. In the communication process a change of distance can signal a change of relationship. I have noticed that when older people put out chairs in preparation for a church meeting they will tend to place them in straight rows and arrange them further back from the speaker. This reflects the emphasis on 'status' and the formal school classroom layout which was more prevalent in former years.

When the receptor receives and decodes the message in order to uncover the meaning, the operation is no less complex. He will be concerned with the status of the source; statements may be accepted quite uncritically from a peer whom the receptor admires and emulates. He will examine the credibility of the source to ensure that he is genuine and sincere. As we have previously noticed, he will perceive the message within his own frame of reference and proceed on the basis from the known to the unknown. He will assess the person on his voice quality, mannerisms and dress. If the message is to influence him it must have an appropriate degree of impact (Kraft 1979:149). Due to the fact that we are all constantly being bombarded with stimuli, we have learned from an early age to be very selective in our response. Our listening ability is related to the relevance of the communication, its intelligibility, and a level of predictability. We listen more quickly than we speak, and when we can anticipate what is coming next then we switch off. Often what we 'hear' is not what is said, but what we think we are going to hear! Where there is a high level of predictability then there is a low impact. One gifted preacher known to the author frequently resorts to the shock statement to break through the 'selective hearing' of his audience. He began one address with the statement that, '1 Corinthians chapter 13 is *not* about love . . . it's about the need to exercise gifts in love.' In another he riveted the attention of his hearers with the statement, 'Samson was the weakest man in the Bible!' Sometimes what we expect to hear is predetermined by cultural influences as well as the ways in which facts have previously been presented to us. At every stage in the communication process we can detect the powerful influence of culture.

4.3 The role of the Holy Spirit in the communication process

Up to this point in our discussion we have been preoccupied with the *mechanics* of the communication process. We must now turn our attention to the spiritual *dynamics* which operate in relation to the communication of the gospel. In addition to the cultural blocks there is a spiritual blindness in the hearts and minds of people which prevents them from hearing the Good News. Paul explains to the Corinthians that those who do not believe have minds which have been kept in the dark by the evil god of this world. 'He keeps them from seeing the light shining on them, the light that comes from the Good News about the glory of Christ.' (2 Cor. 4:4).

Therefore, the application of communication techniques, no matter how skilled and imaginative, will not of itself ensure the effective transmission of the gospel message. The Holy Spirit is the essential communicator. If he is absent, the message will not get through. The Old Testament prophets knew the impossibility of making any impression on those who were stiff-necked and hard of heart (Is. 6:9, 10; 29:10). Even our Lord experienced the frustration of trying to communicate to those who did not have ears to hear (Luke 10:16; Matt. 13:14; Mark 6:52).

Spiritual understanding is only possible through the work of the Spirit of God in the human mind. The Old Testament looks forward to the new covenant written not on tablets of stone but on the heart. And it is God who will do the writing. As a result, 'None of them will have to teach his fellow countryman to know the Lord, because all will know me, from the least to the greatest.' (Jer. 31:33, 34).

Our Lord, with his disciples in the upper room, taught them about the role of the Holy Spirit as communicator. He would lead them into all truth (John 14:17; 16:13) and would 'convince the world concerning sin and righteousness and judgement' (John 16:8 RSV).

Paul the missionary, that master of cross-cultural communication, admitted that the message about Christ's death on the cross was nonsense to those who were being lost (1 Cor. 1:18). For God in his wisdom made it impossible for people to know him by means of their own wisdom (v. 21). How, then are they to know him? Paul replies, 'by means of His Spirit'. He continues, 'So then, we do not speak in words taught by human wisdom but in words taught by the Spirit, as we explain spiritual truths to those who have the Spirit.' (2:13).

If the New Testament witnesses were truly to communicate, they had to speak in the 'power of the Spirit' (1 Thess. 1:5; Rom. 15:19; Acts 1:8; 4:33; 6:8; 1 Cor. 2:4). At the same time the Holy Spirit was at work on the receptor's end of the communication process (1 Thess. 1:6; Col. 1:9).

None the less the awareness of the Christian communicator of this essential role of the Holy Spirit does not provide him with a short cut to instant communication. Rather the role of the Holy Spirit is to heighten our awareness of the problem and enable us to identify with those to whom we are called to speak. There is no true communication without genuine incarnation. And the incarnational route is always costly intellectually and emotionally. It requires a special gift of the Spirit (Eph. 3:7).

5 Culture and church structure

The relationship between conversion and culture is of enormous importance to the task of evangelism and church planting. These activities inescapably take place within a specific cultural context, which may be a clearly defined mono-cultural situation, or, more frequently, within a multi-cultural environment. As we have seen, culture permeates the whole of life and has a profound influence on the meaning which people attach to the messages they hear, the way they make decisions and the social and institutional structures which they build around their creeds and values. The insights of the church growth movement in showing the impact of culture in these areas has been a major contribution to the Church's understanding of its missionary task in recent decades. These perceptions are as relevant to the mission of the Church in the United Kingdom as in Asia, Africa and Latin America.

5.1 The spread of the gospel through homogeneous units

In his examination of the working of the Great Commission, McGavran draws attention to the significance of *ta ethne* in the phrase translated in most English versions as 'all nations', but rendered more accurately as 'all peoples' in the Good News Bible. 'Go, then, to all peoples everywhere and make them my disciples. . .' (Matt. 28:19). McGavran and Arn point out that *ethne* does not mean 'modern nation states' such as India, the United States, or China. *Ethne* means the castes, tribes, peoples, ethnic units of mankind (McGavran and Arn 1970:38). This distinction has been widely overlooked in modern missionary strategy to the extent that when a church has resulted in a particular country, it has been assumed that an adequate base for evangelisation has been established. However, the extent of the command in the Great Commission is not simply the spread of the gospel outwards territorially but down through the cultural layers.

McGavran describes society as honeycombed in a 'cultural mosaic'. Individuals need a social identity – a sense of peoplehood – if they are to identify, develop and function in society. They therefore form themselves into various groups in which they identify themselves as 'we', as distinct from those who are outside and described as 'they'. He defines such sociological groupings as 'homogeneous units', which he admits 'is an elastic concept, its meaning depending on the context in which it is used' (McGavran 1970:86). Simply stated, the homogeneous unit is a group in which all the members have some characteristic in common. The homogeneity may be represented by a political unit, a culture or a language, a tribe or caste or tribal sub-unit. Within western society it might represent a socio-economic group, people in a particular employment, a young people's counter-culture, etc. These are groups which share a particular life-style, language, and assumptions so that they feel at home with one another. Each develops its own behaviour pattern. 'Thus, within each homogeneous unit, individual action is considered typical or atypical as judged in the light of the social roles determined by the group' (Wagner 1979c:59).

Peter Wagner has attempted to develop a model to describe homogeneous units in North American Society based on '*ethclass*' which is a subsociety created by the intersection of the vertical stratification of ethnicity with the horizontal stratifications of social class (Wagner 1979c:61–74).

In Britain denominational planning has depended too exclusively on the 'geographical map'. Within the Church of England this has been influenced by the parish structure inherited from rural society with a feudal structure. While the geographical map may be helpful to ensure a measure of blanket coverage, it can at the same time be very misleading if used as the only planning model. The 'ethclass' concept provides a valuable alternative map by which to gauge the Church's effectiveness in relation to the 'mosaic' of peoples which make up the population of the British Isles. When applied to particular urban or rural situations it will reveal the dynamics which, while attracting some into the fellowship of the churches, are at the same time excluding others.

Church growth theorists have observed that churches tend to grow within homogeneous units. Peter Wagner claims that between ninety-five and ninety-eight per cent of churches are basically homogeneous (Wagner 1978). While it is impossible to either prove or disprove this estimate, as a matter of observation it is true that a high proportion of churches seem to attract 'their kind of people'. The reason for this is stated by McGavran as, 'men like to become Christians without crossing racial, linguistic or class barriers' (McGavran 1970:198). If people outside the Church can see people among its membership like themselves, and who make a favourable impression, they are more likely to want to identify themselves. On the other hand, when people outside the Church see no one within the Church with whom they can readily identify, they will not be so easily attracted. They will conclude, as people on a South London council estate expressed it when they observed the middle-class congregation going into their local church each Sunday, 'That church isn't for the likes of us.'

The other major contribution to missiological thinking by McGavran has been his stress on the corporate dimension of the decision-making process. He has provided a much needed corrective to the over-individualistic approach to conversion which has been characteristic of many western evangelists and missionaries. Such strategy he describes as 'one by one against the tide' (McGavran 1970:299). Against this, McGavran points out that historically in the Christianisation of Europe individuals have come to Christ in great numbers through 'people movements'. 'People become Christians as a wave of decisions for Christ sweeps through the group mind, involving many individual decisions but being far more than merely their sum. This may be called a chain reaction. Each decision sets off others and the sum total powerfully affects every individual' (McGavran 1970:12).

McGavran has been taken to task by his critics on two counts. Firstly, on account of his ill-chosen illustrations. John Howard Yoder asks, 'Can there be a Christianisation of a whole population that is so superficial that they are not really Christian at all?' In response to McGavran's positive assertions about the age of Constantine and Charlemagne, i.e. of the historical Christianisation of Europe by the prince, he retorts, 'I trust there are people movements that are more valid than that' (Shenk 1973:19). A similar criticism has come from Latin American theologians with their background of the 'Christianisation' of Latin America by the Spanish 'conquistadores'. To safeguard himself from misunderstanding McGavran needs to be clearer in describing what he means by group conversion. The follow-my-leader (or else!) illustration which he gives in his initial statement in *Bridges of God* in 1955 was not helpful.

In addition to the '*follow-my-leader*' pattern of people's movements there are a number of other varieties which have a much firmer biblical support. We read of *crowd conversions* through the preaching of the Christians in Jerusalem after Pentecost (Acts 2: 37–41; 4:4). There are a number of instances of *household conversion*. The extended household of the centurion Cornelius (Acts 10) and the business woman named Lydia in Philippi (Acts 16) were all baptised, presumably following family deliberation. This pattern can be extended to become a *community decision*. The villages of Lydda and Sharon turned to the Lord (Acts 9:35). The fifth pattern is that of a *web movement* when the decision of one person triggers other people with whom he is in contact. In this way Andrew influenced his brother Peter (John 1:40–42) and Philip found Nathaniel (John 1:45). This is perhaps the most common pattern by which the gospel spreads. To this list we might also add a sixth, *media movement* which is seen in the rise of the 'television church' through congregational sponsored televised services in the USA (Olson 1979:133–142).

The second criticism levelled against McGavran is in regard to his speaking of a 'group mind'. It has been rightly emphasised that people are accountable to God individually and that each person must turn from his sins in repentance and faith. From the divine standpoint each person is created as a unique individual and God is not just concerned about humankind in general, but deals with us as individuals.

Fifteen years after writing *Bridges of God* Donald McGavran in *Understanding Church Growth* provides further elucidation. 'The kind of conversion on which people movements are based is the root of the difficulty. The crucial question is: Do people movements rest on group conversion? The answer is No. There is no such thing as group conversion. A group has no body and no mind. It cannot decide anything whatever. The phrase group conversion is simply an easy inexact description of what really happens.' He then decides what actually takes place is 'multi-individual, mutually interdependent conversion' (McGavran 1970:302). Although there is a powerful chain-reaction or 'knock-on' effect, each individual is personally responsible for his decision within the total group dynamic.

Whenever there is a widespread turning to Christ there is a very real danger of superficiality leading to nominality. Steps must be taken to ensure that each decision is genuine, and adequate post-baptismal (or post-conversion) counsel and care must be provided to ensure a good environment for the nurturing of the new life (McQuilkin 1973, 74:48).

5.2 Values of the homogeneous unit concept

This concept heightens the Church's awareness of the unreached groups within a nation, county, or local district. It provides an alternative map to complement the geographical one most commonly used, which, when exclusively, may mask as much as it reveals. It also helps congregations understand why they are finding it so difficult to reach 'resistant areas' for which they feel a responsibility. As we noted at the beginning of the chapter, white, middle-class churches in Britain have a poor 'track record' in relating to artisan, West Indian and Asian cultures. It underlines the need to adopt methods appropriate to the group which is to be reached. Part of their resistance may be explained in terms of the inappropriate methods pursued in the past by well-meaning people who were 'foreigners' to the area.

It also helps to sensitise the Church to the dangers of cultural imperialism. Earlier in the chapter we outlined the various views on the relationship of gospel to culture. Here I would identify with the position held by Charles Kraft, namely that God, whilst being above culturel, chooses to work through culture (Kraft 1979:113–115). In such instances the Church can become more of a barrier than a channel in the communication of the gospel (see Fig. 3).

We will now unpack that statement in a series of affirmations:

5.2.1 *The gospel redeems cultures*. It is unlikely that there is any culture which is wholly evil. Every culture represents a mixture of good and bad, of ennobling and degrading elements. We must, therefore, seek to discover what the gospel has to say to our culture. What elements does it affirm, what does it reject, what does it accommodate, and which need to be redeemed? Wagner states that 'cultural integrity is part and parcel of human identity, and any system of thought or behaviour that denies cultural integrity is dehumanising' (Wagner 1979:97). He is strongly opposed to an extractionist approach in evangelism. 'When a gospel is presented that explicitly or implicitly teaches that becoming a citizen of the Kingdom of God requires a denial of peoplehood, its authenticity must be called into question' (Wagner 1978). The same point is emphasised by Tippett: 'Church growth theory believes that the Lord wants converts who can live the Christian life within their own social structures – be they industrial, nomadic, or subsistent. We ask the question: what does it mean to be a Christian in this or that kind of society? If our missionary methods extract converts from their society and leave them as social isolates or misfits, there is something wrong with our missioning' (Tippett 1970:34).

Such insights are more easily applied to animistic tribal cultures than to Islamic, Hindu, Buddhist or Marxist societies where social structures revolve around a core which is inimic to Christianity. The former are increasingly being weakened by the challenge of economically and technologically powerful cultures, which have encroached upon them and thereby created new conditions with which traditional beliefs are unable adequately to come to terms. In such circumstances the Christian missionary must, however, act with discernment in order not simply to exploit but rather to redeem the situation. For the gospel may have as much to affirm in the traditional beliefs, which are being undermined, as to decry in the alien culture with which the missionary may too closely associate (or even represent).

In the case of the powerful and widespread cultures mentioned above, while the Church might achieve culturally compatible features in terms of aspects of lifestyle, architecture, liturgy and communication forms, there will still be a basic incompatibility in relation to the person of Christ and a whole range of distinctive Christian values. Nevertheless, the challenged presented by Tippett and Kraft is that even these fundamental distinctives need to be interpreted and explained in terms which will be meaningful to the host culture, be that Moslem, Hindu or whatever. The Christian communicator must seek reference points in the other's frame of reference. There must be an open dialogue as a result of which the participants will not only enter each other's world-view, but

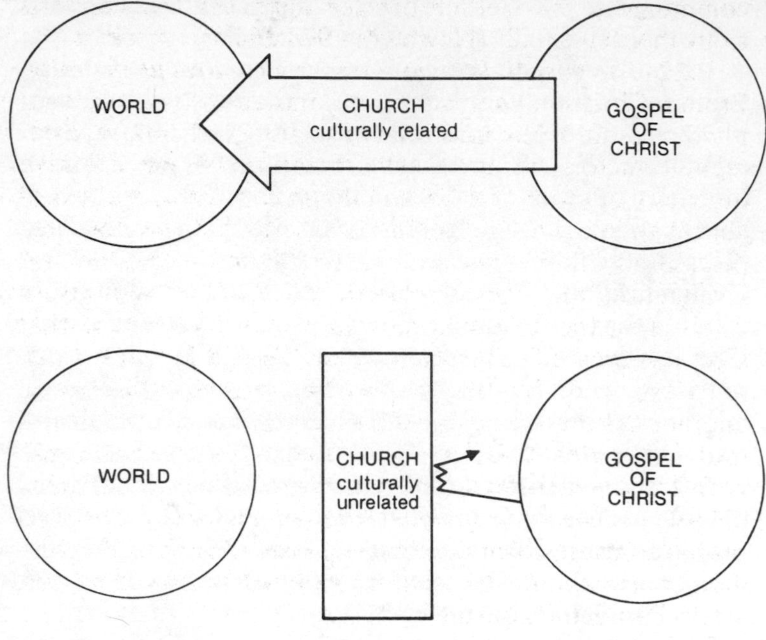

Fig. 3
The Church: a communication channel or barrier?

will as a result have re-evaluated their own position. An American Indian proverb cautions, 'One man should say nothing to another until he has walked in his moccasins'.

On the one hand the gospel does not destroy culture, and on the other it cannot simply be accommodated. It sifts culture, rejecting, affirming and fulfilling. Bishop Lesslie Newbigin describes the practical dilemma which faces many a Christian involved in cross-cultural communication. 'How, in seeking to preach the gospel to people of another culture, does the Church find the proper path between a kind of accommodation which robs the gospel of its power to challenge traditional ways of life, and a kind of intransigence which either fails to communicate altogether or else alienates the converts from their culture?' (Newbigin 1978:164).

5.2.2 *The gospel does not impose a cultural uniformity*. From a Christian perspective cultural diversity is not simply the result of the interplay of sociological and environmental factors, it is a demonstration of the creative ingenuity of God. In 1978 an international group of evangelical theologians gathered in Pasadena under the auspices of the Lausanne Committee for World Evangelisation. They declared, 'We are unanimous in celebrating the colourful mosaic of the human race that God has created. This rich variety should be preserved, not destroyed, by the gospel. The attempt to impose another culture on people who have their own is cultural into a colourless uniformity is a denial of the Creator and an affront to his creation. The preservation of cultural diversity honours God, respects man, enriches life, and promotes evangelisation. Each church, if it is to be truly indigenous, should be rooted in the soil of its local culture' (Pasadena Consultation 1978:3).

Such cultural diversity we should expect to find expression in the structures and institutional life of the churches. Overseas too many missionary-planted churches are over-influenced by their imported histories, which reflect controversies and emphases which may be irrelevant to their environment into which they have been transplanted. Here at home there are denominations which, while they may boast a doctrinal comprehensiveness, manifest a cultural exclusiveness. They impose liturgical traditions, organisational structures, communication methods and leadership models which are alien to their environment. This is not to say that the world dictates the pattern for the Church to adopt, but to point out that the Church must be constantly examining itself to ensure that it is remaining true to the gospel and that the only barrier is the inescapable offence of the atoning message of the cross which stands at the centre of that gospel.

5.2.3 *The gospel brings reconciliation*. Sometimes the

common traits of homogeneity which bind people together are evil; these may be expressed in the form of hostility or antagonism to those outside. This is reflected in the attitude of the National Front towards new commonwealth citizens in the United Kingdom at the present time. At other times cultural groups regard themselves in a superior relationship to other cultures. In the New Testament the gospel is depicted as a power of God to deal with enmity and superiority. 'For Christ himself has brought us peace by making Jews and Gentiles one people. With his own body he broke down the wall that separated them and kept them enemies.' (Eph. 2:14, 15). The Jews had to accept the fact that Gentiles could become Christians and that in so doing they did not have to come to Christ via Jewish cultural conditioning. They did not have to take on board the Jewish ceremonial Law. When Paul was writing to the Galatians he was confronting the Judaisers who were trying to act as cultural imperialists. Their attitude is firmly rejected by Paul as 'another gospel' which was in reality no gospel at all. In protecting the minority rights of the Gentile believers he states, 'there is no difference between Jews and Gentiles, between slaves and free men, between men and women; you are all one in union with Christ Jesus' (Gal. 3:28, 29).

The gospels brings about a reconciliation between groups which were formerly antagonistic to one another. Yet the unity for which Paul strongly argues is not a uniformity. He is not urging the Jews to become more Gentile, or the Gentiles to become more Jewish. If such were his meaning here, it would make a nonsense of his other statement that 'there is no difference . . . between men and women'! Rather he is declaring the abolition of enmity and favouritism.

5.2.4 *The gospel encourages mutual support and enrichment*. Negatively, the New Testament says that believers should take care not to offend one another (Gal. 2:11, 16) and positively that they should recognise that they belong to one another and take active steps to welcome and support one another (Rom. 15:7).

The supracultural dimension of the gospel must be demonstrated in the strife-torn world of today. The Church should not simply reflect the divisions and distancing present in its social context. At this point I am therefore forced to disagree with Peter Wagner's hypothesis that, 'The local congregation in a given community should be only as integrated as are the families and other primary social groups in the community, while intercongregational activities and relationships should be as integrated as are the secondary social groups in the csommunity or society as a whole' (Wagner 1979c:150). If the gospel has truly brought reconciliation and a mutual appreciation, then the local church should demonstrate the reality of this theological truth in practical terms as a testimony to the community. The members will also reciprocate with one another in recognition that it is in each hearing the other that our understanding of the gospel is enriched as it is released from our cultural blinkers.

This attitude is reflected to the Pasadena Consultation at which the delegates agreed 'that in many situations a homogeneous unit church can be a legitimate and authentic church. Yet we are also agreed that it can never be complete in itself. Indeed, if it remains in isolation, it cannot reflect the universality and diversity of the Body of Christ. Nor can it grow into maturity. Therefore, every Homogeneous Unity church must take active steps to broaden its fellowship in order to demonstrate visible unity and the variety of Christ's Church. This will mean forging with other and different churches creative relationships which express the reality of Christian love, brotherhood, and interdependence' (Pasadena Consultation 1978:4, 5).

At every level of church life, international, interdenominational, intercongregational and intracongregational structures must be developed to express both the unity and the diversity of the Body of Christ (1 Cor. 12:12, 13).

In this search the closer one gets to home the more difficult it becomes. Where white and black churches exist side by side, some congregations are now meeting to worship together on a quarterly basis. This has resulted in a great deal of mutual education, and most would not want to worship together any more regularly than that! Other churches have endeavoured to build effective congregational structures to express both homogeneity and heterogeneity. The main congregation is divided into ethnic groups for time of worship, study and fellowship. This is sometimes done as part of Sunday worship, or, more frequently, in mid-week fellowship. The groups come together regularly for acts of celebration worship, cultural interchange (a Caribbean evening) joint action over community concerns, and to share and challenge each other's perception of the gospel and understanding of contemporary Christian discipleship.

5.3 Dangers in overemphasising the homogeneous unit concept

By elevating the homogeneous unit concept into a principle which is normative and universal the church growth movement has laid itself open to misunderstanding and misrepresentation. Some critics look on it as a device for maximising the numerical growth of the Church whilst minimising the social-context challenge of the gospel. At the Lausanne Congress on World Evangelization Rene Padilla launched an attack on what he termed 'Culture Christianity'. 'The God of this type of Christianity is the God of "cheap grace", the God who constantly gives but never demands, the God fashioned expressly for mass-man, who is controlled by the law at least possible effort and seeks easy solutions, the God who gives his attention to those who will not reject him because they need him as an analgesic' (Padilla 1975:126). While this criticism is directed at conservative evangelical Christians who tend to equate the Christian faith with the American way of life, it also has relevance to European Christianity. It is a third-world challenge which must be heeded. Here in Britain we need the constant reminder that God is not an Englishman!

Second, when the homogeneous unit concept is elevated into a normative principle we are forced to present convincing evidence to show that the New Testament Church was structured on homogeneous lines. There is no clear evidence that this was the case. In his otherwise excellent book, *Our Kind of People* C. Peter Wagner is at his weakest in his chapter entitled 'Church Growth in the New Testament Mosaic'. Because the New Testament is nowhere explicit about the homogeneity of the churches founded, he is constantly having to resort to special pleading and to read between the lines. While it is true that eleven of the twelve disciples were Galileans, they represented different trades and political convictions (an explosive topic in occupied Israel). There was heterogeneity alongside a degree of homogeneity which contributed to the learning situation as they rubbed against each other. The existence of Hellenists alongside the Hebrews introduced practical problems and friction among the Christian community in Jerusalem. But the appointment of the seven deacons to deal with the problem cannot be used as conclusive evidence that they became leaders of separate Hellenistic groups. '. . . the solution was not to divide these people according to their ethnic and cultural differences. The solution was to handle the problem administrationally. Thus deacons were selected to give special attention to such matters that there might be unity in the Church' (Dubose 1978:127).

In his discussion of the church in Antioch he states, 'There were in all likelihood two distinct clusters of house churches' (Wagner 1979c:125). This is an unconvincing argument from silence. The fact of the matter is that we simply do not know. Assuming that in many cities Paul visited Christian groups were founded which were either predominantly Jewish or mainly Gentile, the term 'gentile' i.e. non-Jew, is far too broad to be interpreted as a 'homogeneous unit'. Who is to say that churches then, as now, were not organised along both homogeneous *and* heterogeneous lines? Churches in all ages have grown in a variety of ways and cannot be limited to a homogeneous strait-jacket.

Third, an over-preoccupation with homogeneity and cultural identity to the exclusion of cross-cultural perspective can just as well inhibit as stimulate growth. McGavran's picture of a 'mosaic of cultures' is too static a model. Rather, in today's fast-changing and shrinking world he should think more dynamically in terms of a kaleidoscope of cultures with constantly changing patterns as some groups are assimilated, others separate, and hybrids and entirely new cultural groups emerge, some of which will endure and others will quickly pass. Consequently, 'The danger inherent in all programs for the "indigenisation" or "acculturation" of the gospel is that they involve the Church with the conservative and backward-looking elements in the society' (Newbigin 1978:162). This is as true for twentieth-century British tribalism as in Africa or Asia.

Fourth, the homogeneous unit concept presents an incomplete strategy for urban church growth. In urban society people move between a number of homogeneous groups and heterogeneous situations. In the city, life is lived on more than one crossroad. There is a continuous process of mutual influence between groups. This complexity should be reflected in the urban church which demonstrates attitudes and structures which make for creativity rather than conflict. A church which identifies exclusively with one group may live a self-centred, impoverished life. If that group dwindles, so the church will face extinction. Furthermore, given the high population density and high level of heterogeneity in many urban areas, for a church to run exclusively on homogeneous lines may result in the spiritual isolation and exclusion of the majority of the surrounding population.

Having faced some of the dangers of exalting the homogeneous unit factor to a universal principle we conclude by reiterating its positive value of making the Church take seriously the cultures of those with whom it is seeking to communicate and incarnating the message of Christ's redeeming love and regenerating power. Different approaches are required among the artisan, non-book culture, the aristocracy, the black-community, Asian Moslems and Sikhs. Churches which predominantly identify with each of these groupings will take on distinctive cultural characteristics in their worship and personal and social expressions and applications of the gospel. While ethnic churches may be legitimate in a given situation, they must be open to the other churches around them which minister to a different constituency, for each needs the other to enrich their perceptions and challenge their obedience to the Gospel. The apostle Paul, aware of the need for such mutual enrichment, wrote to the Christians in Rome, 'For I long to see you, that I may impart to you some spiritual gift to strengthen you.' He was not shy in stating that he believed he had something to give, but then he checks himself, 'that is, that we may be mutually encouraged by each other's faith, both yours and mine' (Rom. 1:11, 12 RSV).

5 *Summary*

In this chapter we have opened up some of the complex issues raised by the impact of the gospel on culture. My purpose has been limited to increasing a level of awareness, rather than attempting to supply solutions. In reality there are no pat answers, for each situation has its distinctive cultural milieu and must, therefore, be approached with an open a mind as we can achieve. Such open-mindedness is an essential part of the missionary gift which the Church needs in order to function effectively in any cross-cultural situation.

As we engage with the culture in which we are located or which we are seeking to reach, we need to keep a whole range of questions continuously in mind: What elements in this culture reflect gospel values and should consequently be highlighted and affirmed? How does the gospel relate to those areas with which the culture is least able to cope, or which have a dehumanising influence? What practical steps are we taking to discover how the Church appears from the outsider's perspective and how its message is being interpreted; remembering it's not what *we say* but what *they hear* which really counts? What aspects of our ecclesiastical tradition facilitate and what create a barrier to our communication attempts? What are the most effective communication channels in this culture, and how can the Church gain access to them and speak authentically through them? If we were starting from scratch what would we do differently? And even after years of existence here, should we now start doing any of those things?

CHAPTER FOUR

Measurement and Meaning

ONE OF THE great services which McGavran has rendered to the missionary enterprise has been his insistence on the need to gather objective and accurate data in order to disperse the fog in which it has operated for so long. He argues, 'The numerical approach is essential to understanding church growth. The Church is made up of countable people and there is nothing particularly spiritual in not counting them. Men use the numerical approach in all worthwhile human endeavour' (McGavran 1970:83). The persistent tendency to cover up for our lack of effectiveness by using vague language must be strongly resisted. Such head-in-the-sands mentality is particularly evident in areas such as Britain, where prolonged and serious church decline is the prevailing trend.

James Scherer, writing in the *International Review of Missions*, makes the following appreciation of McGavran's emphasis on data gathering. 'So rigorous is he (i.e. McGavran) in dispelling romantic notions and false theological rationalisations of non-growth that he may be said to have de-mythologized this subject. His own interpretation stresses measurable environmental factors and insists that situations be weighed in terms of their social and cultural complexity. The rigour and honesty brought to the task will put students of church growth in Dr McGavran's debt. Much to his credit, the author is even-handed in his criticism of conservative evangelical and ecumenical groups for the rationalisations (theological and promotional) which both employ in justifying or covering up non-growth situations' (IRM 1971:127).

Church growth data gathering needs to be undertaken at least at two levels, national and local. The accuracy of the former will depend on the quality of the information gathered by the individual churches and their readiness to make their results more widely available. Denominational headquarters also need sound data-handling methods to ensure an accurate national picture. At both national and local levels trends can be analysed not only within churches and denominations, but across denominations, to learn from those who appear to be exceptions to the general rule. Only by painstaking research are we able to paint an accurate picture of what is really happening. Without such essential information we cannot plan responsibly for the future. We must take account of the cause and effect relationship which God has built into his created order, by unearthing and facing facts.

What are the most basic areas of research which the Church needs to undertake if it is to take growth seriously? McGavran identifies the following:

1 Church membership and attendance totals and the rate at which they are changing.
2 Homogeneous unit totals (to determine the degree of penetration into the different sub-groupings of society).
3 An analysis of the kinds of church growth, to identify how much represents conversion growth from the world into the Church.
4 A family analysis to determine how many full families, partial and singles.
5 A leader and worker analysis to ascertain the proportion deployed in extending the Church's witness in the community.

At this stage we merely introduce them in passing; we will return to them in greater detail later on. Demographic and social characteristics are also important in the interpretation of all the above data.

Before delving into the practicalities of the subject we must first examine four of the main questions about data gathering in the context of church life which lurk in the minds of many committed Christians.

1 Answering objections to data-gathering

1.1 "Data gathering is unscriptural"

On the basis of 1 Chronicles 21, where it is recorded that David incurred divine displeasure because he ordered a national census, some Christian leaders refuse to gather statistics of their membership. They feel that to embark on such an undertaking might spiritually jeopardise their work. But the incident recorded in Chronicles must be balanced by other parts of Scripture. For instance in the Book of Numbers (sic!) Moses is expressly commanded to count the people upon entering the Sinai wilderness to ensure that they can subsequently be accounted for. He is told, 'You and Aaron are to take a census of the people of Israel by clans and families. List the names of all men twenty years old or older who are fit for military service' (1:1–3). He needed to know both the size of the total community for which he was responsible and the strength of the army he would soon have to deploy (see also Num. 2:32–34; 26:1–4, 63–65).

Why then is David punished for counting in 1 Chron. 21? On this occasion we are informed that the idea was prompted by Satan and not by God, who did it 'in order to bring trouble on the people of Israel' (v. 1). David insisted in proceeding with his intentions despite the opposition of Joab, his commander-in-chief, who sensed the wrong motivation for the exercise. Tippett suggests that, 'Such temptation was possible because David was now proudly aware of his kingdom and his military strength and organisation. The numbering was a sin because it was self-glorification' (Tippett 1970:15). At this time David failed to recognise that his strength lay in the arm of the Lord rather than in his own military capability.

The principle of counting to ensure pastoral care and effective deployment of manpower is carried over into the New Testament. In our Lord's parable of the lost sheep (Luke 15:3–6) we see that it was as a consequence of counting his sheep into the fold each night that the shepherd discovered that he was one short. If he had failed to take this action he would probably have been unaware of the emergency. But as soon as his regular check brings to light the absentee he is able to take prompt and appropriate action.

From the gospel record we know the precise number of Jesus' select team of disciples and that on one occasion seventy were sent out two by two on a mission to prepare villages for Christ's coming (Luke 10). Other ancient manuscripts give the number as seventy-two which shows that even then there was some confusion about statistics!

In his account of the performance of the Church in the Book of Acts, Luke displays no inhibitions in speaking about numbers. We are informed that there were a hundred and twenty believers meeting in Jerusalem (1:15). Three thousand were added to the Church on the day of Pentecost (2:41), and before long the number of male believers grew to about five thousand (4:4). Paul likewise informs us that on one occasion our Lord appeared to more than five hundred believers at once (1 Cor. 15:6).

While it must be conceded that the New Testament displays no great preoccupation with data gathering – which is not surprising considering the complexity of numeration in both the Hebrew and Roman world! – there is no positive evidence to suggest that Christ's mission should be pursued in ignorance of obtainable facts.

1.2 "Data gathering is inappropriate"

Many people discount the value of statistical analysis by

saying that what matters is quality, not quantity. This viewpoint is upheld by no less a missionary statesman than Max Warren. He speaks of 'the strictly limited value of all statistical assessments of the value of missionary work. Scripture provides no justification whatever for taking statistics seriously. This is one of the quantitative fallacies of far too much missionary thinking. Quality is undefinable and known only to God' (Warren 1979:155).

While Max Warren is right to caution against an obsessive preoccupation with numbers, I believe that he overstates the case when he is so dismissive of all quantity measurement. McGavran highlights the fact that, 'Luke did not scorn numbers. He rejoiced in the large numbers becoming Christians and carefully recorded them. The early churches did not scorn numbers. When they heard that multitudes in Samaria had received the word of God, they gladly sent them Peter and John; and when they heard that in Antioch a great number had believed and turned to the Lord, they at once despatched Barnabas who, when he came and saw, rejoiced' (McGavran 1959:25).

The task of mission, while depending on the empowering and guidance of the Holy Spirit, also requires human planning. The interventions of God do not set aside the need for careful evaluation. The surprises of God are not intended as a substitute for strategy. Responsible decision-making requires well-researched data. Such research does not set aside the need for divine guidance, but the evidence produced by investigation forms some of the ingredients. The Holy Spirit guides us through discernment as well as by signs. McGavran and Arn spell out the attitude which should characterise the Christian in his decision-making. 'Father, I've endeavoured to gather all the facts available, and still I'm uncertain which is the best decision. I need your guidance and direction. I'm asking for your leading. I am listening for your instruction' (McGavran and Arn 1977:29).

Baptismal, confirmation, membership and communicant figures do not tell the whole story. They constitute only some of the ingredients in the evaluation and diagnostic processes. When a doctor takes the temperature of a patient, his reading gives him no more than one item of information. Neither will his examination alter the situation, for the thermometer has not yet been invented which can bring down the temperature of the fever-stricken patient. It does, however, provide helpful data which, when combined with the results of other investigations, reveals the state of health of the patient.

The point to emphasise is that the data is only of help to those who know the patient and can build up a case history. McGavran, in addition to emphasising the importance of data gathering, balances this statistical emphasis by underlining the need for careful and competent interpretation. 'It cannot be over-emphasised that statistics, if these are to have any meaning, should be gathered by those who know the churches well and who are concerned that the statistics reveal the truth. They should also be accompanied by a full description of the churches, their natural groupings, and their geographical, social and spiritual environment. Statistics are a summary of significant information and care should be taken that they convey true meanings' (McGavran 1959:27, 28).

Church growth is not imply a matter of baptising converts and filling pews. It is also concerned with the content of the message which forms the basis for the convert's decision-making, and with the quality of life which he can be expected to encounter in the church in which he is to be incorporated.

In my judgement, church growth thinking in its early days tended to over-emphasise numbers in an effort to provide a necessary corrective to the widespread avoidance of the issue. For instance in 1959 McGavran wrote, 'Numerical increase presupposes and necessitates good spiritual care. No Evangelical Church can grow greatly in numbers which has a programme unsuited to men's needs. Men turn to those places where their actual needs are met. True, it is possible for them to be swept into some congregation, but unless they receive real food they will not stay there. Growing churches are precisely those whose members believe they enjoy a life superior to that they had before. Otherwise men would neither come in nor stay' (McGavran 1959:16). This clouds a number of issues. Agreed that men join churches where their needs are met, but this might relate to educational opportunities and material and social advancement, rather than the need for forgiveness and new life in Christ.

1.3 "Data-gathering is unnecessary"

This may be the case in a small house fellowship, or of a small church in a face-to-face village community where everyone knows everybody else. In such locations the leader who knows both his congregation and community and is aware of the facets of growth to keep under surveillance may not need to do a formal count. However, most churches in today's world, with its high population density, complex relationship networks and mobility will need to take a more sophisticated approach to alert themselves to the significant trends.

This is part of the explanation of the lack of statistical concern to be found in the Scriptures. There churches were just beginning. For the most part they consisted of small groups of people meeting in homes. Individuals were also part of extended households so their absences would immediately be noticed. This is a very different situation from many churches today which meet in large buildings and with eclectic congregations, the members of which are unlikely to meet unless they plan to do so.

It is inadequate and misleading to rely on general impressions in such churches. We need to isolate significant measuring points to assess current trends and the influences at work which produce them. Time after time, ministers who thought they knew their churches inside-out discover new factors relating to their growth or lack of it, of which they would have remained blissfully unaware if they had not taken the trouble to investigate.

Ministers as a professional group tend to be averse to data gathering because they are more people than organisation orientated. Another hesitation arises in the minds of some ministers who are men of action and feel that data-gathering and detailed long-term planning are simply a cover-up for procrastination. They want to get on with the job, and are afraid of what the Archbishop of York, Stuart Blanch, has described as 'analysis paralysis' setting in. This needs to be said, because some churches feel more competent at the analysis than the action. So any activity which serves to postpone involvement in a church growth programme is to be welcomed!

1.4 "Data-gathering is uncomfortable"

Some denominations and local churches reject data-gathering because they are not prepared to face the truth about themselves. They are like patients, who, suspecting that something is seriously wrong, steadfastly refuse to see a doctor in the hope that their troubles will clear up without the need to be told the truth about themselves or undergo painful treatment.

Some growing churches which have broadcast their 'success' do not want to look too closely at where their new growth has been coming from. They rejoice that their pews are full, without facing the sobering fact that they are only filling them by emptying someone else's. One further aspect needs to be mentioned for churches which have experienced prolonged decline. Their data-gathering can be a disheartening exercise. If they merely project their ski-slope profile membership and attendance graphs, they will plan for continuing decline. Retrenchment will be the order of the day, with the result that we get what we have planned for. In the knowledge that so much of the central and parochial planning has been based on these kinds of projections, many ministers want to ignore the evidence from the past and present, and work in the hope that God will do a new thing.

2 The value of data-gathering

Having considered the objections, we now turn briefly to outline the advantages of collecting relevant statistical information about the progress of the Christian Church in a locality or nation. These have been mentioned in passing in the previous section, but they are summarised here for the sake of convenience and for added emphasis.

2.1 To be aware of general trends

As situations grow in size and complexity it becomes increasingly hazardous to rely upon hunches and rule-of-thumb measures. Furthermore, it is likely that trends will be well advanced before they begin to become apparent. The more entrenched unwelcome developments have become, the harder it will be to reverse them. Data-gathering provides an early-warning system so that the situation can be analysed soon after the trend has begun to take shape and plot a course.

For the past two years Roy Pointer (Bible Society Church Growth Consultant) and I have been conducting basic church growth seminars for local church leaders up and down the country. Nearly four hundred of the churches represented have furnished membership and attendance figures for a ten-year period. In undertaking this exercise many churches have rued the absence of information from the past, and a number have testified to the value of graphing the information, which has brought to light factors of which they were not previously aware.

2.2 To evaluate their significance

It is frequently said that you can make statistics say what you want them to say. This is a half truth. You can use them arbitrarily when you are speaking to those who can neither verify the accuracy of the data, nor have insufficient knowledge of the situation from which they are drawn to appreciate their significance. However, when the data are studied by a group of people who are all intimately involved in and have detailed knowledge of the situation they describe, they become an invaluable tool.

If you want to put this to the test, simply present your membership, attendance and income and expenditure figures to the church committee in graph form without comment beyond that of simple clarification. Then divide the committee into groups of three to spend twenty minutes drawing out their significance and listing questions to which they give rise. On a blackboard or overhead projector write the heading 'WHAT THE FIGURES SAY ABOUT US' and list the points identified by each group.

2.3 To allocate resources to responsive areas

In marketing terms you sell where you are selling best. In terms of the mission of the gospel you put your human and financial resources to reap where God has prepared a ripe harvest. Many a temporary gain has been lost because the significance of the development was recognised too late in the day and additional resources could not be made available. As we will describe in the final chapter, we should plan from strength and not from weakness.

Effective planning for mission in Britain has been hampered at every level by lack of reliable data. In 1972 the report of the Committee on Mission for the British Council of Churches entitled 'Stand Up and Be Counted' expressed the conviction 'that a fresh approach to the collection and use of statistical information is the basic prerequisite of any realistic planning for mission in the United Kingdom' (p. 1). For future planning the report recommended the regular collection and review of statistics at four levels:

(a) At the *national* level, by improving, standardising and centralising the categories of data collection so that these provide a more reliable basis for research in depth and reflect changes in the work of the Church.

(b) At the *regional* level, by relating material to demographic and socio-economic statistics and deriving projections as a guide to strategic forward planning.

(c) At the *local authority* level, by the constant monitoring and adjustment of resources to meet changing needs and the changing social situation.

(d) At the level of the *local church* to enable them to formulate their missionary task in the area and assess their work in a creative manner.

2.4 To draw up long-term plans for resistant areas
Emphasising the responsive does not mean neglecting the resistant. So what was said under the previous heading needs to be counter-balanced. McGavran argues that resistant areas should be occupied lightly. While this strategy may be appropriate for a 'mission area' where only a few pockets of Christians are to be found and they have to decide between going to one place at the expense of another, it must be applied rather differently in a situation where the Church has extensive geographical coverage. Here in England there are identifiable resistant areas of society, representing particular kinds of people. Each may require a distinctive kind of approach which will take much prayer, research and expertise to develop. What are required are a large number of pioneer, experimental projects, each carefully conceived and evaluated, with opportunities for those involved in similar undertakings to share their findings. We must seek to discover through small teams which approaches have the best chances of success, before committing the battalions. Such schemes require adequate data-gathering, otherwise we will continue to hear ingenious theories unsubstantiated by facts.

At this point in the chapter we turn from principles to practice. First, taking England as an example, we will look at church-going trends to see what we can learn from the available data, and then we will narrow the focus to data-gathering in the local church.

3 Church membership and attendance trends in England
From the year 600 to 1800 there is a complete lack of reliable data on church attendance. But as during the period between the Reformation and the end of the seventeenth century it was a punishable offence to be absent from worship, presumably the percentage of worshippers was high. People were not so much assumed to be practising Anglicans as compelled to hold that church allegiance. The latter half of the eighteenth century witnessed the decline of Anglicanism with the growth of Nonconformity. Between 1771 and 1810 the Wesleyans increased five-fold, and the General Baptist New Connexion four-fold. By 1810 it is estimated that Nonconformists in Britain totalled 312,000 (Currie, Gilbert and Horsley 1977:23).

It was not until 1851, when for the one and only time a religious section was included in the National Census of England and Wales, that a comprehensive and reasonably reliable picture of church-going emerged.

The organisation and interpretation of the data was in the hands of the noted barrister Horace Mann. The day of the count of religious attendances was fixed for March 30, to be undertaken by the ministers and pastors of the churches and chapels.

The results were as follows:

Church of England	5,102,805
Roman Catholic	375,257
Free Church	4,432,866
All Denominations	9,910,928
Total Population	16,764,470

(Gay 1971:223)

The total of 9,910,928 needs to be adjusted to account

for those who attended more than one service. Using Mann's estimate for England and Wales, this gives an adjusted total for England alone of 6,604,642 actual people who attended, which is thirty-nine per cent of the total population.

A more detailed regional analysis of the census results revealed that most of the absent millions were to be found in the towns. 'Mann compiled a special table for the seventy-three large towns (in England and Wales) which had populations over 10,000 and taking these towns collectively it was discovered that only about twenty-five per cent of their inhabitants were in church on Census Sunday' (Gay 1971:58). It was not simply that these urban dwellers had been lost from the Church; the more likely explanation is that they were never in it. As far as the Church of England was concerned Gay concludes that 'in the areas where population and industry were growing most rapidly the Anglican Church had failed to expand its parochial system and hence failed to gain the allegiance of the people' (Gay 1971:74). The Census thus spurred the Church of England to create new parishes and provide more services, and stimulated the Free Churches in a spate of chapel building during the 1860s and 1870s. The ecclesiastical authorities of the period had failed, until faced with the evidence of the census, to detect the effects of urbanisation, resulting from the Industrial Revolution, on national patterns of church-going.

The last three decades of the nineteenth century represented a period of growth and reform. The Anglicans gave attention to correcting the scandals of absenteeism and pluralism in the rural parishes and encouraged mission centres in the slum areas. The re-establishing of the Catholic hierarchy provided the necessary structure for the organisation of a Church to meet the needs of a rapidly growing Roman Catholic community, for by the end of the century the Catholic population was between six and seven per cent of the total. And as far as Nonconformity was concerned, the period represented their zenith of power, not only numerically but in terms of their influence in the community, giving rise to the 'Nonconformist conscience' and contributing to the Parliamentary victory of the Liberal Party in the elections of 1906.

This present century has, however, witnessed a sharp reversal of those promising trends as far as the Anglicans and Nonconformist mainline denominations are concerned. In Appendices A-D can be found the membership graphs of the major Protestant churches, all of which have experienced serious and sustained decline.

With regard to the membership decline of the Church of England, Linda, my seven-year-old daughter, recently made an amusing comment. While on a visit to the Lake District she wanted to know what a shepherd's crook was for. We explained that it was for catching sheep who wander off. Her curiosity momentarily satisfied, she thought for a moment and then asked, 'Is that why Bishops have them? To catch people?' And then came a flash of insight, 'Why don't they have lassoos instead? They would be much better!'

Appendix E shows the Catholic community and Mass attendance trends. This graph reveals a steady increase in the size of the community while Sunday Mass attendance reveals a trend in the opposite direction. What is the explanation of this phenomenon? The increase is almost entirely due to immigration from Ireland and Catholic countries on the Continent. The decline in Mass attendance is evidence of a growing nominality problem as upward social mobility breaks down the cohesiveness of the Catholic community. Appendix F represents a composite graph of the smaller churches (these figures are for Great Britain and not England only). The steady growth in the number of Adventists is almost entirely explained by immigration from the West Indies. Nearly half the entire membership is now drawn from the black community.

Space is available in the graphs for you to plot the

trends in your denomination during the next few years. You might also like to pray for specific growth targets.

The two most significant developments in English church life during the past twenty years have been the emergence of the independent black churches in the inner-city areas and the independent house-church movement.

Of the former groups the largest of the denominations are the New Testament Church of God with 4,466 members and attenders reckoned at 20,000 in 1975 (this is part of the American 'Church of God'), the Calvary Church of God in Christ, the Church of God of Prophecy, which split from the Church of God in 1923, and the Apostolic Church of Jesus Christ.

In addition there are a number of black-led independent churches such as the Holy Order of Cherubim and Seraphim, the Celestial Church of Christ, and the Aladura Church, also the African Methodist Episcopal Church, the Pilgrim Wesleyan Holiness Church and the Ethiopian Orthodox Church (Root 1979:4, 5, 7, 8).

The house-church movement on the other hand has been largely among whites with its strength in suburbia. The house-churches initially grew through the transfer of Christians who had become disillusioned and frustrated with the institutional Church and were looking for less structured forms of worship and more personal life-related ministry. It is impossible to quantify this movement with any accuracy. Membership is variously estimated between twenty and fifty thousand. Some of the groups have become static and introverted, others are becoming more institutionalised as they grow. They are moving out of homes into rented premises and are establishing inter-congregational structures and oversight. Some of these groups are seeing conversions from the world and are making an impact in areas at both ends of the social scale, which have hitherto been resistant to the Church's mission. One indication of the growing strength of the house-church movement is seen in the conventions which they organise. The two most famous of these are the Dales (Yorkshire) and the Downs (Sussex) Bible Weeks which attract thousands for a diet of informal worship and practical Bible exposition. However, not all who attend are from the house-churches. Such events also attract many from the traditional denominations who have been influenced by the charismatic movement.

When we bring together all of the denominational membership statistics in a common graph we see dramatically displayed the reversal of trends which has taken place in the present century. The graph opposite (Fig. 4) is compiled from statistics for Great Britain as a whole drawn together by Currie, Gilbert and Horsley in *Churches and Churchgoers*, which represent the most thorough-going analysis of national and denominational trends to date. Superimposed on the membership graph is a graph of the total population of Britain from National Censuses since 1851 (Annual Abstract of Statistics 1979:HMSO). The sharp rise in Protestant membership was cut off at the turn of the century. After the two world wars there was a brief period of recovery lasting for about a decade after which the twentieth-century decline trend reasserted itself, with the slope becoming increasingly steep.

However, since the mid-1970s a more helpful picture has begun to emerge, which will be analysed in detail in the following section.

4 The current situation with regard to church-going and church membership trends in England

The most comprehensive picture of church-going and church membership trends in England ever to be produced is presented in '*Prospect for the Eighties* – based on a 1979 Census of Churches in England', a survey conducted by the Nationwide Initiative in Evangelism. This was the first occasion on which all of the main Christian groups co-operated on a joint statistical project, and on which the combination of membership and attendance has been explored to see their relationship within denom-

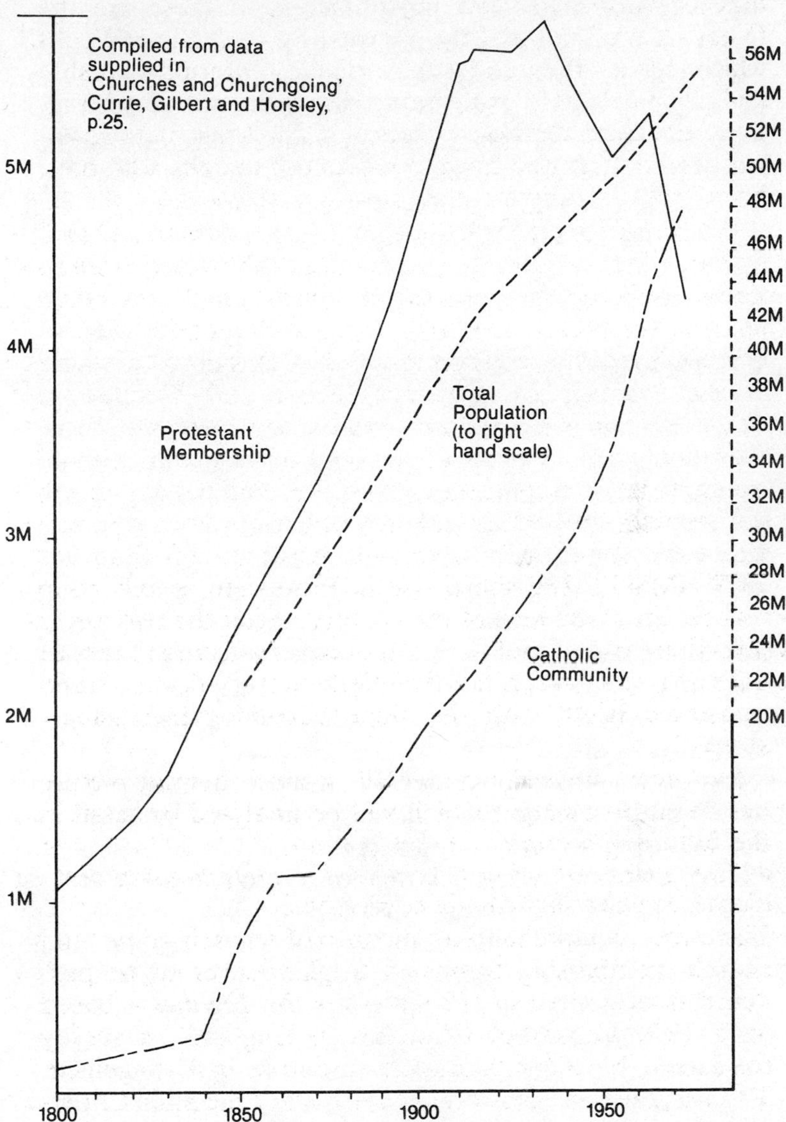

Fig. 4
Church membership in Great Britain 1800–1970

inations and across denominations and counties. Figures from seventy-five per cent of English churches were utilised in compiling the report. Thirty-nine per cent was supplied directly to the NIE by individual churches in response to a questionnaire accompanied by a letter signed by the appropriate denominational leader. The remaining thirty-four per cent was acquired through the Church of England, Roman Catholic, Methodist and Baptist central offices.

The following represent the main findings:

4.1 There are 39,269 churches. As the total adult population (15+) of England is 36,429,200, this means that there is on average one church for every 930 adults. Given the recent history of serious denominational decline and the current response rate, it is difficult to conceive of the possibility of church growth in terms of any large-scale church building programme. In situations where there has been population movement we will need to think of re-locating buildings, and many structures which are unsuitable for today's patterns of ministry will need to be replaced or re-designed. The priority church growth tasks are in the areas of discipleship training, the multiplying of cell-groups and the radical reappraisal of our traditional church-based worship, fellowship, educational and outreach programmes. There is, however, an imbalance between counties regarding the provision of church buildings, ranging from one church per 387 people in the mainly rural county of Lincolnshire to one per 1,660 in Greater London. As will be seen from the table supplied in Appendix E, the more densely the area is populated, the fewer the churches available. Or to interpret the data another way, the more rural and scattered the population, the more churches are required per head of population.

4.2 There are 6,739,000 church members, who represent 18 per cent of the total population. Of these, 3,114,000 are Protestants, 3,530,000 are Catholic and 95,000 are Orthodox.

However, care must be exercised in interpreting these data due to vastly different understandings of 'membership' by the various denominations. This means, as McGavran points out, that 'membership' data is often not comparable across denominations (McGavran 1970:93). The Roman Catholic figure represents the total adult Catholic population. Very few Catholics, no matter how nominal, would fail to have their children baptised. The Episcopal membership figure of 1,908,000 (which while being overwhelmingly Anglican, does include the Free Church of England and the Moravians) is made up, in the case of the Anglicans, of electoral roll membership, for which the basic qualifications are Baptism and a residential requirement, rather than an indication of commitment. The fact that over sixty per cent of the total population have been baptised at an Anglican font while only four per cent bother to take this simple step of identification gives some indication of the extent of the nominality problem faced by the Church of England. Until 1972 this roll gave an inflated figure as names were allowed to accumulate. In that year a fresh start was made and now the roll is revised every six years, when everyone is required to re-enlist. This means that people must be 'committed' to the extent of bothering to fill in a form, and therefore it has become a more realistic figure in recent years.

While in the case of the main-stream denominations membership exceeds attendance, the converse is true for the Independent and Pentecostal churches. For them 'membership' signifies their personal response to the gospel, demanding a deeper level of commitment to the local church.

4.3 3,850,000 adults attended church on a typical Sunday in November, 1979, in England. This figure represents 11 per cent of the total adult population.

Although, as this figure is based on a typical Sunday, it is inflated by those who attended twice or more on the day of the count, but excludes the less regular attenders who were absent on that day. This will not significantly affect the totals of those churches where it is traditional, as in the Catholic and Orthodox Churches, to attend only once per Sunday. Assuming only twenty per cent of Anglicans are 'twicers' and thirty per cent of the Free Churches, this would give an adjusted total of 3,500,000, which represents 9.5 per cent of the total population. This ratio almost certainly varies considerably between surburban and inner city locations, and probably between urban and rural areas, but the report unfortunately does not provide this significant breakdown. However, when we analyse the county table (Figs. 5 and 6) we can postulate that church attendance is lowest in areas:

> Where there are dense conurbations (Greater London, Manchester and West Midlands – though Merseyside is an exception due to Irish Catholic migration and a more militant Protestantism).
>
> Where there is mining and heavy industry (Cleveland, Tyne and Wear, Humberside, S. Yorkshire, Staffordshire, Derbyshire and Nottinghamshire).
>
> Where there is a commuting population which has destroyed the sense of 'community' which the local church has been established to serve.

Some analysts put church attendance as low as one per cent in some inner city areas.

The figure of 9.5 per cent is far more realistic than the remarkable results of the Marplan poll conducted for *Now* Magazine in December 1979 in which sixteen per cent claimed to go to church weekly, twenty-three per cent every month, and thirty per cent every three months. Admittedly this poll covered the whole of the United Kingdom, showing a significant regional variation ranging from thirty-nine per cent in Scotland and the north of England who claimed to have been in church during the previous three months on occasions other than weddings, funerals and christenings, to twenty-eight per cent in Wales and the Midlands and twenty-four per cent in London and the south. Presumably many of these people were there in spirit rather than in body!

4.4 Between 1975 and 1979 the churches collectively experienced a 0.4 per cent drop per annum in membership and a 0.6 per cent drop per annum in attendance.

This overall trend can be further subdivided as follows:

Membership (in 000s)	*1975*	*1979*	*% Change per annum*
Total all churches	6,838	6,739	−0.4
Protestant	3,231	3,114	−0.9
Catholic	3,513	3,530	+0.1
Orthodox	94	95	+0.4

Attendance (in 000s)	*1975*	*1979*	*% Change per annum*
Total all churches	3,945	3,850	−0.6
Protestant	2,521	2,533	+0.1
Catholic	1,418	1,310	−2.0
Orthodox	6	7	+0.7

When we compare Membership and Attendance figures we see significant divergent trends. The Protestant churches are experiencing a decline in membership at the same time as they are beginning to experience a slight increase in attendance. When we compare this recent development with the sharp decline of the 1960s and early 70s, it appears that a notable change may be taking place, unless present experience is no more than a brief hiccup. These statistics indicate that although churches are beginning to attract adherents, they are failing to translate this

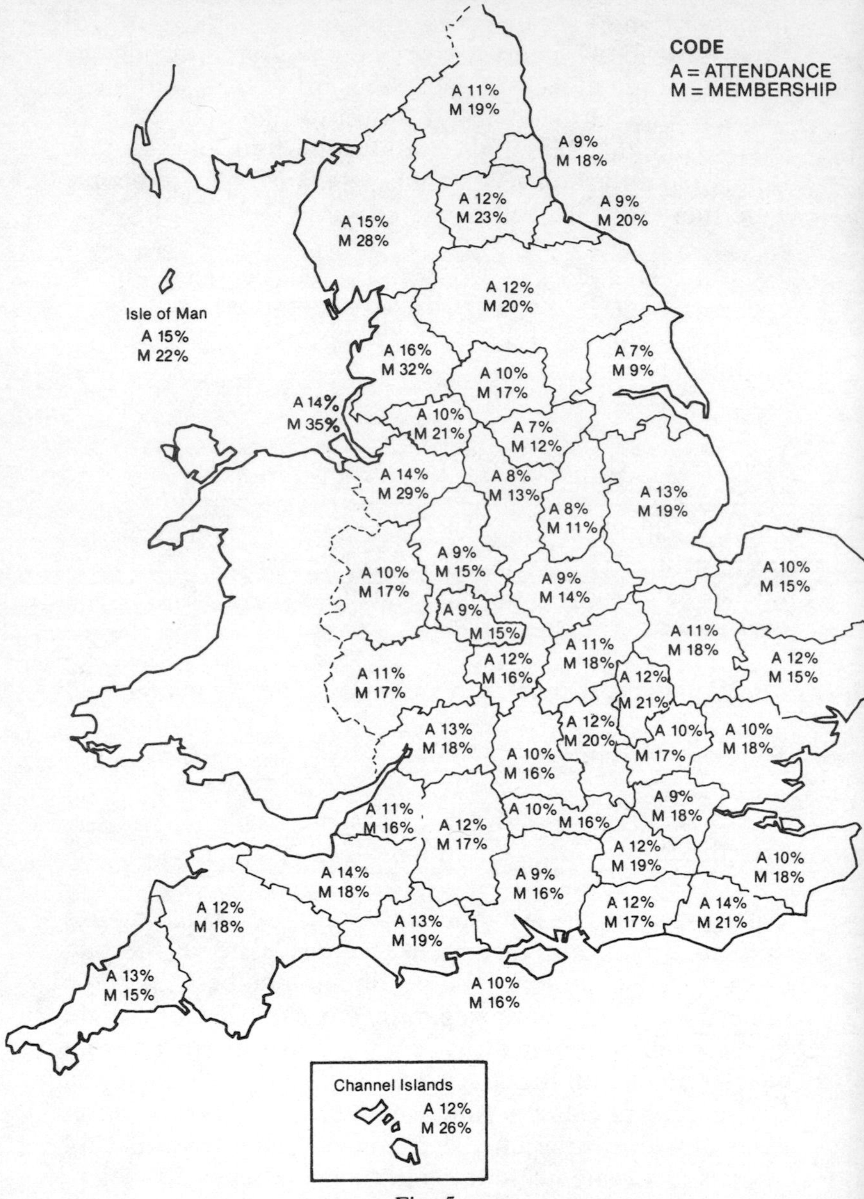

Fig. 5
Adult church attendance and membership in England by county, 1979

Fig. 6
The counties of England

into membership commitment. At various points in subsequent chapters we will return to this problem, and make some practical suggestions as to how the problem might be rectified.

The Roman Catholic Church is continuing to experience a growth in its total community, which is almost entirely explained in terms of Irish and European migration into Britain. However, it is also seeing a drop in Mass attendance. The figures for England *and Wales* are that in 1966 there were 2,114,219 attending Mass, which had dropped to 1,694,175 by 1978.

The real increase in the number of Protestants attending church may be greater than the marginal 0.1 per cent given in the NIE survey, due to the fact that there has been a change in the pattern of Protestant church attendance during the past fifteen years following the North American custom of attending church only once on Sunday. If there were more 'twicers' in 1974 than 1979 this would increase the attendance totals for the earlier year.

Fig. 7 shows those counties where each of the major denominations is experiencing growth in attendance. This data deserves closer analysis especially when it represents an exception to a national trend.

4.5 The following denominations are experiencing an increase in membership and attendance: Independent, African, West Indian, British Pentecostal, Other and Orthodox:

	Membership			Adult Attendance		
	1975 (000s)	1979 (000s)	% Change per annum	1975 (000s)	1979 (000s)	% Change per annum
Independent	136	169	+5.4	167	206	+5.4
African, West Indian	38	47	+5.5	55	66	+4.7
British Pentecostal	43	47	+2.3	78	88	+3.0
Other	141	142	+0.8	122	128	+1.2
Orthodox	94	95	+0.4	6	7	+0.7

These are all smaller denominations, and some, such

Fig. 7

Counties in which the larger denominations are experiencing an increase in church attendance

as the Independents, the Fellowship of Independent Evangelical Churches, Union of Evangelical Churches, Christian Brethren and the House Church Movement may be growing at the expense of the larger denominations. This may especially be the case with regard to the House Church Movement. However, with regard to the other older established groups the transfer traffic is not confined to one direction. The African, West Indian category represent the Black Church movement which has emerged strongly during the past twenty years, with an accelerated growth rate from the late sixties. The two principal Black Churches are the 'New Testament Church of God' and the 'Pilgrim Wesleyan Holiness Church'. The British Pentecostal and Holiness category includes: the Assemblies of God (35,000 adult attenders), Elim (25,000), Church of the Nazarene (5,000) and Emmanuel Holiness (500). The 'Other' category includes Salvation Army, Society of Friends, Seventh Day Adventists, Lutheran Council, Evangelical Lutherans, Churches of Christ, Countess of Huntingdon's Connexion and Churches of Overseas Nationals.

4.6 Among the main-line denominations the Baptists are the only denomination experiencing an increase in attendance but this is not yet reflected in their membership, which continues to decline.

Baptists

Membership			Attendance		
1975 (000s)	1979 (000s)	% Change per annum	1975 (000s)	1979 (000s)	% Change per annum
168	162	−0.9	193	203	+1.3

These figures suggest that although Baptists are attracting adherents they need to give closer attention to more effective membership incorporation procedures. But part of the explanation may simply be a matter of time-lag between the person beginning to attend and then asking and being prepared for believer's baptism. After reaching an all time low in 1970 with 4,5000 baptisms, numbers have begun to increase during the past few years (see 'Signs of Hope' Graph for Baptisms in England and Wales 1952–79) (Fig. 8). A further factor is that, 'Some churches have a trust which denies voting right to members under 18', thus although they are old enough to receive believer's baptism they are not eligible to be included in the membership totals. (Roger Hayden 'A Report on the relationship of Baptism to Church membership' prepared for the Assembly of the London Baptist Association). Furthermore, some growing Baptist Churches are increasing in membership through the transfer of Christians from churches which practise paedo-baptism, but because of their closed membership policy the increased attendance will not be reflected in their membership until the new attenders agree to be re-baptised. Commenting on the overall growth pattern of the Baptists, Independents, Afro-West Indian and British Pentecostal Churches, Gavid Reid observes that a clear pattern can be seen: 'The mainstream large denominations which practise infant baptism are still in decline, while the more highly committed, gathered congregations which practise adult baptism are growing' (NIE 1980:15, 16). Growing churches tend to be conservative in theology and impose stricter membership demands. They also make a strong appeal among young people.

Until 1971, the graph indicates the total number of baptisms in all returning churches: thereafter, it refers only to those in churches affiliated to the Baptist Union.

4.7 More young people under 15 years (1,483,000 out of a total of 10,111,800) are involved in church activities than would be expected.

The annual decline for all churches is −0.6 per cent, which gives ground for encouragement when it is realised that the national child population is falling by two per cent per annum. However, as John Tigwell reminds us in

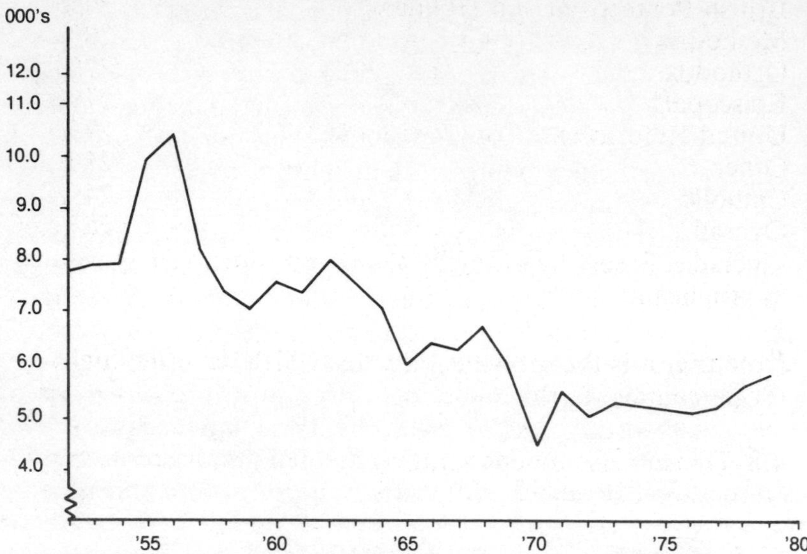

Until 1971, the graph indicates the total number of Baptisms in all returning churches; thereafter, it refers only to those in churches affiliated to the Baptist Union.

Fig. 8
Believers' baptisms in England and Wales 1952–1979

his commentary on the data, 'Thirty years ago church attendance for children was well over 30 per cent of the child population' (NIE 1980:25). He also observes that, 'As we study the regional statistics, we notice that those areas that we might consider "hard" or "a man's world", Northumberland, Durham, Lancashire, Yorkshire and Humberside, are less successful in attracting children' (NIE 1980:25).

Percentage of National Population under 15 years	21%
Percentage of Total Attenders under 15 years	
African and West Indian	38%
Independent	31%
Baptist	30%

British Pentecostal and Holiness	29%
Methodist	28%
Orthodox	27%
Episcopal*	27%
United Reform and Congregational	27%
Other	25%
Catholic	24%
Overall	26%

*Includes Free Church of England and Moravian as well as Anglican.

Note that it is the growing churches which have the highest percentage in this table.

4.8 There is also an encouraging level of response among young adults from 15 – 29 years.

15-19 Year Olds		*20-29 Year Olds*	
(National	*8%)*	*(National*	*11%)*
Catholic	12%	Catholic	12%
African and West Indian	12%	African and West Indian	10%
Orthodox	12%	Orthodox	6%
British Pentecostal and Holiness	11%	British Pentecostal and Holiness	13%
Episcopal	9%	Episcopal	10%
Independent	9%	Independent	13%
Other	9%	Other	11%
Baptist	8%	Baptist	9%
Methodist	5%	Methodist	5%
United Reform and Congregational	5%	United Reform and Congregational	7%
Overall	9%	Overall	10%

The potential responsiveness of young people has recently been evidenced in a national survey of religious attitudes conducted by *Buzz* Magazine and the Bible Society among 980 fourteen to eighteen-year-old school children in 1979. This showed that 42 per cent declared an interest in Christianity, 51 per cent believed the Bible has something worthwhile to say, 52 per cent agreed God helps young people, and 45 per cent had talked about God outside the classroom in the past month. However, 77 per cent said they either never went to church or only went occasionally, and 49 per cent declared they found church services to be boring. Where the Church demonstrates its commitment and credibility in terms which are meaningful to young people it has a considerable growth potential. These results compared closely with the poll sponsored by *Now* Magazine (Sept. 14, 1979) among fifteen to twenty-four-year-olds, 58 per cent of whom said they believed in God, but of those asked to list what they enjoyed doing best out of a choice of eighteen activities only five per cent said going to church. The remainder placed church-going bottom of their list.

However, belief in God appears to be significantly less among young people in comparison with the older generation. Compared to the 58 per cent of 15–24 year olds, according to the Gallup poll sample of 918 adults conducted in April 1979 (*Sunday Telegraph* April 15, 1979), 76 per cent of the British population believe in God. However of those, only 41 per cent believe in him as a personal being; for 37 per cent he is some sort of spirit or life force. The Marplan poll gives an even higher figure for belief in God at 82 per cent, with 76 per cent claiming to be Christian.

A principal reason for less belief in God among young people is the secularising influence of current education, which is reinforced by television. In addition to non-Christian philosophies which underlie general teaching, religious education is a cinderella subject in many schools. Of the *Buzz* sample only 34 per cent of those interviewed felt that religious education was well taught, as compared with 69 per cent for history and 75 per cent for mathematics.

Churches must, therefore, come to terms with the fact that they exist in a secularising and multi-faith environment, and take steps to ensure that they develop an integrated Christian education programme for young adults.

The NIE Report concludes with a projection of existing data to the year 1984 (Fig. 9). It will be interesting to see to what extent the prognosis will need to be revised as congregations and denominations become encouraged by the possibility of church growth!

5 Data-gathering at local church level

In many ways this is the most important level of data-gathering. People are intimately involved in the situation which they are endeavouring to analyse so they are well placed to assess the accuracy and relevance of the information and also to interpret its significance. The local church also plays a strategic role in building up a regional and national picture, the accuracy of which will depend upon the quality of the data which churches have amassed and are willing to divulge.

Before embarking upon data-gathering exercises some of the potential pitfalls must be recognised so that as many as possible can be avoided. People's suspicions are quickly aroused, so from the outset the congregation must appreciate the purpose and significance of the exercise and be assured that confidentiality will be preserved. This latter point is not easily achieved, expecially when questionnaires are used with small numbers. Individuals may be identified by their handwriting, or their answers to the range of questions may serve to point clearly in their direction. If such a possibility is likely to arise, then the analysis of the actual forms must be confined to one person who will act in complete confidence, destroying the forms as soon as his analysis is complete and there has been adequate discussion of the data; or preferably, an outside person should be invited to undertake the task.

In most situations it is advisable that the research project be given a 'low profile', with the actual work of data-gathering and analysis confined to a small group of

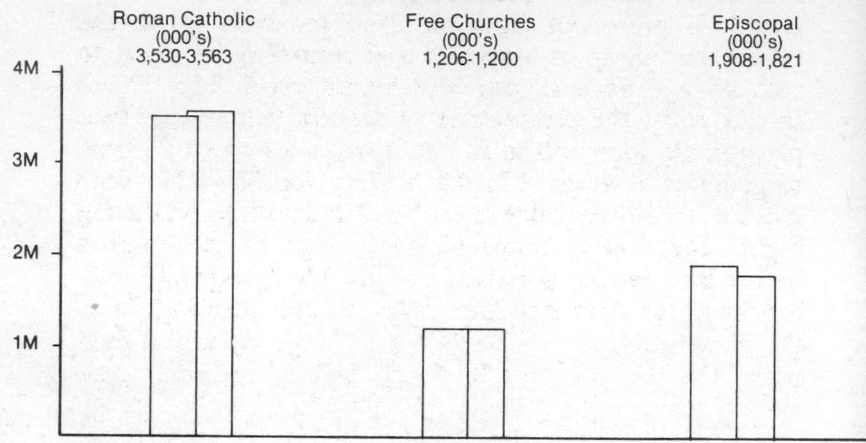

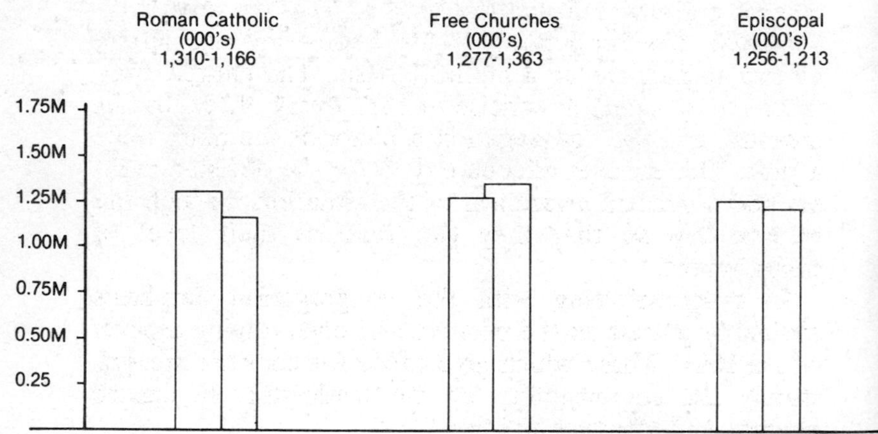

Fig. 9
Church membership and attendance projections 1979–1984

four or five suitably qualified people. By this means the church is preserved from 'analysis paralysis', with the church curtailing its activities and returning its plans to cold storage while it contemplates its navel. The church should resist the temptation to merely tick over. Once programme momentum is lost it becomes twice as hard to generate it again. Church leaders should gather data much as an airliner pilot reads his instrument panel during flight. There is a comprehensive range of information before him and his practised eye quickly detects any malfunction. He does not then relay all the information to the passengers, for to do so would serve no useful purpose. On the contrary it would merely increase their anxiety level, even if there was nothing to worry about. The information is mostly of concern to the crew in the pilot's cabin, who will then make the necessary course, altitude and speed corrections, and note items of equipment which may need a maintenance check, once the aircraft has reached its destination.

In a larger, more complex church, the minister should receive relevant information such as worship service attendance, Sunday School, Youth Fellowship and Home Group attendance on a monthly basis. The church committee may need a concise report every three or six months, and the congregation a pictorial summary once a year. This ensures adequate data for the decision-makers and a general awareness of the situation through the membership so that they can reassess their level of commitment.

In communicating with the congregation emphasis should be placed on the positive and encouraging aspects of the data. Those which give cause for concern are primarily the responsibility of the leadership to ensure prompt and effective action.

A further point to remember in the presentation of data is that most people cannot 'take in' lists of figures, so ensure that they are always presented in a diagrammatic form to show clearly proportions, relationships and trends. While a plain line graph may be adequate for the church committee, it is advisable to re-present the information to ordinary church members in terms of concrete symbols of people for members, and pounds signs for financial graphs. These communicate far more effectively.

5.1 Membership

This is the most readily available statistic in most churches. It is of most value as an indication of commitment in Free Churches, especially where the membership roll is kept up to date. However, it does present problems for Episcopalians and Roman Catholics, who think of their 'membership' as their total community. To illustrate the problem let us pose the question as to who are members of the Anglican Church in England? Are they the 39 per cent of the total population who are baptized as infants? Or the 16 per cent who are confirmed, or the 5 per cent who take the trouble to obtain and return a completed electoral roll form, or the 4 per cent who fulfil a basic 'membership' requirement of taking communion at Easter? (1979 figures). For historic reasons the infant baptism figure more accurately represents the 'external constituency' of the Church of England, that is, those who are favourably disposed, but most of whom do not bother to attend.

If we are to speak meaningfully in terms of membership it is probably better to define it in terms of communicant or active membership. How this is measured will vary from denomination to denomination. In Catholic and High Anglican circles it may be done on the basis of weekly attendance at Mass. In Presbyterianism it will be by attendance at the quarterly communions, and in Anglican Churches with a central or evangelical tradition the most accurate measure will be the numbers at Easter and possibly Christmas communion, although in some churches these two seasons will present difficulties if there is a tradition of members going away for holidays or to visit relatives at these times. Therefore, each church must work out for itself the best way and time to measure 'membership' which most accurately and helpfully reflects their situation. The important thing to ensure is that the measure is done in the same way each year so that true trends can be discerned by being able to compare like with like.

A revealing refinement in collecting membership data is to take notice of the number of full families (where husband and wife are both Christians) in the total as distinct from part families (where only one partner is Christian) (McGavran 1970:92). If you then discover that of your part families a high proportion consist of the wife in membership to the exclusion of the husband, this should lead to some questions being raised about your programme which is obviously proving more effective in one area than another. And what about the children in adolescent years? What proportion have neither one, nor both parents as members of the church? What do these results indicate you should be doing to minister to the situation?

Once you have established the rule of taking a membership count each year, after a period of time you will be able to represent these figures on a graph to compare one year with another. Having displayed in this clear format what has been happening, you will then be able to interpret the general trend, and raise questions regarding those years which proved to be exceptions to the overall picture. We will discuss the trend measures in greater detail in section 5.4 (p. 170)

5.2 Attendance

At first glance this might seem to be a more straightforward operation than gathering membership statistics – after all, attenders are visible on church premises and therefore easily counted. On further thought it is soon evident that it is not as easy as that, because the same people are not at church every week, some come more than once on Sunday and will, therefore, be counted twice, and there is an attendance fluctuation depending on the state of the weather and the time of year!

While smaller churches may be able to count every week, this may prove impractical for large churches, especially with more than one exit, without some fairly elaborate means of arriving at a total for each service. One of the simplest means is to buy a tally counter. Alternatively in churches where hymn books are given out is to note the empty spaces in the shelves where they are stacked or count those that remain and deduct them from the total. Many large churches, however, provide hymn books in the pews. An alternative scheme is to keep a record of the service sheets which are frequently distributed in churches of this size.

In order to compare one year's attendance with another, it is important to count at the same time each year. For England I suggest the best time is between late September and the end of November, avoiding Remembrance Sunday. This is when the new annual church programme gets under way after the summer holidays, and is before the bad winter weather sets in (hopefully!). Choose four typical Sundays during this period, i.e. excluding festivals and other special occasions, and divide your total attendance on those Sundays by four. This figure will be inflated by those who have attended more than once on a Sunday, but, providing churchgoing habits do not change, you will still have an accurate trend measure over a number of years, which is our primary interest. If, over the years, you suspect that there has been a swing to or away from attending more than once a Sunday, you may want to take the trouble of further refining your data. You can do this each year on a percentage basis which you set for that year on the basis of your knowledge of the churchgoing habits of the congregation. Alternatively on the 'count' Sundays you can ask people to register their attendance by placing a disc in a box just *once* during the day. The total number of discs will give you the total number of different people who have attended church that day.

Another way of tackling the problem is completely to separate morning and evening attendance figures so that you can evaluate churchgoing and the appropriateness of your morning and evening programme of services.

In addition to the 'four typical Sundays' measure, we recommend that churches keep a record of attendance at the most popular services on the major festivals of Easter, Mothering Sunday, Harvest and Christmas. It is these occasions which attract the 'fringe' members or the 'external constituency'. Growing churches tend to be those with the widest circle of 'fringers'. If your church is one which succeeds in attracting the crowds for special occasions, these people should constitute your prime target for deeper Christian commitment and church membership.

Churches with an active membership in excess of two hundred should also keep a record of those who attend primary and secondary groups (these are defined in Ch. 6) in order to identify those who only attend Sunday worship and are involved in no other activity. These people will constitute those who are at greatest risk, in that such people can easily go missing from a large church without being missed until it is too late to recover them.

More detailed practical guidelines on how to collect membership and attendance data, graph the results and measure growth rates is given in a number of handbooks. The following are recommended: *The Church Growth Survey Handbook* by Bob Waymore and C. Peter Wagner available from The Global Church Growth Bulletin, P.O. Box 66, Santa Clara, California 95052, USA., *Can British Churches Grow?* by Robin Thomson, Bible and Medical Missionary Fellowship, 352, Kennington Road, London SE11 4LF, and *Tools For the Task* by David Wasdell of the Urban Church Project, St. Matthias Vicarage, Poplar High Street, London E14 0AE.

5.3 Finance

The weekly offering is one of the most sensitive indicators of the extent of the commitment of the membership to the local church. Of the total annual income this figure should be separated from money which comes through legacies and other sources of income such as the hire of the hall and investments. Churches which achieve inspiring worship and operate a meaningful programme seldom have insurmountable financial difficulties. The level of giving is a barometer of church health. But as you graph your annual giving year by year, remember that to give an accurate impression you will need to correct for inflation. Many churches, in comparing their giving with previous years, neglect to take this sufficiently into account, thus giving a false picture, which may breed complacency if the church is succeeding in paying its bills. To correct for inflation start from a base figure, e.g. one pound sterling in 1962 represents a hundred per cent and then using the Retail Price Index, represent the pound as a percentage of this figure and divide your giving total for each year by this factor. These figures are available from the Central Statistical Office, Great George Street, London, SW18 3AQ (01–273 6193 or 6135). Thus the correction factor for 1979 was 0.231. With the high inflation rates commonly experienced in recent years, it soon becomes necessary to establish a new basis for calculation, so that 1970, for instance, becomes your basic pound value. (For correction table see Fig. 10.)

Year	Index for 1st Jan.	Mid-Year Equivalent	Correction Factor
1962	100	101.4	0.986
1963	102.7	103.7	0.964
1964	104.7	107.1	0.934
1965	109.5	111.9	0.894
1966	114.3	116.4	0.859
1967	118.5	120.05	0.833
1968	121.6	125.4	0.797
1969	129.1	132.3	0.756
1970	135.5	141.25	0.708
1971	147.0	153.0	0.654
1972	159.0	165.2	0.606
1973	171.3	181.6	0.551
1974	191.8/100	210.9	0.474
1975	119.9	256.85	0.389
1976	147.9	307.2	0.326
1977	172.4	347.1	0.288
1978	189.5	380.4	0.263
1979	207.2	433.9	0.231
1980	245.3	501.2	0.200
1981	277.5		

Fig. 10
Department of Employment cost of living index 1962–1981

Having represented the giving for a number of years on a graph, next ask what the figures have to tell you about the relevance and quality of your programme.

5.4 Trends

Establishing trends from the past is of enormous help in determining precisely where we are at present and where we should be going in the future. Year by year we should be concerned to know precisely the *rate* of growth or decline. This can be done on an annual basis with a bar graph which reveals the annual growth rate. The following represents the findings of one suburban Anglican church (Fig. 11). The annual growth rate can be calculated by subtracting the earlier year's membership from the later year's. Divide the answer by the earlier year. Then multiply this answer by a hundred, which gives you the percentage figure.

One word of caution. A new church with a rapid initial growth rate should beware of an over-optimistic future projection. This is not to limit faith, but to recognise that it is increasingly difficult to maintain a high figure based on small numbers. The normal pattern is for the initial expansionist phase to give way to a marginal state, which eventually leads through recession to the residual phase. This sequence is not inevitable, but is highly likely to occur eventually unless adequate steps are taken to prevent it.

5.5 Gains and losses

In their church growth analysis, Currie, Gilbert and Horsley distinguish between *autogenous* and *allogenous* growth (Currie, Gilbert and Horsley 1977:80). The former represents those accruing from the families of those already members, while the latter represents those recruited who are from families of non-members. In simpler language, autogenous growth may be described as *biological*, that is the children of church members coming to Christian commitment or church allegiance, while allogenous growth we may describe as conversion from the world.

Growing churches should seek to identify where their growth is coming from. Biological growth of itself will not increase the size of the congregation, at least in the case of white Protestant churches, for the simple reason that white Protestant families tend to have fewer children.

A second classification is *transfer* growth, which means people are leaving other churches in order to join ours. It therefore represents a tidal flow, without any overall increase. One church is growing at the expense of another.

A third possibility is *conversion growth*, which is the most important category in terms of church growth. A church must regularly identify those are coming to faith in Christ from a non-church background or with minimal previous church contact (McGavran 1970:87).

To these we may add a fourth, *restoration* growth, which is a significant category in areas which have witnessed serious church decline. These are people who have been restored to membership after a lapse of some years. They have usually been caused to reconsider their position vis-à-vis the church through contact with a zealous Christian friend or by the church demonstrating a quality of life which was previously unknown to the disillusioned 'back-slider'.

At a mid-week meeting of one thriving suburban church, I asked the hundred and two adults present how many had been brought to that church by their parents. Five hands were raised. I then enquired how many had joined that church within the last ten years. Sixty-one people put up their hands. They were asked to keep them in the air while a further question was put to them, 'How many of you came to this church from another church? If so, would you put your hand down?' Forty-nine hands were lowered, leaving twelve who represented those converted from the non-church constituency. Among those who had lowered their hands were some who had come to a vital faith while at their present church, and, due to rapid population turnover, there were, no doubt, some who had been converted and then moved on elsewhere during that ten year period. But the ratio of one to four between those who had been converted to those who had transferred in was significant and fairly typical of a growing suburban church.

The purpose of such an exercise is to reveal the true state of affairs. Clearly that church had an attraction for Christian people. It was doing the kind of things which Christian people were looking for in a local church, and was doing them well. The church quoted has a country-wide ministry, visiting other churches, sharing in experience of renewal and growth. At the same time the study revealed that the church needs to give further attention as to how to contact and communicate effectively with

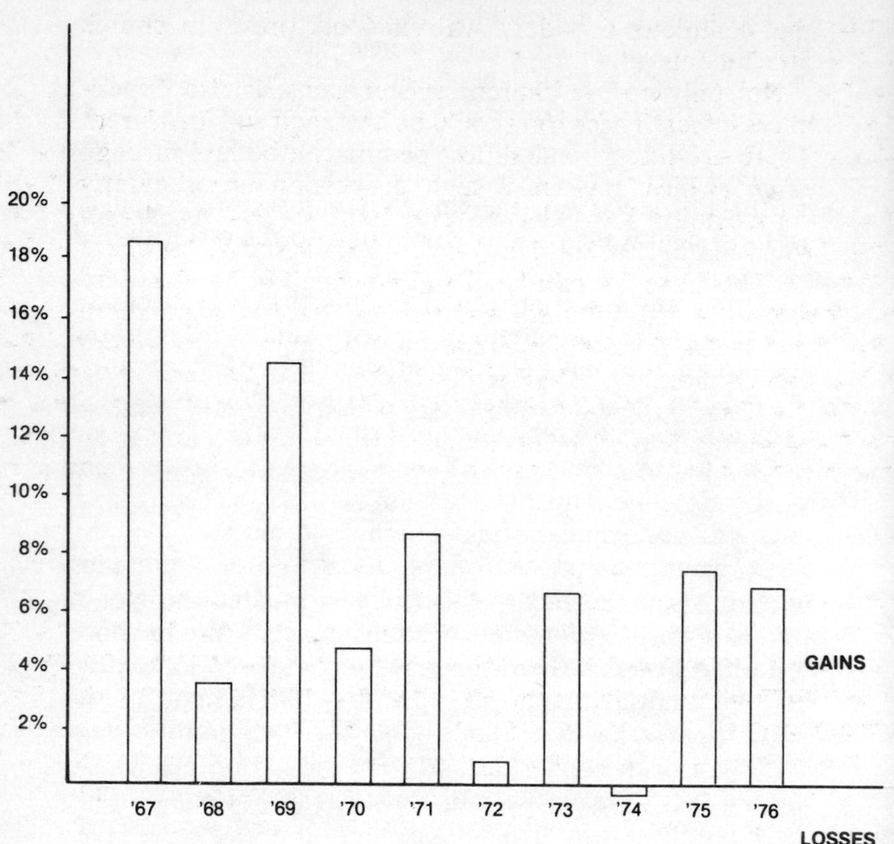

Fig. 11
Suburban Anglican church; electoral role annual rate of growth/decline

the complete outsider, who has no previous church attachments.

Not only does a church register gains, it also experiences losses. These too should be classified and measured. There are three possibilities; people can be lost through *death* (which may be a high proportion in an elderly congregation located in a retirement area), *transfer out* (high in an old community due for demolition, or where people move in search of employment or as they are relocated or promoted, or *reversion* (may be high where the social pressure is hostile to the church, or where church morale is at a low ebb).

Charting the gains and losses will help to give a more accurate picture of the church's growth profile.

Let us briefly consider the profiles of four hypothetical churches, whose gains and losses during a given year are represented in the bar graphs below (Fig. 12).

Church 'A' is Green Acres Estate Church. It is seven years old and located in a new development area of detached houses. Their prices are such that they are beyond the means of most first-time buyers. The estate is just five minute drive from the motorway and fifteen miles distant from an international airport. It therefore attracts men in middle and upper management positions. The development is now four-fifths complete. When the final group of houses is occupied it will have a total population in the region of ten thousand. Through its attractive worship, effective publicity, well-planned visitation campaigns and interest groups it has attracted 375 worshippers.

Looking now at the gains and losses bar graph for the year we see that the main explanation for their growth has been the addition of thirty-two members through transfer. The fact that Green Acres is an expanding and highly mobile community with a high percentage of nominal churchgoers means that it is relatively easy to bring them into church services. As they were mainly couples who had been married for a number of years and were

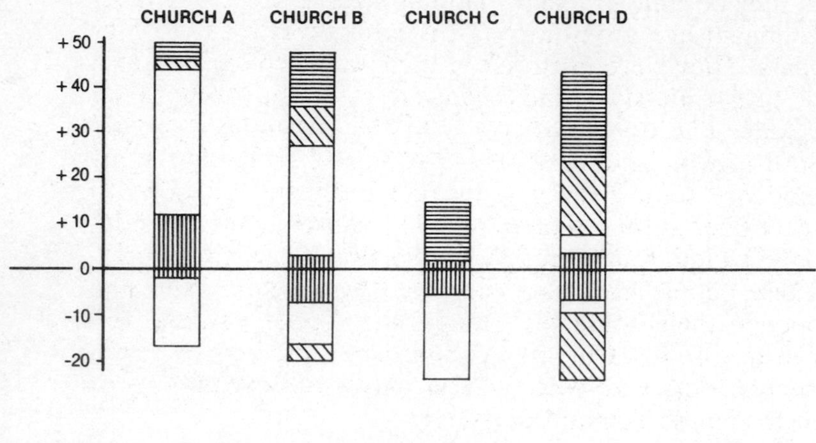

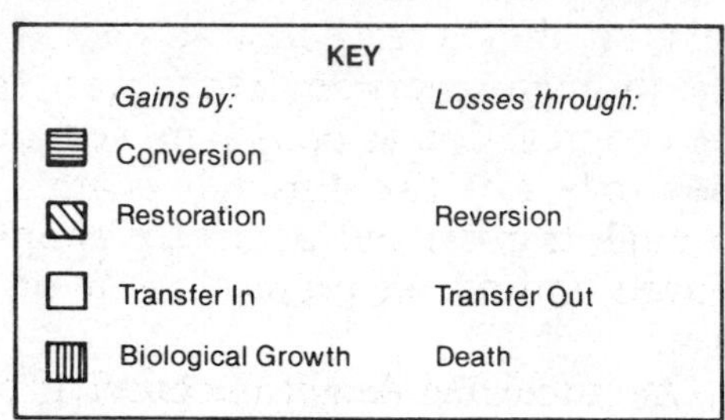

Fig. 12
Membership gains and losses

now able to move to a larger, more expensive home, their children ranged in age between seven and nineteen years. Thus the church added twelve through 'biological growth' as they became of age for church membership. The most dominant age group among the adults was thirty to fifty years. They were fairly set in their ways, committed to a particular life-style, and anxious to climb the promotional ladder. The non-churchgoers in the community proved hard to win, and those who had lapsed from church attendance some twenty years previously saw no need to reconsider at their time of life. The church, consequently, only added four through conversion from the world. These people had been contacted by a couple who had opened their home for evangelistic supper parties. The two restored to Christian commitment and active church membership were brought back through the testimony of their teenage son and daughter.

During that year the church had lost seventeen members. As they were a new and active church they lost no one through reversion. There were few elderly people in the congregation as people moved away at retirement, so they only lost two through death. The major loss was through transfer out as fifteen people were relocated or moved abroad on promotion or on changing to a new firm.

One suburban Anglican church in Surrey discovered on doing this exercise that they had to gain on average thirty-four new members each year just to stay where they were in terms of membership, such was the high level of mobility in their community.

Church 'B' is located in Perivale, an urban area of mixed housing, some of which is a pre-war estate owned by the local council and the remainder older semi-detached houses constructed between 1900 and 1920. The Perivale Church is a hundred and twenty years old. From the post-war years until the mid 1960s it had experienced steady decline. But in the mid 1970s things began to look more promising, with the arrival of a young new minister which coincided with movement into the area of young couples who found that older properties were the only type of house they could now afford as a first buy.

Young marrieds represent one of the most responsive groups in Britain today, as is witnessed by the popularity of family services. The Perivale church had grown to a Sunday morning attendance of two hundred. During the year twelve people had been converted, eight of whom were young wives brought to Christ through a young wives group. A further two mothers from single parent families had been brought into the fellowship through the understanding and practical help offered by the group.

Among the young couples moving into the area were those who had dropped out of church life when they had left home to go to university, or when they got married. However, now that they had family responsibilities and were beginning to put down roots, they returned to their former churchgoing. This occurred when they had their children baptised or mothers came into contact with other Christian young mums through the play group organised by the church. As most of these young people would move on before their children reached their teens, the church experienced little 'biological growth' in its adult membership. Some of the older properties were occupied by elderly couples, and as the life expectation of women is seven years longer than for men, there were a number of widows in the area. Many of these had had church links in the distant past, and were brought into the church's fellowship by elderly members of the Women's Bright Hour group.

During the year the Perivale church lost seven through death, nine moved out of the area, four of whom were elderly people who transferred to an old people's home in another part of the town, and five to a 'better neighbourhood'. In addition, four people in the fifty to sixty-five age bracket left because they didn't like the family service and other changes which the young new minister had introduced.

Church 'C' we will call Station Road Mission. It is located in a run-down, vandalised, inner city area which is due for redevelopment. The old terraced houses are being demolished to make way for a new shopping precinct. The church no longer has a Sunday evening service and the morning worship is attended by about thirty-five 'old faithfuls'. Although few people now reside in the immediate locality, it is a gathering point for young people in the area, who hang around the shopping area and occupy the bench seats located in a landscaped approach to the precinct. A local evangelist working with a youth mission saw the potential of the Station Road mission premises for coffee bar evangelism. He gained the permission of the elders to occupy and renovate a section of their hall, and enlisted the support of Christian musicians from other churches in the town.

The coffee bar saw thirteen young people converted during the year, who were baptised on profession of faith. The coffee bar evangelist had identified with the Station Road Mission to the extent of becoming a member, but as a newcomer he was not able to influence the traditional pattern of Sunday worship. In consequence, many of the young people drifted off. Other factors contributing to the high loss rate were lack of parental support, ridicule by their peers, and no examples of maturer Christians with whom they could identify. As there was no movement into the area, the church was unable to grow through either transfer or restoration.

Church 'D' is a black independent church, now seventeen years old. It is located in an inner-city residential area. Originally it met in the hall of the local Anglican church. Five years ago the host church was made redundant and was purchased by the independents. This church added sixteen members through restoration. These had been regular churchgoers in the Caribbean but had not felt at home in the more restrained worship of the British churches, and some had felt cold-shouldered by the white members. However, once there was a church in the area which reminded them of life 'back home' and with black leadership, they were restored to membership. This opened the way to twenty conversions from the world, through the extended family network to those who had no previous church connections. On the debit side the church also witnessed a high proportion of reversions, particularly among their young people through the secularising influence of their English education and the fact that they did not share their parents' nostalgia.

Of all the areas of local church data-gathering the identification and classification of membership gains and losses is one of the most important. To understand the dynamics of the situation, one must be aware of *who is joining*, where from and why, and *who is leaving*, where to and why. A church with a static membership may equally describe a stable community or a church in rapid transition which is just managing to hold its own. The water level and dip-stick don't tell you everything. We need to know if the tap is on and whether the plug has been removed from the plug hole!

Having identified who has joined the church in the past year we need to know what were the main influences which caused them to make their decision. In this way we can learn more clearly about the strengths of our church in order to improve on them further. Information can be gathered by means of a questionnaire which new adherents are either invited to fill up themselves, or which can be completed in an interview by one of the church leaders (see Fig. 13).

When you have analysed a number of completed questionnaires you will probably discover that the most influential factor in introducing people to your church is the personal invitation of a friend. One of the greatest impediments to effective out-reach on the part of local congregations is their lack of meaningful contact with non-Christian people. But when the church breaks through this isolation it has created a potential for growth. A recent Gallup survey of churchgoers reveals that '58 per cent of those who now go to church regularly, first began going when they were invited by someone they knew. Conversely, 63 per cent of those who do not go to church report that none of their friends of acquaintances has ever invited them' (McGavran and Hunter 1980:33, 34).

On the other side of the picture it is also instructive to know who has left the church during the past year and their reasons for leaving. We are particularly concerned to identify those who have lapsed while continuing to live in the locality. Such people obviously cannot be approached to fill up a questionnaire! But they will almost certainly have friends and perhaps relatives who are still church members who can be approached to discover the real reasons for their departure. Most churches, when asked, claim that they are friendly churches. But the committed membership are not those best able to give an accurate assessment. Their very 'friendliness' towards each other may have excluded others by its exclusiveness.

Once you have collected the data from those who have joined the church and about those who have left, then decide what action you will need to take to correct any deficiencies in attracting and holding people. In subsequent years when you prepare your gains and losses bar charts you will then have objective data on which to evaluate the effectiveness of your plans.

6 Quality of commitment

McGavran cautions that numerical increase 'is not adding mere names to the roll or baptising those who have no intention of following Christ. Roll padding, aside from being dishonest, is useless. The numerical increase worth counting is that which endures from decade to decade. Roll padding and dishonest baptising will never produce lasting growth' (McGavran 1959:16). As we emphasised in the opening chapter, church growth is far more than increasing the head count of those who profess to be Christians.

Tick the appropriate boxes

WHAT ATTRACTED YOU TO THIS CHURCH?

1. It was the nearest of my denomination and so I took the initiative to make contact ☐
2. It was the nearest church to my home and so I took the initiative to make contact ☐
3. My family invited me along to the.. (name the occasion) ☐
4. My friends invited me along to .... ☐
5. Church members visited me and invited me to .... ☐
6. I learned about the church from the local newspaper, ☐
   radio, ☐
   advertisement hoarding ☐
   church magazine/newsletter ☐

WHAT APPEALS TO YOU MOST ABOUT THIS CHURCH?

State three features which have meant most to you during your first year:

1. ....
2. ....
3. ....

HOW CAN THE CHURCH BECOME EVEN MORE EFFECTIVE IN WELCOMING NEW PEOPLE?

Please reflect on your own experience and the attitudes towards church of your non-Christian friends

1. ....
2. ....
3. ....

Fig. 13
Sample questionnaire

In developing measuring tools for the local church we are concerned with quality control as much as quantity measure, to use commercial language. Responsible leaders want to know how people are growing in their understanding of the Christian faith, whether relationships are deepening and extending throughout the church-fellowship, and to what extent the Christian presence is evident in the community outside. Such information cannot be gathered with such precision as numerical data, but it is essential that each area be investigated to ensure that there is a balance between worship, fellowship, learning, evangelism and service. Healthy organic growth is proportionate, with each area and function developing in relation to the other.

Quality of church life can be measured in the following three ways:

6.1 Continuous assessment

The true shepherd knows his sheep. This becomes increasingly difficult as the flock increases in size. The time comes when under-shepherds will need to be appointed to maintain growth in numbers and quality. We must be observant to detect what is happening and continually be asking questions to test knowledge and measure reactions.

6.2 Sample interviews

From time to time draw up a questionnaire on some aspect of Christian truth or church life or community concerns and use those in contact with different segments of the congregation to interview selected individuals in order to sample opinion and collect suggestions. This method might be used to gather ideas for the next course of sermons, for example.

6.3 A congregational questionnaire

Such questionnaires have been used extensively in the Leighton Ford's Reachout campaigns in Vancouver and

Melbourne. But congregational questionnaires can be very threatening to the individual and should only be used in churches where there is a high degree of cohesion and commitment to agreed goals. Otherwise they may prove divisive and generate defensive attitudes. They are best used in an inspirational setting as part of a total church-life conference. For the responses to be regarded as in any way representative of the views of the congregation, there should be at least a seventy-five per cent response rate.

Such congregational questionnaires are available from the Bible Society, Church Programmes Department, 146 Queen Victoria Street, London EC4V 4BX. A series of four Fact Finders has been produced each including a Bible Study, questions on the set passage and a related congregational questionnaire covering the four dimensions of growth – Growing Up in Christian knowledge and understanding – Growing Together in meaningful relationships – Growing Out in service – and Growing More in numbers through evangelistic outreach.

7 Use of facilities

Our buildings are an asset to be used to the full. In some areas the church premises represent the only public amenities; they must, therefore, be utilised to meet the needs of that community to which God would have his people minister. How many hours a week is each room, the hall and the church, sanctuary used, and by how many people each week? In what ways can their use be rightly extended? What alterations need to be made to our programme and the structure and decor of the building to make them more adaptable and attractive? Again, by measuring each year, we can determine what progress we are succeeding in making.

8 Community profile

Both David Wasdell of the Urban Church Project, St Matthias' Vicarage, Poplar High Street, London E14

OAE, and the Nationwide Initiative in Evangelism, 146 Queen Victoria Street, London EC4V 4BX, produce workbooks to enable churches to conduct a survey of their community. At the outset the church needs to identify the geographical area or kind of people it is seeking to reach with the gospel. For the city-centre Anglican church this will mean working with a map of the entire city, in recognition that the majority of their congregation will be living in someone else's parish! Estimate how many people live in the area you cover, and then describe the different kinds of people within those boundaries in terms of socio-economic levels, race, employment, age groups and interests. Describe and quantify each group as accurately as you are able.

Next identify the other churches in the community and identify the kinds of people they appeal to and the numbers they are successful in reaching. Such an exercise is, therefore, best done not in isolation but in co-operation with the other churches. This reduces the workload and helps in the production of a more comprehensive and accurate picture. Having worked together in the area of analysis, it is then more likely that you will be able to co-operate in developing a corporate strategy. In such an exercise we should be especially alert to identify the unreached, contact new arrivals and respond to unmet needs.

Such a community profile must have an eye to the future. The churches should seek to discover the community trends and local authority plans for the coming years. This will save the church from planning for yesterday rather than tomorrow. As a generalisation it is a fact that new churches grow better than old (which is borne out in *Prospect for the Eighties*, a report on churchgoing trends in England). So growing communities need new churches to develop within them.

9 Future projections

Data-gathering should only be undertaken if we intend to act upon the information which has been accumulated. One of Murphy's Laws states that if the statistics don't prove your point then you obviously need more statistics! We might extend this in many church investigations to state that even when the statistics prove your point, your next course of action is to gather yet more statistics. James Engel defines research as 'the gathering of information for use in decision-making' (Engel 1977:13). Thus research must be phased into strategy. The consistent failure to implement findings has given rise to cynicism regarding research. Engel explains, '. . . research must be undertaken for the right reasons. It is especially essential that those who are responsible for implementation must have a thoroughgoing commitment to change if research is to be anything other than counterproductive' (Engel 1977:176).

Our efforts in data-gathering are to maximise our chances of making right choices and decisions. Having drawn up our membership, attendance, financial and other relevant graphs, we can then project them forward not simply as an extension of the existing trend, but as a 'faith projection'. This will represent what we believe it is possible, by God's grace, to achieve. It is called a 'faith projection' because it relates to the measure of faith which God has granted as we have analysed our performance, related these to biblical priorities, and prayed through our response.

If we simply allow events to take their natural course it is likely that the church will follow the life phases of most other institutions. The rapid-growth *progressive* phase, characterised by conversion growth and a high loss rate due to instability and immaturity, will eventually settle in the *marginal* phase, in which the institution is maintained by a high level of biological growth and a lessening appeal to non-members. This in turn will give way to the *recessive* phase as the external constituency from which the institution recruits its membership dwindles and biological growth declines. Eventually the institution will find itself in the *residual* phase, in which the external constituency has ceased to exist and the biological growth is eroded by the loss to the movement of the uninterested children of the members (see Fig. 14).

To prevent such a sequence of events the church must seek continual spiritual renewal; deploy a high proportion of its members to work in the external constituency; in McGavran's terminology, to turn them into class two leaders and workers (for his classification of four worker types see p. 201), i.e. 'members whose energies are primarily directed to serving and evangelising non-Christians in their ministry area in an effort to bring them into the Body of Christ', and to establish new groups and plant new congregations.

10 Summary

One of the drawbacks in presenting such a wide range of analytical exercises in quick succession is that we become so overwhelmed by the options that we end up by doing nothing.

As a start, using the graph provided in the Appendices, you might decide to monitor progress nationally during the coming years from the statistical information supplied by your denomination. Then you will be able to compare the performance of your church against the country-wide trends.

In a one-off data-gathering exercise the results are a highly perishable commodity; they date immediately. Therefore, before embarking on any research project we must make clear that we intend to act on the results.

Review your situation in the light of the preceding pages asking yourself, 'Are there areas of church life where we are operating in the dark, and where hard evidence would help us do things better?' The responses to this kind of question should help you pin-point where to begin.

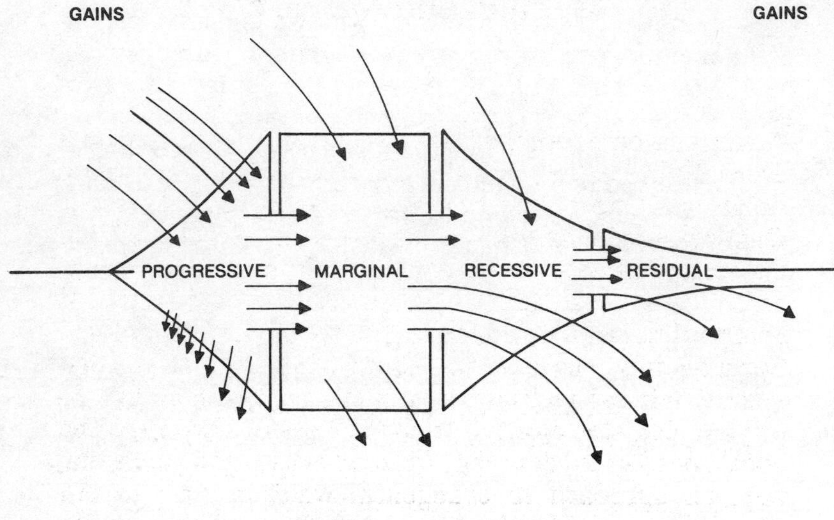

Fig. 14
Phases in the life of an organisation

CHAPTER FIVE

Medium and Message

A NUMBER OF excellent books are available on personal evangelism, dealing with the one-to-one and small group situations. One of the best to appear in recent years is *Out of the Saltshaker* by Rebecca Manley Pippert (IVP). She describes how she was 'turned off' by the way evangelism was presented as a stereotyped technique. It appeared to be an assembly-line processing methodology. Consequently, she admits, 'There was a part of me that secretly felt evangelism was something you shouldn't do to your dog, let alone a friend' (Pippert 1980:16). The book goes on to describe, in a reflective and anecdotal way, an approach to evangelism which is true to our experience, moulded by our personality and sensitive to the needs of the individuals to whom we believe it right to share openly our faith. For personal evangelism to be effective it must be spontaneous, flexible and sensitive.

When we turn from personal evangelism to community-focused church-based evangelism there are far fewer books which provide practical help in this area. This is a serious omission because the church is both medium and message in the process of gospel communication. Evangelism does not simply happen through persuasive individuals, but through communities of believers, who give credibility to the proclamation, by demonstrating something of the reality of what they speak. Our concern in this chapter is, therefore, to highlight a number of considerations which a local church should bear in mind in pondering its evangelistic effectiveness and overhauling its strategy. In our concern that evangelism should happen spontaneously we cannot ignore the need for planning and structure. The church is intended to facilitate, not hinder, growth.

Our purpose in this chapter is not to offer a blueprint, but to outline basic requirements which are applicable to almost any evangelistic programme. When a church has established the prior requisites, then it will be in a position to consider and experiment with a number of alternative approaches maximising their potential.

1 Make prayer meetings the power house

The concern of this book to provide practical guidelines to assist churches in developing growth-enabling strategies must not be pursued to the neglect of the spiritual dimension. No matter how helpful some of the tools presented seem to appear, they will prove useless and even harmful if taken up by those with eyes which are spiritually blind and whose hands lack spiritual strength.

As one studies case histories of growing churches there is one recurring factor – they are all *praying* churches. The Pentecostal movement in Chile was born in a prayer meeting. The Lord spoke to a nightwatchman in the port of Valparaiso in a dream, instructing him to go to his pastor and tell him to gather his most spiritual people together to pray every day. For the Lord revealed, 'I intend to baptise them with tongues of fire' (Wagner 1973:16). Within months revival began, and overjoyed Christians overflowed into the city streets. Seventy years later the Pentecostals of Chile, now numbering over a million, regularly meet for their *vigilias* – their nights of prayer.

Presbyterian ministers from South Korea have told me of their daily dawn prayer meetings, many of them attended by thousands. And around the British Isles ministers of growing churches in all denominations testify to the fact that it began as they met with those in their churches burdened by God to confess their spiritual apathy or impotence and to seek his power to heal their defeated lives and divided churches in order to become the people he intended them to be, not only in the Church, but in the world.

Yet prayer meetings for the renewal of the church and for revival in the nation are not an automatic answer to decline. I have sometimes been saddened by encapsulated groups praying along these lines. They are nostalgic rather than expectant, thinking only in terms of God doing a 'repeat performance' rather than a new thing. Although their sentiments sound very pious as they earnestly cry, 'Lord, send revival', what they are in fact engaged in is not so much a prayer meeting as a spiritual buck-passing session. For coupled with the voiced appeal for revival is the unspoken rider, '. . . and until you do we are not budging'! One learns to grow suspicious of cosy, predictable and sentimental prayer meetings.

Effectual prayer is 'in the name of Jesus', which ascription means, 'according to his character and purpose' – and *we* are part of that purpose! If, while we are praying for the Lord to do a new thing, we are failing to take action in areas where his intentions are perfectly clear and his resources for their implementation guaranteed, then he is unlikely to respond to our appeals to do more. Indeed, if he were to accede to our request, we would probably become so alarmed by the manifestations of his power that you wouldn't see most of us for dust!

Expectation is generated not through the effervescence of the enthusiasts, but through the intercession of the people of God. We plead not simply that God will change our circumstances, but that he will change *us* so that we can become catalysts to his plans to work through them. We must be prepared to face the cost of being a part of the answer to our own prayers. Such an attitude underlies all of the strategy described in this chapter and those that follow.

2 Establish a positive attitude

In some churches a casual visitor gets the impression from the mournful atmosphere of the service that the congregation must be rehearsing their own funerals! Where such an atmosphere of gloom persists it needs to be dispersed by affirming the Christian hope. This was delightfully expressed at the national Roman Catholic Pastoral Conference held in Liverpool in 1980 where Christians were described as 'Easter People'. The people of God should never consider themselves as being the people of yesterday. The authentic Church is part of a Kingdom which is not on the way out, but on the way in. The people of God, therefore, have a stake in today and an inheritance for tomorrow. No matter how unpromising the immediate situation may seem, they have an unshakable hope that the best is yet to come. Nostalgia needs to be replaced by expectancy. While on the one hand we must avoid the temptation of a triumphalism which attempts to transfer too much of the hope of the coming age into the present dispensation, we must also resist the other extreme of postponing all but a few wispy strands into the never-never future.

Remnant theology exercises a powerful influence in the Protestant churches of Western Europe. When the future seems to be filled with storm clouds, it may appear that the Church has no other recourse but to batten down the hatches and attempt to ride the storm. Our Lord did indeed warn of persecutions, heresy and growing violence in the last days. These 'last days' have in measure been with us since his crucifixion two thousand years ago. The Church was born in troubled times. In many places it advanced in the teeth of opposition. But the policy then was not to lie low until a more favourable climate developed. When the Jerusalem authorities, both Jewish and Roman, attempted to gag the Christian witnesses by threats and the token arrest of Peter and John, the Christians responded by taking the matter to the Lord in prayer. They placed the facts before God, declared their faith in his complete control over circumstances, and resolved to carry on despite the dangers, and requested that the Lord should continue to authenticate their testimony through signs and miracles (Acts 4:27–31).

It is strange that remnant theology has such a stronghold in churches within the Puritan tradition. In their defeatism and pessimism they betray that tradition which was so pregnant with expectation. This is demonstrated by Iain Murray in *The Puritan Hope*, in which he traces the Puritans' understanding of unfulfilled prophecy, by extensively quoting their writings on the subject from the sixteen to the nineteenth centuries. The majority of the Puritan leaders during these four centuries came to the conclusion that the Scriptures lead us to expect a time of wider blessing for the Church before the Second Advent of Christ. Moreover such a spiritual awakening would not be dependent on favourable conditions to make it possible. Murray writes:

> The gospel of grace does not need promising conditions to make its reception a certainty. Such a result depends upon the will of him who declares his love to the ungodly. Thus in various centuries revivals of apostolic Christianity have broken out in the most improbable circumstances and have powerfully, rapidly and extensively affected whole communities. 'When the enemy shall come in like a flood, the spirit of the Lord shall lift up a standard against him' (Is. 59:19) (Murray 1971:xx).

The impetus and direction of our missionary endeavours will depend on our view of what God has planned for winding up this world's affairs as well as our understanding of what salvation means.

> In the light of history we can hardly say that matters prophetic are too secondary to warrant our attention. The fact is that what we believe or do not

> believe upon this subject will have continual influence upon the way in which we live. The greatest spiritual endeavours and achievements in the past have been energised by faith and hope. By comparison how small are our efforts! And can we disregard the possibility that this stands related to the smallness of our anticipation and to the weakness of our faith in the promises of God? (Murray 1971:xxii).

We are not abandoned waifs or orphans, but adopted sons in a growing family. The future is not a blank wall to line up against, but a way to be walked. Establishing a positive self-image does not depend on a cheery morale boost, but on appropriating the promises of God and praying and planning expectantly for their outworking in the situations in which God has already placed us or challenged us to become involved.

3 Build an adequate base

In missionary strategy people come before buildings and equipment. On a new housing estate the priority task is to establish Christian cells rather than launch into a brick-by-brick building scheme. New residents are at their most receptive during the first six months. If the opportunity to reach them is missed through a preoccupation with building plans and bricks and mortar, then a never-to-be-repeated golden opportunity has been lost.

From the four Gospels we can see the extent to which our Lord invested his time in people. In addition to addressing the crowds as he journeyed through Galilee and around Jerusalem, he drew aside to be with his closest associates. They represented his investment in the future. The twelve disciples were the core of the new people of God which had originally been organised in its twelve tribes. The writers of the four Gospels show their awareness of this strategy by the emphasis they place on his relationship to the twelve and the teaching he shares with them.

1.1 Rebuilding a run-down situation

The need to build an adequate base is not only relevant to the pioneer missionary situation, but also to many run-down, inner city locations – only here the problems are even greater because of a history of decline, premises which are impossible to maintain in good order and totally unsuitable for the task in hand, and demands made upon inadequate resources by the needy people in the community and overstretched social services trying to meet their needs. Sometimes the building is a major stumbling-block to progress. Its maintenance costs can absorb a major proportion of the available funds. It is more of a liability than an amenity.

Some of the Victorian monstrosities are less inviting as a place of worship than a cold-store warehouse. I remember visiting one such on a freezing winter's day. Clouds of vapour formed as we sang the opening hymn and three people walked out before the sermon from sheer cold. To heat the building to a reasonable temperature would have cost so much that they would have needed to charge a two pound entrance fee! I read the account of an architect who was consulted by a church with unsuitable premises which they wanted to adapt. After his inspection, he tried to think of something positive to say. His only comment was, 'Well, at least it's militarily defensible!'

Another church suffered from a lack of adequate base not in terms of buildings, but of people. This was a Nonconformist church in an inner city area with a modern dual purpose building surrounded by high-rise local authority dwellings. From the outset the denomination planned that the church should serve the local community in two principal ways: through an open youth club and by providing sheltered accommodation for elderly people housed in purpose-built flats alongside the church. However, the new minister on arrival soon found that he was faced with a seemingly impossible task. On the one hand he had to contend with a tough gang of young people attracted to the youth club, and on the other to care for the elderly people who made up a considerable proportion of his congregation. The local authority had provided half the capital for the dual purpose church and the salary for a youth leader, so the church had obligations to maintain the club open despite continuous vandalism and verbal abuse directed at the elderly people, who became understandably reluctant to attend church. To sustain the ministry among the youth and elderly people demanded a substantial core of local leadership. It was this vital element which was lacking.

1.2 A need for a missionary team

Most run-down inner city churches need more than an isolated minister, however, devoted, to get things running again. They require a missionary team, which, in addition to having a gifted leader, comprises a task force with an allocation of funds. Experience of urban mission in other areas of the world needs to be applied to the British situation. If there is little or no local Christian presence, then a team from outside needs to be brought in. Ministers for such tough assignments need pioneering gifts (i.e. they need to be made in the apostolic mould) and cross-cultural training if a church is to put down local roots. Unfortunately, theological colleges give little specialist training in the area of new church planting or moribund church rejuvenation.

A significant contribution is being made by university students who are committing themselves to struggling churches during their years of study. They provide pro-tem leadership for youth groups and home meetings until locally trained leadership is ready. They inject musical talent and mime and drama skills to enrich worship. And their presence helps to correct the impression of the church as a moribund institution for the elderly, or as a convenient child-minding service. As young people they have the necessary flexibility, and the fact that they are struggling on meagre grants means that they can identify with some of the financial problems of the local church! The Rev. Martin Gooder of Brunswick Parish, inner Manchester, acknowledges their enormous contribution to the growth of his church. Some of the young people who get involved with the inner-city mission choose to look for a home in such areas when they leave college for employment. They take this step not with a sense of costly sacrifice but out of preference.

Still other churches lack an adequate base not through a shortage of church attenders but an absence of a committed core. If such a church is to grow, its congregation must become a body of people who are worth knowing. Relationships may need to be healed. The congregation must be brought to the point of rededication, and agreement reached about their priorities as a community of God's people.

4 Agree on your evangelistic goal

Before it embarks on the task of proclaiming the gospel of Jesus Christ the local church must have a clear idea as to the hoped-for result of such an undertaking, and should make appropriate plans to maximise the chances of achieving it.

4.1 The Great Commission

Of the four activities mentioned in the Great Commission recorded by Matthew – going, baptising, making disciples and teaching – the objective of these activities is to 'make disciples'. The going is in order to establish effective contact. The baptising is the act of initiation into the community of the redeemed. 'Teaching' is about the personal life-style, ethical standards and world-view consistent with discipleship. The content of that teaching is to be found in the discourses of our Lord recorded in the Gospels. No new word is added by the Lord after his resurrection. His relationship with his disciples prior to the crucifixion provides a model for the fellowship that believers are to enjoy in subsequent centuries.

4.2 Make disciples

A *mathetes* (discipline) is one who has heard the call of Jesus and joins his company. In its Jewish context it means much more than in secular Greek. For the Greek it meant student, pupil or apprentice. In the New Testament it means total allegiance. This is reflected in the teaching emphasis in making disciples. Such teaching is not simply with the object of enlightening the mind or to satisfy curiosity, but to mould the personality and give direction to life. Our Lord's teaching is presented to us not as information to be sifted, but as guidelines to be followed. It welds together understanding (Matt. 13:52) and commitment (Matt. 27:57).

The objective of evangelism is to make disciples. Disciples are recognisable, countable people. In saying this we must, however, recognise that a 'disciple' is never a finished product, but always a life in formation. Whereas the disciples of the rabbis normally expected to become as good if not better than their masters, the disciples of Jesus must learn never to lose their 'L' plates. Discipleship is not a status following automatically on baptism; it represents an abiding relationship and a continuing response to the known will of our Lord. Furthermore, discipleship does not represent a second level confined to an elite corps. The term describes the essential characteristic of authentic Christian profession.

In any assessment of evangelistic effectiveness the church growth movement stresses the need to focus attention not so much on decisions registered but on disciples made. This is a healthy shift of emphasis, although in itself it does not completely clarify the goal. Discipleship is far more than initiation into a particular congregation or even accepting the terms of membership prescribed by a particular denomination. The significance of the individual's decision in terms of 'responsible church membership' will depend on the congregation's understanding of 'discipleship' and its quality of life and breadth of vision in working that our in practical terms in today's world.

A. W. Tozer makes this timely and uncomfortable reminder:

> Many of us Christians have become extremely skilful in arranging our lives so as to admit the truth of Christianity without being embarrassed by its implications. We arrange things so that we can get on well enough without divine aid, while at the same time ostensibly seeking it. We boast in the Lord but watch carefully that we never get caught depending on him (Tozer 1955:49).
>
> The man of pseudo-faith will fight for his verbal creed but flatly refuse to allow himself to get into the predicament where his future must depend on that creed being true (Tozer 1955:50)

If the local church engaging in evangelism has not worked out for itself the implications of discipleship in its concrete situation it is in danger of subverting that mission rather than forwarding it. It may succeed in producing converts – but converts to what? The older and more prestigious the church, the more this can become a problem. The church becomes a prey to what Dean Kelley calls the 'dynamics of diminishing demand'. 'Stringency – the spontaneous self-governing strictness of the early movement – all too soon gives way to stricture – the imposed, external imitation of it' (Kelley 1972:110). While this may enable the church to tread water for a time, before long the charade will be exposed and the requirements quietly shelved through embarrassment or convenience, leading to a further lowering of membership requirements.

Perhaps it is because we are so aware of the unsatisfactory nature of so much of contemporary church life that we are so reluctant to define our evangelistic goal in terms of disciples made. We are not convinced that the object of the exercise is to make yet more people to become like ourselves! If there is little to distinguish the Christian from his non-Christian neighbour, then discipleship can have little significance. This is a further reason why the renewal of the Church cannot be divorced from evangelism. By inviting people to follow Christ, we must also be in a position to include the invitation to join us in the pilgrimage. The Church is more than the herald announcing the message, it is a demonstration model which gives credence to the effectiveness of that message.

5 Identify the evangelists

Peter Wagner has described the ineffectiveness of attempts to mobilise the whole Church by putting the entire membership in the front-line of evangelism (Wagner 1971: Chapter 7). Such a strategy, he says, rests upon the mistaken premise that every Christian is called to exercise the gift of evangelist. To attempt to dragoon people to fulfil a role for which they are not equipped by God is to invite frustration and instil feelings of guilt as Christians become aware of their inadequacies and ineffectiveness in this area.

Every congregation is none the less called to fulfil the evangelistic mandate. It must, therefore, ensure that it has the means within its membership to fulfil this inescapable obligation. Accepting that evangelism is no optional extra, the church must seek to identify, train and deploy those with the evangelistic gift. And while not everyone has the gift of evangelist, everyone must be prepared to contribute their gift and fulfil the role of witness in the church's evangelistic programme.

5.1 The difference between a witness and an evangelist

At this point it may be helpful to try and distinguish between a witness and an evangelist. A witness is someone who can and is ready to speak from personal experience of what Christ has done in his life. This verbal testimony stems from the silent witness of a quality of life which demands an explanation. When questioned he should, therefore, be able to give adequate and appropriate testimony. 'Be ready at all times to answer anyone who asks you to explain the hope you have in you, but do it with gentleness and respect' (1 Pet. 3:15, 16). He should be able to interpret his experience and assurance in the light of the revealed truths of the gospel. All Christians are called to fulfil this role without exception. Our Lord heavily underlines this responsibility. 'If anyone declares publicly that he belongs to me, I will do the same for him before my Father is heaven. But if anyone rejects me publicly, I will reject him before my Father in heaven' (Matt. 10:32). A witness must be clear and open about his own position, but this does not necessarily imply that he will be effective in convincing and persuading others. To do this requires the particular gift of the evangelist.

Peter Wagner defines the gift of evangelist as 'the special ability that God gives to certain members of the body of Christ to share the gospel with unbelievers in such a way that men and women become Jesus' disciples and responsible members of the Body of Christ' (Wagner 1979:173). It is clear both from Scripture and in the long experience of the Church, that only some Christians can do this effectively. Some are better in a one-to-one situation, others before large crowds. One can speak more effectively to one particular age or cultural group than others. Some can only operate within their own cultural setting, while others are able to adjust their style and content to cultures other than their own. Some are limited in their evangelistic skills to bringing the individual through the joys and traumas of decision, and then their effectiveness tails off quickly, while others couple their evangelistic gift with a nurturing and church planting role. Some Bible expositors would identify this last mentioned manifestation as an apostolic gift, in the secondary sense of the term, i.e. apostles of the Church as distinct from apostles of Christ.

5.2 Identifying the potential evangelists

Accepting the fact that not all Christians have the gift of evangelism, it is important to know who do, and by what means they may be identified, especially when such persons might seem in very short supply or completely non-existent in the local church. On the basis of extensive research in a number of congregations in the United States, Peter Wagner has postulated an estimate of ten per cent who are either effectively or potentially gifted as evangelists. If this percentage potential could be considered to hold true outside the U.S.A., we would certainly have to ask of the great majority of congregations, 'What has happened to your ten per cent'? If it exists at all, their efforts must be going unrecognised, or have been rendered inoperative, or were never activated in the first place. The fact that there is little or no evidence that a gift is operating does not necessarily mean, however, that it is not present. Gifts can atrophy. Timothy was admonished by Paul to reactivate the gift which has been bestowed upon him (2 Tim. 1:6).

For the evangelistic gift to emerge within the life of the local church, *evangelism must be high on that church's list of priorities*. It must be the concern of the minister, the church council of board of deacons, the range of organisations, the home groups and the membership as a whole. The challenge of the evangelistic task must be faced in the preaching, discussion and prayer life of the church. The issue of such a challenge must not be in the form of breast-beating and berating the congregation, which before long will only be counter-productive. Rather it should consist of carefully prepared long-term strategies to communicate the gospel message in ways which are appropriate to specific target groups. Evangelism is a feature performance and not a sideshow. All too often the sporadic bursts of activity have been a hiccup in the life of the Church rather than its heartbeat.

The second requirement for the activation of the evangelistic gift is *effective leadership in this area*. Nothing is so sure to diffuse the explosive of evangelism as ineffective attempts, especially when those continue to be repeated in the hope that they will work next time. Such activity only serves to make the congregation want to have nothing to do with evangelism. However, when the congregation has a minister who is effective in the area of evangelism, he can make the whole congregation feel the thrill and privilege of being present at times of spiritual birth, of being challenged afresh themselves about their own commitment, and even to stir some sufficiently to share in that ministry.

5.3 The five classes of church leaders

Donald McGavran challenges churches to examine the deployment of its personpower (McGavran and Arn 1977:109). He describes five classes of workers.

> *Class 1 Workers* – members whose energies are used primarily in the service of existing Christians.
> *Class 2 Workers* – members whose energies are primarily directed to serving and evangelising non-Christians in their ministry area in an effort to bring them into the body of Christ.
> *Class 3 Workers* – volunteer or partially paid leaders of evangelistic Bible study groups, new fellowships, chapels or small churches.
> *Class 4 Workers* – full-time paid professional staff.
> *Class 5 Workers* – denominational or interdenominational leaders

Growing churches are those which concentrate on class two workers – unpaid workers who are effectively reaching outsiders. In the institutional church this activity tends to be squeezed out by the pressing need to keep the existing machinery turning. Ministers and church leaders should examine their leadership structure and the deployment of their membership to assess the strength of the known resources they are deploying for evangelistic goals to be achieved.

5.4 Church-based evangelism

If no effective evangelistic leadership is operated in the local church, the answer is not to rely exclusively on the occasional fillip provided by an itinerant evangelist. Rather the church must develop its own or import its medium or long-term leadership from elsewhere. Some churches have appointed an assistant minister to lead in this field. This may not be economically feasible for many churches, so they will have to grow their own unpaid leadership.

One way forward in such circumstances is for the minister to initiate a programme of visitation or home group evangelism. He does not pose as the expert, but is one with those involved who are praying that gifts will emerge as they embark upon the exercise. The only way you can discover whether you can do it is by trying. Alternatively the church can send a team on a training course to another church which has a well-developed outreach ministry. They then return to share what they have learned and to launch similar projects in their own church. The minister can make it clear that as soon as leadership emerges through their activities then he will hand over the direction of the programme and future training. It may even turn out that he will discover he has the gift himself as a result of his initiation and participation in the programme!

Once a regular evangelistic programme has been established, but not before, it is good strategy to encourage as many church members (and especially the new converts) as possible to gain some experience. In so doing they will discover whether or not they have the gift. If the results are not very promising, they will not have wasted their time, as they should at least be more articulate witnesses.

What kind of people are evangelists? They are likely to be fairly extrovert personalities, who are clear and confident in their approach to people and can easily relate to a stranger by establishing immediate contact. We all have people in our churches who have this sunny disposition, who can 'chat-up' the shy and defensive newcomer, and so relax them that quickly and imperceptibly he takes them from small talk on to more serious matters. These people may either develop into evangelists or degenerate into gossips. Perhaps some of our gossips are unemployed, untrained and unrecognised evangelists!

In pleading, however, for home-grown evangelists we are not excluding the role of the itinerant evangelist. It is always helpful to have a fresh voice with a different approach from time to time. And there are those with an exceptional gift which the church has recognised and set apart to serve the Church at large. They either operate through independent organisations or, as is becoming increasingly the case today, are based in a local church, which anchors them, provides a support team, and keeps them in close touch with the need for post-evangelistic care and of the difficulty widely experienced of integrating the convert into the life of the local church. Such gifted people will, however, be most effective in churches where there is a prayerful concern and sense of expectancy and which have an ongoing programme of evangelism. Unless the inviting church can show that it has the capacity within itself to attract and retain the outsider, it is unlikely to do so as the result of a brief visit from an itinerant evangelist, no matter how gifted.

6 Train the Christian community to communicate

The character of the members, the priorities and performance of the organisation and the appearance of the premises all communicate something. The question is, do they enhance or impair the church's evangelistic ministry? There must be a correlation between the medium and the message, for the medium is an essential part of the message in the communication process.

Within the evangelical tradition there has been a strong emphasis on the need for clear proclamation in evangelism. It draws attention to the centrality of preaching in the New Testament. This form of communication must not, however, be equated with the formal, structured monologue which may reflect classical Greek influence rather than the Judaic – Christian tradition. In addition in 'heralding' the gospel the New Testament mentions discussing (Acts 17:2, 17; 18:4, 19; 19:8) and arguing and debating (18:28). Communicating, then as now, was a two-way process.

6.1 God's multi-media revelation!

In his monograph *Communicating The Good News in a Television Age* Tom Houston has an important section on the Bible as Media. There he writes:

> It is clear that many media underlie the revelation we have in the Scriptures. The progressive dominance of print since the invention of the mechanised production of books in the fifteenth century has given us a very prosaic and flat image of the Bible that hides its true nature. If we try to identify the media pressed into the service of God's revelation of himself in the Bible, there is an astonishing variety (Houston 1978:7)

He then goes on to list and classify a lengthy and diverse list: visions, dreams, voices, discussions, parables, speeches, proverbs, rituals, laws, songs, drama, poetry, letters, ciphers, anthologies, history, records and stories, and for each he gives chapter and verse. In the unimaginative and uniform way that we present this exciting range, we give the impression that God's appointed way of gaining our attention is by throwing a book at us! Tom Houston reminds us that 'it takes a community to communicate' (Houston 1978:12). The task cannot be handed over to the superstar preacher and those with 'the gift of persuasive oratory'. The message has to be presented in a multitude of ways, recognising that different people respond to different approaches. In addition to the sermon, others will be reached through song, drama, dance and mime, poetry, or dialogue. Monologue is certainly not the only medium.

6.2 Exploring multi-media communication

Recently, the practical implications of the above were explored at a GEAR (Group for Evangelism and Renewal) Conference of the United Reformed Church. We envisaged a special church service at which the large majority of attenders would be people who were not usually in church. The entire service was planned to be a 'total communication event' (Tom Houston's phrase). The objective was to communicate in contemporary terms the message of Psalm 137. This Psalm was selected because at the time the opening words 'By the Rivers of Babylon' were well known as a pop song by the black singing group 'Boney M'. The lyrics of the song, however, understandably omitted the second half of the Psalm (which concludes 'Babylon, you will be destroyed. Happy is the man who pays you back for what you have done to us – who takes your babies and smashes them against a rock!') and substitutes Psalm 19:14. The conference was asked to stick to the original and grapple with the problem of Babylon.

The result of the pooling of ideas was:

1. Begin either by playing the record (recording and P. A. talents needed here!), or by inviting a black group to sing it.
2. While the song is being sung project the words using an overhead projector (artistic gifts).
3. Describe the situation out of which the story arose by a TV 'News at Ten' report, depicting the events which led up to Israel's Babylonian Captivity.
4. Interview a prisoner of war who had suffered at the hands of his captors during the last war, asking how he felt towards them.

5 A sketch showing a member of the congregation humming a hymn tune while he worked. His workmates then poke fun at him, parodying the hymn, illustrating Israel's experience in verse 4 'How can we sing a song to the Lord in a foreign land'.
6 The last part of the Psalm which describes the utter destruction of Babylon was dealt with by a straight explanation that Babylon was the symbol of defiant wickedness. The only way of dealing with it was annihilation. The gospel, however, presents an alternative way of confronting evil. This could be illustrated with a reading from the Soviet prison camp experiences of Wurmbrandt or Solzhenitsyn.

The celebrated actor Alec McCowen has captivated theatre audiences on both sides of the Atlantic with his one-man show in which he recites the whole of Mark's Gospel in the Authorised Version(!). In a *Sunday Times* weekly review article he describes how he worked on the project. 'I was no longer an actor but a storyteller. A storyteller should enjoy himself. A good storyteller's enjoyment is infectious. The good storyteller not only gets absorbed by his story, he engages with his audience.' McGowen not only cast himself into the part, he cast his audience; at one time he spoke to them as though they were disciples, then as Pharisees, as the blind beggar, etc. 'I wonder, who was my audience? Were they friends? Were they enemies? Were they cynics or were they sympathetic? It made a great difference to the telling of the story. I practised with various imaginary audiences. As I rehearsed in my living room, I sometimes made dummies and placed them on the sofa facing me. Dummies made with coats and hats – large photographs of friends and acquaintances . . . sometimes a very surprised old teddy bear watched me. . .' (Feb. 17 1980).

When one begins to take passages of Scripture and to ask how those can be so presented that they speak with equal force and with the same intended meaning as when they were originally communicated, all kinds of possibilities emerge. These will involve a wide range of communication from skills supplied by teachers, writers, interviewers, dancers, actors, artists, photographers, electronic experts, as well as the preacher. Of course, too much should not be attempted at any one time, and the ideas should not run ahead of our abilities to put them into effect. It is better to keep things as simple as possible and to avoid mere gimmickry. The style of presentation must be suited to the audience. A gimmick is a communication attempt which has failed.

It is also self-evident that these more creative and varied presentations cannot be mounted every week. It is probably best to begin by planning two or three a year, so that the regular, more formal, pattern of worship is not threatened, and to give opportunity to learn from one's mistakes and appreciate one's limitations.

A group should be organised to take charge of these presentations, representing a range of skills, preferably including someone with some knowledge of educational theory. In order to experiment without threatening the Sunday services, some churches have found it profitable to hold 'creative worship' services on a week-night. Those attending can choose between a number of groups, electing to do either music, drama, poetry, collage or banner work, etc. This helps to identify the hidden talent and to capture a vision of the wide range of communication possibilities.

7 Identify receptive groups and individuals

In Church growth thinking the distinction is made between three kinds of evangelism. These are Presence Evangelism, Proclamation Evangelism and Persuasion Evangelism. Consideration of the first of these categories will hold over to the next section. With regard to proclamation and persuasion one of the major difficulties in urban society is, how do you bring together those who want to tell with those who want to find out? The sharer needs to be brought into contact with the seeker (Reid 1979:32–36).

At the group level, McGavran encourages the churches to concentrate their evangelistic endeavour on the receptive to win them while they are still winnable (McGavran 1970:Ch. 12). In a Third World context these are especially likely to include the new urban migrants, animistic tribes-people whose culture is being threatened by encroaching 'civilisation' which poses questions and introduces a world view, and creates social disruption which the traditional culture is unable to combat successfully. Sudden changes in political, economic and cultural patterns can also cause increased receptivity at least for a limited period. Though such situations may provide unprecedented evangelistic opportunity, they also need to be responded to with Spirit-inspired sensitivity. Our missionary endeavour is not to exploit such situations but to redeem them. The Church must neither identify with the Westernising technological/materialistic influence, nor provide a bolt-hole in which to hide and avoid the challenge of social disruption. The role of the Church is to act as a catalyst with contextualised models of Christian discipleship to work both critically and creatively within the total context.

Within British society, what are the most likely responsive sectors (these may also apply in some measure to North America and Australasia)?

7.1 New residents

When people move house to take up residence in a new community they are likely to be more open to change. Their old behaviour pattern has been interrupted, while they adjust to their new neighbours, work, school, shops, recreational centre, etc. Churches located near areas where new housing estates are being built or where there is a high population turnover should be alert to this fact. It is significant that most of the growing congregations in Britain are located where there is a new and growing population. As a general rule, the older and more stable the community, the more difficult it is to penetrate.

This pattern is reflected in other areas of the world. Many of the fast-growing 'super-churches' in the United States are located in the sunbelt which extends through Florida, Texas and California. During this century there has been a vast population influx into this region. It is a similar story in Latin America. Most of the phenomenal church growth in Brazil has happened in the industrialised south, which lures millions in from the rest of the country in search or work and the attractions of city life.

Among new residents the contact should be made as soon as possible after their arrival. Some churches alert to the opportunities operate a 'welcome wagon' scheme consisting of a pack of information about the locality – half-day closing of shops, local schools, doctors and dentists, bus times, recreational amenities and information about the church. In many areas such schemes are operated by the local chamber of commerce or residents' association. When this is the case the churches can ask to provide their material to add to the pack, and then ensure that they follow up with a personal call.

Many churches which have area-based house groups give them the task of contacting new arrivals. As soon as the removal van is spotted by a neighbourhood group member, the new family is welcomed into the area with a few pastries and an offer of practical help. This initial contact can then be followed up through subsequent casual encounters in the street or at the local shops, and through an invitation to a coffee-chat or meal to meet other neighbours.

As a general guide it is preferable that the initial contacts be pursued by the church member rather than the clergy. The appearance of the minister on the doorstep may drive the family on the defensive. Whatever he says, they will tend to feel that he has come to enlist them into church membership. And if they do not at that stage feel motivated to respond it may make it all the more difficult later on. The laity can keep the contact at a more casual level, without the danger of frightening people off. They can also provide background information in those instances where a visit from the clergy would be appropriate.

In one Anglican parish the vicar, having spotted a removal van outside a house, called to welcome the new family into the parish on behalf of the local church. When, in the course of conversation, he paused to enquire where the family had moved from, they replied, 'Oh, we have only come from just around the corner'! Exit the red-faced minister overcome with embarrassment. A neighbour making the visit might not have made that kind of faux pas.

The Rev. Jess Yates of Bamford Chapel, Rochdale (United Reformed Church) reports that, 'Just over a year ago a visitation was carried out on the newest estate in the community. Before the visitation not one family came to our church from the estate. One good contact was made and followed up. Now twelve couples and their seventeen children are integrated into our fellowship. They were strangers to each other before, now there is a real sense of community amongst them. They open their homes to each other and are always seeking to bring new friends to "their" church.' Within a four year-period Jess Yates has seen two hundred and fifty people join Bamford Chapel, seventy of whom had never been church members before. This is a measure of the responsiveness of a new residential, middle-class, area in Lancashire.

Such a ready response needs to be contrasted with that of the Rev. Martin Gooder in an inner-city redevelopment area in Manchester. His church's faithful, year-long, door-to-door visitation covering two thousand homes resulted in just one family joining the church. But their dogged determination has brought its rewards. From thirty worshippers seven years ago, they now have a multi-racial congregation of over two hundred, meeting each Sunday for family worship. Many other churches in the inner city have been equally faithful without as yet seeing anything like this level of response.

7.2 The people visiting your church

This is so obvious that at first sight it might seem superfluous to state it. Yet experience shows that such people are frequently both overlooked and mishandled. One family known to the author, on moving house, went one Sunday to their local church. Having arrived early, they sat in their car until other members of the congregation began to arrive. Sitting there, watching the 'faithful' go into church with mournful faces and dragging feet, caused them to change their minds. They turned the car around and drove home. Happily, in their case, that early unfavourable impression has now been corrected. The incident raises the question, 'When people see us on the way to church, do we give any impression that it is worth going to and that our neighbours and friends are missing out by not coming too?'

When people do cross the threshold of the church, do we make it easy for them to do so? Many church buildings are so austere and fortress-like from the exterior that the visitor not only has to pluck up a great deal of courage, but also has to exert considerable effort to force open the creaking, heavy door.

What can we do to make it easier for the potential visitor? Can the entrance be 'opened up' in any way? Goldhill Baptist Church in Buckinghamshire has built a glass-sided extension to their chapel which allows the casual passer-by to catch a glimpse of their lively worship and capacity congregation.

Do we need a strategically placed welcoming notice outside? Does the lighting need to be improved? And when people step inside, what will happen to them? First impressions are of enormous importance.

As regular, well-known members of the church it is difficult to put ourselves into the shoes of the first-time visitor. To find out what it is like, why not arrange for a member of another church to come unannounced one Sunday morning, playing the role of a visitor. Then get him to recount his experiences and suggestions to the church council. It is salutary to learn how we appear not simply through our own eyes, but through the eyes of an objective assessor.

It is important that the visitor be made welcome on the way in rather than left until he is on the way out. Practical arrangements for the conducting of public worship should be finalised as far as possible before Sunday, leaving the minister free to welcome people as they arrive. In addition, the stewards handing out the hymn books require alerting and training to their responsibility in making the visitor welcome. Some churches with large congregations find that they have to make additional arrangements. The minister gets waylaid by members of the congregation who want to discuss urgent matters or exchange pleasantries. The stewards are also preoccupied stacking books, inserting leaflets and handing them out. They cannot hold up a stream of people to talk to an unfamiliar face.

St Thomas's Church, Kendal, the gateway town to the Lake District, attracts many holiday visitors. To ensure their welcome the church has a host and hostess rota, with a married couple stationed by the door whose sole task it is to shake people by the hand, welcome them to the service and enquire where they are from.

Many churches have a major influx of visitors and fringe people at monthly family services and major festivals. At such occasions it is important to open the service with words of welcome to set people at ease, and to give some brief explanation to help people find their way around the service. Later in the service when (hopefully!) a positive impression has been made, people can be invited during the notices to fill up a card placed ready in the pew and hand it to a steward on the way out.

Where church facilities make it possible refreshments after the service can be made available either at the back of the church or in an adjoining hall. One north London church serves over two hundred cups of coffee after both Sunday services. There is, however, the danger that the newcomer will be lost in the crowd and left on his own. To prevent this it is helpful to have a team of 'lookouts' detailed to spot those who have been left on their own, and to periodically remind all the members of their responsibility to befriend the lonely and welcome newcomers.

7.3 Those experiencing the major events of life

There are specific occasions in life when we are more open to God:

1 At the birth of a baby when we marvel at the appearance of new life.
2 During adolescent years when we face the responsibilities of adulthood and the prospect of choosing a career and making a living in the world.
3 When facing the prospects of marriage, bringing personal adjustments and added responsibilities.
4 Serious illness and the prospect of death and what lies beyond.

To these we might also add:

5 The threat of unemployment and the prospect of retirement.

The church must seek to develop its spiritual and personal resources to minister imaginatively and responsibly in all of these situations in its care of people from the cradle to the grave.

One Anglican vicar in a church on a housing estate in the Coventry area concluded that his methods of dealing with families bringing their babies for baptism and couples coming to make wedding arrangements needed radical reappraisal. His sincere and careful counselling was ineffective in introducing them to the life of the church. After the 'great event' they were not seen again in the church until the next 'rite of passage' came along. He decided on an entirely new approach. Instead of seeing them individually in the privacy of his study, he arranged regular 'Sharing Jesus' evenings to which the baptism families and wedding couples were invited. There they met an equal number of members of the congregation, people like themselves, who would be invited to share their experiences. The vicar opens up the conversation by simply saying to two of his church folk, 'John and Mary, you have been married for a year now, what are the lessons you have had to learn in getting used to married life which might help Philip and Eunice and Albert and Sylvia who are to be married in our church in three weeks' time?' Their response then leads to an open discussion. Similarly, those with children share the joys and responsibilities of parenthood with those bringing babies for baptism. In such a situation Christian testimony emerges naturally, voiced by lay people in a language which other lay people can understand and identify with. The couples are more relaxed as part of a group, talking to people like themselves, whom they are likely to bump into subsequently in the street and local shops. This new policy has paid dividends. Some of the couples coming to the church respond to the claims of Christ upon their lives as they see the evidence in the lives of the church members.

With increasing unemployment and early retirements, the Church will need to do fresh thinking in the area of ministry to those with time on their hands, opening up opportunities to learn new skills and engage in spheres of community service. In the United Kingdom perhaps churches have been too ready in the past to leave such concerns to the local authorities. The current serious cutbacks in adult education and the social services due to economic difficulties are perhaps an indication that the Church should step in to make available its local resources in building plant and volunteer personnel.

8 *Emphasise a biblical theology of conversion*

Growing churches recognise the radical nature of conversion to Christ and preach the need for a decisive commitment to him. They are not prepared to accept an 'easy believism' by baptising the status quo. They require a genuine allegiance to Christ demonstrated by a new quality of life. While churches may differ in their understanding of the timing and mode of water baptism, they must emphasise the decisive spiritual reality depicted by the sacrament. It represents both the *washing* from the stain and defilement of sin, and also *death* to the old way of living and the beginning of a new resurrection life.

8.1 Conversion

This is the act of turning by the individual. It represents a complete turnaround rather than a minor course correction; a turning away from sin to salvation and service in Christ. As an initial act it is a once-for-all, unrepeatable experience. It is a turning from darkness to light, from the domain of Satan to the Kingdom of God, from slavery to sin to freedom to service and worship of Christ as Lord (Matt. 18:3; Acts 3:19; 4:15; 26:18; 1 Thess. 1:9). Its essential components are: negatively, a turning from sin in *repentance*, and, positively, the exercise of *faith* in the atoning work of Christ (Mark 1:15; Acts 20:21). It embraces a change of heart, mind and will.

However, conversion does not refer exclusively to the initial act of reorientation. For as we mature in the Christian life so we come to recognise that there are still unconverted areas in our life which need to be repented of and handed over to God. As Keith Miller has pointed out, 'all a man does when he commits his "whole life" is to commit that of which he is conscious. . . . So the totally committed Christian life is a life of continually committing one's self and problems day by day as they are slowly revealed to his own consciousness' (Miller 1965:60).

Conversion, which emphasises the human response, would be impossible without the accompanying initiative-taking and power-enabling act of God. There are five key theological terms: Reconciliation, Redemption, Justification, Regeneration and Adoption, which express God's involvement in the total process.

8.2 Reconciliation (Rom. 5:10f.; 2 Cor. 5:18f., Eph. 2:13; Col. 1:20)

This word means the ending of a quarrel by which former enemies become friends. The New Testament clearly teaches that man in his natural fallen state is opposed to God (Rom. 5:10; Col. 1:21; James 4:4). The seriousness of this condition should not be minimised. Until people are unequivocally taught this unpalatable truth there can be no preaching of good news. If they are left unaware of impending judgement they will not appreciate the significance of salvation.

Man's rebellion has roused God's anger as well as his sorrow. The wrath of God is described by Dr James I. Packer as a technical term 'for the outgoing of God in retributive action, by whatever means, against those who have defied him' (Packer 1973:165). It should not be caricatured as God 'seeing red', but understood as God's judicial indignation, without the slightest trace of vindictiveness.

Furthermore, Christ did not act independently to change the attitude of his heavenly Father to humankind. It was precisely because *God* so loved the world that he gave his Son (John 3:16); it was *God* who showed us how much he loved us in the death of Christ on the cross (Rom. 5:8). We must, therefore, drive no wedge between Father and Son, thinking that the Son who is for us came to appease an angry God who was against us. The plan of salvation is a product of all three persons of the Trinity.

This incredible, undeserved act of God demands a response from man. So Paul calls upon all men everywhere to be reconciled to God (2 Cor. 5:20). Our acceptance is not represented as a reward for good conduct. No probationary period was required before the prodigal son was received by the waiting father. He ran towards him as soon as he came in sight, and he was still a long way from home when the father first spotted him (Luke 15:20). It was while we were yet sinners that Christ died for us (Rom. 5:8). Furthermore, we are not left in any doubt as to whether we are fully accepted. Reconciliation is not an event in the future to be anticipated but to be received now, because it is offered now (Rom. 5:11).

8.3 Redemption

This expresses the means by which reconciliation is made possible. It describes how deliverance from evil is achieved through the payment of a price. Thus prisoners of war may be released or slaves freed on the payment of an agreed sum being received. In the New Testament those who do not enjoy salvation in Christ are regarded as slaves of sin (John 8:34; Rom. 7:14). Christ's atoning death on the cross is regarded as the price paid to release the slaves and free the condemned (Eph. 1:7; Rom. 3:24; Heb. 9:15; 1 Cor. 6:19f; 7:22f).

The cost to God of his redemptive act is underlined by the fact that it was only achieved through the death of his Son. In other words it was on the basis of *substitution*. The innocent one stood in place of the guilty (Gal. 3:13; Mark 10:45). While the concept of substitution is not the only way in which the atonement may be understood, it is an essential feature as represented in Scripture.

8.4 Justification

This is a legal term meaning to 'acquit' or declare righteous. God, in Scripture, is represented as judge of all the earth. And because he is at the same time King, he is also responsible for the executive as well as the judicial aspect. He not only passes the verdict, but also implements the sentence. In the New Testament it is Paul who develops the concept of salvation in terms of justification.

> Justification means to Paul God's act of remitting the sins of guilty men, and accounting them righteous, freely, by His grace, through faith in Christ, on the ground, not of their own works, but of the representative law-keeping and redemptive blood-shedding of the Lord Jesus Christ on their behalf (Lilley 1962:683) (Rom. 3.23–26, 4:5–8; 5:18f).

Thus having passed the appropriate sentence, he then, through the atoning work of Christ, stands in the sinner's place and stead. The sinner is thereby declared righteous, not because he was innocent of the charges brought against him, but because of the righteousness which belongs to Christ and is bestowed on him. Technically this is known as 'imputed righteousness'. (See also Gal. 2:15–21; 2 Cor. 5:16–21; Phil. 3:4–11). The ground of the sinner's justification is by faith, that is by placing his confidence in Christ for salvation, and not in the his own good works. Justification is on the basis of God's grace not human merit.

8.5 Regeneration

This describes the new beginning and permanent change brought about by the presence of the Holy Spirit in the life of the person who has responded by faith to Christ. Indeed that very initial act was only made possible through the Spirit who bestowed the gift of faith (Eph. 2:8). The new birth (John 3:3–8; 1 Pet. 1:3, 23) has brought us into God's new creation (2 Cor. 5:17, Gal. 6:15). The new beginning has permanent and far-reaching effects, as individuals become part of God's plans for the future as citizens of his coming Kingdom.

8.6 Adoption

This concept is closely allied with the previous one. The idea that all men are the children of God is not found in The Bible. To be able to call God 'our Father' is a covenant privilege, not a universal right. John, in the prologue to his Gospel, makes it clear that we do not become God's children by natural means, that is, by being born as children of a human Father, but by receiving Christ as God's son and our saviour (John 1:12–13). Our adoption is only made possible through the exercise of God's grace and the operation of his Spirit (Eph. 1:5; Gal. 4:1, 3; Rom. 8:15; Gal. 4:6). The gift of Sonship does not come through our being born, but through our being born again.

Dr James I. Packer describes 'adoption' as 'the highest privilege that the gospel offers; higher even that justification' (Packer 1973:230). While 'justification' is the primary blessing it is not the highest blessing. 'Adoption is higher, because of the richer relationship with God that it involves' (Packer 1973:231). Because we have been made children of God, we carry the family likeness through the indwelling of the Holy Spirit, we want to live so as to please our Heavenly Father, and we enjoy his Fatherly protection and generous provision.

In these few paragraphs we have not been able to do more than provide a sketchy summary of these rich concepts. But it is only when we see conversion as a miraculous, radical and gracious act of God, that there is an adequate basis and motivation for church growth. Without such a theological grasp, demonstrated in personal and corporate experience, there will be no significant progress. If this vital element is missing, then the application of the many other church growth principles will be to no avail. We must have experienced a deep work of God ourselves and believe that it can happen to people around us and that God intends it to happen conceivably by reaching them through us.

9 Develop a long-term strategy for resistant areas

9.1 The need for an inductive approach

So much of Christian attempts at communication begin where we would like people to be rather than where they are actually at. Our minds are so full of the (pre-packaged) message that we have not stopped to think how it relates to those for whom it is intended. George Hunter reminds us that 'Effective communication of the gospel begins with a demonstration of its relevance . . . the point of contact between people and the gospel is people's needs, hopes, yearning, fears, longings, and deepest motives' (Hunter 1979:39). This was the communication principle which our Lord himself used. With the adulterous woman who came to the village well to draw water, he spoke first of the water and then of the men in her life. When the impetuous wealthy young man rushed up to him, he turned the conversation to the subject of money. Surrounded by the crowd, among whom were many subsistence farmers, our Lord's opening words were, 'A sower went forth to sow.' They were with him immediately. With the demon-possessed, disintegrated personality, our Lord exposed the situation after the direct question, 'What is your name?'

An inductive approach to communication means knowing the audience, whether that audience is an individual or a group, and beginning in the area of their known or anticipated needs. If it is a group, then you will need to identify the elements of community. Whilst the Spirit is ready to help the prayerful communicator to guide him to hidden personal needs of which otherwise he would be unaware, he also expects us to take practical steps to discover the needs around us. Robert Schuller, of the Garden Grove Community Church near Los Angeles, built up his congregation on the motto, 'Find a need and feel it, find a hurt and heal it.' This, however, was more than a slogan – it was a strategy. He spent several weeks calling on the homes around his church to discover the needs of the community and the inhibitions which kept them from church attendance (Schuller 1974:81).

Nearer home this same strategy has been applied to good effect. An Anglican church in Cambridge recognised that there were a lot of elderly people around the church. The gospel touched their lives at the point of loneliness, so the church opened a day care centre providing a lounge with comfortable chairs and a hot meal as an alternative to depending on the local authority 'meals on wheels'.

A Nazarene church in Hertfordshire located on a housing estate was finding it difficult to make meaningful contact with the residents. They then began to enquire about local needs, which brought to light the fact that there was no bread shop in the locality, so they opened one. They now have daily contact with scores of people.

An Anglican church in London's commuter belt realised that there was often the need for a suitably qualified person to be at hand to meet a domestic emergency. Elderly people could not get to the department stores which were situated ten miles away without transport. A housewife frying chips spilt hot fat on her young child holding on to her apron. She needed to get him to the hospital but her husband had the car, and who would be at home to meet the children when they came out of school? In conjunction with the other churches serving the community they therefore initiated a 'contact' phone service with a line manned twenty-four hours a day, seven days a week. The person at the phone had in front of him a list of people offering a variety of services so that the appropriate home could be selected to meet the need. The number to phone is prominently displayed in local shops and on notice boards located outside churches and in public buildings.

9.2 Maslow's hierarchy of needs

We must begin at the point of the individual's, or group's, needs and perceptions. Abraham Maslow has drawn up a model of seven motivational needs, all of which are basic to human personality. He lists them as follows:

1 Physiological needs
2 Safety needs
3 Love and belonging needs
4 Esteem needs:
   a. self esteem,
   b. esteem by others
5 Need for self actualisation
6 Desire to know and understand
7 Aesthetic needs

While all these elements are continuously present, not all are to the forefront of our consciousness. At any given time one or more will emerge to motivate a particular train of action. Effective communication occurs when the relevant motivational need is identified and addressed.

But such a model must be applied with caution. Considered in isolation, it may lead us to tell people only what they *want* to hear, which may be very different from what they *need* to hear. Our Lord's ministry, for instance, provides examples to guard us against this danger. In identifying and responding to real needs he did not shrink from touching the painful spots. We may have to sound a warning note of challenge as well as minister a word of comfort. Beginning at the point of need does not imply changing the gospel to suit the situation. The gospel is changeless and is centred on the saving power of Christ and his lordship over our lives. Here we are focusing attention on the point of contact which will vary from person to person. But, by whichever door they enter they will then need to come to terms with the whole gospel, which applies equally to all.

9.3 The Engel scale

Awareness of need must be coupled to an understanding of the decision-making process. In terms of response to

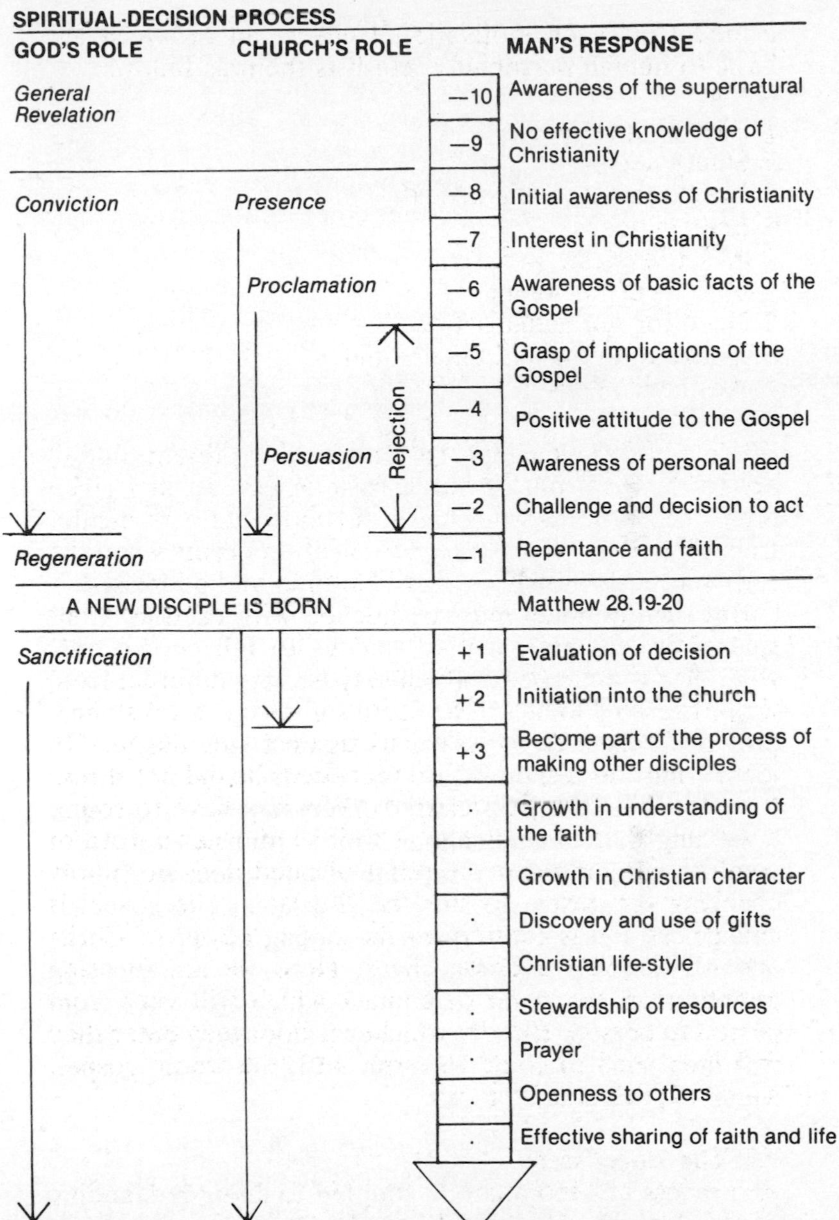

Fig. 15 *The Engel scale (adapted)*

the gospel this has been worked out in the 'Engel Scale' by James F. Engel of Wheaton College. He classifies man's response in the stages represented in Fig. 14. This has appeared in a number of versions. The one we give represents an adaptation which is used in the Bible Society Church Growth Course material.

In order to interpret the stages represented in the scale, the following notes may prove helpful:

−10 *Awareness of the Supernatural.* Man is aware that he is not alone in the universe, he is aware of 'presence'. He may fear it as in animism or study it as in extra-sensory perception. Nevertheless he is aware of the supernatural.

−9 *No effective knowledge of Christianity.* Unaware of the content or character of the Christian faith, though the name 'Jesus Christ' may be familiar.

−8 *Initial awareness of Christianity.* This comes from a consciousness of the presence of the Church. But such awareness is open to misunderstanding and caricature.

−7 *Interest in Christianity.* The presence of the worshipping and serving community of God's people has provided interest and acceptance. There is a willingness to listen to what the Church has to say. However, there may be an acceptance of the communicator before an acceptance of the communication.

−6 *Awareness of basic facts of the gospel.* Here proclamation is built upon presence and the witness of words follows the witness of works. The significance of the saving acts of Christ is heard and understood.

−5 *Grasp of the implications of the gospel.* What is demanded by the gospel in terms of personal response and commitment is understood. What is involved in being a Christian has been clearly communicated.

−4 *Positive attitude to the gospel*. The demands of the gospel and the Christian life are considered reasonable and attractive.

−3 *Awareness of personal need*. The benefits of the gospel are seen to be relevant and necessary.

−2 *Challenge and decision to act*. The challenge to turn from sin and trust Christ as Saviour and Lord is accepted.

−1 *Repentance and faith*. The individual response to the working of the Holy Spirit leads to repentance and faith.

0 *A new disciple born*. Regeneration has taken place and the man has been born again. John 3:3. 'Jesus answered "I am telling you the truth: no one can see the Kingdom of God unless he is born again." '

+1 *Evaluation of decision*. Very soon after commitment a period of uncertainty and questioning arises and Satan is active to undermine and confuse (1 Peter 5.8).

+2 *Initiation into the church*. The Church is responsible for incorporating the new believer who is initiated into the Church through new members procedures.

+3 *Become part of the process of making other disciples*. Further responses are as indicated in the diagram. These points are not numbered as they are not sequential.

In Western Europe, North America and Australasia much of our Christian communication has assumed that the bulk of the population was no further back than −5. If this was the situation in the past (which is doubtful) it is increasingly not the situation today. While the Engel Scale cannot be applied mechanically, it does provide a helpful guide to gauge where the people we are trying to address are located. Having estimate that, we will be in a better position to know where to pitch the message and to what extent persuasion is appropriate. Furthermore, if people are well up the scale between −6 and −8, then we must recognise that it might be a long haul before they reach the point of decision. Our evangelistic strategy will therefore have to be long term, geared to moving people along step by step, ensuring that we leave every contact and conversation where we can take it up again at some future date. Persuasion is only appropriate at a certain point. Wrongly applied it will simply close doors to the possibility of further contact. Too much of our evangelism is still of the 'hit and run' type, expecting an immediate response. We must recognise that we are now in a missionary situation which requires a capacity to develop an acute sense of hearing, and inexhaustible patience.

10 Recognise the evangelistic potential of groups

Most congregations are subdivided into groups of one kind or another. One of the most significant developments in English church life during the past fifteen years has been the mushrooming of home groups. Such groups may now number more than a hundred thousand, and represent potential launching pads for mission. The sad fact is that the vast majority are failing to realise their evangelistic potential, preferring to concentrate on spiritual nurture of the group members. They are locked in on themselves out of a sense of fear or inadequacy.

Where such nervousness has been overcome and groups have invited their neighbours along, they have often been surprised by the level of response (Gibbs 1977:13; 1979a:22).

For many groups this is an idea so novel and daunting that it is unlikely to happen spontaneously. It will need positive leadership and in many cases the provision of a skilled person to initiate and guide the home group evangelistic programme. We will, however, postpone further discussion of this important topic until chapters six and seven.

11 Achieve visibility

While it is probably advisable for the church to aim for a low profile in the small, stable, face-to-face village community, the opposite is almost always the case in the urban and suburban scene. Where there is a high population density and a rapid population turnover, the church must achieve visibility. This is achieved not by headline-grabbing sensationalism, which method Jesus repudiated in confronting Satan (Matt. 4:5–7), but by its members being seen whenever possible in the community, contributing to its life and responding to its needs. The church will be seeking to serve, expecting nothing in return, which is an essential characteristic of self-giving love as described and demonstrated by our Lord. But in addition to the church's calling to be the invisible yeast leavening the whole dough and the salt savouring the whole meal, it is also called to be a light placed prominently and strategically upon a lampstand so as to light the whole house. It is to be as visible as a city built upon a hill. The illumination is not the neon-sign of self-advertisement, but the outshining of a spirit-filled life. The light is the Shekinah glory of God's presence which is not restricted to the Tabernacle and Temple as in Old Testament times, but shines through every believer and Christian community.

In modern urban life, prominence involves skill in handling publicity.

11.1 Magazine/news sheet

Most churches produce a *magazine or news sheet*. If we have such a periodical the key question to ask, and to keep on asking, is, 'Who is it written for?' Is it a domestic journal intended primarily for the church members? If so, then one would expect it to read like an extension of the church notices. However, if it is intended for the community, the contents must reflect the concerns of the community, with comments on the wider world and put together with a certain degree of journalistic skill. When church events are mentioned, they need to be 'angled' to the community, with plenty of human and local interest to catch the eye. Many church magazines attract a readership far wider than the congregation, so it is strategic that these be prepared as attractively as possible both in content and format to create a favourable response.

11.2 Local newspaper

The next significant area is the *local newspaper*. While national newspapers have to work hard to increase their readership levels, the sales of local newspapers continue to rise. Their editorial resources are, however, limited, so the church will be welcomed if it can provide good story 'copy' and clear photographs, thus saving them the expense of sending their own paid staff along to the various functions. There is always the danger that if they do send someone, it will be a junior reporter who does not know how to handle 'religious' news or is unsympathetic. Newspapers welcome with open arms a regular, efficient news service on which they can rely.

In addition the church might consider placing paid *advertisements* from time to time, highlighting forthcoming events which could be made especially attractive to the outsider. The themes and wording should be related, not to the regulars who will be there anyway, but to the felt needs of the additional people you are hoping to reach.

A couple of years ago I visited a thriving church on New York's Staten Island. The minister was a chirpy Italian American by the name of Dan Mercaldo. With the help of the Fuller Evangelistic Association his church researched the surrounding community to discover that the unchurched population were of Roman Catholic and Jewish origins. At the time the church went by the name of 'Calvary Temple' which they came to realise was not very appropriate to their constituency. So with typical North American pragmatism they changed the name to 'Gateway Cathedral'. They then sustained a prolonged advertising campaign in the Staten Island newspaper to put the church on the map. Beginning in 1965, the church grew slowly to a hundred and twenty members. Within two years they reached the two hundred mark. In the following two years they grew from two hundred to five hundred and fifty. Before long they had to duplicate the morning service.

Pastor Dan Mercaldo also noticed that a large percentage of the New York Police Force chose to live on Staten Island, so he advertised in the Police Gazette and arranged a special service for policemen. As a result a number have become regular members of his congregation.

Here in the United Kingdom local churches have little access to the television networks, as there is no possibility of buying time. Thus ministers cannot become nationally known TV personalities as they can in North America. However, the advent of local radio stations, both BBC and commercial, has opened up new opportunities for news slots and interviews, to which local churches should be alert. Often the religious affairs broadcaster and programmer is recruited from one of the local churches. Some churches in areas covered by local stations have taken advantage of the situation by building a simple recording booth in which they can record suitable material to an acceptable standard. St George's, Leeds, has equipped itself in this way, and has, in consequence, been able to supply regular features.

12 Implement new members procedures

Most churches have membership classes which consist of a course to teach basic Christian beliefs and membership requirements. Usually such classes only run once a year, which may leave someone who has come to the point of decision too late for that year's class in limbo for several months. During the waiting period he may fade from the scene. A further problem arises in relation to those who return to church life after an absence of many years, or who transfer from one church to another. In many churches their arrival receives no public recognition. Individuals slip in and out without most people being aware of the fact. New converts and transfers in should be introduced to the church leaders and members of the congregation. They need to feel that they are part of the family. St Andrew's, Chorleywood, has started an annual welcome evening which provides an opportunity for the Parochial Church Council to meet all those who have started coming to the church during the past year. Some larger churches can be so impersonal that to think in terms of 'joining' is as meaningless as joining the cinema! Do people have a clear idea how to become members and to transfer that membership? Are the procedures for doing so effective in practice?

12.1 Sponsorship

Even in the case of the large church with a regular new members' class, this may need to be supplemented by a sponsorship scheme in which the convert is matched with a church member of the same sex and similar age and background, to help him find his feet and be introduced to the family. If such a scheme is implemented, there must also be procedures established to deal with any possible mismatch. Someone in charge of the scheme will need to establish contact with both parties to assess how things are working out.

12.2 Initiation

One of the church growth debates has been on the issue of 'discipling' and 'perfecting', to use a McGavran distinction. For McGavran, 'discipling' includes all that is involved in bringing people to Christian initiation, while 'perfecting' refers to post-baptismal instruction and care (McGavran 1970:325–329). While we may take issue with his semantics in restricting discipling to the moving of individuals or peoples 'over the threshold of minimum commitment to the Christian movement', rather than describing the ongoing status of the believer, the issue remains as to what is essential for Christian initiation, and what can be held over for post-baptismal instruction. On the one hand a simple confession of 'Jesus Christ is Lord' might lead to an 'easy believism'; on the other, a prolonged period of ethical instruction and requirements might run the danger of implying a gospel of works rather than of grace. As the requirements become more rigid, so the number of the disqualified rises, until we are left wondering who does qualify. Clearly membership of his family is on the basis of God's grace and not human merit. And for one going to spend a lifetime coming to terms with the implications of the gospel for one's motives, standards of behaviour, areas of commitment and world-view, baptism cannot be made into a 'last rites' ceremony!

More recently McGavran has distinguished between three separate uses of the verb 'to disciple' which he had coined in 1955 in writing *Bridges of God*.

> Firstly, it was used – as I had used it – for the movement of a *non-Christian society* under the influence of the Holy Spirit such that large numbers of its members became baptised and committed Christians, and becoming a Christian no longer meant 'leaving the tribe or caste'.
>
> Second, it was used to describe the initial conversion of individuals in a nominally Christian society. A person was discipled when he was led to belief in Jesus Christ as Lord and Saviour and baptised membership in His Church.
>
> Third, the word was used for the later stages of the process by which an individual Christian becomes an informed, illuminated, thoroughly dedicated follower of Jesus Christ. . . . A discipled individual was

> like a college graduate, he had been through the entire course and passed all his examinations. He was a complete Christian (*Church Growth Bulletin* 1979:265–270).

The central act must be the acceptance of Christ as Saviour and a willingness to place one's life under his complete control as Lord. At this early stage in the new convert's experience he must gain his impressions of what this step implies from a knowledge of the character and claims of Christ as portrayed in the Gospels, and from the image of the church which is set to receive him. The safeguards against 'easy believism' are that he should have read carefully at least one of the Gospels and that the church must show in its life some proximity to its teaching.

Bearing in mind our highly mobile society and the numbers of Christians who transfer their membership from one church to another (and from one denomination to another), it is advisable for such people to be expected to attend some introduction classes as part of the transfer procedure. Furthermore, in cases where the church has a chronic nominality problem, it is often necessary to encourage as many as we feel appropriate to cover the same curriculum in rededication or baptismal or confirmation-reaffirmation classes.

12.3 Membership requirements

Some churches have found it helpful to set out a few simple guidelines to indicate what is entailed in 'responsible church membership'. Here is a suggestion:

1 I will endeavour whenever possible to worship with God's people each Sunday.
2 I will endeavour to be a consistent witness to Jesus Christ in the way I live and speak.
3 I will join some group within the church so that I relate to others on a personal level.

4 I will become a functioning member by involving myself in a specific area of regular Christian service within my church.
5 I will contribute financially in a systematic and sacrificial way.
6 I will uphold my church and especially the leaders in my daily prayers.

13 Summary

In this chapter we have looked at twelve issues relating to the church's task in communicating its message effectively. Not every point will be applicable to every situation. But pondering each may heighten awareness or trigger new avenues of thought to help us break through the double walls which arise around every church: one built by the members and the outer one constructed by the community. List the points you have identified as especially relevant to your local situation and keep them particularly in mind as you read through the remaining chapters. Let us think beyond the problems to the opportunities and potential which lie before us. To prevent our visions degenerating into day-dreams they will sooner or later need to be earthed in goals and plans.

CHAPTER SIX

Groups and Growth

THE PROLIFERATION OF small groups has been one of the most significant developments in church life in recent years. While no statistics are available of the percentage of churches in Britain which have encouraged the formation of groups, I would estimate that in England at least, it is probably in the region of sixty per cent. I base this estimate on my questioning of clergy and laity at many conferences and training courses. Every time I ask people to raise their hands if they have home-based groups as a regular feature of their church programme, over sixty per cent indicate that this is the case. In Wales, Scotland and Northern Ireland, however, the percentage appears to be rather less.

While no detailed research has yet been undertaken here in Britain there are clear indications that most growing churches would regard the establishing of fellowship groups as being a significant factor. An analysis of 131 church profiles, representing a cross-section of denominations, shows a correlation between the existence of groups and their growth prospects. Each of these churches had been represented on a Bible Society church growth course, in connection with which they supplied data about themselves covering a ten-year period. The results are as follows:

	No. of churches	*With house groups*
Declining steadily	25	40%
Declining erratically	25	76%
Plateaued in membership	11	55%
Growing erratically	38	79%
Growing steadily	32	91%

This small sample indicates that starting groups does not in itself guarantee growth, but that if you do have groups then there is a higher probability that you are a growing church.

This chapter will mainly be concerned with groups which are linked with a local church. I have not complicated the discussion by dwelling on either ecumenical groups or the House Church Movement. The former have been omitted due to the fact that I have had no personal experience of them to draw from. The latter is only mentioned in passing, not because the House Church Movement is of little significance, but in recognition of the fact that it is a complex recent phenomenon which, to do it justice, requires a detailed study of its own.

By a 'home group' I mean a small group, generally numbering between five and twenty persons, meeting in homes for the purpose of mutual encouragement, Bible study, discussion, prayer and sometimes including community service and evangelism.

God has not made man to live in solitude and independence. Neither does he intend him to be lost in a crowd and so made to feel a nonentity. From the very beginning of the Christian church small groups have played a significant role in helping Christians build up their faith and extend their witness.

1 Groups in the New Testament

Within the New Testament we can see the strategic significance of the small group at every phase of the development of the Christian Church.

1.1 The synagogue

The synagogue is a Jewish place of meeting. From the time of the Babylonian exile it has come to fulfil both a religious and social function. It was a place set apart for worship, study and interpretation of the law and prayer. It was also the gathering-point for the community to discuss important local affairs. Much of the early Christian preaching took place in the synagogue. Our Lord was instructed there and himself ministered both in the one at Nazareth (Matt. 13:54; Luke 4:16) and at Capernaum (Mark 1:21; John 6:59).

Synagogues began in a small way. A new one could be formed with ten men as charter members. According to various traditions, Jerusalem had between 190 and 480 in the year AD 70. Worship was informal in style, yet firm control was exercised by the elders who were empowered to exercise discipline and punish members. The synagogue provided a model for the organisation of Christian congregations within the Hebrew Christian culture.

1.2 Jesus and the twelve

Our Lord invested the major part of his three years of ministry in the training of a small team. These were to continue his ministry and to form the nucleus of the new people of God. The pattern on which they themselves had been taught would be influential in their own future ministries. They in turn would catch men in the same way as they had been caught by Christ. The disciples were commissioned to the mission of making disciples, and discipleship was a distinctive learning process. Although discipleship groups may take a variety of forms due to the changed circumstances, the principles of discipleship are true for all time and locations. This learning pattern has been analysed in an excellent book by Robert Coleman entitled *The Master Plan of Evangelism* (1963). He details the steps as follows:

a. *Selection*. Christ's concern was not with programmes to reach the multitudes, but with men whom the multitudes would follow. The decisive factor in his choice was not brilliance, but a readiness to learn, and to respond to his teaching. Their changed lives would in turn influence others.

b. *Association*. He stayed with them. He himself was the curriculum. They learned through being in intimate contact with him, and through rubbing shoulders with one another. Discipleship learning is learning in community, which provides an immediate point of reference for the application of principles learned.

c. *Consecration*. Our Lord required obedience. He exposed the impossibility of trying to be the slave of two masters – God and money (Luke 16:13). You will not survive for long if you have a divided loyalty. There is an all-or-nothing implication to discipleship.

d. *Impartation*. Our Lord gave of himself daily in ministry, and gave his all at the cross. But that was not the end of his self-giving. In the upper room discourses he encouraged his followers to expect 'another comforter', that is not someone different from himself but essentially the same. This same attitude of self-giving is seen in the missionary motivation of the apostle Paul. Writing to the Thessalonians, he reminds them that he not only gave them the gospel, but also gave them himself (1 Thess. 2:8).

e. *Demonstration*. Jesus showed them how to live. His classes were always in session, and there was nothing predictable about the timetable! They learned to pray use Scripture, heal the sick, deal with objectors, and win individuals, not by hearing talks on the subjects, but through seeing Jesus in action.

f. *Delegation*. He assigned them work. They had to put their hands to practical jobs such as gathering food, row-ing boats and arranging rooms. They were also sent out unsupervised, and with the minimum of provisions on preaching missions. The twelve were sent out first (Mark 6:6f), and then seventy-two disciples (Luke 10:1). They received specific instructions as to what to do and were given the spiritual resources and authority to carry out their mandate. These missions were a preparation for the global mission which Jesus entrusted into their hands at the time of his death, and burned into their souls with the flame of Pentecost.

g. *Supervision*. He also kept a check on their activities. They were accountable for their actions, so were required to report back at the conclusion of their missions. And throughout his ministry he continued to ply them with questions.

h. *Reproduction*. He warned them that, as branches, if they failed to produce fruit they would be cut away. When they bore fruit they would be cut back in order to bear more fruit. The followers of Christ who had spent two and a half to three years in the school of discipleship were themselves to go and make disciples.

We may summarise discipleship under three 'Cs':

1 Commitment – there is a yielding of oneself;
2 Community – learning is a corporate activity;
3 Communication – what is experienced is intended to be shared with the wider world.

1.3 The church in the home

Throughout the New Testament there is an emphasis on the home. Jesus was teaching at his home base in Capernaum where the paralytic was lowered through the roof. He visited people's homes to heal the sick, raise the dead, converse over a meal, and advise those who had begun to follow him. When he sent out the twelve and the seventy-two they were to go in pairs to people's homes (Matt. 10:14; Luke 10:5).

His intention was that they should find a welcome there as their greeting of peace was received.

From its inception the Church took root in homes. In Jerusalem the Christians met together for fellowship in addition to attendance at temple worship. 'Day after day they met as a group in the temple, and they had their meals together in their homes, eating with glad and humble hearts. . .' (Acts 2:46). Acts 5:42 makes clear that Christians used their homes for more than eating. It was there that 'they continued to teach and preach the Good News about Jesus the Messiah'.

When Peter was imprisoned with the fearful possibility of execution, believers in the home of Mary, the mother of John Mark, were earnestly praying for his release. Their prayers were answered beyond their expectations so that Peter through a miraculous deliverance was able to join them briefly (Acts 12:1–17). At Troas Paul was making a long after-dinner speech in the upstairs room of someone's home when Eutychus fell out of the window (Acts 20:7–12). Later in that same journey, when he gathered together the elders of Ephesus he reminded them, 'You know that I did not hold back anything that would be of help to you as I preached and taught in public and in your *homes*' (Acts 20:20). Not only were homes used for preaching, they also became the regular meeting place for groups of Christians. Aquila and Priscilla made their home a base for the church both in Ephesus (1 Cor. 16:19) and Rome (Rom. 16:3–5). In Laodicea a group of Christians met in the home of Nympha (Col. 4:15), and in Colossae they were given hospitality by Philemon (Phil. 2). For the first two hundred years of the Church's life, it was a home-based movement. No special church buildings were constructed for Christian worship until the close of the second century.

The home-based church enabled the Church in the New Testament to expand at a phenomenal rate with the minimum of human resources. Commenting on Floyd Filson's article on house churches and their influence in ancient Corinth, McGavran writes, 'Lacking church growth insight, Filson misses the most important influence of house churches: that they enabled the tiny church to grow mightily. At one stroke they overcame four obstacles to growth which the church met as it liberated new populations. (1) *The cost of a church building.* Without any cash outlay at all, house churches provided as many places to worship as there were groups of Christians. This first common obstacle to multiplying churches never appeared. (2) *The obstacle of the Jewish connection.* House churches pushed the church away from the synagogue into the Gentile population. (3) *The obstacle of introversion.* Each new house church exposed a new section of society – a new set of intimates and relatives – to close contact with ardent Christians. (4) *The obstacle of limited leadership.* Each house church thrust the responsibilities and prestige of leadership on able men of the new congregation. These, within the elastic bonds of the Old Testament, oral tradition of the life of the Lord, and a letter or two of Paul's were free to follow the leading of the Holy Spirit' (McGavran 1970:192, 193).

2 The strategic importance of groups

The availability of church buildings does not do away with either the need for small groups or the continuing use of the home. As we have already demonstrated, the small group learning situation is essential for discipleship training. Alongside worship with the crowd at the Temple the followers of the Christian way in Jerusalem also supplemented that experience with fellowship meals, prayer and teaching in homes. Many churches today are likewise feeling the need to divide their congregations into home-based fellowship groups. There is a continuing need for small groups and there are aspects of our urban and rural society today which make them even more important.

2.1 Intimacy

Today's urban society combines many powerful depersonalising elements. We are strangers in the crowd on the streets, in the shops and on public transport. We make many casual contacts, but there are few abiding relationships because the crossroads of contact are constantly changing in our mobile, manipulated society. There is in consequence a deepseated hunger for face-to-face contact; to know and be known. Yet, paradoxically there is also a hesitancy and reluctance to expose oneself or become too involved with other people. For some people the small group is so threatening that they don't feel able to cope emotionally. This has tactical implications which we will consider later.

Intimacy is essential for establishing an atmosphere of mutual trust, to the point where we are prepared to remove our masks. The primary group provides the structure for face-to-face relationships and accountability. I have to have confidence in people if I am to share a confidence with them without the fear of being betrayed. As we get to know one another so we are prepared to lower our guard and share our sorrows, joys, frustrations, feelings of rejection and perplexities. We do not minister to each other from any superior standpoint but as 'wounded healers' of others who also bear this same wound (Clemmons and Hester 74:38).

In Britain we are more nervous than most about becoming involved with others at a deep personal level. This is partly due to the national characteristic of reserve and maintaining 'the stiff upper lip'. In the USA there seems to be a greater openness and informality enabling churches to make use of the insights of the secular small group movement. Osmaston has observed that 'in England, the Church has tended to fall into the opposite error of feeling that close sharing groups are vaguely dangerous, probably immoral and certainly upsetting' (Osmaston 1977:7). While being alert to the dangers of over-intense relationships developing, we must find ways of expressing that intimacy and frankness which is assumed in the letters of the New Testament. These are addressed to groups of Christians who recognised their responsibility to encourage and admonish one another.

2.2 Flexibility

While urban society can keep people apart, it can also bring together people from a variety of backgrounds. Communities are made up of people who have come from all points of the compass, and from locations near and far. They will represent different personalities, social levels and types of employment. This variety of clientele can be catered for in groups. There is no need for an extensive church campus if fellowship activities are located in homes. This will not be a practical option for every group; it will depend on the group's size and the nature of their activity. Snyder comments that 'because the group is small, it can easily change its procedures or functions to meet changing situations or to accomplish different objectives. . . . It is free to be flexible as to the place, time, frequency and length of its meetings. It can easily disband when it has fulfilled its purpose without upsetting the institutional seismograph' (Snyder 1975:140).

2.3 Community

Discipleship is not a claim to self-reliance and independence. It is a frank acknowledgement of our vulnerability and interdependence. Christian fellowship in the small group is designed to help counteract the extreme of diffidence on the one hand ('Because I am not a hand, I don't belong to the body' 1 Cor. 12:14) and arrogance on the other ('I don't need you' 1 Cor. 12:21). In pre-industrial society this sense of belonging existed in the village, face-to-face community and through the network of the extended family. Urbanisation, employment opportunities and housing availability have destroyed these relationship networks so that the Church in the city has the task of recreating community.

As far as those outside the fellowship of the Church are concerned the existence of a Christian community in their street or place of employment should ideally serve as a model of what the Church is seeking to demonstrate. Ron Trudinger likens them to an oasis: 'An oasis beckons by just being there; the greenness and water attract the thirsty desert traveller' (Trudinger 1979:88).

2.4 Mobility

As McGavran observed, home-based cells enable the Church to multiply economically and speedily. It can quickly move to where people are and put down local roots.

Home-based groups are a good way of 'soil testing'. If the ground proves to be productive, then the groups can meet together in a local schoolroom, community hall or other suitable premises. One 'daughter church' in a County Durham parish holds its services in a local public house as an interim arrangement. Not every chuch will find this an acceptable solution!

Eventually, the time will probably come when the size of the work and the demands of ministry make it necessary for the group to obtain their own premises. This will bring added freedom, with the church able to arrange their activities to suit their own needs; this is frequently not possible in rented premises which are hired out to a variety of groups. Having one's own church building, however, is not all gain, as a number of new churches have discovered. In those areas where there is a wide cultural gap between church and community, the fact of having a distinctive building labelled 'church' can keep many people away who would have been prepared to attend when services were held on 'neutral territory' such as the school or community hall.

Conversely, in middle-class urban areas in Latin America it has been discovered that a church building is a distinct advantage as a 'back-up' to home-based evangelism. Groups which do not have a church building to relate to are regarded with a certain amount of suspicion.

There people are culturally conditioned to worship in church with the service conducted by professional clergy.

2.5 Sensitivity

Home groups enable the church to keep its ears to the ground. They are like detectors scattered around the area to pick up a variety of signals. Through the home groups the church can keep track on who is moving in or out, those who are sick or in trouble and those who have lapsed. They can alert the church to community concerns and can gauge how their image stands in the neighbourhood.

3 The purpose of groups

It is recognised that a healthy church will have a variety of groups. In this section we are confining our attention to the cell unit which is a primary face-to-face group. In the next chapter we will move on to consider larger groups which are less personal and more programme orientated.

3.1 To provide a learning situation

The home group circle provides an opportunity for Christians to air their doubts and voice their opinions. For obvious reasons this is not possible in the more formal context of a church service; consequently if no opportunity is provided for 'come back', people are left with their questions unanswered and their views unheard. As educationalists are eager to remind us, no one has taught anything until somebody has learnt something. There is no impression without expression. In the informal atmosphere of a living room and seated among friends, individuals become relaxed and confident enough to raise questions and invite the response of the others in the group to their ideas and concerns.

However, a cautionary note needs to be sounded at this point. If the group never gets beyond discussion, it is in danger of eventually running into the ground. The object is not to talk ourselves to a standstill, but that the talk should challenge us to reassess our presuppositions and priorities. Many groups, especially in suburban parishes, are more a meeting of minds than of people. They have an ingrained tendency to keep the discussion abstract and impersonal. The theme is examined from all angles until intellectual curiosity has been satisfied, and then they move on to the next item on the programme. But nothing actually happens as a result of all the talk. As someone has commented, 'when all is said and done, too much is said and too little is done.' 'In most matters, we move in either of two directions: from "words" to "things", or from *things* to *words*. That is to say, if we do not make the journey from theories and ideals to concrete situations, then the concrete situations will be lost under a smog of words' (Coleman 1963:10). In which direction are we moving in our home groups?

3.2 To develop meaningful relationships

Juan Carlos Ortiz, the Argentine pastor, has drawn attention to the fact that the object of discipleship is not simply the information of the mind but the formation of the life (Ortiz 1976:ch. 14). Faith in Christ entails a life of obedience. The truth of the gospel is made known 'so that all may believe and *obey*' (Rom. 16:26). It is designed to bring about a transformation in the way that we live in every department of life. Such a change is made possible by the work of the Holy Spirit in the life of the individual. But this does not imply that his operations are exclusively individualistic and privatised. The Holy Spirit speaks to a Christian community as well as to the individual. When we read the letters of the New Testament we have to remind ourselves constantly that when the recipients are addressed to 'you', the word used is second person plural and not singular. This simple, yet significant fact, is obscured in our modern English translations. The primary group provides both a context and a support group to implement our dedication.

An essential part of our development occurs as we respond and relate to other people. Without the stimulus and challenge of other Christians we would be in danger of carving out a gospel to our own liking and which we found comfortable to live with; a gospel which confirms our prejudices without challenging our presuppositions. The Church today needs the constant stimulus to think and act. Che Guevara, the Marxist guerilla who was killed in Bolivia, was described as 'one of those ready to risk his skin to prove his platitudes'. This pinpoints the issue of credibility which faces us all.

Fellowship seldom occurs when pursued as an end in itself. It emerges as a by-product of other activities. Lyman Coleman describes three essential steps in fellowship building; these are:

1 *history giving* – the creation of an atmosphere in which people feel at liberty to speak about themselves, relating their hurts, fears and aspirations.
2 *affirmation* – the development of an improved self-image through self-acceptance and the affirmation of group members who accept us and help us to identify and develop our gifts. This provides a fertile soil for the personality to blossom.
3 *goal setting* – this entails the setting of personal and group objectives in the belief that we can help each other to achieve our potential and cooperate in joint enterprises.

Step Four is *Koinonia* as the group 'jells' through the sense of mutual commitment and fulfilment. (See Coleman 1972:26–27).

The home group situation in which there is a degree of mutual commitment, accountability and the readiness to incarnate the truth as it is revealed in Scripture and applied by the Spirit, may provide a life-generating structure. Within the Roman Catholic Church in Latin America a promising, widespread renewal movement is taking place through *comunidades do base* (basic communities). In Brazil alone there are eighty thousand such groups.

Recreational activities provide a way for group members to get to know each other. Church groups need to learn to relax together and be themselves. We are intended to enjoy each other's company, and relaxation has a rightful place alongside edification, for God is concerned for the well-being of the whole man. Groups should therefore be encouraged from time to time to vary their activities by having a meal, participating in a games or hobbies evening, going out for a picnic, taking part in a sports event, going for a ramble, enjoying a holiday together. Such activities help other leadership gifts to emerge.

This is important for all the family: the over-stretched businessman, the home-bound housewife and mother, the manual worker in a monotonous job, boisterous children whose parents seem too tired, preoccupied or unimaginative and fail for one reason or another to provide treats and outings, lonely, single or elderly people.

For most children home groups often seem adult and studious. Home group night means that they have to go to bed early and they feel excluded while the meeting drones on downstairs. When it is held in someone else's home the meeting is associated with being left with baby sitters while parents go out. It is important that children be included from time to time, with a special meeting in which they can participate, or by the occasional outing when they can enjoy a day out with 'Aunts' and 'Uncles' and children from other families in the group. Our youngsters should be able to look back on their childhood in later life with happy memories of a church which enlarged and enriched the family, rather than dividing it and leaving them in foster care.

3.3 To identify gifts

The small groups situation is the ideal context in which to begin to identify and develop one another's gifts. Opportunities to do so should arise naturally as the group responds to each other's needs and to those which arise within the community. Among the members will be those who reveal gifts of discernment and wisdom as personal problems are tackled or possible lines of action considered. There will be those with gifts of healing who will pray and lay hands upon the sick. Others will display a gift of hospitality in the way that they host the meetings, making everyone feel relaxed, comfortable and cared for. People from the neighbourhood will feel inclined to pop in for a chat, to ask for help, or to share a confidence, because it has become known as a warm and welcoming home. There will be those with practical skills who will be delighted to make and mend in the home and garden. And there will be some who are especially effective as witnesses who will be introducing new people to the group.

Within the confines of a small group latent gifts can bud and flower in modest and unobtrusive ways. Such blossoming of life is frequently inhibited by the more formal structures and public worship services where people feel they have to be polished performers before they can contribute acceptably. Shy and diffident people are easily overlooked in the crowd, whereas in the small group they can be coaxed along to reveal their hidden talents for the immediate benefit of the group, and in preparation for a wider context.

3.4 To train new leaders

Another highly significant aspect of the cell group for church growth is that it provides an ideal structure for leadership training. Whereas the centralised pyramid structure severely limits the number of leaders who can be usefully incorporated, the cellular structure can multiply infinitely, continually creating a growing number of leadership vacancies. This is most dramatically illustrated in the growth of the Full Gospel Church in Seoul, South Korea, which in March 1979 had a membership of a hundred thousand divided among over 5,771 house groups around the city. A similar pattern is also to be found in the Jotabeche Methodist Pentecostal Church in Santiago, Chile. It has now a membership of eighty thousand distributed in a large number of house groups or shack churches. The pressure of numbers is so great on the central place of worship that groups are only allowed to attend on one Sunday in four! Here in England the church which best demonstrates this aspect is possibly St Michael's, York, with thirty-eight home-based neighbourhood groups, with 69 people involved in leadership and with 508 people officially attached to groups, although by no means all attend. In my own parish of St Andrew's Chorleywood, north of London, there are currently twenty-five home groups with an estimated 280 attending. Multiplicity of cells provides both the need for leadership and training ground for the leaders not only of today but for tomorrow.

3.5 To ensure greater pastoral care

As a congregation grows so the pastoral demands increase upon the minister. If the church relies upon a one-man ministry then experience shows that the effectiveness of the individual caring minister will begin to tail off within the 65–150 member bracket. Pastoral care then increasingly comes to mean occasional contact and emergency calls. You have to have very urgent needs to gain attention, and even then there is no guarantee that you will be noticed. If no special needs are detected then you are left to drift on. When the flock becomes too large for one man to care for, the shepherd finds himself becoming little more than a vet! This is a far cry from the kind of pastoral care envisaged in the New Testament. A growing church needs a growing number of pastoral elders who will act as undershepherds of the flock. While larger congregations may be able to provide such training resources themselves, this is not the case in the majority of smaller parishes. A high proportion of clergy who received their training over fifteen years ago have themselves had little training in group work, so they are in need of help themselves before they can facilitate others.

Where the group is responsible for a geographical area, the pastoral care may well extend beyond the group members to include all of the church members who are located within the group's area of responsibility. Regular contact can be maintained through a visiting rota. Group members can also distribute the church magazine or newsletter which provide a reason for calling.

3.6 To demonstrate concern for the neighbourhood

Christian cells to not simply exist for the nurture of their own souls, they are there to try to recognise and then help meet the needs of the neighbourhood. They should be alert and responsive to domestic emergencies – doing the shopping and taking care of the washing for a sick housewife, driving the elderly to hospital appointments or to the departmental stores when public transport is unreliable, looking after children when they cannot be met at school. The home group should also keep a look out for the arrival of removal vans to welcome new arrivals into the district and help them with their orientation. They should be prepared to spend time listening sympathetically to tales of domestic troubles without reprocessing the information as gossip with a high retail value! A broken confidence can mean a loss of credibility for the whole group. And, when appropriate, they should give assurance of prayer either personally or on behalf of the group. The Christian cell provides a means of showing that someone cares. And it is good when Christians can be numbered among those who put themselves out for neighbours in need.

3.7 To establish local basis for evangelism

In contrast to American experience there is little evidence to date of home groups being used effectively in on-going evangelism here in Britain. Why should this be the case? The problem is not that the people are unwilling to accept invitations to hear the gospel in homes. Most parish missions today are based on home meeting contacts rather than central meetings. While very few non-churchgoers attend the 'evangelistic rally' or the 'mission service' they will come in large numbers into the homes of neighbours and friends. This is the experience of evangelists and missioners across the country who have adopted this strategy. The inhibition therefore seems to be located in the group rather than the community.

Part of the problem arises from the fact that *there is little evangelistic drive within the church's ministry and the ethos of its worship*. If there is no evangelism at the centre there is unlikely to be much at the circumference. However, when evangelism is placed high on the agenda during a week of mission it may be expressed effectively through the home groups. Many evangelists have adopted the small group concept as a strategy to establish contact with the unchurched. But this injection of concern is only temporary, the effects quickly wearing off as the church lapses back into its pre-mission, self-preoccupied routine.

A second reason for the lack of evangelistic initiative stems from *the way the group sees its purpose*. Most of them regard their role to be that of personal spiritual nurture. They are preoccupied with taking their own spiritual temperature, and have either postponed mission indefinitely till they feel spiritually prepared, or have transferred the responsibility to a committee which is responsible for 'that kind of thing' or left it to the initiative of a few individuals who 'go it alone'.

A third factor is that *the group either does not have among its members anyone with the gift of evangelist, or if it has, has failed to relate that person's gift to the activities of the group*. To deal with this situation the church should consider providing a training course in evangelism designed to identify those who have this gift-potential, and to help everyone fulfil their role of witness more effectively, thus providing a spiritual climate in which the evangelist can operate with greater impact. The church leaders should also encourage every home group to feature evangelistic events in their annual programme of meetings.

Many groups may initially feel nervous about responding to such a challenge. This is understandable if it is outside their previous experience. They may not in fact have anyone in their group with the gift of evangelist. They may not know what kind of programme would be appropriate in their circumstances, and they may be frightened of so mishandling the occasion that they lose the friendship of those people whom they have invited. Therefore the church leaders will need to provide guidelines for conducting evangelism in a small group context. They may need to offer programme suggestions. And for groups who feel they do not have anyone with the gift or experience to lead such an occasion, the church must be able to supply people skilled in group evangelism and suitable for the kind of people whom the group are intending to invite for the occasion.

A further inhibiting factor experienced by many groups of Anglican churches is presented by *the Church of England's parochial system*. This divides the whole country into geographical parishes, and locates clergy in each sector. Its strength is that notionally at least everyone is covered as far as pastoral care is concerned. However, since the Industrial Revolution this is more theory than reality. Many industrial parishes are too densely populated for the church to remain in effective contact with the total parish population. And in rural areas the amalgamation of parishes, usually for reasons of economy, has diluted the effectiveness of the ordained minister. Consequently the blanket coverage is becoming thin and moth eaten.

The static parish concept may be ideally suited to the face-to-face community of village life, but it can be artificial and inhibiting in a mobile society. People do not spend their lives within the parish bounds. They travel to work, to shop, to visit friends and relatives and to pursue their leisure interests. Home in that context may be little more than a place where they roost at night! Yet many clergy tend to have a fixation on the roosting area, mainly because, unlike most of their parishoners, they live and *work* within the parish bounds. They are acutely aware of where their territory begins and ends, and that surrounding them are other ministers jealously guarding their patch. Lay people, however, are scarcely aware of these invisible boundaries, apart from when they apply for baptism or weddings.

Frequently a high proportion of church attenders live outside their parish. They shop around for a church to belong to in the same way as they exercise choice in the shops which they patronise and other places which they frequent. Urban society is highly mobile. In the United States people are prepared to travel twenty miles to go to church (Schuller 1974:78); here in Britain families with cars are happy to go up to ten miles, although some travel much further. Recent increases in petrol prices may lead to a more localised society, unless alternative cheaper forms of fuel come on the market. But for the present, and possibly into the future we need a more flexible structure if the gospel message is to flow unimpeded along the existing communication channels which extend far beyond the parish boundaries.

Anglican ministers located in neighbouring parishes should acknowledge that a proportion of their members live in each others' parishes, and must be prepared for them to meet in home groups beyond their church's parish bounds. Furthermore each member has a responsibility in his immediate neighbourhood and should be encouraged to welcome his friends into the group and invite them along to his church if they are not attending elsewhere. McGavran observes, 'The only church you can effectively win people into is your own. If you think that after you win them to Christ they will find a church that suits them, you are badly mistaken' (McGavran and Arn 1977:88). Our concern is the building of the Kingdom and not simply the enlarging of our congregation. Congregations cannot be neatly packaged in parish-shaped parcels. We must be free to follow up contacts uninhibited by parochial jurisdictions, with the important proviso that the neighbouring clergy should keep each other fully informed of developments in each other's area.

The situation does however become more complicated when one large church dominates the scene and thrives at the expense of the rest. When this becomes a danger then extraparochial groups may be organised on an inter-church basis, and the church well endowed in resources should be prepared to share its personnel to help the other poorly-attended churches out of the doldrums.

In this section we have stressed the need for primary groups with a comprehensive function. I concur with David Wasdell in the need for such groups to be 'a microcosm of the larger church, a sub-unit of the congregation, sharing the overall purpose and task of the body of Christ, yet limited to those functions appropriate to the primary task' (Wasdell 1975:29). I do not, however, believe that we can expect to catch every Christian in a net of this size. We will consider this problem in greater detail in the following chapter.

In addition there is need for other small groups with a narrower function relating specifically to prayer ministries, discussion of ethical and other problems arising in particular professions, and for evangelistic efforts among mutual friends and associates.

Whether the purpose of the group is comprehensive or single it needs to be clearly defined and understood so that the members' expectations are in line with intentions, so that effectiveness of the group in realising the declared objectives can be maintained, and in order that appropriate leadership can emerge and be appointed.

4 Problems likely to arise in groups

When a church decides to subdivide the membership into groups as an answer to the problems of the individuals' lack of a sense of identity and belonging, and to lift the congregation from its numerical plateau, it may soon discover that in solving one problem area it has exposed itself to new problem areas. Groups can create as many difficulties as they solve. This fact should be recognised from the outset. By the exercise of a little forethought, and by taking care to build in safeguards we can save ourselves a number of headaches. The following problems are those most likely to arise in a cell group structure

4.1 Introversion

Groups of people can quickly develop an intense relationship. They form a clique which regards others who try to join the group as intruders. This is especially the case if that person is of a different age bracket or economic class, or holds views which are strongly at variance with the other group members. The other people in the group are unlikely to repel him overtly, but a number of subtle innuendos will signal to him that he does not really belong.

The ultimate purpose is not for groups to turn in upon themselves, but for the members to be activated to find and fulfil their mission in the world. The 'inward journey' must be accompanied by an 'outward journey'. To facilitate this two-way movement Elizabeth O'Connor has suggested the following structure. The first stage is to enlist in a school of Christian living which is designed to help members in 'three essential engagements: with God, with others, with self'. The programme involves personal assignments in learning to 'reach a state of inner attention', to establish personal growth disciplines, to discover and exercise new gifts, to relate to others so that we continue to be 'growing people' (O'Connor 1968: ch. 8). Having completed the school of Christian living, people have a wide choice of options in joining mission groups engaged in a specific activity, which may range from intercessory prayer, evangelistic visitation, to operating a coffee shop, or carrying out home improvements. People join a group which is in line with their particular gift and 'call'. If no group exists which corresponds to their leading a new group can be formed. Such mission groups are not simply activity-oriented. They also minister to one another, by appointing members whose main concern is the maintenance needs of the group itself. Thus work is not divorced from worship and mutual ministry.

4.2 Fragmentation

When groups become preoccupied with themselves, they begin before long to pull away from the centre and vie against each other. Many churches have been torn apart in this way because almost from the outset the groups set themselves up as protest groups, to register their frustration at the irrelevance of the central acts of worship and traditional organisations. If the groups are then able to supply what was previously denied to the members, and if the central activities have no distinctive contribution to supplement and stimulate that cell life, then the main structure will lose cohesion and begin to fall apart.

To prevent this unhappy state of affairs developing, the distinctive roles of the cell groups and the congregational activities must be clearly defined and strong links between the two forged. Later, we will look at this in practical detail. The primary principle to be upheld is that the cell is a subdivision of the congregation and not a substitute for it. Therefore the group members' primary allegiance is to the congregation rather than the group.

4.3 Domination

Small groups can suffer through an overbearing leadership. Some leaders dominate through their strong personalities, others through their show of expertise. Their presence in the group is oppressive and inhibiting, rather than relaxing and enabling. The situation has arisen through an unwise choice at the outset, or because of inadequate guidance and supervision, or because no established procedures were devised at the outset to deal with such an eventuality.

This oppressive style of leadership has developed in some sections of the charismatic movement which have exercised 'oversight' or what they term a 'covering' ministry in a rigidly authoritarian and hierarchical framework. Discipleship training should be geared to making people disciples of Christ, not to the processing of individuals to become extensions of any human leader. Michael Harper observes, 'The master – disciple relationship is, of course, used frequently used to describe the human relationship that Jesus had with others on earth, and therefore, can equally describe our relationship to the Lord today. We are still his disciples, and he is still our master. But it is never in the New Testament used to describe the relationship which Christians may have with one another' (Harper 1977:152). Such an emphasis is in response to the need to bring a highly individualistic spirit-led movement under some kind of authority and disciplined commitment to a body of believers. 'But if the language of "discipling" is used in place of "serving", it will simply be a way of replacing anarchy with tyranny' (Harper 1977:74, 75).

4.4 Dependency

This represents the other side of the coin to the problem described above. Some groups demand the complete subjection of the individual's will. They process people into a dull, predictable uniformity. Socially inadequate people may be especially attracted to such groups to provide them with support and a sense of identity. This may be beneficial up to a point, but there is a danger of such a strong sense of 'belonging' developing that 'the group becomes the source of an individual's identity, and he becomes dependent on it rather than on Christ. He lets the group become God for him, in making his decisions and planning his life' (Osmaston 1979:15).

4.5 Stagnation

Birds of a feather flock together, but after a time the feathers may begin to fly as disagreements develop, or the birds may resort to tucking their heads under their wings through boredom. Groups which begin well with members dropping their guards, getting to know one another, affirming each other's beliefs and challenging each other's opinions, may eventually lapse into lethargy. Individuals in the group begin to bore each other as they ride their hobby horses, and frustrate one another as they chase shoals of red herring. Eventually they may reach the stage when they only have to catch the opening sentence to predict with unfailing accuracy what is likely to follow. People then stop listening to one another, and merely wait for the person to finish speaking in order to add their contribution to the ritual conversation. When meetings become routine and predictable, the more resourceful members will begin to look for more stimulating activities to occupy their time.

4.6 Subversion

Groups are vulnerable to subversion by those who seek acceptance for ulterior motives. They may want to push a personal view point, or, more seriously, to disrupt the church by generating discontent and rivalry. Some have utilised the mutual support of the group for personal gain. They have made the group feel responsible for them, and traded upon their generosity. The New Testament letters which are addressed to small group situations, warned against such eventualities.

Our Lord warned against false prophets who would succeed in penetrating the Church's defences, like wolves in sheep's clothing (Matt. 7:15). Paul alerted the recent converts in Thessalonica to deal with the layabouts who were living off the earnings of the more industrious (1 Thess. 4:11; 5:14; 2 Thess 3:6–15). When he met with the elders of the church in Ephesus he predicted that after he left, wolves would devour the flock and that 'some men from your own group will tell lies to lead the believers away after them' (Acts 20:29, 30). He constantly warned against those who preached another gospel (Gal. 1:6–8; 5:10; Eph. 4:14), posed as apostles (2 Cor. 11–13), stirred up envy and strife (Phil. 1:15) and worked evil (Phil. 3:2). He counselled the young Timothy to guard against those who would challenge his authority and undermine believers (1 Tim. 1:3; 4:1, 6; 2 Tim. 2:14; 3:6–9, 13). Titus was similarly warned (Titus 1:10–14; 3:10). This was not simply a hobby horse of Paul. The same line is taken both by Peter (2 Pet. 2:1f) and John (2 John 7, 10, 11; 3 John 10). Such dangers have not subsided with the passage of time; the Scriptures highlight the fact that they will intensify 'in the last days'.

4.7 Overloading

This danger arises when the cell structure is superimposed on existing, centralised organisational framework. As a consequence the committed church members are locked still more tightly into a merry-go-round of church activities. They find themselves committed to so many groups that they are likely to become eventually spiritually as well as physically exhausted! If home groups are to fulfil their twin functions of building up the believers in their spiritual lives and of becoming launching pads for mission, then there will have to be a clearing of the decks of other organisational clutter. From time to time every organisation (including home groups) should be required to justify their continuing existence and to review their programme.

Many church leaders have been all too aware of these dangers, either because they have observed them occurring elsewhere, or have imagined their possible development if their own church were to set up groups. They have, consequently, resisted any moves in this direction. However, where groups have been well-organised and managed as an integral part of an overall strategy for Christian education, pastoral care and evangelistic outreach, they have had a transforming effect on church life. In all of my eleven years of itinerant ministry I cannot recall any growing church which does not encourage small groups.

5 Leadership for groups

The larger the congregation the greater the percentage of passengers and the larger the number of unused and frustrated leaders one is likely to find. This is not inevitable, yet it frequently occurs when the large church does not have an adequate cellular growth structure. By multiplying cell groups the growing church creates leadership positions and an ideal training ground for future leadership. Wasdell describes cell groups as 'leader-breeders'.

Capable leaders of large congregations are sometimes slow to recognise the need to widen the leadership base. Moses, one of the outstanding leaders of the Old Testament, was no exception. He was a workaholic who was heading for a breakdown when Jethro, who was alert to the situation, stepped in. 'You are not doing it the right way. You will wear yourself out and these people as well. Now let me give you some good advice, and God will be with you. . . . You should choose some capable men and appoint them as leaders of the people: leaders of thousands, hundreds, fifties and tens. . . . That will make it easier for you, as they share your burden' (Ex. 18:17–22). At the base of this leadership pyramid were the leaders of tens – the primary group. Ron Trudinger has done some arithmetic on this passage, linking it with Exodus 38:26 where the number of men from 'twenty years old and upwards' was 603,550. On the basis of this population figure Moses would need 600 leaders of 'thousands', 6,000 leaders of 'hundreds', 12,000 leaders of 'fifties', and 60,000 leaders of 'tens'. This makes a total of 78,600 leaders! (Trudinger 1979:25, 26).

5.1 Leadership qualities

The personal qualifications required for leadership among the people of God are spelt out in a number of places. For example, the leaders appointed to assist Moses were required to be capable, God-fearing men who could be trusted and would not yield to offers of bribery (Ex. 18:21). Turning to the New Testament, the qualities expected in an elder, presbyter or deacon would apply equally well to a group leader with pastoral responsibilities for the members. He is to have a blameless reputation, to be faithful to his wife, to be trustworthy, self-controlled, discreet, disciplined, hospitable, able to teach, respected by his children, fair-minded, devout, well thought of by non-Christians, able to get on with people, reasonable, gentle and firm yet patient with difficult individuals (see 1 Tim. 3:1–7; 4:14; Titus 1:5–11).

In order to operate effectively in a primary group context he needs to be able to develop inter-personal relationships. Therefore, he must be a person who is secure in himself, does not feel personally threatened by criticism and is able to evaluate himself and the group. In temperament he is relaxed and restrained; calm, poised and objective. He displays a loving concern for everyone in the group and has an understanding, generous attitude which covers the fault of others. He is sensitive to 'atmosphere'; able to display tact and apply 'antifreeze' to thaw out a tense situation. He recognises that *how* one says things is as important as *what* is said. He displays vitality and an enthusiasm for the job which rubs off on the rest of the group. He is humble and teachable, making it clear that he does not pretend to know all the answers. He studiously avoids overshadowing others, and is appreciative of the contributions made by everyone in the group.

5.2 Leadership tasks

The primary groups envisaged in this chapter, 'should as far as possible express the full nature and message of the church' (Osmaston 1979:11). This being so the leader is responsible for a wide range of tasks. The complexity of his role is often masked by the smallness of the group, and does not become evident until the new leader has worked his way into the job. The scope of the task and the range of responsibilities need to be spelt out and agreed upon before any appointment is made so that no one takes on more than he finds he can manage. The following paragraphs attempt to describe his range of responsibilities.

The leader's prime task is to enable the group to come together to achieve the objectives for which it has been established. He must, therefore, be able to define clearly the nature of the various tasks to be undertaken or the problems to be considered. He must establish rapport between members so that they can relate creatively to one another. 'Leadership involves sensitivity to the feelings and attitudes of others, ability to understand what is happening in a group at the unconscious as well as the conscious level, and skill in acting in ways that contribute to, rather than hinder, task performance' (Rice 1965:5). He works to draw out the insights and views of the group, by encouraging participation which occurs when everyone is encouraged to feel that they have something valuable to contribute. He does not immediately jump in to answer questions, but bounces them back for the group to respond. When someone becomes muddled and confused he saves them from embarrassment by a face-saving interjection, such as, 'Did I understand you to mean. . .?' He looks out for the flaring up of private feuds, the surfacing of red herrings or the emergence of 'hidden agendas' which might subvert the purpose of the group. He calms the argumentative, restrains the over-talkative and spots the shy person who has withdrawn into a mental backwater. When the pace flags he fires the group with a fresh idea or a provocative question. He is not embarrassed by, but rather encourages, periodic silences for the incubation of new ideas. He discourages sloganising and repetitions. He is concerned to see that much talk about God results in a closer walk with God for all. He is therefore, alert to challenge the group in considering ways of applying practically what has been discussed.

He will realise the extent to which behaviour can be influenced powerfully by group ineraction. Kurt Lewin reported an experiment in which a group of women discussed together cheaper cuts of meat. As a result, thirty-two per cent began using them. When the same facts were conveyed by means of a straight lecture only three per cent of the women did so.

The leader is also responsible for ensuring that practical arrangements and details are cared for. He will be concerned to see that the meeting begins and ends on time. He will undertake to introduce newcomers and visit absentees. He will maintain good relationships with the wider congregation and liaise with other groups.

To be an effective group leader requires the acquiring of skills and dedication of time. It cannot be taken on as yet another chore for the already over-taxed church leader.

As we commented earlier, it is essential that the leader understands what the job entails and what is expected of him. This may be achieved by means of a written job description, which is talked over, modified where necessary and then agreed to. The job description might look something like the following (see Fig. 16).

5.3 Appointment

As home groups are not autonomous bodies but sub-units of a larger fellowship, the leaders should not be appointed by the group members but by the minister who has overall pastoral responsibility and will in effect delegate pastoral responsibilities to them. A wise minister under normal circumstances will also take the precaution of seeking

JOB DESCRIPTION: HOME GROUP LEADER

The task of the leader is to direct the group to fulfil its stated purpose:

1 To be responsible for the group to the minister and church leadership.
2 To conduct the teaching programme within the guidelines agreed by the minister or pastoral eldership group.
3 To encourage the participation of all the group members in discussion, prayer times and other activities.
4 To endeavour to establish an atmosphere of trust, in which people feel free to air their problems and concerns and ask for the support of the group.
5 To visit all members in their homes at least one every three months.
6 To help each of the members to identify their gifts and skills, and to encourage their use in the group, the life of the church, and the community at large.
7 To report to the minister or church leadership any special needs arising in the group.
8 In the case of neighbourhood groups, to ensure that group members are monitoring the needs of the locality, making contact with new neighbours, visiting any individuals or dealing with specific needs to the group by the minister; and to require adequate reporting back on results.
9 To initiate at least two invitation evenings each year, one of these to be for church members in the locality who are not group members and the other for group members to share their faith with non-Christians.
10 To train assistant leaders who can act for him in a temporary capacity and eventually take on responsibility for their own group.

Fig. 16

ratification by the parochial church council, deacon's meeting or other appropriate body. In the case of an existing group requiring a change of leadership, it is usually advisable to discuss the matter with the group or consult with one or two members who would be considered representative of the group prior to making an appointment rather than to approach candidates privately and individually. Such behind-the-scenes tactics can have an unsettling influence on the group, and make them feel that they are not considered mature enough to arrive at their own decisions. If the group cannot provide a new leader from within, then the minister must bring in a new leader from elsewhere.

Wherever possible the minister should avoid being a group leader. The presence of an ordained man can be inhibiting to laymen. But most importantly, he should be free from other commitments to call in on groups to evaluate how effective the leader is proving to be, and be prepared to step into the breach should an emergency remove a leader without an assistant being readily available. If the minister has spotted any mistakes in the leader's approach he can then counsel him on ways of improving his performance.

It is advisable for the period of the appointment to be specified both in the interests of the church, the group and the leader. The leader may prove to be unsuitable and the fact of the agreed time limit makes it easier to arrange a replacement, avoiding embarrassment or ill-feeling. Obviously on occasion the minister must act at once for the good of the group. As for the leader, his circumstances in terms of his family responsibilities or work commitments may change, making it difficult for him to continue. Little good purpose is served when the leader is left to soldier on when he finds that he can no longer give the time nor the energy which the job requires. The sight of him in this situation will be a warning to other prospective leaders that they would find themselves in a similar position if they allowed themselves to be persuaded to become home group leaders! A time limit encourages the leader to re-assess his commitments to decide whether or not to agree to a renewal of the appointment for a further period.

The appointment is not simply the concern of the group but is to an office which is part of the total congregational structure. As such it should be recognised and supported by the whole church. This can be expressed in a commissioning service of the leaders held at the beginning of the church's new yearly cycle of activities, which normally gets under way after the long summer holidays.

5.4 Training and co-ordination

It is vitally important for the minister to keep in regular contact with the various group leaders in order to provide them with adequate personal support and to obtain feed-back. This may either be arranged on a one-to-one basis or through a monthly or quarterly group leaders' meeting. Able leaders tend to have many commitments so the minister must be prepared to meet at their convenience and not simply at his own. If all else fails contact can be maintained by a regular telephone call. If the leadership are not regularly comparing notes the cell structures will be in danger of losing momentum and cohesion.

If regular monthly sharing and training sessions prove too frequent to sustain, it may be necessary to work to a three- or six-monthly programme. At the training sessions the teaching programme can be arranged and any alternative agreed to. In programming for groups a degree of flexibility is necessary. Some groups may be of a different social, cultural and age mix from the rest, which may mean they will have to follow a distinctive approach or have a programme of their own.

Training topics may include the following:

1 How to lead a discussion.
2 Encouraging group sharing and prayer.

3 Visiting church members.
4 The art of listening and counselling.
5 Identifying gifts.
6 Visitation evangelism.
7 Holding an evangelistic Bible Study.
8 Relating to community needs.
9 Arranging a local community outreach.
10 What to do when the group becomes too large.

5.5 Avoid the leadership bottleneck

As a church grows, so groups multiply and before long things grind to a standstill through a shortage of trained leadership. To avoid the leadership bottleneck ensure from an early stage that each group has an assistant able to work alongside the leader. He is then ready to stand in should the leader be absent for any reason, and is also available to spearhead new groups. Assistant leaders should be encouraged to participate in all the leadership training opportunities to equip them to run a group of their own. However, they should not be encouraged to assume that they are the automatic choice when the group needs a new leader.

5.6 Distinguish between leader and host

This is a helpful and often necessary distinction to make to ease the burden on the leader. If the meeting is held in his home and he is responsible for all the practical arrangements in addition to the meeting programme he is unlikely to be able to give of his best. This is especially the case with a married man or woman with children. By the time the children have been put to bed, toys put away, room tidied, furniture rearranged and the refreshments prepared, they flop back exhausted as the members begin to arrive and the programme gets under way! When the leader is not the host, he can arrive fresh to conduct the evening's programme. It must be recognised that some leaders, while having the essential pastoral and teaching qualifications, may not possess the gift of hospitality.

A further advantage is that the location of the group can be changed with minimum disruption to the group. If the leader who is also the host suggests moving the meeting elsewhere to ease the hospitality burden from his family, this may seem to imply that he has lost interest in the group, or that he is questioning its importance.

5.7 Female leadership?

Some churches restrict the home leadership to males for theological reasons. They consider Paul's statement that women should not have a teaching authority over men as normative rather than being corrective statements or culturally conditioned restrictions (1 Cor. 14:34–36; 1 Tim. 2:11–15). Personally, I can see no theological objection to ladies leading home groups. My main concern is strategic. Female leadership may discourage single men and husbands from attending. Though I wouldn't want to press this point too strongly. Some ladies might wish to argue that male-dominated leadership keeps them away! Some churches with home groups are breaking out of their traditional attitudes and are discovering as yet untapped leadership potential among the single ladies. And other home groups are successfully led by a husband and wife team which is sensitive to the needs of both sexes and can provide and acceptable compromise solution to this problem.

6 Roles adopted by group members

The leaders need to be aware of the various roles that the individuals assume within groups. In a well-functioning group the members will change from one stance to another. If an individual becomes stuck in one stereotype then the leader (or others in the group) must work to steer him into an alternative stance. The following describe the most common roles which people adopt.

6.1 The expert
He is the resource person for the group, readily providing information or quoting from his store of experience. His presence will at least safeguard the conversation from degenerating into the mere sharing of ignorance. However, care must be exercised to ensure that he does not dominate the group or frighten others off from contributing, through fear of being constantly corrected.

6.2 The spokesman
He interjects to reinterpret a statement or summarise a conversation. He gives shape and direction to the discussion. If, however, he slips into the role too frequently he can easily degenerate into a bore. He, like the expert, must be discouraged from pontificating.

6.3 The lieutenant
He is the leader's self-appointed assistant; a 'Yes' man with no fresh or original thoughts to contribute. If he remains uncritical and predictable, merely echoing the opinions of the leader, his presence can become embarrassing and irritating.

6.4 The loyal opposition
He represents the minority or anti-establishment view. He at least saves the conversation from one-sidedness. His contrary views are not however, expressed in such a way as to split the group to the extent of raising tempers and breaking fellowship.

6.5 The devil's advocate
This represents a contrived opposition. Someone takes up the cudgels on behalf of others not present at the meeting. It is not easy to play this role convincingly. Sometimes the person adopts the stance because secretly he identifies with the view and this enables him to test opinion without feeling the group's hostility or rejection.

6.6 The 'Mr. Everyman'

Some members give the impression that they are just 'ordinary people' with little to contribute. They ask straightforward questions, sometimes with a slightly naïve air, hoping that they are valid and that the group will help to increase their self-esteem by identifying with their question, or commending their perception. Sometimes Mr Everyman will come out with a 'gem' of a comment casually dropped and therefore in danger of being overlooked.

6.7 The joker

He provides the quip which relieves tension or adds a flash to insight. The skilful use of humour enables sensitive points to be made in a non-threatening, acceptable way. If the group is encouraged to laugh at itself, it will be enabled to look at itself with greater honesty. However, humour needs to be controlled. A wit can crack jokes as an attention getter. When the comment is mistimed and inappropriate it can create tension and inflict hurt. Whispered jokes can create disruptive diversions.

6.8 The spectator

Silent partners require understanding by the more talkative group members. People remain quiet for a variety of reasons. If through misinterpreting their silence we respond inappropriately we may cause hurt, embarrassment or antagonism. Some people are silent because they are *reflective* by nature. Though such people do not say much, when they do speak it is worth hearing because they have learned to weigh their words. Others are silent because they are *nervous* and *reticent*. They need assurance and easy ways into the conversation. Still others are silent through an attitude of cool detachment. Feeling superior to the group, they mentally switch off from the conversation. This is akin to the silence of *boredom*, which can only be broken by a change of subject or of tack. Lastly there is the silence of the *passive objector* who simmers with frustration and anger, feeling that his views will make no impression on the present company. Such a silence can only be broken by the group demonstrating that they are prepared to listen. A useful tactic, when a group member senses such an attitude, is for him to voice the objection he perceives is in the mind of the passive objector, thus providing an opportunity for him to follow through.

7 *Group communication patterns*

In addition to detecting roles which group members adopt it is also helpful to understand some of the communication patterns which emerge. These patterns may arise spontaneously or be deliberately suggested to help the group make progress in opening up a subject or arriving at decisions. I acknowledge my indebtedness to Ada Lum and Ruth Siemens for the following descriptions (see Fig. 17).

7.1 Lecture situation

The lecturer presents a prepared speech without allowing for interruption or inviting a response. Such an approach is inappropriate for a small group except as a brief introductory statement, providing a basis for group discussion.

7.2 Teaching situation

The teacher interacts with his pupils, posing questions and inviting comments. He involves them in the learning process by opening up avenues for them to explore.

7.3 Dialogue

This occurs when two members engage in a debate which is overheard by the rest of the group. Its advantage in the group situation, when pursued by a pair equally matched is that it provides a way to present the pros and cons of an issue. These establish the opposing poles for subsequent general debate. Listening to the 'experts' talk means that the other members are not required to state

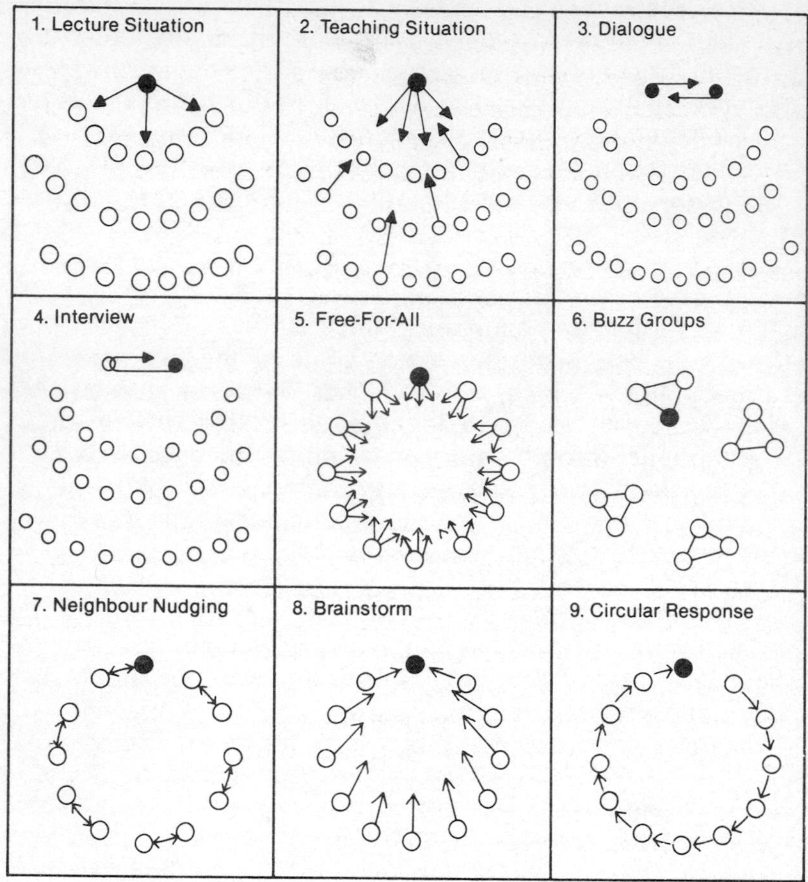

Fig. 17
Group communication patterns

their views and possibly expose their ignorance of the subject, and thus have time to gather information and formulate their own views. As the debate progresses so the group member can usually identify with one or other of the protagonists or come to his or her own independent conclusions.

7.4 Interview
This consists of question and response. In a small group it allows the group members to confront the person being questioned and to identify with his answers. In some sensitive areas it can be used as 'a third party gambit', allowing issues to be aired in a non-threatening way. While addressing one individual the interviewer is in fact also speaking through the person he is questioning to the other group members.

7.5 Free-for-all
In this instance everyone talks at once. Generally this approach is not recommended, though a short burst may help to get the reticent person to open his mouth without fearing that his contribution will prove to be a conversation-stopper!

7.6 Buzz groups
This is a structured free-for-all. The group is divided into subgroups of three for a short period for opinions to be tested or ideas gathered. Each buzz group then shares its findings with the others.

7.7 Neighbour-nudging
The group pairs off, speaking to the person either to their right or to their left, without moving their seats. They discuss the point at issue for a few moments and then each person reports what the other has said, or one of each pair, acting as spokesman, shares their separate views, how they have modified each other's thinking, or their joint conclusion. This technique provides an opportunity for 'nudging' each other's thinking.

7.8 Brainstorm
This is a quick way of gathering ideas, without stopping the flow of inspiration to comment and evaluate. As each suggestion is put forward it is simply listed on an overhead transparency or blackboard. Only when the flow of ideas

has dried up is the list then evaluated for effectiveness and practicability.

7.9 Circular response

Each person in turn gives his views on the issue. No interruptions are permitted until everyone in the circle has spoken. The group leaders may note the spread of opinion and then summarise the views of the group and how they are weighted (Lum and Siemens 1973:11, 27).

Part of the art of good group leadership is not only to be aware of the different kinds of group communication patterns, but to know which method might be the most applicable for the task in hand and when is the most appropriate moment to introduce it. The novelty of the procedures must not detract from the business in hand, but serve to facilitate its most effective implementation.

In summary the leader needs to understand the dynamics of small groups to keep the discussion on the subject, to involve as many people as possible and to try to reach where appropriate a conclusion.

8 Summary

This chapter has attempted to demonstrate the importance of small groups for the growth of the church both in regard to quality of corporate life and by multiplying points of contact with and outreach into the surrounding community. Assess their significance to date in the life of your church. How can they become more meaningful for those who attend? By what means can other members of the congregation become involved? How can their leadership be improved? How can new groups be formed to undertake specific tasks, while at the same time ministering to one another? How can the resources given by God to the Church be channelled into the community to get done what God wants us to achieve? These are key questions which every growing church must squarely face if its growth momentum is to be maintained. Otherwise it will simply grow flab rather than muscle.

CHAPTER SEVEN

Structures and Strategy

Human growth entails, in addition to the multiplication of cells, the development of the skeletal structure to support them. For the body of Christ to grow, structure is equally important. Without an adequate and expansible framework the Church will be in danger of an organisational overload leading to institutional collapse. In order to prevent such an unfortunate eventuality many churches operate a self-limiting structure which determines the ceiling level of performance.

David Wasdell of the Urban Church Project presented a report to the General Synod of the Church of England which showed conclusively that the answer to the problem of achieving an increased level of penetration in a densely populated urban parish is not merely to increase the numbers of clergy. 'In parishes of over 2,000 the single-clergy model church levels off at an average congregation of 175 regardless of parish population' (Wasdell 1974:5). He quoted an earlier piece of research which had shown that a two-person team adds an average ninety Christmas communicants, and increasing the team by a further full-time worker added an extra eighty-one Christmas communicants. He writes, '. . . the only way to break out of the self-limiting church structure is to increase lay mobilisation in mission and to minimise lapse rate. In other words we need structures of high motivation, maturation, education, training and pastoral care, together with a sense of belonging' (Wasdell 1974:12).

In the previous chapter we examined the small group, emphasising its importance for providing a sense of belonging and pastoral care. In this chapter we will be concerned with further structures for education and inspiration. Chapter seven will focus attention on lay mobilisation.

The study of local church structures is a neglected area in the thinking of many clergy because their main preoccupation in ministry is with people rather than structures and organisation. Some suspect all organisation as having a depersonalising influence. However, when properly understood and worked out, organisation can help a growing church to retain its emphasis on the importance of the individual, by providing channels of communication which can help everyone to know what is happening and through which they can be heard and are able to participate. The Church in today's urban world with its mushrooming population needs structures which facilitate its own ability to mushroom.

1 Defining groups

Peter Wagner in his analysis of growing urban churches in the United States, identifies as his fourth vital sign of a healthy growing church the interrelationship of a three-tier structure, which he expresses in the formula: celebration + congregation + cell = church. Each tier is represented by a different size of group, designed to fulfil a distinctive function. Sociologists distinguish between three types of group which differ in size and function (see Fig. 18). The smallest of these is the '*primary group*' which consists of twelve members or less. This is the intimate face-to-face unit, which provides the possibility of developing in-depth, personal relationships. But as numbers grow much above twelve it becomes difficult and then impossible to maintain this level of intimacy.

The next stage is the '*secondary group*' with a membership ranging from thirteen to a maximum of 175. Within this range it is possible to know everyone by name, be on casual speaking terms and experience a group identity. The group stresses social activity rather than personal interaction. It is more task- than people-orientated.

The third tier begins at 175 plus with no upper limit. This is the '*tertiary group*' in which it is not possible for people to know one another. The tertiary group provides the opportunity for community, celebratory events. The focus is not on those sitting or standing in the crowd, but on what is happening up front. However, on such occasions the activity 'on stage' may be suspended for a while, to give opportunity for a relational exercise in small groups. This occurs, for example, during the Anglican Series III communion service when 'the peace' is exchanged along and between the pews. Such an exchange only really works well with a fairly large congregation with the pews will filled. It also occurs in charismatic gatherings in which strangers greet one another, or at celebration events such as a 'Come Together'.

The establishing of relationships with people immediately around us in the crowd helps to encourage a greater degree of participation.

Primary, secondary and tertiary groupings each have a significant role to play in the life of a growing church. In modern urban society the small group is not the whole answer. We therefore need to appreciate the distinction between the three levels of groups, understand their distinctive dynamics, and establish a dynamic relationship between them.

In the previous chapter we examined the nature of groups at the primary level and their leadership. We now proceed to describe the secondary and tertiary levels.

2 Secondary groups

The secondary group is more task-orientated than person-centred. With up to 175 members, it is large enough to contain an interesting variety of people, yet small enough for each person to know everyone by name. For the small church the 'secondary group' will be the

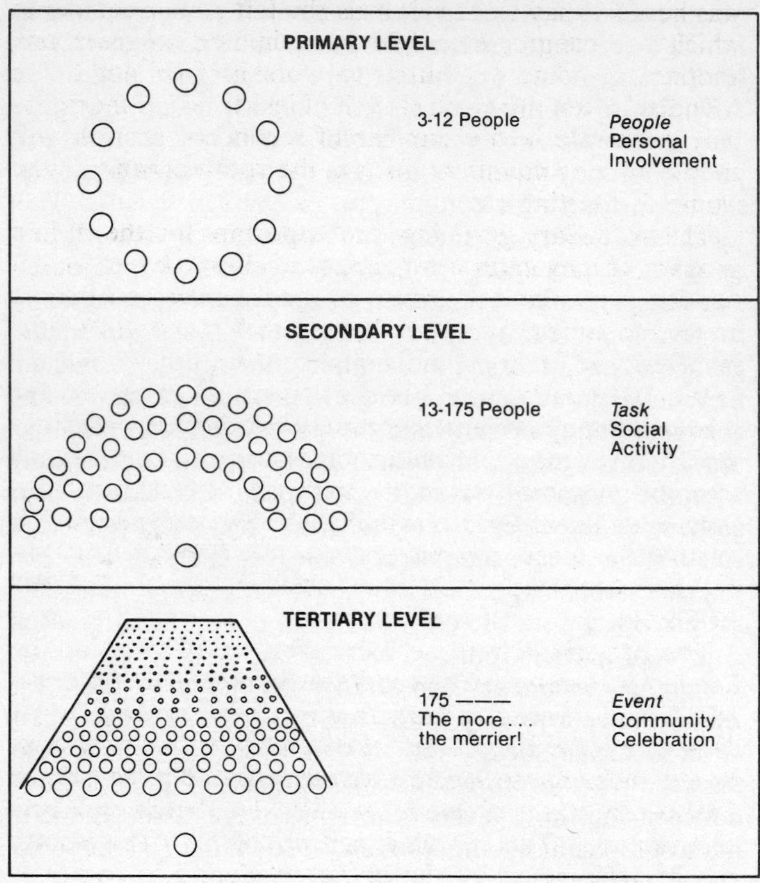

Fig. 18
Structures for growth

congregation. When people come to the church service there is a likelihood that the worshippers know one another, although recognition is usually minimal due to the seating arrangements of the building or the members' understanding of worship. One South Wales worshipper was heard to say to her vicar as she left after a service in which the congregation had been invited to greet one another, 'I come to church to worship God not to be friendly!' Even the small church of less than 150 members may subdivide into a number of secondary groups with twenty to sixty members, such as the youth organisations, women's meeting etc.

The secondary groupings are important for the church growth, as they cater for a variety of church-based activities for particular age groups or special interests. People are made to feel that they belong and can begin to get involved and make an individual contribution.

When a small church becomes too large to function as a healthy single unit, it becomes what Lyle Schaller describes as a 'supersaturated solution with more members than can be absorbed into one group. These congregations usually are able to assimilate replacement members to take the place of members who move away, drop out or die; but rarely are they able to grow' (Schaller 1978b:59).

The groupings become increasingly important as the Sunday services grow beyond the point where it is possible for all the worshippers to know one another, or for members to be able to spot the newcomer and take steps to get to know, welcome, and introduce him to others. Frequently this problem is signalled by church members commenting, 'This church is getting too big.' This should not be interpreted by the church leaders as a comment on *size* but on *structure*. What they are really saying is, 'Help, I'm lost here' or, 'I no longer count around here.' The organisational structures have begun to creak or break apart under the strain of additional mass. If the growing church fails to build intermediate structures then the growth dynamic will be destroyed. Strangers will go unnoticed among the crowd of regulars. While these gather in groups, the visitor stands near the wall to hide the fact that he has been left out, or simply slips quietly away.

In large churches people are much more likely to 'stick' when they have been successfully incorporated into face-to-face groups either at the primary or secondary level. The unspoken questions are: Do people know my name? If I am absent am I likely to be missed? Do people want to know me bettter? Would my contribution be invited and welcomed?

Many churches are a hive of activity throughout the week, especially when public amenities are scarce in the area. They provide premises which are attractive and adaptable to a wide range of activities – uniformed organisations, dance, drama, social clubs, badminton, judo, painting, pottery etc. The trouble is that in most cases the church acts as little more than a landlord. This can cause complications with financial haggling and competing claims.

2.1 Mid-week activity groups

I believe that the church should be the focal point of a hive of diverse activities, because urban society brings together different kinds of people in large numbers. But wherever possible it is preferable for the church to identify and anticipate the likely interest and to initiate activity groups with able Christian leadership. In this way the church can avoid being driven into fulfilling a landlord role, hosting activities over which it has little or no control, and can integrate those activities as aspects of its total mission in the community.

The key problem area for implementing such a policy is to identify appropriate leaders who are technically competent to lead the activity and are spiritually mature to relate the specific activity to a wider Christian framework.

The significance of the secondary groupings is likely to increase in the foreseeable future, with the prospect of more people out of work, shorter working weeks and earlier retirements. The church will have an greater opportunity to help people cope with the increased amount of time they find on their hands.

In the present economic climate, government education cuts mean that many of the adult education and creative leisure opportunities will now have to be provided on a voluntary basis. The level of demand increases as the opportunities and options shrink, as people become disenchanted with television and increased petrol prices restrict their mobility.

I would like to see more churches encouraging family nights, providing an opportunity for the whole family – mum, dad, teenagers and youngsters to go *together* to the church for an evening of fellowship, relaxation and fun. A well-equipped and spacious church hall can provide facilities not normally available at home. So often the church has tended to divide, rather than draw together families. In an age when there are so many influences at work to break down the family unit, such an activity night will help to provide a much needed corrective. The programme could include table tennis, badminton, five-a-side football, games for young children, handicrafts (with the whole family making things for the Missionary Sales or Christmas Market), barbecues, 'spic and span' (when we join forces to decorate, clean or garden). Such occasions can be great fun, and particularly effective in bringing the menfolk together.

Gavin Reid, however, sounds a warning bell with regard to activity groups. He observes, '. . . some churches have run social activities hoping that they would "bring people in". But church dances only "bring people in" to church dances . . . when we set up clubs for social and recreational activities we must be quite clear that they will not win people for Christ, but they will end up by attracting people because of their activity and not because of their associations with the church' (Reid 1979:47). I agree that this is frequently the case. Equally, because of the church link many will think there is a hidden trap and just stay away. But when such groups serve to provide a relaxed atmosphere in which Christians and non Christians can mingle, when the leadership is clearly Christian, when the church members are fully involved with everyone fulfilling their role of witness and those equipped to do so exercising the gift of evangelist, then social activity groups can provide the occasion when individuals are befriended and introduced to Christ.

2.2 Multiplying congregations

Some churches do not believe in becoming too large. They, therefore, take steps to ensure that they do not grow beyond the 'secondary level'. This is ensured through the imposition of self-limiting structures such as the seating capacity of the church premises or a restricted leadership base. Such a maintenance attitude reflects a static concept of the church. A more dynamic small church approach is for the congregation, when it grows beyond the 150–200 membership mark, to begin to think about dividing and establishing a new church elsewhere. These can be regarded as completely independent offspring, or as satellite congregations relating to a mother church which continues to provide celebration events, training facilities and personnel and financial assistance.

David Wasdell advises, 'Where the secondary group is reached, it should not be expanded into a tertiary group and destroyed in its fundamental character, rather, other secondary groups should be established. The tertiary group thus becomes a federation of secondary groupings, which in their turn may well be federations of primary sub-groups. The Church of England would appear to be strangled by its insistence on one secondary group at the heart of each parish' (Wasdell 1975:13).

An alternative approach to establishing satellite congregations is to duplicate services on the one premises in order to keep the worshipping congregations to a size in which it is still possible for people to relate to one another. If this seems the best option, it is inadvisable to attempt this by trying to divide the existing congregation into two. As with home groups, such a strategy frequently destroys the dynamic rather than stimulating further growth. Whereas previously the church was full, with the crowd serving to attract a crowd, now that the congregation has been split into two congregations meeting at different times, the church has suddenly become half-empty, and people become disheartened. To avoid this danger, the second congregation may be developed from a small nucleus of 30–40 people who have the vision and drive to involve themselves in a fresh undertaking. Should this experiment fail to get off the ground the originating group can go back to the parent congregation without any damage having been caused.

Sometimes the motivation to create a second congregation is not lack of space but the need to provide a contrasting style of worship. Some members prefer a traditional form of service, in contrast to younger people, or those with no church-going background, who prefer a more informal and spontaneous style of worship. Tension frequently arises in churches with family service in which the children are present for most or all of the time. The noise and disruptions are off-putting to older people who no longer have the patience with children that they once possessed. They find they need quiet and dignity to enable them to worship.

When services are duplicated because of numbers, or even more when alternative types of worship service are offered, careful thought must be given to the increased demand which this extra work places on the leadership. If the service is a straight repeat with only a measured output of nervous energy (as in a liturgical service with a brief, coolly-delivered message) then the one minister may be able to cope. Where there are contrasting styles of worship, requiring the minister to adjust from the quiet, predictable, formal service to the heavy demands of the lively family service or the youth service requiring a high level of energy, output, creativity, and thinking-on-your-feet, it may be necessary to appoint assistants to pastor these congregations. A multi-congregational church has the drawback of causing a degree of fragmentation. However, this is a preferable option to our impersonal crowd which is too big for people to get to know one another. Its advantage is that it enables the church to offer worship options to meet the needs of members and provide the atmosphere which they find most conducive to worship. It also calls forth a wider range of openings for leaders. The formal church choir, for instance, may not attract the gifted young folk, jazz or pop musician, while the family, youth or newcomers service will provide scope for creative talents to blossom and express themselves in a Christian context.

2.3 All-age Sunday School

So far we have considered the 'secondary group' in terms of a midweek activity group and as a Sunday congregation. The secondary group's most significant form in the North American pattern is in the all-age Sunday School. Families come to church around ten o'clock and divide into a range of classes for the first forty-five minutes to one hour. In addition to the graded classes for children and the crêches and play groups for tinies, there is a range of groups, for young marrieds, singles and senior citizens, all engaged in programmes which relate to their differing interests and stage in life. At the end of an hour all the groups come together for an act of worship with a brief inspirational message.

In Britain we have relied on week-day activities to provide secondary groupings. These supply the needs of young people, the elderly and mothers who are not able to go out to work. But they are not so effective in attracting fathers, working mothers and singles. Furthermore, lack of a regular teaching curriculum means that we have a congregation of adults who are theologically ill-equipped, spiritually undernourished and lacking the skills to apply Bible teaching to their everyday lives. Brief monologue sermons on isolated topics provide an inadequate diet of teaching, so most Christians who want to grow in their spiritual understanding have to rely on

Christian literature; hence the Christian paperback publishing boom.

In recent years a number of churches in England have responded to the problem of pioneering the all-age Sunday School. In doing so they have had to face three major problems. The first is a time constraint which is not shared in North America. Here in Britain there is a tradition of 'the Sunday roast lunch', so that many Mums have half their mind on the oven during the Sunday morning worship. Among middle-class churchgoers in the USA the tradition is to go from church to a restaurant with many going on to a 'ball game' afterwards. Most only go to church once on Sunday, so are prepared for a full Sunday morning programme.

The second problem is a serious lack of teaching materials to sustain an adult Christian education programme. These constraints probably mean that the all-age Sunday School may be most applicable to the city-centre church with resourceful members who can develop their own curricula, and provide luncheon facilities.

The third problem relates to inadequate facilities in the form of classrooms for a number of groups of up to sixty members. I am reminded of the contrast between English churches and Calvary Chapel just outside Los Angeles which has an education block the size of an English comprehensive school!

Experience in introducing the all-age Sunday School in Britain is limited, but the following points may be of help to churches contemplating such a move.

a) *Groups should not be too small*. A large percentage of the congregation will not readily be prepared to go into a primary group. The sight of seats placed round in a circle indicates that they will be expected to contribute. If people accustomed to formal church services are to be coaxed from an anonymous tertiary group into an interpersonal primary group they may find it too big a jump. As we have already indicated, attempting to push the congregation into primary groups will only succeed in driving many into rapid retreat. To encourage a high percentage of the congregation to participate, ensure that the group operate at the secondary level, with the chairs placed in an arc around the speaker. This provides the opportunity to respond without imposing an obligation to do so. The large group situation leads eventually to small group experience. 'Large groups always tend to split into smaller ones anyway if the activity they are indulging in seems to warrant it. Large groups of up to forty, fifty or more usually possess all the charisteristic bonds of smaller groups when they are moved by intense feelings or absorption in the task' (Douglas 1978:58).

b) *Don't continuously disrupt the groups*. Some churches have organised their Christian education programme according to subjects. Individuals are encouraged to sign up for the subject and the group then disbands at the end of the 'term'. This may work when such a programme has become firmly established and when people have become used to participating in small groups. But even then I have my doubts about its appropriateness for a heterogeneous congregation.

I prefer 'classes' with an element of homogeneity. People are not allocated to classes but can opt for groups according to friendship networks and age and interest groups. The group then stays together, electing what subject it wants to study each term. Individuals should be left free to transfer from one group to another should they so wish.

c) *Distinguish between the class leader and teacher*. The leader is long term. He is pastorally responsible for the group and seeks to interpret its needs. A teacher for each subject will be chosen for his competence to deal with the study. They may be drawn from the group itself or be transferred from another group for the duration of the course.

d) *Choose the themes to be studied with care.* They should be relevant to the needs of the group and pitched at the right intellectual and language level for the membership. Illustrations should be chosen to be particularly appropriate to the kind of people characteristic of the group. If the class meets immediately before worship, highly controversial subjects should be avoided as you cannot walk straight from a heated debate into worship. The emphasis should be on Bible Study. In addition it may be helpful to have a group for the elderly and people from a traditional background who like a contemplative and formal programme, consisting of devotional addresses and guided meditations or intercessions.

Another advantage of the Sunday morning all-age Sunday School is that it enables a church to have a contrasting programme for the evenings. For a long while I have puzzled over why some churches are able to sustain an evening congregation while others can do nothing effectively to combat dwindling numbers. This disparity does not seem to be satisfactorily explained by geographical location, denominational affiliation or theological emphasis. In some cases the membership content of the big evening congregation is quite different from the one in the morning. The morning congregation is locally based, while the evening is eclectic, but those attending limit their church going to a single Sunday attendance. Where churches achieve a high proportion of members who regularly attend twice on a Sunday it is almost always because they have a contrasting form of worship in the evening from the morning. There is abundant evidence that people these days will not turn out twice on Sunday for the 'same thing', whether this be Anglican morning or evening prayer or the stereotyped Free Church hymn sandwich.

2.4 Groups for men

Although figures are not available for the proportion of men among church attenders in the United Kingdom, for many churches it is in the region of one quarter to one third. Why should it be that women outnumber men? Is the explanation that women are more spiritual than men? It seems hard to justify this biblically. What then is the reason for the imbalance? I would offer the following five suggestions which either singly or in various combinations could explain the fact.

(i) In many churches, of all theological persuasions, there is a dependency style of ministry in which women are more prepared to acquiesce than are men. To rectify the situation, ministry must be regarded as the activity of the whole congregation with responsible leadership positions open to men. If men are shaping policy and deciding on courses of action at work, they are unlikely to be attracted to churches where they are blocked from contributing at this level. This area will be considered at greater length in chapter eight.

(ii) In the adult programme of most churches the organisations and teaching content are more geared to the needs of women than of men. The pulpit approach tends to be individualistic, introspective and domestic in application. Menfolk come to church with a range of work and family problems to which the church seldom addresses itself.

(iii) Men on both sides of industry face moral problems relating to their work which their wives, especially if they are at home or in part-time employment, do not face. They therefore have to weigh up the cost of Christian discipleship, which in some types of employment may be very high.

(iv) Because women are more often at home when the minister is free to do his visiting – namely during the afternoon – they are contacted more readily. This is especially the case with young wives who are unable to work while the children are on their hands due to inadequate pre-school, play group facilities. Wives therefore get together for coffee chats and invite one another to the church women's fellowships, pram services etc, and so begin to get involved while their husbands remain largely uncontacted. In some cultures the result of winning the women first is to make it all the more difficult for their husbands to follow. The women's circles are then left to pray for their unconverted husbands – as a direct result of this faulty strategy. Ways must therefore be found at an early stage to contact the husbands through other men.

(v) When a women attends church on Sunday she is far more likely than her husband to know other people in the congregation. She will have more contact with the neighbours and is more likely to belong to a 'primary ' or 'secondary group' in the church – the Mothers' Union, Women's Fellowship, Coffee Chat, Bright Hour etc. She therefore feels a sense of belonging, which her husband does not share because most likely he does not see people with whom he mixes socially on or off church premises.

In middle-class areas men can frequently be reached through home-based groups. This is especially the case where men are articulate and are accustomed to attending social functions with their wives. It is however less easy in an artisan culture where men find it difficult to join in discussion when wives are present, especially when the subject is 'religion'. In general men are less likely to be attracted to the 'talk shop' kind of meeting as distinct from the 'planning occasion'. They are more attracted to the task-orientated group or to sport pursuits. There should be not one route but many ways into membership of the local church, through a wide variety of activities. People are most likely to get involved through the avenue in which they feel they can contribute most.

One minister in a Hertfordshire parish has a novel method of contacting men effectively. His church holds a monthly evening women's meeting. Having glanced in to see who is there, he and a group of Christians then spend the evening visiting the husbands most of whom are at home child minding! In a Western culture and most difficult, yet strategically most important member of the family to win is the husband. We must therefore resist the temptation to concentrate on mothers and children as an easier option, in the hope that fathers will be won at a later stage. By concentrating more effort on reaching men there is more likelihood that complete families will be won, leading to greater family unity and stability.

Tertiary groups

Tertiary groups number 175 or more members, with no upper limit on numbers; in fact, the more the merrier. Wagner describes this as the 'celebration' level. He writes, 'One of the things a large church can do well is to celebrate. . . . When a lot of people come together hungry to meet God, a *special* kind of worship experience can occur. That experience is that I want to call "celebration" ' (Wagner 1976:97). This is a level of corporate religious experience with which most European Protestant Christians are unfamiliar. The great majority of Protestant churches are small, or if the buildings are large the congregations occupying them are depleted. In the religious sphere, unlike sporting events, we are unaccustomed to crowds. Furthermore, our remnant theology has idealised smallness so that we are suspicious of 'popular' religious events. When one speaks of the mammoth super-churches to be found in Latin America, Asia and North America, many Europeans respond negatively, declaring, 'we wouldn't want to belong to a church like that!' If we instinctively react adversely at the thought of crowds we should reflect that we are going to have to get used to crowds one day, for heaven will be crowded! John had this vision of life on the other side. 'After this I looked, and there was an enormous crowd – no one could count all the people! They were from every race, tribe, nation and language, and they stood in front of the throne and of the Lamb, dressed in white robes and holding palm branches in their hands. . . .' (Rev. 7:9).

The celebration event is not however postponed until then. It has great significance for church life today. It comes as a great surprise to many British Christians to learn that there are between seven and nine times as many people in church on Sunday as at professional soccer matches on Saturday afternoon. We do not recognise our numerical strength because we are scattered throughout 51,000 Protestant and Catholic churches in the United Kingdom, with little opportunity or inclination to gather together in strength.

3.1 Celebration expresses identity

'The individual believer must be able to feel himself a part of the larger corporate unity of the people of God' (Snyder 1975:106). Our fragmentation horizontally into different congregations and vertically into denominations has destroyed our sense of 'peoplehood'. Visitors from other congregations are treated almost as though they were adherents of another religion and no concern of ours. Loyalty to *our* church or *our* denomination can take precedence over our loyalty to Christ.

The people of God in the Old Testament preserved their identity not simply through their distinctive way of life, but through their sense of 'belonging', heightened through regular pilgrimages. In March/April as many as could make the journey went to Jerusalem for the feast of the Passover. Seven weeks later the crowds gathered once more for Pentecost, which marked the end of the grain harvest. September/October was heralded with a fanfare marking the Jewish New Year. Special celebrations were followed by the solemn Day of Atonement when the nation confessed their sin and asked for cleansing. A few days later the people observed the Festival of Shelters – a national camp-out, when they built shelters of branches to remind themselves of their wanderings in the desert and of God's provision for his people. This came at the end of the olive and grape harvests. Israel was a nation of pilgrims, not hermits. They loved to congregate to express their identity. Such gatherings helped to keep scattered clans together. This was needed in a hilly terrain which tended to divide communities. The Jews did not build bridges!

3.2 Celebration provides inspiration
It can be a moving experience to be part of an enormous crowd. When the crowds converged on Jerusalem there was a sense of occasion and expectations were heightened. The significance of the celebration event today is recognised more within the Catholic than the Protestant tradition. In Southern Europe, Poland and throughout Latin America there are popular pilgrimages. These capture the imagination of masses of people, causing hundreds of thousands to gather at popular shrines. I write these words soon after the visit of Pope John Paul II to Northern Ireland and the United States. On most days of that exhausting tour (superbly stage managed), celebration events drew crowds of between 25,000 and one million. They gave a sense of identity and provided inspiration to the Catholic community.

Yet, celebration doesn't just happen. It requires a 'charisma' of leadership. Many an ecumenical occasion has gone off like a damp squib through lack of ability to handle such an event or understand the dynamics of the occasion. The dignitaries drone on, and the choir render their anthems with esoteric detachment. Such events are endured rather than enjoyed.

For the celebration event to fulfil its inspirational role there must be a sense of occasion, with individuals gifted to hold the attention of the crowd, and musicians spiritually motivated to lift the entire gathering in worship.

Speaking of the church where he worships regularly, Lake Avenue Congregational Church, Peter Wagner declares 'that 52 times a year 2,500 people go home to

Sunday dinner feeling that they have just had a important meeting with Almighty God and that because of it they are not the same' (Wagner 76:59). He also recognises that to achieve this a great deal of work goes on behind the scenes, for good worship doesn't just happen. On this scale it normally depends on the consecrated professionalism of a lot of people with a wide range of gifts.

Here in Europe where there are very few, if any, Protestant congregations to match this size, when 'celebration' has been experienced it has been outside the local church. The Billy Graham evangelistic crusades of the fifties and sixties gave many people in Britain their first taste of worship 'en masse'. I can still remember vividly the sound of 90,000 people singing hymns in Wembley Stadium. More recently the need and appetite for celebration events have been reinforced by the popularity of the 'Come Together' worship presentations and the charismatic renewal conferences and festivals of praise.

3.3 Celebration crystallises intention

One of the reasons why 'Come Together' proved hard to follow, and why the charismatic renewal meetings are difficult to sustain, is that they lack the structure to implement the expectations aroused. The inspiration then turns either to disillusionment or fantasy. The celebration even can only serve to supplement what is happening at the grass roots level; it cannot substitute for what is not happening. Howard Snyder underlines the need for *covenant* experience which reminds us of God's faithfulness and our obligations. He describes four functions which such acts might fulfil.

1 Celebration of the acts of God. Reciting with joy and praise the acts of God in biblical history, in Jesus Christ (especially the incarnation, resurrection and Pentecost) and in the history of this particular subgroup of God's people.
2 Covenant renewal.

3 Evaluation and definition.
4 Renewal of a vision for the future (Snyder 1975:109, 110).

The problem however is to ensure that something happens after the meeting. So often in the past, people have returned to their locations to continue doing what they have always done, oblivious to the rest. What happened at the celebration left a warm glow but was as remote as a day trip to heaven!

The churches must strive for more effective structures to act at national, regional and district level. Such structures would help to earth the celebration events, which have hitherto been frustrated by isolation, individualism and mutual suspicion. Here in Britain at the present time it is hoped that the Nationwide Initiative in Evangelism backed by all the main denominations, and the Evangelism 80's programme of the Evangelical Alliance, will provide some of those structures.

3.4 Celebration restores confidence

Elijah felt that he was struggling on alone. He was unaware of the existence of 7,000 others who had not succumbed to pressure to worship Baal. If our experience of the church is limited to the one or two places where we have regularly worshipped, then we will tend to imagine that all the rest are like these – or worse! Here in the United Kingdom it is estimated that about five million people are in church on Sunday. When we make the effort to meet with the many other Christians in our area we begin to realise that we are not just a surviving handful, but a numerous army with enough manpower to make an impact on the entire nation.

3.5 Celebration establishes visiblity

The Protestant Church in Latin America is a minority movement fragmented into hundreds of factions. As such they could be ignored. However, through nationwide

Evangelism-in-Depth campaigns thousands of evangelical Christians were reported in the press and on radio and seen on television marching in procession through the streets of the capital cities. Whole nations began to waken up to the fact of the Protestant movement. In Brazil and Chile the indigenous Pentecostal movements have developed an effective structure for church growth especially suited to urban life. People are coming in their millions to the big cities in search of work, schooling and housing. These new arrivals are contacted by the church and house groups in the shanty towns and new housing developments. They are welcomed by people like themselves into those small support groups. Then at the week-end they go to the mammoth mother church where they meet tens of thousands of fellow believers. Those who have been attracted from the country by the bright lights of the city are delighted to find that the company they have joined has its prestige place among those bright lights. The 25,000 seater São Paulo Church and the 15,000 seater Jota beche Methodist Pentecostal Church give the denomination visibility. The city centre streets of the big Latin American cities are crowded during the week-end so that the Christians converging on their mother churches cannot go unnoticed.

Crowds also attract the attention of the media. Around the world hundreds of millions of people have seen the Pope address a sea of faces stretching to the horizon during one of his Papal visits. Large churches in North America use their financial resources to buy television time and their professional resources to sustain a series of programmes, which would be beyond the capacity of the small church. In some urban situations the only ways into the home are often via the television or the telephone. Home calling is rendered very difficult by the security systems installed in apartment blocks.

In the United Kingdom time cannot be bought on the commercial television channels. It can only be earned by the quality of the communication or the significance of the event. A programme of celebration events which had the whole-hearted backing and support of Christians in the regions where they were to be held would, I believe, attract media coverage, if not at national level then certainly through the local radio station and press. This would serve to replace the one-sided presentation of the outmoded, irrelevant and dwindling Church so often portrayed in current affairs and light entertainment programmes.

For the church of two hundred plus members, 'celebration' level of worship can be experienced at congregational level, provided that is not dispersed in a seven-hundred-and-fifty-seater building. Most European and North American churches have a membership below the two hundred level. This being the case, the 'celebration' event has to be staged at a multi- congregational level, organised denominationally or ecumenically. One town in Kent which has run a programme of such meetings on a Saturday night once a month from time to time attracted a crowd of 600–900 people. On one occasion the police station rang the organisers to be kept informed of future meetings so that they could provide traffic control!

The celebration level becomes significant when a fresh surge of spiritual vitality is being experienced within the local church, when churches are open to each other to be mutually encouraged by each other's faith (Rom 1:11, 12), and when they have a united evangelistic vision to share the Good News with their locality. But if these conditions have not developed then the celebration can prove more of a diversion than provide a dynamic.

4 Incorporating newcomers into membership

It is not sufficient for growing churches simply to establish a three-tier system of primary, secondary and tertiary groups and then just leave individuals to find their way around. There needs to be a clearly defined structure which shows how the various groups relate to one another in the achievement of overall objectives. Each group must see its own specialist contribution within the context of a wider strategy and framework. The leaders must have a vision which reaches beyond their group activities, otherwise the groups will begin to compete and this will only serve to fragment the church's life rather than provide the building-blocks.

All the groups should be seeking to enable the people they are attracting to eventually become responsible members of the church. How this objective is pursued will depend on the nature of the group. The question which churches with more than 120 members need to face is, 'To what extent do our structures act as a maze to confuse and divert people, rather than a channel which leads them into the heart of the fellowship and into a personal relationship with Christ as Saviour and Lord?'

The diagram on page 298 (Fig. 19) represents a congregational structure which is commonly found in the United Kingdom. After studying the model, make any necessary adaptation to fit your particular church. The numbered arrows on the diagram represent the various points of entry into your church life. Each of these should be studied carefully from the vantage point of the newcomer. From within the groups, the point of entry might seem as easy to cross as a chalk line drawn on the pavement, while for the outsider the barrier to entry might seem as daunting as the Berlin Wall.

Think of specific individuals who have come to one of your activity groups (Arrow 1, secondary), or who have been invited to a home group (Arrow 2, primary), or who have simply turned up at a Sunday service (Arrow 3, secondary or tertiary, depending on the size of the congregation). Ask yourself three simple questions regarding each person:

1 What was meant to happen to incorporate them into the worship, fellowship and witness of the church? Do you have any clearly defined procedures for incorporating new members?

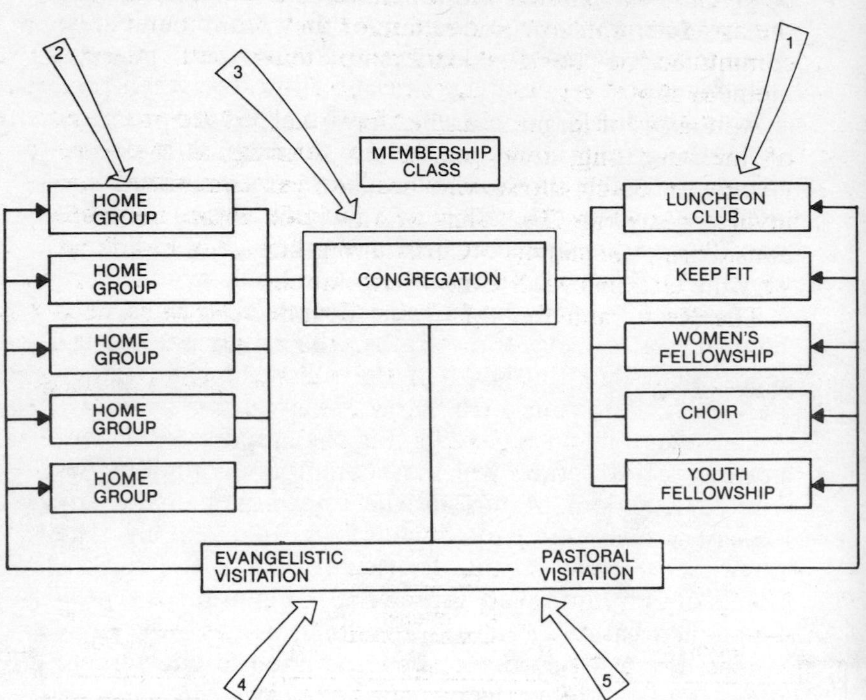

Fig. 19
How are potential members contacted?

2 What happened to them in practice? Assuming you have laid down procedures, are they effective?
3 How can you improve on the effectiveness of your approach?

Then do the same exercise with respect to those who have been contacted during the course of your evangelistic (Arrow 4) or pastoral visitation programmes (Arrow 5).

Should the results of your investigation prove to be disappointing, showing that people are getting locked into the small groups, lost in the crowd or are being allowed to drift off unnoticed, then urgent attention will need to be given to the church's new members procedures. Either the arrangements are inadequate or they have been badly communicated to the leadership team and general membership.

A number of larger churches have tackled the problem of incorporating new people by forming a *Welcome Group* to which those who are not yet committed are invited (see Fig. 20). This will include those who are considering the claims of Christ upon their lives and those who have transferred from other churches.

The Rev. Paul Berg of Christ Church, Clifton, a resi-

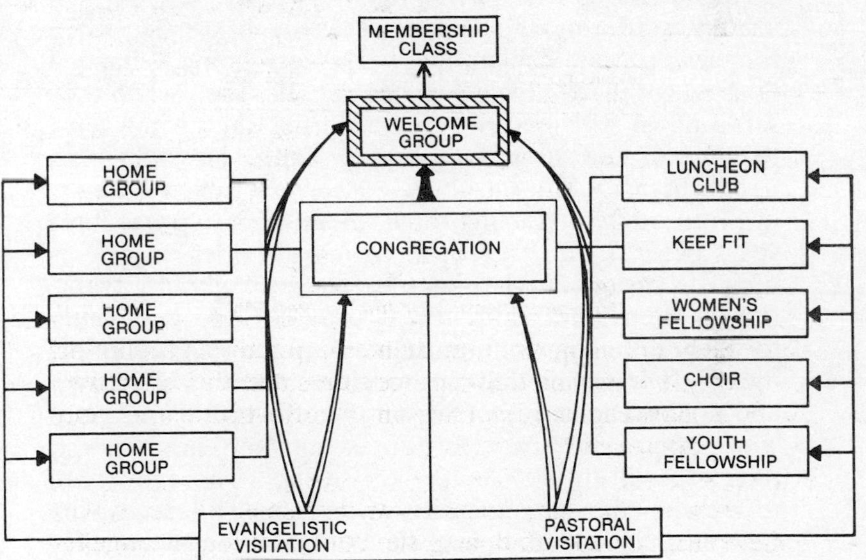

Fig. 20
How do potential members join?

dential suburb of Bristol, runs eight such Christian Basics Groups a year which have resulted in a steady trickle of enquirers. These then go on to a beginners group before being integrated into one of the neighbourhood groups. A similar scheme is operated at St Thomas's, Crookes, an inner city district of Sheffield. The Rev. Robert Warren reports that they run five six-week courses a year with an average attendance of between twelve and fifteen. The new members are then introduced to one of their twenty-four area-based home groups.

In what ways does the Welcome Group differ from the Membership Class? It provides an immediate 'half-way house' for the enquirer who is not yet at the stage of wanting to commit himself. There are those who were baptised in infancy and formally received into membership in adolescence without any personal commitment. Soon afterwards they quickly fell away to live in a spiritual wilderness during the disruptive years of 18–28, when they went from college to work, left home, changed houses, got married and began a family. Then when they settle down with family responsibilities they come back to church, and come to personal faith. How do such people *join* their local church when they have already been through denominational membership procedures years before? The Welcome Group provides an opportunity to re-lay foundations. As for those who are transferring from other churches, it provides an opportunity for them to familiarise themselves with the spiritual priorities of their new church and to learn abouts its objectives and organisations. New Christians in the group and those who come to faith or wish to make further enquiries can then proceed to the Membership Class. Those restored to membership or who transfer from elsewhere can be welcomed immediately into the congregation by publicly extending the right hand of fellowship.

Considering the high lapse rate in many churches, as much emphasis needs to be placed on their restoration as on contacting non-members. Lyle Schaller suggests four ways of strengthening the notion of membership (Schaller 1978b:219, 220).

1 Treat the transfer of members as a celebration event and not just a paper routine. The new person or family should be publicly welcomed.
2 Each member is asked to come forward and publicly reaffirm his membership vows annually.
3 Establish a probationary membership which is a preliminary step before achieving full membership.
4 Develop clearly stated expectations of the responsibility of membership in that congregation in operational terms.

The Rev. Jeffrey Yates of Bamford Chapel, a United Reformed Church near Rochdale, Lancs. also lays great stress on clear new members procedures. His church, located in a growing middle-class area, sees a high level of response as a result of their house-to-house visitation programme, their range of recreational activities and lively Sunday services. During the past four years 250 people have come into the church, seventy of whom had no previous church membership. They are prepared for membership in classes led by the minister. As an additional point of contact four new couples are invited to the manse once a month.

As we saw in the previous chapter there does seem to be a correlation between church growth and the existence of primary groups. However, with few exceptions it seems that the new church members are not being recruited by these groups. Rather, the groups provide the opportunity for the Christian community to develop so that when they gather on Sunday there is a new quality of friendliness, acceptance, trust and 'family feeling'. This sense of community communicates itself to the newcomer who then wants to come again on another Sunday and eventually gets further involved, until he also finds himself within a primary or secondary group.

Most groups have not proved effective so far in the area of evangelism because they consist of groups of long-standing church members with a programme designed to meet their needs. These may not be appropriate for the enquirer or beginner in the Christian life. The best group for the nurture of the new believer is a group composed largely of people who are just starting out.

New churches which have grown through neighbourhood groups eventually find that these groups have moved so far away from 'base' that they have opened up a communication gap and as a result they no longer attract new people so readily. There are two ways around this problem. One is to hold the occasional evangelistic group meeting, with any converts then being escorted to the 'Welcome Group' for the duration of the course and then brought back into the group where having been given the basic they will be better able to cope. The other way is to be continually forming new groups of new Christians led by people who can relate to the perceptions and problems which they face.

5 *Evangelism at all three levels*

We conclude this chapter with a brief look at the evangelistic significance of the primary, secondary and tertiary groups, for each has a distinctive role to play in a total evangelistic strategy.

5.1 Evangelism in primary groups

The small neighbourhood group can provide an ideal base for contact visiting, that is, identifying the seekers, and also for the following-up of contacts in a home visitation programme. For this to happen, church members in these groups must have both concern for and contact with their neighbours. Regrettably many churches have an over-full programme based on a 'come-to-us' philosophy which keeps their committed people so busy that they have no time to develop friendships in their immediate community. A large church has the advantage of providing a full and varied programme, but church members must be disciplined enough to be selective, and in particular, to resist pressure to support those activities which appear to have long since outlived their usefulness.

Primary groups which have been preoccupied solely with the spiritual nurture and social intercourse of the existing membership need to be gently but firmly challenged to face their evangelistic responsibilities. Within every group each member is called to fulfil the role of witness. The group must also seek to discover whether one of more of their members appears to have the gift of evangelist. If not, then it may be necessary to import someone who is gifted in this area to be present when they hold an evangelistic event.

Evangelism in a small group situation is most appropriate among people with whom we have had previous contact and experience a measure of compatibility. The people we decide to invite may be either neighbours or work colleagues, etc. When the small group consists of complete strangers it is extremely difficult to break the ice and to conduct a conversation at a deeply personal level.

Conversely, where people know one another, the small group situation provides a positive, informal atmosphere for frank speaking.

While the overall programme for the outreach meeting should be informal and flexible, it is advisable to have a well-thought-out conversation opener. Some begin with a brief statement, lasting for no more than ten minutes, of the central issues to be discussed, after which opinions are invited leading into a dialogue situation. This part of the programme may either be conducted by a spokesman for the group or be in the hands of an invited, outside speaker. Others prefer to base their discussion on a specific passage of Scripture. If this approach is adopted it is essential that ever one in the group has the same version of the Bible so that page numbers can be given, and people are not confused by chapters and verses and a variety of renderings. Instead of using whole Bibles some groups have individual Gospels or even brief Scripture selection leaflets for use in such evangelistic groups. The advantage of this approach is that invited non-Christians can then take the booklets or pamphlets home with them to continue to consider the passage studied at the meeting.

When basing the evangelistic programme on a text of Scripture it is important to let the passage speak for itself. Rather than drawing up a list of prepared questions, an alternative approach is simply to ask individuals in the group to say what the passage has said to them. Having invited one person to express an opinion or voice a response, find out from others in the group if the passage made the same impact on them. This avoids the problem of posing questions to which there is a 'right' or 'wrong' answer or which introduce issues which are of no immediate concern among the individuals present.

One rapidly growing house fellowship considered that one of the secrets of their success in attracting new people was their refusal to precipitate an 'us' and 'them' situation. They included newcomers as 'insiders', leaving them to discover for themselves that they had not yet arrived at the point of commitment or level of experience described by others in the group. By that time they had picked up enough knowledge to make a meaningful decision.

The handling of evangelism in small groups requires particular leadership skills and sensitivity on the part of Christians in the group. In order to avoid any appearance of undue pressure the non-Christians should outnumber the Christians present. Some people with experience in this field would also recommend that the meeting be held in the home of an interested person who was not yet a committed Christian or church member. It is important that the Christians present be as ready to listen attentively as to speak themselves. We must look for opportunities to affirm all that the other person is saying and not merely look for points of confrontation. When people come to groups aware of their personal needs, they are not so much looking for answers to their problems as for people who can help them. The great advantage of the small group is that it provides the opportunity for two-way communication on the basis of shared experience.

Only occasionally do individuals come to the act of commitment to Christ during the actual meeting. It is therefore important to conclude the programme at the pre-arranged time, allowing opportunity for those who want to talk further to do so. This may be the time when someone will take the life-changing step of faith. Others may come to the point of decision during a subsequent contact when members of the group are in personal conversations with an invited person.

It is important not to overstep the mark in our eagerness to influence our neighbour and friends for Christ. We must always leave the conversation where we can take it up again on a subsequent occasion. Those with little or no contact with the Christian message and community may take months or years to be won. We must therefore think in terms of both a short and long-term strategy.

5.2 Evangelism in secondary groups

The small face-to-face primary group may not provide the best environment into which to invite the comparative stranger, or be suitable in areas where it is not the custom to open one's home to the neighbourhood. Furthermore, some people would recoil at the thought of being exposed in a small group. They may find conversation difficult or are fearful of their ignorance being exposed. This, incidentally, is one reason why those who are long-time office bearers in the church but have little understanding of the fundamentals of the faith and no personal commitment to Jesus Christ as Lord, keep at a safe distance!

For both the types of people mentioned above the secondary group may provide a more relaxed and gradual pathway to Christian commitment. People are invited to join with Christians to engage in activities which already interest them. As they work and play alongside each other, openings will eventually arise during the course of conversation for personal testimony in specific areas of life and for an explanation of the content of the Good News.

The secondary group is small enough for personal relationships to develop between members and for subgroups to form spontaneously. Yet the secondary group is also large enough for the new person not to feel himself the focus of attention. He can therefore progress at his own pace. Many people in coming to faith do not follow a steady path of progress. Usually they fluctuate, taking three steps forward and two back. Sometimes they may encounter a 'sticking-point', and if too much pressure is applied to drag them forward they may turn tail. Such long-term response patterns are more easily handled in the larger group with which the individual can merge.

In order that a secondary group may realise its evangelistic potential the leader must exercise pastoral care over the members who in turn must function effectively in their role of witness. Furthermore, at least one person in the group should have the gift of evangelist.

St Thomas's Church, Aldridge on a housing development in Walsall just north of Birmingham, has established an effective method of following up contacts made at church-based secondary groups and baptism and wedding contacts. They arrange for two and three-person teams of Christian lay people to visit enquirers in their homes to conduct a Christian Basics Course, which lasts for six weeks. The minister, Rev. Michael Wooderson reports that eighty of his 120 members have so far taken part. At the time of writing they have used their course with 120 individuals representing seventy-two homes. Of seventy-nine people who made a commitment to Christ, only five have lapsed, and fourteen have left the area, hopefully to join up with churches elsewhere.

Other growing churches operate a similar home visitation scheme among their fringe contacts using the Evangelism Explosion gospel presentation and lay-training scheme. The Rev. John Banner of Christ Church, Liverpool has seen between eighty and a hundred respond to this approach. Of this number he estimates that approximately one third have so far come into church membership. This reflects something of the cultural distance between the church and the community experienced in an artisan situation. One other church in comparable social situations using the Evangelism Explosion methods reports a similar percentage response rate. For churches in middle-class locations the commitment rate is generally much higher.

5.3 Evangelism in the tertiary groups

Some people who shrink from contact either with a primary or secondary group are prepared to listen while lost in a big crowd. They wish, for the time being at any rate, to be left alone to come to their own conclusions. Then there are those who are impressed by the colourful, big-scale event, because they are gregarious by nature or larger-than-life personalities. Such people are more likely to respond to the 'celebration event'. Such occasions provide the opportunity for church members to invite their personal friends to something out of the ordinary, and for the church to circularise the institutional fringe. Within the community at large a well-publicised celebration event makes an impression, rouses curiosity and becomes a topic of conversation. Such an impression is considerably enhanced by good media coverage.

However, effective celebration evangelism depends upon widespread support from the local churches. It must be a scaled-up version of what they are regularly doing at local level. If the celebration event is no more than a substitute for, rather than a supplement to what should be happening in individual congregations, then it will prove to be an expensive diversion. Regrettably this has been the case in much of our experience in mass evangelism in Britain during the last thirty years. Nevertheless, when such events are an integral part of an ongoing strategy they can play a highly significant role.

Large churches which operate Sunday by Sunday at the celebration level need to give a great deal of careful thought as to how the visitor is to be identified and welcomed and how the enquirer is to be followed up. In this area many of the large churches in the United States are more efficient than their European counterparts. It is the custom in some for everyone present to fill in an attendance card, so that absentees can be spotted and newcomers identified. New people are then contacted by phone during the next twenty-four hours and visited that week by a lay person in the church. I know of no church on this side of the Atlantic which has succeeded in persuading church attenders to fill up a card on a regular basis.

Some larger churches do invite visitors to fill up a Visitor's Card with varying degrees of success. Where the system is adopted the minister making the invitation should hold up the card to identify that piece of paper he is referring to. The card should be readily available in the pew or on the seat. If the system proves to be effective it is recommended that the cards be kept tidily in a special holder on the pew lodge or seat back to prevent becoming dog-eared or buried under the hymn-books, pew Bibles and service sheets. The wording needs to be friendly and minimal. One church has devised the following wording:

We are a large family, and it's easy to get lost in the crowd. Please help us to get to know you by supplying your name, address and telephone number.

Name ....

Address ....

Tel. No. ....

We sincerely hope that you have enjoyed worshipping with us.

Having filled in the card the visitor must be given clear instructions as to what to do with it. If it is to be handed to the stewards (or sidesmen), they should wear an identifying badge, and be given training in what to do when they are handed a card. They should welcome the visitor warmly and introduce him to another member of the congregation with whom he is most likely to have something in common. An increasing number of churches follow their services with coffee, which provides a further ready-made opportunity for a newcomer to be introduced to other church members.

The visitor's card should be left in the vestry or parish office for the minister to see and for it to be handed ultimately to the appropriate home-group leader in those churches which have area home groups. It then becomes his responsibility to establish contact that week, to chat about the various activities which may be relevant to the needs of that person, and possibly to extend an invitation to the home meeting; although, except for the most keen, this should probably be postponed to a subsequent visit. People don't like feeling that they are being stampeded. And if they represent the 'cool fringe' they may need to learn some Christian basics before being launched into the home meeting programme. The Welcome Group might be the most appropriate next step.

In order that the church leadership may be aware of new people joining the church and provide an opportunity to meet them, St Andrew's, Chorleywood, in the North London commuter belt, has initiated an evening occasion when those who have linked up with the church during the past year are invited to a reception to meet the clergy and the Parochial Church Council and to hear about the church, its activities and its plans for the future. This occasion is valued as much by the council members as by the newcomers.

Evangelism also has its rightful place within the main worship service. Occasions such as Christmas, Easter, Mothering Sunday, Harvest and Remembrance Day provide opportunities for a clear and winsome presentation of the claims of Christ to people who are unlikely to be in church at other times of the year. Four days before writing these words I was with the Rev. John Delight of St Mary the Virgin, Aldridge. To a packed Remembrance Day congregation he spoke of man's desire for peace and of that peace which the world cannot comprehend but which Christ alone can offer. If people wanted to know more they were invited to take a leaflet which outlined how to know God's peace. Forty people asked for one on their way out. Many people come to church uttering a silent cry for help, yet leave without being given the opportunity to be heard.

Evangelism should be built into the church's programme at every level, using a variety of methods, so that by the use of all means we might at least succeed in saving some.

6 An example of a comprehensive urban strategy

For the urban church to sustain growth it must learn the art of generating cells, gathering them into congregation, and providing growth-orientated leadership. This is the pattern of church growth in such places as South Korea, Brazil and Chile. Aware of this dynamic, the Anglican diocese of Auckland, New Zealand has set up an imaginative scheme to plant churches in the city of Auckland which between 1966 and 1986 will grow in population from 550,000 to 1,200,000.

Each neighbourhood of 3,500–4,000 people, it is intended, will have their own resident, self-supporting priest. One of his priority tasks will be to foster indigenous leadership in the house churches. When groups are formed they will meet in the community primary school for services. Each congregation will be encouraged to set its own goals. With no buildings to maintain it will be free to concentrate on its missionary responsibilities and pastoral opportunities.

The town planners have grouped six to eight neighbourhood areas into *District Shopping Centres*, which will each serve 25–30,000 people. Each of these will in turn have a parish church to serve as a resource enabler to the neighbourhoods and house churches. They will also provide a base for the ethnic groups of the area – Maori, Tongan, Samoan, Tokoluan, Ninean and Cook Islanders. At the moment this scheme is still in an experimental stage.

Manukau City is the administrative centre of South Auckland and is designated a *Sub-Regional Shopping Centre*. Its population will grow from 230,000 to 400,000. The church is determined that the denominations should not vie with each other, investing vast sums in building projects. They have therefore combined on a project to minister to the special needs of a commercial centre. 'The day the city centre commercial area of over 800,000 sq. ft. was inaugurated, Friendship House, two prefabricated houses joined together by a wide attractive entrance foyer, was opened for business. A temporary building, attractive and functional, adjacent to the site chosen for the permanent building, this centre already tells a moving story in its first year of operation' (Buckle: 1978:15).

Here is a bold plan to overcome the twin problems of parochialism and separatism which hinder the development of a comprehensive urban strategy here in the United Kingdom. The missing element in the report is the need for the Celebration Event to provide cohesion and inspiration to the new groups and to establish visibility in the total community. One longs that this might be just one of many attempts at strategic thinking.

7 *Summary*

This chapter has argued in some detail the need for appropriate and extendable structures to facilitate growth. Churches with a regular attendance of more than sixty must begin to develop primary small-group structures. Congregations of more than 150 must pay close attention to the need for secondary in addition to primary groupings. They may decide to plant new churches or to subdivide the existing congregation into several worship educational and fellowship groups. If it fails to develop an adequate structure it will end up with an increasing proportion coming in semi-anonymity to the Sunday worship without making relationships with others in the church, which will be to their own spiritual detriment and that of the church. The desire for and experience of renewal does not obviate the need for facilitating structures. Our structures should reflect the faces and shape of our fellowship.

Examine your congregational roll to ascertain how many are in primary and secondary groupings. Are the groups to which they belong enabling them to identify their gifts and to contribute to one of more of the many ministries of your church? Who are excluded from any of the groups, and for what reasons? How many of your groups have proved to be effective avenues into the fellowship of your church in the past year? Let us seek ways of realising the growth potential of groups in the life of the church in the coming months.

CHAPTER EIGHT

Equipping and mobilising

CHURCH GROWTH CANNOT be sustained unless the laity are mobilised to fulfil their distinctive ministries both in the Church and the world. The problem of how to motivate and sustain lay participation concerns many, if not the majority, of church leaders. Someone has indelicately commented that the trouble with the Church as a body is that it is all mouth and bottom! The majority of church members have little understanding of their place and function as members within the body of Christ. For them belonging to a church means turning up, singing up and paying up, and that's about it. Developing an adequate theology of the laity is an urgent task which faces the Church. Nothing less than a lay people's liberation movement will be adequate to release the Church's manpower resources to meet the challenges and opportunities in the world today.

The missionary and ecumenical theologian Hendrik Kraemer observes that while the Reformation emphasised the doctrine of the priesthood of all believers, it failed to give the concept an ongoing practical expression. 'In spite of the fact that the layman's place of responsibility in the church and the principle of the universal priesthood of believers were strong ingredients in the Reformation Movement, in respect of Continental Europe it is largely true that, after the consolidation of the Reformation in various countries, the laity receded into the background and the ministry or clergy, although with different motivations and in different forms, was again established as the "office" and body which represent the Church' (Kraemer 1958:25). We might add that this clericalism was not restricted to Continental Europe but crept through Britain as well. The priest moved from the altar to the pulpit, but the people remained undisturbed in their pews!

From the Catholic side Yves Congar also emphasises the priestly and apostolic role of the whole people of God. 'Lay people, each one according to the conditions of his life and his state in the Mystical Body, truly bring something to God's Temple and help to build it up. It is in and through the life of the faithful (and of the clergy as members of the faithful) that Christ's saving powers are made manifest within the dimensions of history and of the world, so as to bring back to God all the richness of his creation, of which Christ is the first-born and the king' (Congar 1959:109). He views ministry both in the traditional Catholic framework of a clericalised hierarchy (the warp) and as the collectivity of the faithful (making up the weft of the fabric of ministry). By this means he endeavours to integrate the ministry of the laity, avoiding the tendency of the hierarchy to reduce them to a mere appendix. Specifically in relation to gifts Congar writes, 'In some of his finest passages St Paul shows each of the faithful members active according to the diversity of his gifts, for the benefit of all the members of the whole Body (Rom. 12:4–8; 1 Cor. 12:4–14; Eph. 4:7–12,16). Thus the body is built up, the purpose of each one's gift being simply to ensure the growth of the body by promoting the growth of its members, each in himself for the benefit of all (Eph. 4:11–16). What each has, all have, intended indeed for his personal life but also and inseparably for the life and service of others' (Congar 1959:318,319).

As a consequence of the contribution of the lay apostolic movement 'Catholic Action' and the influence of Congar among other Catholic theologians, the role of the laity found its way on to the agenda of the Second Vatican

Council. 'This was the first time in the history of the Church that a council had concerned itself with lay people as such' (Schillebeeckx 1973:106). In the resulting document, *The Dogmatic Constitution on the Church*, lay people are described as 'all Christian believers outside the members of the priesthood of holy orders and of the religious state recognised by the church; those Christian believers namely who have been embodied into Christ by baptism and set up as the people of God, who participate in Christ's priestly, prophetic and royal office in their own way and who consequently for their part carry out the mission of the whole Christian people in the church and in the world' (4,31). We see here a significant move away from a paternalistic attitude towards the laity, with a growing recognition of their importance if the Church is to fulfil her mission in the world.

With such an emphasis placed upon the laity in both Protestant and Catholic theology how is it that the majority of lay people still keep to the side-lines?

1 Why people are reluctant to get involved

There are a variety of reasons for the serious lack of lay participation in many churches. In attempting to deal with this problem, ministers and church councils must be prepared to face the causes within their particular situation. The views not only of the clergy but also of the lay leaders must be taken into account, and the situation must be perceived from the perspective of those who 'follow' (and maybe are excluded from participation) as well as from the appointed leadership. An accurate and balanced assessment can only be reached by examining the situation from all sides, in an open and frank spirit. In order to create a positive atmosphere in which there is the possibility of changes for the better, people must be as ready to affirm one another's strengths as to expose weaknesses. Frank speaking is a characteristic of true friendship. 'A friend means well, even when he hurts you. But when an enemy puts his arm around your shoulder – watch out!' (Prov. 27:6).

The following represent the principal causes of lack of lay involvement:

1.1 *The majority of the congregation have not yet placed their lives under the lordship of Jesus Christ.* This is the problem of 'nominality' which to some degree or other afflicts almost all churches. Nominal Christians are Christians in name only. They are second, third, or fourth generation Christians without a personal experience of God's saving grace. They are present in church largely for reasons of historical association or cultural conformity rather than out of personal commitment. They lack a basis of belief and a vital personal faith. In such a situation there will be no spiritually significant growth until the minister provides a sound basis of biblical teaching, coupled to a life-related, personal challenge to commitment. If the minister is failing to obtain a response he must ask whether the cause is in the way he is endeavouring to communicate. 'Am I achieving truth with impact?' Or is the cause located in the rebellious wills of his hearers? 'I hear what you are saying. It makes sense to me in my situation. But it's not for me.' Some people have heard and resisted for so long they become 'gospel hardened' – a common condition to be found in many churches of an evangelical tradition. Rarely, if ever, does the preacher experience a hundred per cent acceptance of his message. But the effective communicator seeks to understand the reasons which underlie the attitudes of his audience to his message.

1.2 *Many churchgoers undervalue the corporate nature of the Christian faith.* This is especially true for Western Christians for whom religion is essentially a personal and private matter. People must be encouraged to establish relationships with other members in the body before they can begin to function through the fulfilment of a role within the life of the Christian community. It is usually a futile exercise to try and encourage people to do a job in the church through a general announcement to the congregation when the majority of those listening to the exhortation are on little more than nodding acquaintanceship with each other. Relationship precedes function. As people feel accepted so they gain in confidence to contribute.

1.3 *Many churches have no clearly defined aims and in consequence no cohesive programme*. Some congregations would be hard pressed if asked to give an agreed statement on the reason for their existence. Their activities serve to conceal a lack of purpose rather than to achieve one. 'A congregation without specific goals may be compared to an apathetic football team engaged in a "game" on a field without goal lines. The players are content to kick and pass the ball but no one tries to score. If one were to cross the line where the goal ought to be no one would be sufficiently interested to record the points' (Curry 1968:63). The participants in a 'kick-around' become disinterested after a time, and such an activity is unlikely to attract others to see what is happening and to move from the touch-line on to the field of play.

1.4 *Lay people may not be convinced of the relevance of the church's programme or of its chances of success*. Many churches saunter along with pedestrian programmes which lack imagination and challenge. People of ability and vision feel frustrated and don't want to get involved. This is especially the case in churches where the leaders insist on repeating events which have not worked in the past either because they have shut their eyes to the results or haven't bothered to consider them. No one wants to be identified with a lost cause. Those with the insight to see what will not work and to appreciate why it will not need to get alongside those with vision to picture what might work, and to redirect those with dedication from the futile to the more promising!

Sometimes the obstacle lies more in the absence of leadership skills than in the inadequacy of the programme ideas. If this is the case then the church must take urgent steps to extend its base of leadership.

1.5 *Lay people may be discouraged by their ministers from taking leadership initiative.* There are some clergy who regard themselves as omnicompetent and resent any lay initiative. They regard the congregation as little more than customers and consumers, whom they are called to satisfy. Members who do become involved are largely confined to practical matters relating to the running of the church as an institution and the care of its property. They have little place in formulating policies, or in establishing objectives with regard to the spiritual ministries of the church. Their expertise is regarded as being principally in such areas as property maintenance, raising funds and running organisational activities.

1.6 *Lay people may be excluded by the established lay leadership from joining their number.* This is especially so in small churches which can often be dominated by a small tight-knit group of powerful personalities. As the church tries to develop, it may attract for a while people who are more able and consequently pose a challenge to the existing leadership. Instead of welcoming those with leadership gifts the church committee or board of deacons closes ranks. The newcomers are thereby relegated to the sidelines and may eventually move elsewhere where their gifts will be recognised and used and their desire to contribute can be satisfied.

1.7 *Lay people may be reluctant to get involved because they fear that their willingness will be abused.* Many churches find themselves having to sustain a programme which is too large for their available manpower. The short-cut expedient to deal with the situation is to make yet more demands on the already over-committed. Such a practice is self-defeating in the long term. Not only does it exhaust those who shoulder the additional responsibilities; it also warns off those who might otherwise have offered their services, but who suspect that they in turn would end up in the same situation.

2 The resources which the Lord supplies

If the church is to grow and move forward in effective mission, then it must solve the unemployment problem within its ranks. It must deal with the underlying causes whether they be in the area of clerical domination or lay abdication. It is not that jobs do not exist or that there is no work to be done. The church urgently needs to mobilise its manpower to tackle more effectively its global commission. Lloyd Perry exhorts the clergy, 'We must learn to look at the laity as people of potential rather than people with problems' (1977:106). People with problems help the minister to feel wanted. To regard them as people with potential might make him consider them as a threat. Despite all the teaching of the New Testament on ministry as the function of the total membership there is still a persistent tendency to make a dichotomy between the sacred and the secular. The 'spiritual' ministry is the concern of the clergy, while the 'practical matters' are largely cared for by the laity.

As we have already seen, often where there is lay initiative and a desire to get involved the way for them to do this may be blocked. 'Laymen are often disillusioned, dissatisfied and disorientated, because they cannot figure out how to become vitally involved in a church which appears to be merely struggling to survive rather than seeking to fulfil a God-given mission' (Lloyd Perry 1977:107). It is our concern in this chapter to seek ways to identify and bring together in a creative relationship the full range of resources that God has bestowed upon his church so that it can function imaginatively and effectively.

The Lord has not left it to his Church to generate her own resources. From the moment of his ascension into Heaven he did not expect his followers to go it alone. They had more than the stimulus of their fading memories to rely upon, and those whom they would recruit would be given more than second-hand evidence. The fact is that the Lord keeps in vital day-to-day contact with the entire operation because he is present with them by his Holy Spirit. For this reason he had instilled in his disciples that it was to their advantage that he was going away (John 16:7). In the future he would be with them far more intimately and universally, because his Spirit would indwell every believer. In practical terms this stupendous truth means that the risen Lord is not merely master-minding a grand strategy at Supreme Headquarters level, but is also present with the smallest group and the most isolated individual.

The Holy Spirit is able to fill each believer and every Christian community with power so that they can become channels for the implementation of the divine will. Such first-hand experience will enable them to become prime witnesses to a doubting, questioning and accusing world. They will bear witness to the fact of the Lord's crucifixion and resurrection as recorded by apostolic testimony, and from their own experience they will speak of the power of the gospel at work in their own lives (Acts 1:8). They will both point people to Christ and invite them to join their company. A spirit-filled community is able to communicate powerfully. But for the Church to fulfil adequately such a witnessing role it must be able to speak from first-hand experience. 'What we have seen and heard we announce to you also, so that you will join with us in the fellowship that we have with the Father and with his Son Jesus Christ' (1 John 1:3). The 'fellowship' of which John speaks is much more than human comradeship, it is the communion in the Holy Spirit, who indwells each member, and binds them together as adopted children in the family of God (Rom. 8:16; Gal. 4:6).

2.1 The Holy Spirit shapes our character

The evidence of the presence of the Holy Spirit in a person's life is to be seen not primarily in sensational exploits but in Christ-like character and conduct. His instantaneous work of regeneration is followed by his gradual, progressive work of sanctification. This character formation is described as 'the fruit of the Spirit' in Galatians 5:22. His life within us produces discernible qualities. Paul lists these as, 'love, joy, peace, patience, kindness, goodness, faithfulness, gentleness and self-control' (Gal. 5:22,23 NIV). Such qualities are in marked contrast to the 'works of the flesh' which Paul identifies in the verses immediately preceding.

Fruit tells us two things about a tree. First, it enables us to identify what kind of tree it is. Many people may fail to recognise an apple tree by the shape of the leaf, or the appearance of the blossom. But all doubt is removed when the fruit begins to form. The appearance of the apples enables the least expert to identify it unmistakably as an apple tree. That is also the way to tell a true prophet from a false one, according to our Lord's teaching. 'Watch out for false prophets. They come to you in sheep's clothing, but inwardly they are ferocious wolves. By their fruit you will recognise them. Do people pick grapes from thornbushes, or figs from thistles?' (Matt. 7:16,17 NIV). The clear answer is 'No'. Secondly, the appearance of the fruit tells us something about the health of the tree. A well-nourished tree produces an abundant crop of large, juicy fruit. A diseased tree produces unhealthy and inedible fruit. 'Likewise every good tree bears good fruit, but a bad tree bears bad fruit. A good tree cannot bear bad fruit, and a bad tree cannot bear good fruit. Every tree that does not bear good fruit is cut down and thrown into the fire. Thus, by their fruit you will recognise them.' (Matt. 7:17–20).

It is no wonder then that the letters of the New Testament lay such great stress on the character of the Christian and on the personal qualities which are essential for Christian leadership (1 Tim. 3; Titus 1). The fruit of the Holy Spirit provides the Christian's mark of identity and guarantee of authenticity.

The fruit is the evidence of the 'abundant life' which Christ came to give (John 10:10). Such life cannot simply be contained by the tree, it must burst out in fruit. This represents the give-away life of the Church. It is life which others can pick and sample. The fruit contains the seeds which can in turn germinate in the receptive soil of other people's lives. Without such fruit the Church's activism may produce congregational enlargement but it will not be authentic church *growth*. Above all else growth depends on the quality of life. A barren tree may succeed in gathering birds on the leaves of its activism, but it will never produce saplings, for that requires seed-bearing fruit.

While Peter does not use Paul's phrase, 'fruit of the Holy Spirit' he has a similar list of qualities which are the evidence of 'God's divine power'. Having listed them he goes on to say, 'These are the qualities you need, and if you have them in abundance, they will make you active and effective in your knowledge of our Lord Jesus Christ' (2 Pet. 1:3–8). The secret of effectiveness lies not in a frenzy of activity but in the fruit of character. Mission is not issuing an invitation to passers-by to inspect and pick their own fruit! The coming of the Holy Spirit stirred the Church into action. It was to take the initiative. Its first members were enlisted in a seek and find mission. Their starting point was local and their target universal. They were to go to all peoples everywhere (Matt. 28:19). They were to work outwards from Jerusalem, to the surrounding province of Judaea, then northwards to Samaria and then in all directions 'to the ends of the earth' (Acts 1:8).

Whether the journey is one of three yards to the nextdoor neighbour or one of three thousand miles to the edges of the known world, the most difficult part of the journey is always the last eighteen inches. It is at the point of eye-ball to eye-ball confrontation that we either succeed or fail.

Many churches and individual Christians today suffer a severe loss of nerve when they find themselves in the front line. It is then that we realise that we do not have a sufficient grasp of the essentials of the message we are called to explain, neither do we have an adequate first-hand testimony to its effectiveness in our lives. If our individual and corporate lives do not bear close inspection then we want to keep people at bay. In saying this, we must recognise that what people are looking for is not perfection but reality. When individual believers and local churches are filled with the Spirit of God they are propelled into the world and attract others from the world. There is both mission and magnetism, a centrifugal and a centripetal movement.

2.2 The Holy Spirit equips us for service

Ministry, as envisaged in the New Testament, is not the prerogative of one man, or an élite corps. Ministry is the function of the whole people of God. It is integral to their call to Christian discipleship. Our call to serve Christ entails a call to serve one another. Our sphere of service is not restricted to our Christian brethren in the Church, but extends to our neighbour in the world. 'Neighbour' is not a narrow concept, but includes all with whom we come into contact.

Every Christian shares in the mission of the Church. He does this through his personal witness, which he should be constantly bearing as he takes Christ to all the world. In addition he is equipped to fulfil specialist roles. God's mission entails a vast range of activities. Each of these is to be undertaken with thoroughness and skill. So God equips different individuals in distinctive ways so that they can make specialist contributions. We are all generalists in our witnessing role, and specialists as we exercise the specific gifts which the Lord has bestowed on each of us.

During the past decade there have been a number of excellent books dealing with the subject of gifts of the Spirit. All we will attempt to do here is to raise the most common questions which are still in the minds of many Christians, and give a brief answer to each. For a fuller discussion the reader is advised to consult one of the books listed in the bibliography.

3 Gifts for Service

3.1 What is a 'gift of the Spirit'?

The *Dictionary of New Testament Theology* edited by Colin Brown defines 'charisma', the principal word used by Paul to denote a 'gift of the Spirit' as, 'The manifold outworking of the one grace in individual Christians through the one Spirit' (Vol. 2 p. 121 H.-H. Esser). Arnold Bittlinger provides the following definition. 'The concept of charisma is understood in the New Testament as "the concrete realisation of divine grace". It characterises a function – whether "ordinary or extraordinary" – that serves to build up the body of Christ' (Bittlinger 1974:16). For Peter Wagner, whose special contribution to the subject has been specifically to relate the topic of spiritual gifts to church growth, 'a spiritual gift is a special attribute given by the Holy Spirit to every member of the Body of Christ according to God's grace for use within the context of the Body' (Wagner 1979b:42). From these definitions we can see that the gifts are related to the grace of God. As such they are neither acquired skills nor are they rewards for devotion or service. They are given by God according to his sovereign will. Following one of the lists of gifts in Paul's letters he goes on to say, 'All these are the work of one and the same Spirit, and he gives them to each man, just as he determines' (1 Cor. 12:11).

3.2 Who are given gifts of the Spirit?
The New Testament makes it quite clear that the gifts are distributed throughout the entire body of believers. Every Christian has at least one of the gifts and many Christians have more than one. However, no individual Christian has by any means *all* of the gifts of the Spirit. Unlike the manifold fruit, the gifts are dispersed among the body.

1 Corinthians 12:7	'To *each* is given a manifestation of the Spirit for the common good' (RSV)
Ephesians 4:7	'But grace was given to *each* of us, according to the measure of Christ's gift' (RSV)
1 Peter 4:10	'As *each* has received a gift, employ it for one another, as good stewards of God's varied grace' (RSV)

This underlines the truth that no Christian is self-sufficient. We are all in need of other members of the Body of Christ. 'So, the eye cannot say to the hand, "I don't need you!" Nor can the head say to the feet, "Well, I don't need you!" ' (1 Cor. 12:21). There is a mutual dependency at every level. We stand in continuous need of one another. Everybody makes his distinctive contribution to the whole. The gifts are given irrespective of sex, age, social standing, intellectual level, or academic attainment.

3.3 How many gifts of the Spirit are there?
Many of the books on the subject written from the classical Pentecostal position speak in terms of nine gifts, which neatly match the nine-fold fruit of the Spirit described in Galatians 5. Nine gifts are in fact listed in

1 Corinthians 12:8–12. But towards the conclusion of the same chapter still more gifts are mentioned (1 Cor. 12:28–30). In Romans 12 yet another list is to be found, and Ephesians 4 lists five leadership roles which are described as the gifts of the risen Christ to his Church. 1 Pet. 4:10–11 mentions two broad categories of preaching and service. Even then the list is not exhausted, because in other places in the New Testament reference is made to isolated gifts. When we turn to the Old Testament, mention is made of the Holy Spirit coming upon individuals to equip them to perform specific acts of service to fulfil the divine will. It is, therefore, evident that none of the five main lists of gifts is meant to be exhaustive. John Stott comments that, 'No single gift occurs in all five lists, and thirteen gifts occur only in one of the five lists. The arrangement seems almost haphazard, as if to draw attention to the fact that each is a limited selection from a much larger total' (Stott 1975a:88). For instance it seems that Paul made his selection in 1 Corinthians 12:8–12 because there was misunderstanding and malpractice in the church in Corinth over these particular ones.

To give an idea of the scope and variety of the gifts of God we will attempt to give a fairly comprehensive list of those mentioned in Scripture, on pp. 333–344. The New Testament makes no distinction between what we might call the extraordinary and the ordinary, or the supernatural and natural. It is not possible to draw up a complete list. Each of the lists in the New Testament is illustrative rather than exhaustive. Peter Wagner argues that there are apparent gifts in the New Testament which are not explicitly called by that term. He lists for instance: intercession, exorcism and missionary gifts. There may also be further gifts which are not even mentioned in the New Testament.

3.4 Should every congregation manifest the complete range of gifts?
Gifts are given on God's initiative in order that the Church may fulfil its mission in a specific locality. God will therefore select those which are relevant to the needs of the hour. He may gift one church in one area and another church in a different direction, because each is facing a different situation. The range of gifts in evidence should not be the result of the church's theological filter or cultural disposition, but represent those which are essential and strategic for the church to fulfil its mission. Furthermore, as Scripture nowhere provides a fully comprehensive list we do not know the complete range.

3.5 Are all the gifts of equal importance?
The New Testament makes it clear that not all the gifts are of equal importance. While none is to be despised, for all are from God, there are some which are described as 'higher gifts' which are to be earnestly desired (1 Cor. 12:31). The higher gifts are those which edify, i.e. do most to build up the Body of Christ. The advice Paul gives to the miracle-mongering believers in Corinth was, 'since you are eager for manifestations of the Spirit, strive to excel in building up the church' (1 Cor.14:12 RSV). The speaking of intelligible, relevant words from God has top priority in the building up of the Church. 'Make love your aim, and earnestly desire the spiritual gifts, especially that you may prophesy' (1 Cor. 14:1 RSV). People need to hear truth from God if the Church is to grow. John Stott writes, '. . . the teaching gifts have the highest value, for nothing builds up Christians like God's truth. It is not surprising, therefore, to find a teaching gift or gifts at the top of each of the five New Testament lists. The apostles' insistence on the priority of teaching has considerable relevance to the contemporary Church. All over the world the churches are spiritually undernourished owing to the shortage of biblical expositors. In areas where there are mass movements they are

crying out for teachers to instruct converts. Because of the dearth of teachers it is sad to see so many people preoccupied with, and even distracted by, gifts of lesser importance' (Stott 1975a:112).

3.6 What is the relationship between our natural talents and our gifts of the Spirit?

We have noted above that not all of the gifts of the Spirit appear as 'miraculous' phenomena. Some of them appear to be very 'natural' and ordinary, for instance teaching, helping, administration, serving, hospitality, performing acts of mercy and craftsmans' skills. These maybe exercised by a non-Christian as well as by the Christian. What then is the relationship between natural talents and gifts?

Peter Wagner draws a sharp distinction between the two. He heads a section dealing with the distinction, 'Don't Confuse Spiritual Gifts with Natural Talents' (Wagner 1979b:85). He writes, 'Spiritual gifts are reserved exclusively for Christians. No unbeliever has one, and every true believer in Jesus does. Spiritual gifts are not to be regarded as dedicated natural talents. There may be a discernible relationship between the two, however, because in some cases (not all, by any means) God takes a natural talent in an unbeliever and transforms it into a spiritual gift when that person enters the Body of Christ. But even in a case like this the spiritual gift is more than just a souped-up natural talent. Because it is given by God, a spiritual gift can never be cloned' (Wagner 1979b:86, 87).

I do not agree that gifting can only take place subsequent to a person's conversion. The Holy Spirit is active in our creation as well as in our regeneration. Wagner concedes in response to the question, 'Where do these natural talents come from?' – 'Ultimately, they are given by God, and as such they should be recognised in a sense as gifts' (Wagner 1979b:86). Prophets like Jeremiah and John the Baptist were set apart to be prophets from their mother's womb (Jer. 1:5; Luke 1:15, 76). 'This fundamental truth that God has planned the end from the beginning should warn us against too facile a discontinuity between nature and grace, between pre-conversion and post-conversion life' (Stott 1975a:91). To fulfil his purposes and bring glory to his name. God in his sovereignty may use the gifts that he has given to people who do not acknowledge him. But far better that the talents which God has given be recognised as such and offered back to him in rededication. Howard Snyder declares that 'A spiritual gift is often a God-given ability which has caught fire' (Snyder 1976:133). As they are subsequently used in response to the prompting of the Holy Spirit and under his direction, they will bring all the more glory to the risen Christ and be more clearly identified as gifts of the Holy Spirit. 'These gifts are too often buried in the natural man, and they are often misused and distorted in their application independent of God. But if we put our lives at the disposal of God, he will animate all the gifts and talents he has placed in us, and through them he will show his grace and Spirit in a new way. Our natural gifts thereby become gifts of grace' (Bittlinger 1974:14).

However, it cannot be automatically assumed that every natural talent will be converted into a gift of the Spirit. Some Christians who have exercised some great gift before their conversion do not feel moved to do so by the Holy Spirit after their conversion. This can occur for a variety of reasons. They may have so misused, distorted and debased the gift in the past that it is difficult to resurrect and apply it to the work of the Kingdom. As new and immature Christians they may be held back from exercising a spectacular gift, at least for a time, because it might destroy them spiritually, leading them to pride. God may say, 'Not yet', until they have learned how to utilise their gift for the glory of God.

Furthermore, we should not be limited to think purely in terms of the gifts we had before our conversion as we make ourselves available to God for his service. We must be open to the 'surprises of the Holy Spirit'. He may wish to equip us in new ways for fresh spheres of ministry. There are some gifts which it is extremely unlikely that we will have exercised prior to our conversion, as for instance that of evangelism or praying in tongues.

3.7 Are gifts a permanent possession?

They are gifts from God and not personal acquisitions. He gives when and how he will, and is free to withdraw a gift again at any time. We therefore must guard against a presumptive attitude, taking for granted that the gift is there for us to use when and how we like. 'Charismata' are by definition gifts of *grace*. On the other hand God does not play games with us. There is a consistency in his operations. Gifts are not given and withdrawn arbitrarily. They may be withdrawn because they have been grievously misused, or allowed to become dormant because they are no longer relevant to our present opportunities. Peter Wagner argues that gifts are, normally speaking, a lifetime possession. He explains, 'This rather dogmatic opinion is derived from Romans 12:4, where Paul established the analogy of the physical body as the hermeneutical key for understanding spiritual gifts. If spiritual gifts are to the Body of Christ as hands, tongues and other members are to the physical body, there is no question in my mind that once we know what our gift is, we can depend on keeping it' (Wagner 1979b:106). The fact that the three main lists of gifts in the New Testament occur in the immediate context of teaching about the body adds further weight to his line of argument.

Others take a different line, arguing that 'gifts' are distinguished from 'ministries' in that the former are temporary while the latter are permanent. Ph.-H Menoud writes about Paul's list in 1 Cor. 12:29–30, 'He designates them by terms which are abstract and not personal, for they are beyond doubt spontaneous and sporadic manifestations of the Spirit, which do not possess the permanence of a ministry' (J-J. von Allmen Ed. 1958:265). The distinction may however lie more in the area of official recognition and leadership implications than in permanence. The ministries represent those activities which are essential for building up the body. The fact that Christians are exhorted to utilise their gifts responsibly as 'good stewards' (1 Pet. 4:10; 11) also implies a measure of permanence, and implies that we are accountable.

3.8 Were the gifts withdrawn at the end of the apostolic age?

Many Protestant Christians in the reformed tradition have argued that the supernatural gifts of the Spirit were characteristic of the apostolic times. When the period of 'redemptive history' was replaced by 'church history' these gifts ceased to operate. They were phased out with the passing of the last of the apostles.

This line of argument is based upon a desire to safeguard the normative nature of apostolic tradition and of the completeness of revelation as enshrined in the canon of Scripture. This is argued at length by Oscar Culmann in *The Early Church*. He regards the period from the birth of Jesus to the death of the last apostle as a time of direct revelation. This was recognised by the Church in the second century when it fixed the canon of Scripture. 'The Church was getting to the point where it was too distant from the time of the apostles to be able to guard the purity of the tradition so she drew a line under apostolic tradition. In doing this she demonstrated a clear line of demarcation between apostolic and the church period; between the time of foundation and of construction' (Culmann 56:89).

There are three other principal considerations which have further underlined this negative stance. Firstly, they look back through two thousand years of church history and note that many of the gifts have fallen into disuse for much of this period. Secondly, looking at the crude religious magic of the medieval Church, and some of the practices of 'folk catholicism' at the present time, 'It is not surprising that main-line Protestantism, . . . suspicious of anything mysterious or miraculous, . . . turned its face against a revival of the apostolic gifts' (Bridge and Phypers 1973:30). Thirdly, in observing the manifestation of some of the 'supernatural' gifts within the classical and neo-Pentecostal movements, they have been unconvinced about their authenticity.

In response to these genuine concerns, I would make the following brief comments. First, there is undoubtedly a uniqueness about the period of our Lord's ministry and the apostleship of the Twelve. Therefore, the terms 'apostle' and 'prophet' have undergone some modification when applied outside their ranks and after their period. Indeed, within the pages of the New Testament there is evidence of these terms taking on a wider, secondary meaning. We will look at this more closely in the following section.

Secondly, the Bible nowhere explicitly states that the gifts, or certain of them, have been withdrawn. On the contrary, 1 Cor 13:8–10 infers that prophecies, tongues and knowledge will be needed until the 'perfect comes' i.e. until Christ returns. Ephesians 4:11 teaches that the gifts of apostles, prophets, evangelists and pastors and teachers are all required to prepare God's people for works of service, so that the body of Christ may be built up until we all reach unity in the faith. Surely, the need for this is as great today as it was then?

Thirdly, when the Epistles speak about the gifts, it is to instruct Christians in their proper use – 'never how to phase them out' (Bridge, Phypers 1973:28).

Fourthly, as we have previously noted, the Scriptures nowhere draw a distinction between 'ordinary' and 'supernatural' gifts. They are intermingled without comment. By what authority therefore have we the right to perform a scissors-and-paste exercise to edit out certain gifts which we consider have been withdrawn?

Part of the problem may be more cultural than theological. As Western Christians we have serious inhibitions in coming to terms with the supernatural, which are not shared by the majority of our brethren in Africa and Latin America. Signs and wonders are sovereign acts of God. He causes them to happen as and when he pleases to authenticate his word. Perhaps at times we too glibly say that these are more appropriate in the pioneer missionary situations overseas. The missionary frontier is as much on our own doorstep, and we are not performing so startlingly well without them. Perhaps their scarcity may have as much to do with our little faith (Matt. 13:58), as with their inappropriateness.

Michael Griffiths, principal of the London Bible College and one-time director of the Overseas Missionary Fellowship, who does not identify personally with the charismatic movement, has written concerning the gifts. 'Common objections or apprehensions about certain gifts can be met, not by denying that they are still given, but rather by insisting upon a careful biblical study of what these gifts mean in the New Testament and by exercising them only in the way which Scripture itself clearly teaches' (Griffiths 1978:9).

4 A composite list of gifts mentioned in the Bible

This list does not claim to be exhaustive and a number of the descriptions are tentative, as it is not always possible to know the exact nature of every gift to which the Scriptures make passing reference. In classifying the gifts I am following Michael Green's helpful categories (Green 1974:161–192).

4.1 Gifts of Utterance

(a) *Prophecy* (Rom. 12:6; 1 Cor. 12:10; 1 Pet. 4:11). Prophecy is a message given directly from God through men who have learned to listen to him and are prepared to speak on his behalf. The message may come as a result of study or be spontaneous. It may be a proclamation regarding the present or a prediction relating to the future. It may be addressed to the Church for her upbuilding, encouragement and consolation, to an unbeliever to convict him of sin, or to society at large. Prophecy is a gift which is characteristic of the 'last days'. It is given to all regardless of age, sex and social standing. It is the most commonly referred to of all the gifts.

(b) *Teaching* (Rom. 12:7; Eph. 4:11; 1 Cor. 12:28). To explain and apply the word of God in such a way that people can understand and are encouraged to respond. It is not restricted simply to the imparting of information, but calls people to commitment which produces a behavioural change. It is therefore closely related to the gift of pastor, and overlaps with prophecy and encouragement. Teaching need not be equated with formal lecturing; it may be given in a variety of styles and using different media appropriate to the occasion, content, audience and desired response.

(c) *Exhortation* (Rom. 12:8). The Greek word translated 'exhortation' literally means to draw alongside in order to strengthen. It signifies to challenge, comfort, console, rebuke and encourage, so that people move forward rather than shrink back, and pass the breaking-point without breaking. The encourager is the positive, patient, resilient motivator. His exhortations serve to dry out the gun-powder and light the fuse.

(d) *Tongues* (1 Cor. 12:10). These are generally understood as 'languages' which have not been learned but are given by the Holy Spirit, for private or public use, to express our praise to God or to communicate his message through a divinely anointed utterance. In the latter case it must be accompanied by the gift of interpretation for it to become intelligible. Some Christians understand 'tongues' to mean a definite language form with vocabulary and syntax, while others regard it as an expression of feeling and emotion – 'rather like the love language of a happily married couple, which may not *mean* anything, when the words are analysed; but which *denotes* the intimacy and trust of the couple concerned' (Green 1975:162). Still others interpret the phrase 'various kinds of tongues' to mean simply an unusual aptitude to learn languages (Stott 1975a:112–115, Griffiths 1978:57–60).

(e) *Interpretation of Tongues* (1 Cor. 12:10, 30). This is the ability to give the substance of a message delivered in a tongue. It is not strictly speaking a translation. Those with the gift of tongues are encouraged to pray for this complementary gift so that they will be able to understand what they are saying (1 Cor. 14:13). Without the gift of interpretation the tongues can have no place in the Church (1 Cor. 14:27, 28). Tongues followed by interpretation become equivalent to prophecy.

4.2 Gifts of Action

(a) *Apostolic* (1 Cor. 12:28; Eph. 4:11). This gift, together with Prophet, Evangelist, Pastor and teacher we will be discussing at greater length in section (5) devoted to leadership. Here we take this to mean responsibility for a number of churches, exercised so as to enable those churches to grow in spiritual maturity. It also expresses a pioneering spirit to establish a Christian witness where the gospel has not yet been heard, with a view to gathering converts and planting churches.

(b) *Missionary* (Eph. 3:7–9). Peter Wagner draws attention to this as a distinct gift. He defines it as 'the special ability that God gives to some members of the Body of Christ to minister whatever other spiritual gifts they have in a second culture.' (Wagner 1979b:205.) Most people find it difficult to function adequately outside of their own culture. They are unable to make the necessary adjustments to adopt another language, enter the frame of reference of another culture, and adapt their style of working.

(c) *Evangelist* (Eph. 4:11). The ability that some people have to know to whom, when and how to share the gospel so that others become disciples of Christ and responsible members of his church.

(d) *Pastor-Teacher* (Eph. 4:11). To assume the spiritual care and nurture of a body of believers.

(e) *Gifts of healing* (1 Cor. 12:9, 30). The ability to heal various kinds of sickness whether of the body, mind or soul. The healing may be instantaneous, gradual, complete or partial, with or without the aid of medication or surgery.

(f) *Miracles* (1 Cor. 12:10, 28). These refer to any mighty act of God performed through one of his servants. While including healings, the term 'miracles' embraces other signs and wonders which 'are received by observers to have altered the ordinary course of nature' (Wagner 1979b:237).

(g) *Faith* (1 Cor. 12:9; 13:2). This does not refer to saving faith but a gift of 'mountain-moving' faith to overcome difficulties and achieve the seemingly impossible. It should not be confused with brash presumption which is confidence in one's own abilities, or the mistaken assumption that God places a safety-net under every tight-rope. Rather, it is taking God at his word and acting upon it. It is thanking God for what I believe he is going to do before he does it (Yohn 1974:47).

(h) *Leadership* (Rom. 12:8; 1 Thess. 5:12). The ability 'to set goals in accordance with God's purpose for the future and to communicate these goals to others in such a way that they voluntarily and harmoniously work together to accomplish those goals for the glory of God' (Wagner 1979b:162). The Greek word literally means 'the one who presides'. To fulfil this role effectively he must be able to see the parts in relation to the whole; to reconcile conflicting interests, and to inspire trust and confidence. The Old Testament example of Daniel's God-given ability to act as a supervisor in the Persian court demonstrates that gifts of leadership are not restricted to the ecclesiastical realm. He was gifted for political leadership (Dan. 6:3). Closely associated with the gift of leadership is the following gift:

(i) *Administrators* (I Cor. 12:28). In the New Testament this word is also used of a ship's captain or steersman. It describes the ability to keep the vessel on course and safe from navigational hazards so that it arrives at its destination in good shape. Administration is the drawing up of realistic plans and the establishing of effective procedures, so that goals can be achieved and all involved enjoy job satisfaction as they can see the significance of their contribution to the success of the whole enterprise. It may also have a link with the administration of finance. Arnold Bittlinger points out that 'according to recently discovered papyri the Greek word for administration (*antilepsis*) was a technical term in the field of banking and referred to the chief accountant.' (Brittlinger 1967:70.)

(j) *Helps* (I Cor. 12:28). The word literally means 'to take firm hold of someone, in order to help' (Robertson and Plummer 1911:281). Others apply the gift to the general area of administration. In view of the paperwork burdening every minister simple secretarial and organisational skills are invaluable. In the context of New Testament church life it probably refers to the offer of practical assistance to the poor, the orphaned and the widowed. It is closely associated, if not synonymous with the next gift mentioned in our list.

(k) *Service* (Rom. 12:7; 1 Pet. 4:11). It is from this word that we get the term 'deacon'. It is a task-oriented gift which prompts a person to see what needs to be done and then sets about doing it.

(l) *Mercy* (Rom. 12:8). Like the previous two this gift is practical and unostentatious. It represents kindly acts of all kinds performed out of compassion for those in need.

(m) *Giving* (Rom. 12:9). While it is the duty of every Christian to give sacrificially, regularly and cheerfully to the Lord's work, some Christians have a particular burden to give generously themselves and to stimulate others to give. At this point I am reminded of the work of Vernon Hedderley who through his Missionary Mart auctions raises thousands of pounds each year for overseas missions.

(n) *Voluntary Poverty* (1 Cor. 13:3). Peter Wagner describes this gift as the special ability 'to renounce material comfort and luxury and adopt a personal life-style equivalent to those living at the poverty level in a given society in order to serve God more effectively' (Wagner 1979b:96). It is demonstrated by those who take the vows of monastic order and by many missionaries serving overseas. Many Christians are being led by God into a simpler life-style in response to the selfish over-affluence of the surrounding society.

(o) *Hospitality* (1 Pet. 4:9). The readiness to keep an open home to which the visitor is invited and in which he immediately feels welcome and at ease. Where this gift is present a relaxed atmosphere prevails. There is no unnecessary fuss and bother, and the practical details are attended to in a quiet and efficient manner, so that the visitor never feels an intruder.

(p) *Martyrdom* (1 Cor. 13:3). The ability and willingness to endure suffering to the point of death in a joyful and victorious attitude which brings glory to God.

(q) *Suffering* (Phil. 1:29 Col. 1:24). 'For it has been granted to you that for the sake of Christ you should not only believe in him but also suffer for his sake' (RSV). I am grateful to an Anglican clergyman, a Jewish Christian who lost both of his parents in Auschwitz for pointing out this gift to me. The verb translated 'granted' might equally well be translated 'gifted'.

(r) *Celibacy* (1 Cor. 7:7; Mat. 19:12). Those who remain unmarried in order to be freer to devote their time and energies to the Lord's service (Bridge, Phypers 1973:84).

(s) *Craftsmanship* (Ex. 31:3–6). The Spirit of God inspired Bezalel to give him skill in design and working with wood, precious metals, building stone, in cutting precious stones for jewellery and in weaving curtains and garments.

4.3 Gifts of Knowledge

(a) *Word of Knowledge* (1 Cor. 12:8; 13:2). The God-given ability to understand truth, or knowledge of events or motives, which has not been acquired by normal means. Peter Wagner also understands the gift as the ability 'to discover, accumulate, analyse and clarify information and ideas that are pertinent to the growth and well-being of the body' (Wagner 1979b:218). In either case it includes the ability to apply information so that it has a significant bearing on a situation.

(b) *Word of Wisdom* (1 Cor. 12:8). A special insight to apply knowledge to resolve a difficulty or silence an opponent. It helps a person to remain objective and provides him with a sensitivity to what people are saying and to handle them appropriately. It is the ability to see things as they really are and to work towards an appropriate solution. This gift is necessary both in personal counselling and labour negotiations.

(c) *Discernment* (1 Cor. 12:10). The Revised Standard Version translates the phrase denoting this gift as 'the ability to distinguish between spirits'. It describes the ability to discern whether a person's words or actions, which are claimed to be of God, are in reality divinely inspired or whether they are the manifestations of merely human activity or are satanic in origin. It enables the false prophet to be distinguished from the genuine one. As every genuine work of God is challenged and counterfeited by Satan this gift is of abiding importance.

Attemping to draw together a composite list highlights a number of facts with regard to the gifts of the Spirit. It demonstrates that there are a large number, covering a wide variety of activities. As mentioned at the outset it is not always possible to describe them with any degree of precision.

5 Gifts for leadership

In the New Testament leaders are not thought of in terms of dignitaries but as functionaries. The emphasis there is on service rather than status (Luke 22:25–27). Furthermore, various leadership specialisations are envisaged. No single individual, no matter how versatile he may be, is competent in every sphere. For a church to move ahead in numerical growth and diversification of ministries there needs to be effective leadership in each area. Five such spheres of ministry were in operation among the churches of Asia Minor as recorded in the letter to the Ephesians, which many New Testament scholars regard as addressed not just to one church but possibly to a number in the region. Michael Harper in *Let My People Grow* sees these five ministries as five interlinking spheres, rather like the Olympic symbol. More accurately they may be represented as a Venn diagram in which all the circles intersect one another for all of the ministries are interrelated.

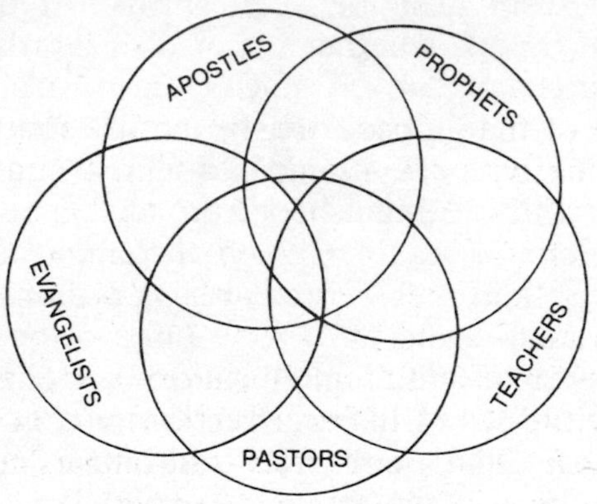

He describes them succinctly as:

Let my people go – the apostolic function of the Church

> Let my people hear – the prophetic function of the Church
> Let my people care – the pastoral function of the Church
> Let my people know – the teaching function of the Church
> Let my people grow – the evangelistic function of the Church
>
> (Harper 1977:44, 45).

For the churches in Asia Minor to sustain their life and spread their influence throughout the province they needed effective leadership in each of these specialisations. As most of the individual congregations were probably quite small, with no adequate premises in which to come together regularly, they possibly were little more than an extended family gathering or large house meeting. The specialist leadership roles had to be provided on an inter-congregational level. The various groups were 'visited' as often as possible by itinerant leaders exercising their particular ministry.

5.1 Apostle

The role of the '*apostle*' was to ensure that the teaching was in line with the sayings of Christ and the body of doctrine which the apostles had established as foundational. Their visits also served to remind the local congregations that the Church was a dynamic, expanding body. In addition to the twelve unique *apostles of Christ* (among their essential qualifications was that they had to be eye-witnesses of his resurrection) were the *apostles of the Church*. They were the trail-blazers and travelling representatives, working on the spiritual and geographical frontiers to bring individuals to faith and establish new congregations. The New Testament names Barnabas (Acts 14:14), Andronicus and Junias (Rom. 16:7), Timothy and Silas (1 Thess. 2:6) and Epaphroditus (Phil. 2:25) as among those fulfilling this kind of function.

The apostles were not cautious, bureaucratic leaders, but bold, pioneering adventurers, ensuring not simply the orthodoxy of the Church, but also safeguarding its continuing mobility and flexibility. Such a steadying and inspiring ministry was particularly relevant to the small, struggling groups of relatively new Christians, many of them fighting for life in a hostile environment.

In addition to the 'ambassador' and 'pastor-pastorum' I would like to see a new generation of bishops, with a truly apostolic gift of the trail-blazing kind. We need leaders who are freed from administrative and maintenance tasks. Once a leader becomes overburdened with management problems he quickly loses his vision and perspective. The urgent crowds out the significant. The confusing of management with leadership has contributed to the dearth of enabling and inspiring leadership which the Church so desperately needs. We need leaders with time to reflect, diary flexibility and visionary qualities who can be with the troops not just for the ceremonial parades and in the casualty stations but share in the strategic advance. They should be released to roam freely on the growing edge. Their task is as much concerned with preparing for tomorrow as preserving yesterday.

5.2 Prophet

Of equal importance was the '*prophetic*' function. Among some groups, especially those predominantly Gentile in membership, the Old Testament Scriptures may not have been readily available. This problem must have become acute as the followers of Christ became more and more distanced from the synagogues where the scrolls were deposited. At this early stage in the Church's life many of the New Testament books had not yet been written. The production problems were immense in a day when every manuscript had to be copied by hand and personally conveyed. When specific issues arose in the Church concerning doctrine and practice, which were not covered by the portions of Scripture in their possession or in the apostolic teaching which they had received verbally, they had to rely on the prophet who spoke a Word from God as the Spirit moved him for the guidance of the Church.

Michael Harper helpfully distinguishes between the role of the prophet and that of the teacher. 'A prophet is not a Scripture exegete. He knows the scriptures, but he does not teach from his knowledge of the Bible, which is the role of the teacher; he hears that which is particularly appropriate for the hour, and he faithfully passes on the message to the appropriate quarter, wherever and whoever that may be' (Harper 1977:52). The prophet in no sense adds to God's self-revelation in Christ, but he does bring a practical word of encouragement, warning, exhortation and guidance, which must then be tested by the Church, in the light of Scripture and according to their Spirit-led discernment.

5.3 Evangelist

The task of the evangelist is located within each individual church. Apart from the mention in Ephesians 4 and the example of Philip as an evangelist in Samaria (Acts 21:8), and the exhortation to Timothy to do the work of an evangelist (2 Tim. 4:5), there is no stress in the New Testament on the office of 'evangelist'. The overwhelming evidence is of the church itself actually engaging in the evangelistic task. We may therefore conclude that the task of the visiting evangelist was to help the local churches to become more effective in their outreach. He evangelised among them as one specially gifted, not to remove the responsibility from their shoulders, but to inspire them by his example. As distinct from the 'apostle' who is the pioneer church planter, the evangelist works from a local church base and in conjunction with local Christians. He will help each local church to identify those within their midst who are the potential evangelists. This will often only be discovered and developed as the congregation responds to the outside stimulus of those with a recognised evangelistic gift.

5.4 Pastor and Teacher

Small groups are prone to foster intense relationships which exclude others, and to generate personality conflicts which are not easily resolved from within. Furthermore, among those joining the Church would be those with pressing personal problems. They would also be stepping into a very different environment as they came in from the surrounding pagan world, bringing a lot of their beliefs, attitudes and habits with them. The fact of their becoming Christian may have resulted in their being disowned by their families, thrown out of home or losing their jobs. Many of these problems would be dealt with by the local leadership, but there were no doubt some thorny issues which would require the attention of a visiting pastor responsible for shepherding a number of groups. Paul's letters reflect his wide-ranging pastoral concerns, and as he travelled he was acutely conscious of the pastoral burden which he carried for all of the churches.

Similarly, not every group would have someone within it capable of fulfilling an adequate teaching role. So there were visiting teachers providing instruction of a more systematic kind, on which the local leadership could base their own exhortations for the coming months.

The Ephesians 4 pattern of inter-congregational ministry makes more sense to me as a result of serving overseas for a brief four years, sharing in a church planting team in Chile, South America. Many missionaries report that such experience provides insights which are seldom reflected in academic commentaries on the text.

6 The mobilising of gifts through the 'modality' structure

In his important article 'The Two Structures of God's Redemptive Mission' (1974:121–138) Dr Ralph Winter argues the case for the Church to maintain what he terms 'modality' and 'sodality' structures. He draws a distinction between two kinds of community. The modality represents the settled community, and the sodality the apostolic band. The former places emphasis on being called and the latter on being sent. The modality is people-orientated and diverse in its concerns, while the sodality is task-orientated and single-minded. In this section we will explore the emergence of gifts in the modality structure, and in the following section of this chapter we will go on to see how specific calls from God draw together people who pool a gift-mix to create a variety of 'sodality' structures.

Within the local, settled congregation the New Testament depicts a variety of arrangements. The church in Jerusalem is governed by apostles backed up by deacons, with the whole congregation sharing in important decisions (Acts 15:22). The church in Antioch is led by prophets and teachers (Acts 13:1). Paul left the churches in Asia Minor in the care of elders whom he had appointed (Acts 14:23), while in Philippi the leaders are described as 'bishops' and 'deacons'. In the midst of all this confusing variety, one thing stands out clearly, namely that there was a plurality of leadership in the local church. Furthermore, the leadership ministries did not displace the charismata distributed throughout the membership. 'The charismata must not be pushed aside by the ministry, nor may the ministry be pushed aside by the charismata. Charismata and ministry belong together, just like the motor and the steering wheel in an automobile . . . A motor without steering wheel is dangerous, but a steering wheel without motor is useless' (Bittlinger 1974:27).

Some writers have played down the significance of gifts on the basis that the Pastoral Epistles lay emphasis not on essential gifts but on personal qualities (1 Tim. 3; Tit. 1). This may seem puzzling from the standpoint of those who have only operated within an established church environment. However, in a pioneering, church-planting situation the dynamics are very different. The people who are officially recognised and appointed have frequently already begun to operate unofficially in that capacity. The emerging situation produces the latent leadership talent, which is later officially recognised by an appointment to office. They come to the notice of the church on the basis of their performance, not simply their potential. By their deeds you will know them!

For many readers much of the material on the subject of gifts will have been fairly familiar ground, as a great deal of attention has been focused on the subject in recent years. The area of concern has shifted now from the theology of gifts to the practical issue of how they are to be identified in the congregation and then deployed and developed. In *Body Building Exercises for the Local Church* I have outlined an exercise for a congregation to measure to what extent it has succeeded in implementing 'body ministry' and how it is progressing from year to year. (Gibbs 1979b:62–65). Here we will concern ourselves with the five basic requirements for gift identification and motivation.

The five leadership spheres described in Ephesians 4 represent supra-congregational ministries exercised by individuals travelling among the groups of Christians scattered throughout Asia Minor. Their roles were appropriate to the structure and needs of the church at that time. Each group would have its local leadership, which was developing to the point where it could assume many of the functions previously exercised by leadership from outside the fellowship. As local congregations become established, developing community life and growing numerically, so their ministries become diversified. In this way the ministries increasingly find expression in the life of the local church.

With the institutionally developed church life of today we must look at the leadership spheres described in Ephesians 4, asking ourselves how they apply to our times and our local situation. They will vary from congregation to congregation according to the ministry emphases of each church and the constituencies which they believe God has called them to serve.

It is the responsibility of the ordained minister, with his church council, to ensure that effective leadership is being exercised in each sphere and that there is cohesion within the leadership team. It is not, however, his responsibility to give a personal lead in each sphere. His ordination did not endow him with all the gifts necessary to fulfil every role. Churches which expect their minister to be effective in every area of ministry will soon become disillusioned. As a consequence of such unrealistic expectations many churches engage in the game of 'scapegoating', in which they compare the weaknesses of their present minister with the strengths of his predecessor. To avoid this futile pastime churches should help their minister identify his gifts and encourage him to develop his ministry in those areas. Some churches have taken the step of drawing up a job description in cooperation with their minister, which recognises his particular contribution. Such an exercise also exposes those areas where he is unable to give an effective lead. These must be met by others within the church who have corresponding leadership gifts.

The diagram overleaf represents the leadership spheres as perceived by a certain church:

If I were the minister of such a church, I believe that according to my gifts I could give a personal lead in the areas of teaching, pastoral care, and exhortation and encouragement. But as I am not particularly gifted, for instance, in administration, finance, music, evangelism and children's and youth work, we would need as a matter of some urgency to look for competent leaders in those areas who would form part of the ministerial team. Each member of such a team carries a great deal of responsibility for developing church life in the area of his gift and is accountable to the other team members to ensure that one area is not pursued to the detriment of another. New work should only be undertaken on a provisional basis until suitable leadership has emerged to ensure its continuance and long-term effectiveness.

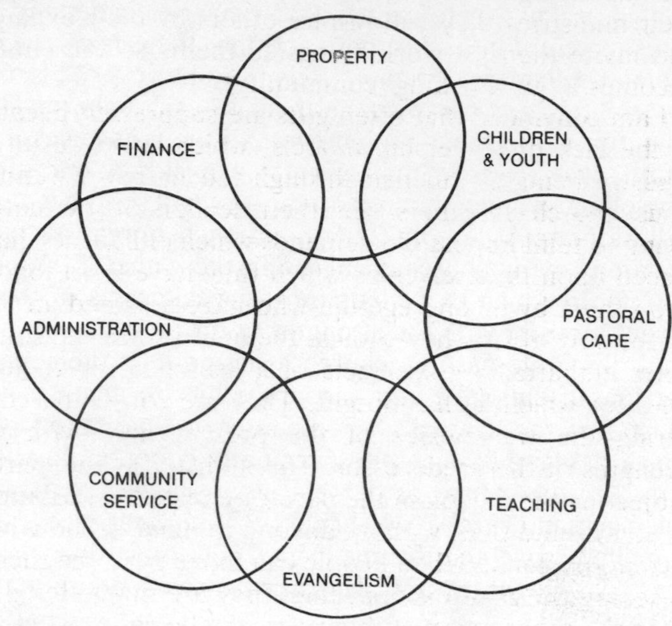

6.1 The need for a leadership team which demonstrates a range of gifts

As a church grows, so its ministries diversify. Just as in Ephesians 4 we have distinct inter-congregational leadership roles fulfilled by different individuals, ('. . . he [i.e. the Risen Christ] appointed some to be apostles, others to be prophets, others to be evangelists, others to be pastors and teachers' [v. 12], so distinctive roles begin to emerge in the local church.

Those who are in a leadership position do not merely exercise their gift on behalf of the congregation and with their official recognition; they are also responsible for stimulating those similarly gifted (but not necessarily with accompanying leadership ability) in the congregation. In their ministries they will inspire others by their example and invite them to work alongside them. So the church becomes a 'gift evoking' community.

I am convinced that often gifts are suppressed because of the lack of leadership models, which is the result of ministry being channelled through too narrow a funnel. Thus church members see their leaders inadequately trying to fulfil impossible demands which either they have placed upon themselves or which they have been loaded upon them by a congregation who have assumed an 'observer only' role. They witness the uninspiring and sometimes embarrassing spectacle of a leader trying to fulfil roles for which he has no gift. They are constantly comparing the weaknesses of the present man with the strengths of the predecessor. The minister for his part is subjecting the person in the pew to repeated exhortations to do this and that, without anyone to hand to show how it could be done. When people can move from the theory to seeing the gift in action, then they are motivated.

At the other extreme, however, the leader must guard against thinking that because he can do something everyone else should be able to perform likewise. This will only serve to cause frustration, with people trying and failing and eventually being forced to the conclusion that they have nothing to contribute. Paul makes this clear to the gift-laden church in Corinth. 'If the foot should say, "Because I am not a hand, I do not belong to the body," it would not for that reason cease to be part of the body.' Feet must not be mistaken for hands. They must be identified, deployed and trained for what they were meant to do!

6.2 The need for a personal pastoral relationship

This picture of a shepherd with his flock of sheep as a model of the relationship between a religious minister and his people, is unique to the Hebrew-Christian tradition among the religions of the world. (Ps. 23; Jn. 10:12;

1 Pet. 2:25; Heb. 13:20; Jn. 21:15ff). An eastern shepherd spent most of his life with the flock. He knew every one of his sheep by name, and noticed when just one went missing. He was prepared to give his life for the sheep. The shepherd has a daily relationship with the sheep. In the church today the relation of the minister to his flock is more like that of the vet or the sheep-sheerer than the shepherd. He can only deal individually with the sheep at infrequent intervals or in response to an emergency or domestic crisis.

The pastor has to know his flock individually if he is to identify their actual and potential gifts. He must know what his members do for a job, what their leisure interests are and if they are involved in community service. These may give some clue to their gifts. For churches with over 150 members this will inevitably mean the pastor delegating some of his pastoral responsibilities to a team of lay pastors. As the pastors get to know those for whom they are responsible a card index can be built up, which shows the gifts each person possesses and is perhaps already exercising in the world, which he has not made available to the church because he either does not see its relevance or has not been given opportunity.

6.3 The need for a group context

It is often within the small group that gifts are first identified and begin to function. I have already dealt with this aspect in our chapter on groups so there is no need to elaborate further here. I make just one observation, namely, the larger the church the more important become the primary and secondary groups for the release of the congregation's gifts. The Sunday worship is on such a scale that gifts have to be highly developed to operate effectively at that level. Many people are therefore discouraged, thinking that they would never utilise their gifts in the presence of so many people. The small group situation on the other hands helps gifts to blossom in the warm, friendly atmosphere of mutual friends. If mistakes are made at this level, they are considered as 'within the family' and can be overlooked or laughed away without embarrassment. As people gain confidence in the primary group they can then begin to function in the secondary group and eventually be introduced, where appropriate, to the tertiary level.

Additionally, individuals may be helped to identify their own gifts through the use of a self-evaluation questionnaire. I am grateful to the Rev. Lewis Misselbrook of the Baptist Home Missions Department for permission to use such a questionnaire which he has developed for this purpose (see Appendix H). A more elaborate questionnaire can also be found in the author's *Body Building Exercises* (Gibbs 1979b:90–94).

6.4 The need for an inspiring, well-publicised programme

Many people are reluctant to offer themselves for service, not because they lack dedication but because they lack information and inspiration. The fault often lies with the leadership, who have not communicated the fact that the church has a programme which is designed to achieve God-given objectives. Jobs are undersold, and those invited to take on responsibilities are not encouraged to 'dream their dreams' to envisage what that work might one day become. In the final chapter I will spell this out in much greater detail. Suffice it to say here, many churches have not identified gifts because they have no programme to which the gifts which God has given could be usefully put. Or if they have such a plan it is concealed behind a 'Top Secret – Restricted Circulation' file cover!

7 Gifts operating through 'sodality' structures

The sodality represents the task-orientated group. It is made up of people who have banded together in a common cause. In his article expanding on the need for a two-fold structure of modality and sodality, Ralph Winter has principally in mind the Roman Catholic missionary orders and the Protestant missionary societies as the sodalities. I believe his model also has application to home mission within Britain, for not all that God wants done is likely to be achieved through denominational structures and local congregations.

7.1 Types of sodalities in the United Kingdom

In order to identify 'sodalities' more clearly I have attempted the following classifications:

(a) *Pioneering Sodalities*, which seek to establish cell-groups and congregations in housing developments, new townships, and places of employment where there is no Christian presence, or where there is only a token presence with an inadequate outreach potential. When modalities fail to respond promptly and imaginatively to such challenges, special initiatives may have to be taken apart from the local church, but hopefully with their blessing and cooperation. Sometimes the modalities themselves will make special arrangements for experimental mission projects, or the denominational authorities will pool resources by forming ecumenical parishes. Pioneering sodalities are represented, for instance, by teams of Church Army evangelists and (hopefully) theological students operating in a church-planting role and in encouraging the formation of Christian cell groups.

(b) *Enabling Sodalities*, providing resources to equip the church to function more effectively in specific areas such as evangelism, creative worship, music and Christian education with various age-groups. Among them we may number: The Church Pastoral Aid Society, the Catholic Missionary Society (involved in conducting parish missions), the Baptist and Methodist Home Missions Departments, Evangelism Explosion and the Fishers Fellowship in the area of evangelism, One Step Forward, Royal School of Church Music, Scripture Union and Bible Society. From the above examples it will be immediately obvious that 'sodalities' vary greatly in their relationship to the 'modalities'. Some exist within a 'modality' framework while others operate quite independently.

(c) *Renewal Sodalities* to quicken spiritual life, e.g. The Fountain Trust which, until it disbanded in 1981, was concerned with charismatic renewal in the main-line denominations, Group for Evangelism and Renewal within the United Reformed Church, the Methodist Revival Fellowship, the Eclectic Society among Anglican ministers under forty years of age (!) and Mainstream within the Baptist Union Churches.

(d) *Target-group Sodalities* which have a specialist ministry to particular groups within society e.g. industrial, university, hospital and Forces chaplaincies and Christian Unions, drug addicts, rehabilitation programmes (Coke Hole Trust, Teen Challenge) Frontier Youth Trust, Newham Renewal Project (concerned with church development in the inner city), village evangelism, Torch Trust for the Blind, Mission to Caravan Dwellers, etc., etc.

(e) *Media Sodalities* concerned with publishing, broadcasting, telecasting, film-making, drama, dance and other art forms.

Such sodalities attract persons who can offer particular expertise to advance the mission of the Church. In many instances the local church modality structure would have neither the scope nor the resources for people to develop gifts in these areas.

8 The gifts at work in the world

In the foregoing pages we have been examining some of the inhibiting factors which have held back the discovery and use of gifts in the local church. To the theological misgivings, clerical reluctance and structural inflexibility we must now add a further constraint – failure to appreciate the significance of the gifts of God to enable the church to fulfil its servant role in the world. Every gift of grace is a first-fruit of the Kingdom of God, and as such it is as relevant to the needs of the world as to the church. The Christian does not leave his gifts at home while he is out earning his living. God is concerned for the whole of life and his gifts are to enable his people to function effectively and creatively in every sphere.

As we have seen, it is in the context of the body of Christ that Christians are encouraged to discover their gifts, challenged to dedicate them to God, and helped to use them in such a manner as to bring glory to God. The New Testament teaches that *being* is as important as *doing*. So the exercise of the gifts of the Spirit is closely linked with the need for the demonstration of the fruit of the Spirit. This ensures that gifts are never used with any sense of superiority or desire for self-seeking, or unscrupulosity to manipulate other people.

In developing the use of gifts within the church context Christians also learn how to relate those same gifts to their life in the world. The Spirit-inspired and Spirit-controlled use of those gifts by lay people in the workaday world will help make it a better place for everyone, and will demonstrate the relevance of the gospel to the whole of life.

God will give to some a prophetic word to expose injustice and dishonesty on the factory floor, in the boardroom and within the professions. He will give a word of wisdom to a group seeking to avert a strike while facing the need for just demands to be met by management, or to counsel a couple where marriage is in difficulties. He will enable his people in times of perplexity to distinguish between spirits to expose the under-cover motives of those who take up sides in a dispute. He will inspire acts of generosity and mercy to meet the needs of the poor and lonely. He will guide administrators in the management of complex processes and situations of conflict, so that efficiency is not achieved without regard to job-satisfaction or the social consequences. He will generate a gift of faith in the politician faced by a seemingly impossible future scenario, giving assurance of a way through to a brighter day. He will inspire the artist, designer, craftsman and technician to produce objects of all kinds – interpreting reality, displaying beauty, relieving drudgery, and able to perform intricate operations or release prodigious power. And when people turn to those who have created them with thanks or admiration, they point away from themselves to the Creator God who bestows his creative gifts and guides them in their expression.

9 Summary

The issue of gifts is crucial for church growth. We have attempted to show that gifts are distributed among the people of God so that no one is exempt. We have also noted the wide variety of these gifts. The task of the ordained ministry is not simply to minister to the congregation but to create and direct a ministering congregation through the detection, development and deployment of God-given resources. The church members are not there to enable the ordained minister to do his job; he is there to enable the congregation to fulfil theirs. This being so, we must examine our situation to discover how these principles are being worked out in practice.

What proportion of the congregation have identified their gifts? What steps do we envisage taking to help everyone identify their gifts? Once recognised, are our structures elastic and diverse enough to encourage people to develop and employ their gifts in fellowship with others?

Increased diversification will necessitate an enlarged leadership team with new specialist skills and the need for coordination so that the diversification does not result in fragmentation and frustration. I believe that there are enormous supplies of untapped resources within the Church. The present high level of unemployment in the nation palls into insignificance in comparison with that which prevails in the Church. Unidentified gifts represent unlived life. Let us find ways of helping each other identify our gifts and affirming one another in their development. The mission which Christ has committed to his Church represents the greatest enterprise with which we can be identified. Its implementation requires the total mobilisation of all our God-given resources in unending waves of committed creativity.

CHAPTER NINE

Leadership and Relationships

THE CHURCH GROWTH literature emanating from North America emphasises the vital role played by leadership in facilitating growth. Peter Wagner, for instance, in *Your Church Can Grow – Seven Vital Signs Of A Healthy Church*, rates strong pastoral leadership as the first of these signs. He writes, 'Vital Sign Number One of a healthy, growing church is a pastor who is a possibility thinker and whose dynamic leadership has been used to catalyse the entire church into action for growth' (Wagner 1976:57). His sheer ability, love and dedication have earned him a place of authority in his church. This is not an authority of status invested by the ecclesiastical hierarchy, but generated from below; built up through living relationships with people. 'Strong pastors of strong churches have earned the fierce loyalty of their parishioners' (Wagner 1976:57, 58).

The Southern Baptist denomination tested out Peter Wagner's seven vital signs in 277 of their fastest growing churches in the United States, and interviewed the pastors of the top fifteen in growth terms. They found that although the leaders of their fastest growing churches were self-effacing, yet they were the undisputed leaders. 'Overwhelmingly, lay persons describe their pastor as "shepherd of the flock" and 78 per cent of those interviewed considered him to be "a strong leader".' Pastor O'chester of Allandale responded, 'I have always been an authoritarian leader, but I'm not the man I used to be. My church didn't always follow me because I wasn't follow-able. Today, my church would charge hell with a thimble full of water if I said this was where God wants us. They would follow me because I would be out front!' (*Home Missions* Magazine Dec. '77).

This kind of language is hard to take from a European perspective. We react strongly against the dynamic image and success language which casts the church minister in the role of the business tycoon. The Rev. Gordon Jones, Education Secretary of the Church Pastoral Aid Society, reflects the sentiments of many British clergy when he exclaims, 'Phew!' in response to Peter Wagner's 'first vital sign', and then comments, 'If that is true most of us had better start packing our bags now. See you at the station' (*Church of England Newspaper*, May 18, 1979). In the second part of his article he expands on the theme, concluding, 'If such charisma and dynamism is essential for church growth then it has to be said that a large number of churches will never grow. Most of us are not in the star-studded first division of the clergy league' (*CEN* May 25, 1979).

A typically British attitude to church leadership is reflected in the following tongue-in-cheek article which has appeared in a number of parish magazines with the title THE ULTIMATE CHAIN LETTER (presumably with the incumbent's approval!)

> If you are unhappy with your vicar, simply have your church wardens send a copy of this letter to six other churches who are tired of their vicar. Then bundle up your vicar and send him to the church at the top of the list in this letter. Within a week you will receive 16,435 vicars and one of them should be all right. Have faith in this chain letter for vicars. Do not break the chain. One church did and got their old vicar back!

It is difficult to hear one another through the 'static'

created by differences of culture and ecclesiastic structure. The North American culture is success and growth-orientated. Achievement is acclaimed and rewarded. Everyone loves a winner. Furthermore, there is a much higher percentage of new churches than is the case in Europe, due to US population growth and urban migration, coupled with an entrepreneurial approach to religion. Churches are incorporated by a group of Christian businessmen who want their church to expand in much the same way as their businesses. They hire their pastor on merit, and fire him if his performance falls unacceptably short of expectations. This is a far cry from the position of an Anglican clergyman in England enjoying the security of his freehold without the constant pressure from his lay leaders to produce 'results', but where he has the freedom to say unpopular things without the fear of being voted out at the next board meeting. There are obvious strengths and weaknesses in both systems.

1 The Need for Leadership

While many of us would want to challenge the super-star approach with all the personality cult-following which it engenders, and the traumas which occasion the star's departure, we cannot duck the important issue of leadership. If we react adversely to the North American stress on ability and achievement we must also come to terms with European constraints on leadership, where so much depends on class, privilege and the 'old boy' network. In their book *Turning the Tide* (to be published by The Bible Society in 1981), Paul Beasley-Murray and Alan Wilkinson quote numerous statistics gathered from 350 Baptist churches throughout England. One section explores this first 'vital sign' by gathering data about the minister, his dominant characteristics, his theology, his relationships with lay members, and his usage of varied activities and techniques.

Their findings broadly support Wagner's premise that the pastor should be a possibility thinker and a dynamic leader for growth. It is, however, just as important that he should have a willingness and the ability to delegate or share his responsibilities with the members in his fellowship. There is a fruitful interdependence which neither party can achieve on its own.

When one considers the totality and variety of the pastoral care, the teaching, the evangelism and the administration needed within a fellowship, it is improbable that any one man – not matter how creative a thinker or dynamic a leader – can cope with the total spectrum. The leadership base must be extended to include others who are appropriately gifted and show leadership potential.

We may be nervous of success-orientated language with regard to leadership for both theological and pragmatic reasons. At the theological level we may feel that the leader will be judged on his faithfulness and effectiveness in fulfilling his calling, irrespective of results. Thus the faithful prophet may be rejected for his bold and frank speaking, while the false prophet who tailors his message to appeal to his audience may pull in the crowds. Success is not necessarily to be measured in terms of a full church and a mountainous budget.

On the other hand we are surely not simply to soldier on without any concern for results. The New Testament clearly teaches and demonstrates that God wants lost people found. He wants them to be introduced to his only son Jesus Christ, who alone can give them eternal life. At the level of pragmatism, we shy away from success-orientated language because it is too threatening in the European context of sustained decline since the First World War. But this is a situation which calls for leadership. Throughout the Old and New Testaments, and across the centuries of subsequent church history, the great periods in the story of the people of God have been characterised by outstanding leadership.

Clearly a few individuals display a distinctive charisma and most well-known leaders certainly have had it, but many others have achieved great things for God and inspired thousands by their example, even though they did not possess such personal charisma. Leadership is not created by image as much as by performance. This is a point which Paul makes in 1 Cor. 3; where he hits out against the factions produced by personality cults among the various Christian groups in Corinth. Some said they followed Paul, others Apollos, a third group were attracted to Peter, while a fourth, apparently out of a false sense of spiritual superiority, said they followed Christ. (1 Cor. 1:12). With regard to Apollos and himself, Paul draws attention away from their personalities to the essential functions which they each performed. 'The one who sows and the one who waters really do not matter. It is God who matters because he makes the plant to grow.'

But supposing after all the planting and regular watering nothing comes up. Do we simply shrug our shoulders and shift the responsibility on to God? Clearly not. Although it does not matter *who* does what, it is of crucial importance *how* it is done. The way we do things affects the outcome. There are more effective ways and less effective. Faithfulness implies more than stickability, it embraces being teachable, gaining skills and remaining expectant.

2 Styles of leadership

Styles of leadership vary. They depend upon a number of factors: the personality of the leader, the nature of the task to be accomplished, and the conditions prevailing at the time. There are also cultural influences which predispose societies to accept certain styles of leadership.

2.1 Autocratic leaders

Some leaders are *autocratic* by nature. They steamroller things along. Some do this in a benevolent manner as paternal autocrats. Others are more bureaucratic in style. They go by the book of rules. Still others are more visionary and inspirational. Olan Hendrix, a North American who has become well known in Britain through his leadership seminars sponsored by the Evangelical Alliance, describes such people as SNL – Strong Natural Leaders. The strength of this approach is that it usually gets things done speedily, but its principal weakness is that it creates a dependency network of reliance on one man which will readily collapse if the key person is removed. There is also the very real danger that as the situation grows and develops under his leadership the key man becomes progressively remote from the grass roots situation. If there are no adequate built-in checks and balances subordinates may become subservient, and the organisation will, like a ship without a compass, veer off course without the machinery to evaluate progress and make course corrections. Passengers and crew then become nervous and angry until the point is reached where they either mutiny or abandon ship.

2.2 Democratic leaders

Other leaders are *democratic or participatory* in approach. This is the style favoured in the majority of Protestant churches. It seeks to give organisational expression to the theological truth that the Church is the Body of Christ, and that we should normally expect the Lord to make his will known through the membership or their elected representatives. This is where the snags begin to arise. For it to work the group must be agreed on their fundamental beliefs and have arrived at a consensus on the objectives that they are constituted to fulfil as a local church. They must be sensitive to God's leading, in tune with one another, and with a breadth of vision to evaluate alternative routes to achieve an agreed goal. Where this is lacking then the church wanders along without either vision or motivation on a 'lowest common denominator' approach to opportunities and obstacles.

Furthermore, many so-called democratic systems are not so truly representative as they would appear on the surface. Sometimes the leadership group has a stranglehold on the situation. New people with a great deal to contribute are held at bay because they present too much of a threat to the less able people who have been occupying the seats of power for many years. The attitude prevails that those new people must serve a long apprenticeship before they begin to think of stepping into leadership positions.

2.3 Theocratic leadership

The democratic processes can be used to neutralise leadership initiative. The leader resigns himself to a laissez-faire approach, allowing everything to run its natural course, knowing that he would be blocked at every turn if he were to propose anything which either threatened his people's security or questioned their priorities.

From the side of the congregation the attitude is that of 'genteel anarchy' which expresses itself in a defiant attitude of 'Whatever you decide, we will continue to do precisely as we have always done, and if you persist in pressing the matter either we leave or you leave.' Faced with this kind of entrenched attitude it is all too easy to succumb to institutional pressures and abdicate from leadership on the basis of 'anything for a quiet life'.

The people of God in both the Old and New Testaments have been governed according to the *theocratic* principle. Perhaps within the modern western Church this has too readily been equated with the democratic approach. The organisational structures through which 'theocracy' – the rule of God – is expressed may vary according to the prevailing conditions and the nature of the task in hand.

Whatever the leadership style adopted the leader cannot escape the fact that he is an agent of change. Lyle Schaller describes the different roles: 'By action or by inaction every person does influence the future. Therefore, in one manner or another everyone is an agent of change. Some people are passive agents of change (let things happen), others are negative agents of change (they stop things happening), and an increasing number are becoming affirmative agents of change (they enable things to happen)' (Schaller 1973:12, 13).

In times of rapid change the church must seek to play a dual role. On the one hand she represents a conservative emphasis, seeking to remain loyal to a body of truth delivered once for all to the saints, and with a long and rich tradition built up through the many changing circumstances of her life. On the other hand she is called to fulfil a rejuvenating role, furthering the impact on the whole of life of the gospel which makes all things new. The Church as a Messianic community lives between the two comings of Christ. She experiences the tension of the 'now' and the 'not yet' of the Kingdom of God. The Church points back to the past, reaches out to the future, and expresses all she can of both in the *now* of day-to-day living.

3 Avenues of change

When considering the avenues of change there are four possible routes that the leader can follow. The path chosen must relate to his assessment of the situation and the degree of change envisaged. The first is that of *evolution*. This is the one most favoured by the conservative elements. It stresses continuity with the past, and thinks in terms of shaping what we have inherited to meet the demands of today and tomorrow. Such an approach is appropriate provided the pace of change in the society you seek to serve is fairly slow and the situation has not deteriorated beyond recall.

The second possibility is that of *reformation*. This also has a 'rear mirror' emphasis, but this time it is more critical. It is an attitude which sifts the past to distinguish between the good and the bad, and the more helpful and less helpful elements in our inherited structures. Some features are retained and reordered while others are discarded as a hindrance to effective performance.

The most radical route to take is the *revolutionary* road. It is also the most potentially traumatic as it entails a complete rejection of the past and overthrow of the established order. Some situations may be so appallingly and fundamentally wrong or corrupted that they have to be eradicated. However, the cost and outcome should be weighed very carefully. Power to turn the tables can so easily destroy the very idealism which motivated the action. 'Revolution' can come to mean no more than a turning of the wheel, with the last state simply a more extreme form of that which it replaced.

The fourth avenue is that of *innovation*. I believe this to be the most appropriate route for a leader to take in most church situations today. The innovative leader does not destroy all that he has inherited as an essential prerequisite for a successful investment in the future. He is appreciative of the insights and achievements of previous generations, and possesses discernment to identify those elements which are of lasting value. He is also aware that the 'latest' does not necessarily equate with the 'best'. So he tempers his enthusiasm with humility as he plans for the future. He is hesitant to sacrifice the existing set-up until he is reasonably assured of the success of its replacement. Furthermore he will have to bear in mind those among his church members who either through old age cannot cope with yet more change, or who have been hurt or disillusioned by traumatic experiences in the shape of unwanted changes which were inflicted upon them.

It will serve no useful purpose to threaten the existing set-up as a first step to introducing new approaches. Such action will only serve to raise barriers and block further progress in other areas. The innovative leader adopts a different strategy. He affirms all that he can in the existing situation. What his people are used to may be meeting their needs. It is an unloving act to inflict further changes with which they can neither cope, nor do they see its relevance to themselves. When confidence has been established through the existing members realising that their leader is on their side, he can then begin to talk, for instance, about the potential church members who may be from a very different background from those who have been church members for most of their lives. Such new people are unlikely to be reached unless the church is prepared to adopt alternative approaches, possibly through a different style of church service and through other avenues than those provided by the existing organisations. Thus, while enthusiastically maintaining what is there already, the new grows up alongside and hopefully each benefits from the other.

There is always an element of risk in attempting to forge new paths and some of the enterprises may fail or need to be revised at frequent intervals. By using the innovative, approach experimentation can proceed with minimum damage to the existing patterns, so that change will not automatically be equated with decay in the mind of the 'old stagers'. Furthermore, the traditionalists can be involved in the planning of new concepts and should certainly be encouraged to take a prayerful interest in what is going on. In the long term, those new ventures which succeed may well eventually attract those who were cautious and suspicious at the beginning. Any cross-pollination which occurs will be to the benefit of all and therefore should be planned for and encouraged.

4 Leadership models

As we have previously noted, different situations require different leadership styles and mode of change employed. A medical team at the scene of an accident has to take rapid and co-ordinated action. To cope with the emergency, when speed and efficiency are vital if lives are to be saved, an autocratic model of leadership is essential. Orders have to be given concisely and clearly. There is no time to argue the pros and cons, they have to be smartly obeyed, at the double!

In the case of long-term planning or deciding on how to deal with a situation which, although serious, does not have to be acted upon immediately, a more democratic approach can be adopted.

Within the church context there are a number of leadership models which the minister or priest may be called upon to adopt. Different individuals will feel easier in one role than in the other, and some personality types are more adaptable than others. Very few individuals, however, are versatile enough in gifts and skills to adopt all the roles. Each must therefore recognise his limitations and seek to supplement these by well-chosen advisers who can compensate for his deficiencies. Let us now consider some of the more common models:

4.1 The able teacher

This is the model most dominant within the majority of Protestant churches. His task is supremely to expound the Bible. When education was a privilege enjoyed by a select few, the clergyman was respected as the man of letters. Thus the academic hood, whether granted by a university or theological college, is part of the uniform on formal occasions. However, the acquisition of learning is not the same as having the ability to teach. Many a polished three-point sermon fails to make a three-point landing!

The Church's established patterns of training for the ministry are partly to blame, as they train men to become amateur theologians rather than able teachers. Happily this state of affairs is beginning to change, but there is still a long way to go.

Far too many theological college lecturers hide behind a barricade of books which provide protection and conceal the world outside from them. They sit 'heads down' pursuing their specialist interest. The ministerial students are invited to share this erudition. As a result they learn a new vocabulary, become proficient at answering abstruse questions set by examination boards and thereby think they have learnt something. To dispel any sneaking doubts they are given a certificate to prove it.

What I have written does not constitute a swipe at theology. I am not intending to be anti-intellectual. But I am pleading strongly for a theology which is earthed in real life – or to use the jargon – a contextualised theology. As a regular feature of training we must be asking, 'How does that relate to situations I have already experienced or might conceivably have to face?' And 'How can I say that in a way which enables me to be understood and which is authentic to me?' I regret to say that while at theological college I had neither the discernment nor mental discipline to do this for myself, and so emerged with sheaves of notes for much of which I could find little subsequent use.

The missionary anthropologist Charles Kraft expressed the issue succinctly with regard to 'hermeneutics', which is the study of the principles of interpreting the text of the Bible. 'Hermeneutics is not, therefore, merely an academic game to be played by supposedly objective scholars. It is a dynamic process that properly demands deep subjective involvement on the part of Christian interpreters operating within the Christian community (which includes scholars) both with the Scriptures and with the life of the world around them in which they live. . . .'

'The life context with which the interpreter is interacting is critical to the whole process. If the life context to which the applications are made is merely an academic context, the nature of the insights derived from Scripture and their usability outside that context are vitally affected. This is what makes much of what goes on in academic institutions and scholarly writings unusable in life contexts other than the classroom' (Kraft 1979:145).

To be fair to theological colleges, most of them have precious little time-table flexibility to build in the dimension which I suggest. The pressure of the syllabus requirements, set either by university or denominational educational boards, squeezes out alternative approaches to the designated topics, and the students are assessed largely on written examination performance. The situation has however become more flexible in England within recent years with the introduction of the Council for National Academic Awards which allows accredited educational establishments to devise their own courses. Some are taking advantage of this opportunity to introduce courses which are more closely related to the job for which ministerial students are supposedly being prepared.

The problem expanded here is not confined to full-time theological students. It can also affect those being trained, as in the Anglican Church, for the auxiliary pastoral ministry and to become 'Readers' (what an archaic title!). Their training is in danger of domesticating and institutionalising them so that they become, in the words of veteran missioner Canon Harry Sutton, 'mini-parsons rather than maxi-witnesses'. The orientation of our training should be to the world rather than the Church.

Dr Donald McGavran sets the following exercise for his church growth students. He asks them to look critically at the basis of faith of their church. Most of these were drawn up within a 'Christendom' situation and describe the church in relation to other Christian bodies which are regarded as in error or deficient in some way. He then requires them to re-write their basis of faith within a missionary context of a non-Christian society, reflecting the priority of the Great Commission to go into all the world and make disciples. When applied to the Thirty-nine articles of the Anglican Church, to which I belong, this makes for a fascinating work project.

In the Church's selection of leadership above the congregational level I believe there has been an over-emphasis on the scholar model, which has adversely affected the growth potential of the denominations. Being skilled in teaching requires, in addition to a thorough grasp of the subject, a profound understanding of the audience and the questions in their minds. School teachers are aware that pupils are seldom prepared to 'pay' attention. Attention has to be 'earned' by exciting their curiosity. Teaching is not to be measured in terms of output but intake. Nobody has been taught anything until someone has learned something. An essential ingredient in Christian education should be the opportunity to respond, for we are required to be doers of the Word and not hearers only. Latin American theologians make the helpful distinction between orthodoxy and orthopraxis. Orthodoxy is what we claim to believe. Orthopraxis is what we demonstrate that we believe. And at the end of the day, they point out, we shall be judged on the basis of our orthopraxis rather than our orthodoxy.

Once, in South America, I was invited to lecture at a Christian night school being set up by a group of Chileans, most of whom were from Pentecostal churches around the port of Valparaíso. As they discussed their plans, one of the church leaders began to express his doubts. He wanted to know what the students were going to *do* with all their newly acquired knowledge. For 'to whom much is given, much is required', he quoted. And if they were not going to do anything as a result of attending the institute, it would be better if they had never come in the first place. Their learning only serves to place them under greater judgement. This is an interesting third-world perspective on theological education!

Many books have been written on the craft of making sermons and the art of their delivery, but insufficient attention has been paid to their reception. What is to be done with them once the benediction has been pronounced? Are they simply to be filed away by the preacher? Will they simply fly out of the minds of the congregation (that is assuming they ever flew in)? What change was the sermon designed to bring about, and what appropriate steps were taken to give opportunity for response? Rarely is there any provision for feed-back or time to discuss attitude changes, or specific courses of action. Because there is no opportunity for response, people are at a loss to know what to do with the sermon once it has been delivered. Being able to teach means far more than the ability to deliver a clear exposition of biblical passages; it embraces the art of raising questions so that people are stimulated to think for themselves. It also involves apprenticeship learning. The teacher cannot confine himself to the theoretical aspects of his subject, but must teach through being involved with his pupils in learning situations.

In the Church's selection of the top echelons of leaders I believe there is an over-emphasis on the scholar model, which has adversely affected the growth potential of the denominations. The wise scholar is a person who can see both sides of an argument. He can shuttle skilfully between the pros and the cons. Yet he may have great difficulty in making up his mind and in determining on one course of action rather than another. While not wanting to dispute that the Church needs erudite scholars, I suggest that it also urgently requires many more men on the ground who have vision, confidence and courage to lead; who have that sixth sense to size up a situation, to set a course and inspire people to go with them. Our performance must be brought into line with our declared purposes. Only then will our public statements sound other than platitudes.

4.2 The protecting father

This leadership style has its roots in the patriarchal tradition. The paternal autocrat is the central figure in the extended family's complex network of relationships. 'A patrilineal extended family is composed of a patriarch, his sons and grandsons and their wives and offspring' (Hiebert 1976:215). He is the anchor man providing stability and cohesion. Today, this model is still to be found within a number of Christian churches with a wide range of traditions. The leader who is a firm-handed father figure is evident in Catholicism and in the Orthodox and Pentecostal churches. Within Catholicism the model arises not simply out of that Church's theology of the ordained ministry as mediating priest and dispenser of the sacraments. It is also explained by the fact that, being celibate, he has fewer conflicting loyalties and traditionally stays longer in one church than does his Protestant counterpart.

In the Orthodox and Pentecostal traditions the sociological explanation is somewhat different. There the leader has probably grown up in the community he serves and regards his pastoring of that congregation as his life's calling. This encourages and enables him to establish a depth of relationship which is not possible for someone who has come from elsewhere and expects that he will be moving on again with the space of five to seven years. The leader, therefore, never fully identifies with his people, preferring to distance himself. Such aloofness was actively encouraged in theological college training. Ministerial students were advised not to make their friends within the parish! When problems begin to arise among his church members he is more prone to complain about them than weep over them.

I remember kneeling in prayer on the dirt floor of a shack church alongside a Chilean Pentecostal pastor. He was a man of his people, indistinguishable from them either in his dress or his speech. He had dedicated his life to their service. Like most of his kind he was an older man with gnarled hands and a weather-beaten face. As he prayed earnestly for his congregation he named each in turn, and poured out his heart for them as though they were members of his flesh-and-blood family. They were like his own children for whom he felt personally responsible. He recounted before God the joys or sorrows which each brought to his heart. After a time tears were streaming down his cheeks. Was this depth of relationship between pastor and people one of the secrets of the incredible growth of the Pentecostal churches in Latin America?

Christian Lalive D'Epinay thinks so. He writes, 'The pastors are the authentic expression of the congregation, and the thing which distinguishes them from the mass of members is not their social origin or their way of living or their intellectual attainments, but simply certain qualities they have as leaders of men' (Lalive 1969:77). A further factor is that seventy-nine per cent, according to Lalive's research, are first-generation converts from the world, so they are acutely aware of what life is really like for their congregation. They themselves have shared its harsh realities, and as the majority of pastors still continue to earn their living in secular employment, they are in daily touch.

I write these words after watching the BBC televised Sunday night worship service 'Songs of Praise'. On this occasion it was broadcast from St George's, Everton, where the Rev. Neville Black is the Team Rector and leader of the Evangelical Urban project. Born and bred in nearby Bootle, he has preserved a close sense of identity with the area and is passionately concerned for the church to put down indigenous roots in this inner-city, artisan area of Liverpool. In the programme he explained how he had learned to do his theology in a new kind of way, and that it had taken fifteen years of ministry there to arrive at his starting-points. Later in the programme, the parish clerk, who worked as a docker in Liverpool, was asked whether he had ever wanted 'to go into the Church'. That phrase is revealing in itself. It suggests that you do not really belong until you have been processed and received ordained leadership status. He replied that he would love to, but did not have the necessary educational qualifications. This highlights part of the reason for the Church's ineffectiveness in the inner city.

One valiant attempt to respond to the need to generate indigenous local church leadership in the inner city was made by the Rev. Ted Roberts at St James-the-Less, Bethnal Green, in the East End of London. He describes the Cockney life-style of his parishioners. 'They are not ashamed of being working class! In fact, if they have thought about it at all, they probably believe that their way of life is as valid and enjoyable as anyone else's. A

Christian visiting East London will soon discover that, for the majority, the church does not constitute part of that way of life.' (Roberts 1972:12). Despite vast sums of money having been invested by the Church, and heroic work done by clergy and lay helpers, little has endured. There have been glorious achievements, Ted Roberts acknowledges, 'But those achievements have been almost exclusively with individuals. For some reason we have failed to create Christian community.' He recognised that 'if a genuinely indigenous church is to grow it must have an indigenous ministry', and so developed an imaginative and innovative scheme to train local people. Six accepted his invitation to begin the five years of training. Two dropped out and four were ordained deacon in 1972, an event which achieved BBC television news coverage. In six important respects his training scheme was different from the normal run of training. He identifies them as follows:

1 – a team rather than solitary ministers.
2 – call by the local church rather than outside appointments.
3 – settled rather than itinerant ministry (i.e. the traditional minister moves elsewhere after a few years).
4 – training – local and practical.
5 – a specific term of service rather than an open ended commitment.
6 – voluntary rather than paid.

These principles are all admirable for the creation of indigenous ministry; they are all according to the missionary text-book. However, when applied to the Anglican Church in the inner city they run up against serious obstacles. There is a long history of an alien, imported pattern of ministry and leadership which cannot easily be replaced either in the minds of the congregation or the surrounding community. The image of the 'vicar' as a middle class, educated, imported leader means that the 'ordination' of a local person appears as a betrayal of his origins, so that he becomes culturally dispossessed. He cannot fulfil the chain of expectations which are linked to the 'dog collar'. The nub of the problem rests in the Church's failure to establish Christian community within the Cockney culture. If local church leadership is to emerge and find acceptance (not with the powers-that-be, but with those they are called to serve), then a new kind of church life will need to emerge which will be distinctive in its forms of worship and the way in which it expresses its mutual commitment and mission within the community. New wineskins are needed for new wine.

4.3 The understanding brother

'Brother' was the term by which the apostle Paul most frequently addressed his fellow Christians. It expressed the bond of spiritual kinship linking believers together. It is particularly emotive when the Church has achieved a high degree of commitment to a common cause and is exposed thereby to hostility and persecution. The Trades Union movement also uses the term to express to fellow trade unionists the sense of belonging together in the defence and advancement of their mutual interests. When, however, the mutual commitment is lacking, the title assumes a hollow ring, and may become an embarrassment. When used between theological students on the college campus it is an indication that 'the brother' has forgotten your name!

The title 'brother' was reinstated for me during my four years of missionary service in Latin America. There you are welcomed as '*hermano*' (brother) with a warm embrace. You are introduced to the congregation as to your family of adoption. Being an '*hermano*' may lead to an invitation home, a meal and a bed for the night. I have no doubt that the same would be true of the churches in Africa and other parts of the world. Here in Europe there is a disturbing lack of 'kinship' in many churches. A handshake is little more than a polite formality – a way of ending an encounter rather than of deepening one. The majority of churchgoers recoil from the thought of personal involvement with one another.

In leadership terms the 'understanding brother' is one who identifies with people and their problems. The 'brother' takes on the local culture. There is no sense of managerial aloofness or clinical detachment. Paul as an apostle sometimes had to lay down the law. But having done so, he then drew alongside as a brother to share his own internal struggles, fears and plans. He had that rare ability to slip from one role into another. He did not use his apostleship to secure aloofness from the personal involvements of brotherhood.

Within middle-class and artisan cultures there is a different attitude to employment which has a bearing on the acceptance of the minister. The middle class are concerned about job opportunities and promotion. The artisan is concerned about job security, status between grades and pay differentials. If a minister leaves his inner-city church he is regarded as leaving 'in order to better himself'. It is a boss who moves, but a brother who stays. The Rev. Bryan Ellis, while working at Burmantofts, a growing church in a down-town area of Sheffield, testified that it took him seven years to *start* his ministry. The imported short-term minister can easily regard the Christian family as foster children. He takes in problem children for a brief span before handing them on with a sigh of relief to someone else! A brother, like the father-figure, cannot adopt that attitude.

To become a 'brother' means not only a readiness to get near to people, but being prepared for them to get close to us. In spiritual warfare, as in military combat, one of the enemy's tactics is to isolate soldiers from the main column and pick them off one at a time. There are many exposed, lonely men in the ministry who have become isolated because they will not be ministered to by others. Ministry is a two-way transaction. The bond of brotherhood helps us to enter the rough and tumble of life together, enjoying both mutual support and accountability.

4.4 The effective manager

In the pre-industrial times of the Bible, the closest we get to 'manager' is the 'steward' (*oikonomos* or *epitropos*). These two terms are used interchangeably to denote the 'house manager'. The steward would be responsible for running household affairs and for managing the estate. From the parable of the three stewards (Matt. 25:14–26) we can see that he is expected to operate faithfully and effectively. Those who demonstrate that they can handle the resources entrusted to them will be rewarded with greater resources and wider responsibilities.

The Bible recognises that individuals have different levels of ability. This is expressed in the parable of the three servants by each one being given different amounts. In Luke's Gospel this is recognised in a different way. There ten servants are given equal amounts – a gold coin each (Luke 19:11–27). In response to the challenge, 'See what you can earn with this while I am gone!', one returned with ten times the original amount while another increased his five-fold. People who start off equal do not end up that way. Some will achieve more than others. But most of us can improve on our performance.

Many churches face serious management problems, though these are often spiritualised to recast them in a form with which the clergyman feels professionally competent to deal. Many of the difficulties arise because management skills are not taught in most theological colleges. We clergymen emerge from training with a theological and historical understanding of the Church, but without sufficient understanding of it as a social institution. As such it is subject to all the pressures of any other secular organisation. If management skills are required for running industry, they are even more needed in the Church, for there the management task is more complex. In the

Church there is no narrowly defined and clearly labelled product, and the labour force consists of volunteers. The management of volunteer workers is far more delicate, with different rules applying, than is the case when people depend on the work for their livelihood. Some men entering the ministry bring management skills which they have learned in their previous employment in business or military service. Where such skills have been sensitively adapted to the peculiarities of church life, congregations feel the benefit. Clergy without this background are 'forced to fly by the seat of their pants'. If they have a sense of direction and succeed in getting a hang of the controls they remain airborne, otherwise they have to bail out or crash land when things get out of control. Fortunately management skills can be learned, and there are many qualified lay people in the Church who would be delighted to render their services if invited to do so.

4.5 The humble servant

A Christian understanding of leadership excludes any idea of power grasping or engaging in an ego-trip. He seeks to serve God not *be* God. Paul, the apostle of Christ, was also his bond-slave and conscious of his fraternal relationship with every member of the family of God. When a leadership struggle broke out among our Lord's disciples, Jesus pointed the contrast between the world's understanding of leadership and that which was appropriate to his Kingdom. 'The kings of the pagans have power over the people, and the rulers are called, "Friends of the people". But this is not the way it is with you; rather, the greatest one among you must be like the youngest, and the leader must be like the servant. Who is greater, the one who sits down to eat or the one who serves him? The one who sits down, of course. But I am among you as one who serves.' (Luke 22:25–27). In his understanding of both leadership role and style our Lord broke through all the conventions of his time. He did this not just by means of his teaching, but through his personal example. He insisted that people are not there for the sake of those who govern, but that government is there for the sake of the people.

This principle was dramatically demonstrated in the Upper Room when Jesus was at supper with his disciples and performed the foot-washing service, which custom required should be the service performed by a household servant. John's account of the incident highlights its significance. 'Jesus knew that the Father had given him complete power; he knew that he had come from God and was going to God. So he rose from the table, took off his outer garments and tied a towel around his waist' (John 13:3–5). This lowliest of acts is set in the immediate context of the loftiest of claims. It was intended as a example for his disciples to follow (v. 15). We are called to minister to one another. This entails being alert to what needs to be done, no matter how lowly the task, and then taking the initiative in doing it. Our commitment to one another is total, to the extent of being prepared to lay down our lives for one another, as Christ laid down his life for us.

Although Christian ministry involves wearing an apron, this does not mean becoming a door-mat. We are called to hold the towel of humility, not the door-mat of subservience which everyone can walk over. Service is not doing everything that everyone else should be doing; rather it is acting in such a way that others are prompted to take up their responsibilities willingly.

In summary, there are a number of leadership models, and which model is appropriate at any given time will depend on a combination of factors. Furthermore, these models are not mutually exclusive, and the one which predominates will depend both on the personality of the leader and the nature of the situation.

5 Skill levels

If any organisation, ecclesiastical or commercial, is to sustain growth, it must be prepared to restructure when the need to do so becomes evident. Moving from one phase to the next often requires a change in management style, and the acquiring of fresh skills. I am grateful to the Rev. John Wimber, an associate professor at Fuller Seminary, for the following model which I have adapted slightly to fit the British situation. He relates church size to the corresponding skill level in industry.

CHURCH SIZE	INDUSTRIAL SKILL LEVEL
1	Unskilled worker
2–65	Foreman
66–150	Supervisor
151–450	Middle management
451–1,000	Top management
1,000+	Chairman of the Board!

5.1 Unskilled worker

When the congregation stands at zero, *unskilled worker* level will suffice! The unskilled worker is merely concerned about his own activities without any need to be responsible for anyone else, or for the quality of the product or service he is working on. There is widespread frustration among lay people at the lack of management skill displayed by their clergy. As a clerical colleague admitted, 'As far as running anything is concerned, some of us couldn't run a tap!' If we lack skills to this extent then we must do some rapid reading on the subject or seek advice from those who have management expertise. We may not have far to look, for on many of our church committees are to be found people who are organising every working day, yet have not seen the usefulness of their skills for the life of the church, often because the minister has never encouraged their use.

A number of churches known to the author are facing this problem with a refreshing openness, and mutual expressions of relief as between the minister and his church council or deacons' court. While vision is an essential quality in leaders, management skills are not indispensable. However, he must understand management principles before he can assess his own management ability. If a leader knows that he will never make a good manager, then his awareness of management principles will help to minimise the frustration he is likely to cause. When a leader, who shows his competence in other areas yet lacks management skills, is in the driving seat, it is essential that he has someone at his elbow who can translate vision and ideas into strategy, otherwise they will not remain on course. The distinction between management and leadership is an important one to maintain. The leader perceives *what* needs to be done. The manager demonstrates *how* it can be achieved.

5.2 Foreman
In a small church with a membership of up to say 65, the management style of the leader will probably be at the level of *foreman* or charge hand. He is one of a work-gang who is able to stand in for any of the members. He is available to be personally involved in every task which comes to hand. So the minister of the small church is expected to be a Jack-of-all-trades. He turns his hand to everything: mowing the grass, stoking the boiler, typing the letter, duplicating the magazine, leading the choir, etc., etc. He can probably sustain this pressure and diversity of work-load until the adult congregation tops 65, and then he will be in danger of driving himself into the ground. The church probably will not grow much beyond that point until he either leaves to establish another struggling church, or changes his ways.

5.3 Supervisor
In churches with a membership of between 66 and 150 the most frequently encountered leadership level is that of *supervisor*. In industry the supervisor is responsible for

a line of people engaged in a number of routine operations or a small department whose job is to provide a service (e.g. invoicing). He shows everybody in his charge what to do, and constantly watches them to make sure that they continue to do it in the approved manner and to an acceptable standard. He is on hand to deal with any emergency and resolve any difficulties which may arise. Church ministers who operate in this way have their phones constantly ringing, or find people for ever at the door and have queues of church members at every service and function. These are people who have been given jobs to do, but have not been given the authority to make decisions relating to their tasks. Consequently, everything has to be referred back to the minister, who then begins to find that it is quicker to do things himself, as he is now spending the major part of his time chasing up other people. The situation becomes impossible as membership nears the 150 mark. Few individuals can cope with more than that number of people at more than surface level. Working relationships begin to break down. Also, as a church grows it diversifies its activities to the point where the leader is unable to make meaningful detailed decisions in every area. The Jack-of-all-trades has revealed himself to be incapable in the circumstances of becoming a master of any.

5.4 Middle management

The leader has to change his management style to *middle management* level to get far into the 151–450 member bracket. Middle management involves delegation *with accountability*. When people are invited to undertake some responsibility in the church they are given appropriate decision-making powers. The musical director, Sunday School superintendent, magazine editor, youth leader, parish administrator, require written job descriptions which spell out the requirements of the job and specify areas where the job holder has decision-making powers to avoid the need to refer back constantly to the minister or one of the church's management committees. (See page 264 for a sample job description for a home group leader.) In a large church the Sunday School superintendent, for instance, must be responsible for the teaching curriculum, training of teachers, discipline and home visitation of the children. He will work through his education committee and teaching team. Policy matters will be agreed with the minister and church committee, and the minister is on hand to offer a listening ear. Yet he must avoid getting over-involved in the detailed execution and allowing all the decision-making to float up the church's organisational structure. People have to be trusted. When others do a job in our place, it is to be expected that they probably won't do it our way. There is a wise missionary saying which reminds us, 'If you want a job done properly do it yourself. But if you want it to last, get someone else to do it!'

Management in a growing church of more than 150 members becomes increasingly complex, because the work force is made up of volunteers. The minister is the one person paid to run the church, and he is the one most likely to be available to attend to the hundred-and-one practical things which have to be dealt with during normal business hours. At this point the church will need to give serious consideration to the enlarging of its full-time staff, to diversify its ministries and provide the necessary administrative support.

5.5 Top management

The church with more than 450 members will have a growing full-time staff, each of whom operates at middle-management level. The minister in charge therefore needs *top-level management skills* to weld his professional team together. He is responsible for over-all strategy and ensuring its implementation in the various departments. But he must leave room for initiative to be exercised by his team members. They will want to be treated as professionals who know their jobs, have ideas of their own and can carry responsibility. They must therefore be left to formulate their goals and draw up plans to implement agreed objectives.

5.6 Chairman of the board

When a church tops the 1,000 membership mark it enters the super-league. Some exponents of church growth theory have serious doubts as to whether churches should ever be encouraged to reach such proportions. They argue that it is preferable to sub-divide to maintain a growth momentum. The larger the church the higher the percentage of passengers it may find itself carrying. Superchurches, they argue, merely drain life from other congregations situated in their extensive catchment areas. Others take a different view, maintaining that urban conurbations with a densely populated, highly mobile society of people with wide-ranging interests and affiliations, require churches which are large enough to achieve visibility in the urban scene, and are able to sustain a wide range of activities corresponding to the community's diverse needs.

Our purpose here is not to enter into the pros and cons of this debate, but simply to indicate the leadership level at which the presiding minister of such a church will need to operate. He functions as *chairman of the board*. He dreams his dreams, formulates his plans, and excites others with the vision of his perceptions of where the church could be five years hence. He is looking for a hand-picked team of able people who can see their individual specialisations in relation to the whole. He ensures that there is free time in his diary to take soundings of the state of affairs at the grass-roots level, otherwise he will quickly get out of touch, and he fulfils a wider ministry as ambassador of his congregation, sharing their vision with the church at large. There are very few examples of this kind of church in Europe, but they are to be found in the Americas and elsewhere. Some have proved to be an inspiration in many places around the world. Such a ministry is however is not without its self-evident dangers.

6 Leadership qualities

While leadership styles vary there are a number of characteristics which are apparent in the lives of outstanding leaders.

6.1 A leader is gifted with perception

Many people get so entangled in the problems that they cannot 'see the wood for the trees'. The leader should be able to step back, to get outside the problem and see things in perspective. He must be able to set the situation out clearly and expose the heart of the matter. A great leader in fact makes few significant decisions, but he isolates the key issues. Having made up his mind about these, many other decisions fall into place. Until that central issue has been identified and decided upon, every other decision has to be considered in isolation, which makes for muddle and contradiction. Henry Ford's key decision was that the motor car should be cheap enough to be available to the average family. The rest of what Henry Ford did follows on from that – a basic model, one colour only, assembly line production etc. Lord Alanbrooke in his position as Chief of the General Staff in World War Two developed his grand strategy of rolling back the Allied map, starting in North Africa and continuing through Italy and southern Europe. During the early part of the war he had to contain Churchill's enthusiasm for the headline-grabbing, one-off daring raids. Task and problem definitions are a key role of the leader. Having identified what needs to be done and having explored and evaluated the possible ways of approaching the task he then must identify the resources he will need. 'Effective leadership diagnoses where the greatest readiness and capacity exists to carry out the commitments and priorities of the organisation. A good leader utilises the best equipped person to act on those priorities' (Perry 1977:73).

6.2 A leader must lead

He must have the courage of his convictions to set a course and to ensure that it is maintained. Like the captain of a sailing ship he must be skilled at reading the weather to take advantage of a favourable wind by hoisting full sail, and he must know how to ride out a storm, keeping the ship's bows to the waves. He needs also to be alert to the subtle influences of tides which would carry the unwary off-course, and to the hidden dangers to which he needs to give a wide berth lest his craft be holed and possibly sunk.

A church must define clearly and concisely what it believes to be its main objectives. It is the task of the leader to ensure that this is done. He is also required to chart the possible routes to their achievement. Leadership means the loneliness of being out front – but not too far ahead. A leader ceases to lead when he is so far ahead that he is either out of sight, or sets too fast a pace which none of his followers will be able to sustain. Leadership entails being in touch with the tail-enders as well as the front-runners.

There is a tendency for some ministers to abdicate from a leadership position. It is safer and more secure to be a neutral chairman ready to accept and implement committee decisions without questioning them too closely. There is a feeble form of democracy which prevents any action until there is unanimity. The result is that many long-overdue decisions are kept in limbo, and the church can only move forward on non-controversial and usually relatively insignificant matters. In reality this state of affairs is not democracy but rule by the minority who hold the rest of the congregation to ransom.

Due either to the influence of training, or the demands of parochial ministry, a number of clergy place the emphasis on counselling rather than leadership. They become so entangled in the problems of individuals that the church as a whole loses a sense of direction and lacks cohesion. A captain of a ship cannot confine himself to the sick bay. He must get back on the bridge. Furthermore his 'non-directive counselling' approach is carried over into his leadership functions with debilitating consequences. While it may be possible to act as a non-directive counsellor, it is a contradiction in terms to be a non-directive leader. A leader must lead.

6.3 A leader inspires confidence

A distinction must be made between the convictions people have regarding the suitability of plans and their confidence in the leadership seeking to implement them. Plans can be turned down without being given serious consideration through lack of trust rather than lack of commitment.

A leader must secure his leadership base by having an adequate support group. Such a group is not composed of pliable 'yes men' but of those who have leadership standing, a degree of discernment and a range of specialist skills.

A new minister, or for that matter an old, established minister, who is seeking to lift both himself and his congregation out of a rut, must work hard to build trust and confidence. The inexperienced and impetuous are tempted to move into the areas of greatest controversy to establish their battle ground and force through sweeping changes. Such changes run the risk of proving to be for the worse rather than the better. Beware of change for change's sake.

A wiser strategy is to leave the more controversial areas until later and begin by affirming what is inherited, wherever possible only introducing change where there is evidence of broad support and which looks reasonably sure of success. This establishes confidence in the judgement of the leader and creates working relationships and team cohesion. When bonds of mutual esteem and confidence have been forged they can then be tested in the more contentious areas. The leadership must reach a stage where they can disagree seriously on issues while still parting as friends. This leads us directly into the next point.

The course once set must be maintained. Nothing erodes confidence in a leader more than switching from one objective to another so that the whole progress of the church becomes erratic. When it's anybody's guess where it might be heading next, no one is prepared to commit himself.

A friend was taking an indoor photograph of a Chilean minister with his wife and young family. As he pressed the shutter release his electric flash gun went off, startling the children. 'That bulb's no good,' declared the bright six-year-old lad. 'You want one like that,' he said, pointing to the bulb suspended from the ceiling. Leadership is not a bright, momentary burst of light; it must supply sustained illumination. 'Stickability' is an essential quality. Great leaders are not easily discouraged. They press forward in the face of seemingly insurmountable odds. They refuse to dig up what they have sown in faith. No pessimist was ever a great leader. An effective leader sees a promised land stretching before him and refuses to let those around him reduce it to problem land. A responsible leader does not ignore problems, but he keeps them in perspective. There will always be obstacles to progress, but he refuses either to sit down under them or retreat before them. It is the task of leadership to blast through, climb over, or find a way round. The leader does not panic. He maintains his poise under pressure. Having accepted responsibility he does not then try to pass the buck or hide behind committee decisions. A leader must be able to live with tension. This demands a sense of personal security, the ability to make difficult and sometimes unpopular decisions, and the capacity to switch off and relax.

6.4 A leader is able to influence others

One of the simplest ways to spot a leader is to notice who people are following! The leader has a winsomeness which enables him to influence the thinking of other people and to motivate them to action. His presence instils confidence, heightens possibilities, and encourages people to get involved. Trust is gradually built up through the quality of personal relationships. Tactically, a minister is wise to spend the greater part of his first year in an established church situation in getting to know who the decision-makers are and in establishing rapport with them. He should concentrate his leadership decisions on fairly safe areas, where he is guaranteed a wide base of support.

When the time comes to introduce innovative ideas, we are saved from disappointment if we recognise that most good ideas are rejected first time and even second time around. The fact that they fail to achieve the necessary majority should not be regarded as the end of the road. It is better to withdraw the suggestion while the debate is still amicable, than precipitate a crisis which may debar the reintroduction of the idea for months or even years. If the discussion is allowed to become heated, on each subsequent occasion that the issue is raised, committee members will re-enter the fray in the same combative spirit. If, however, the idea is introduced first time as no more than a tentative suggestion, the responses, both negative and positive, can be evaluated with a view to its later reintroduction in a form which is most likely to secure the widest acceptance.

6.5 A leader is able to foster good relationships and build up a cohesive team

This follows on from the previous point. The leader inspires confidence through his consistency and a measure of predictability. If those around him do not know where he is likely to jump next, they become understandably nervous and cautious. A leader who has patiently established a consistent and workable pattern of operation can then afford to adopt a more flexible approach from time to time. A totally predictable man becomes dull. The occasional unexpected, adventurous decision keeps people on their toes without setting them on the retreat.

One of the drawbacks of a 'strong natural leader' is that he often tries to project on to other people his high standards and total dedication, which they do not always share. He therefore becomes very critical of his colleagues and subordinates, and in turn they become cautious in their response to him. Thereby are sown the seeds which will jeopardise the future prospects.

The Christian leader is called to be a shepherd, not a jockey! He rounds people up and leads them forward rather than riding on their backs and driving them on to achieve his objectives. Good relationships are fostered through affirmation. We must have a ministry of encouragment to one another, helping each other develop those gifts with which God has endowed every one of us. Only then will we have access through each other's defences to offer constructive criticism.

Summary

A good leader must be prepared to extend the base of leadership by encouraging others to share their particular expertise for the good of the whole. We must be ready to welcome other people to work alongside us, who have abilities in specific areas greater than our own, without feeling personally threatened by their presence. Remember, the chain is as strong as its weakest link. So a team will break apart unless weak links are reinforced.

There will be little in the way of sustained church growth without inspiring and facilitating leadership. Identify the leadership requirements of your church in terms of your spheres of ministry (see page 348). Do each of your leaders have workable job-descriptions? Do they work together as a cohesive team? Are you alert to spot new and potential leaders, or is the leadership a closed circle? Does your leadership encourage initiative among the members, or does it regard any move among them as a potential threat? Do your leaders need further training to upgrade their skills to cope with a larger and more diverse operation? Are your leaders prepared for an evaluation of their performance? Do we pray regularly for our leaders, that their vision might be kept clear, that they will be able to sustain their creative drive, that through their decisions the whole congregation might be challenged, excited, involved and fulfilled?

CHAPTER TEN

Expectations and Planning

SOME CHRISTIANS ARE suspicious of planning and reluctant to get involved with policy statements, strategic thinking and the defining of objectives. Their hesitancy stems from the belief that the mission in which we are engaged is God's mission and not merely the Church's. While it is our responsibility to carry out his will, they argue, the planning and strategy remains in God's hands, and the results of our activities on his behalf are in accordance with his will, rather than commensurate with our efforts. They, therefore consider that we must be prepared to operate on impulse as the Holy Spirit leads, preferring to remain in the dark regarding God's planning, and to rest content, leaving the results in his hands. They quote a number of Scriptures in support of this stance.

As Zerubbabel was pondering how Jerusalem could be restored and the Temple there rebuilt, the angel told the prophet Zechariah to inform Zerubbabel: 'You will succeed, not by military might or by your own strength, but by my spirit. Obstacles as great as mountains will disappear before you. You will rebuild the Temple, and as you put the last stone in place, the people will shout, "Beautiful, beautiful!" ' (Zech. 4:6, 7).

When Christ was in conversation with Nicodemus, the Jewish leader, he underlined the fact that regeneration was a work of God the Holy Spirit. He achieves the seemingly impossible – 'How can a grown man be born again?' And his activities are totally unpredictable – 'The wind blows wherever it wishes; you hear the sound it makes, but you do not know where it comes from or where it is going. It is like that with everyone who is born of the Spirit' (John 3:8). As someone has delightfully commented, 'No weather forecasts are issued!'

Paul, in the course of his letter to the sadly divided church in Corinth, reminds his readers that it did not matter who did the sowing of the seed or the watering. God was the one who really mattered, because it was he who made the plant grow (1 Cor. 3:7). He had invented the germination process, had designed the seed, and was in control of the climate. This puts the part played by man in achieving a harvest in proper perspective.

To the self-assured, James issues this warning: 'Now listen to me, you that say, "Today or tomorrow we will travel to a certain city, where we will stay a year and go into business and make a lot of money." You don't even know what your life tomorrow will be! You are like a puff of smoke, which appears for a moment and then disappears. What you should say is this: "If the Lord is willing we will live and do this or that." But now you are proud, and you boast; all such boasting is wrong' (James 4:13–16).

Such passages of Scripture do not deny the possibility or legitimacy of planning, rather they warn against wrong attitudes in planning. They caution against substituting man-made schemes for a reliance on God's power. They remind us that nothing is impossible with God. They alert us to be prepared for the unexpected to happen, for God is not scheduled by our programmes. They emphasise that no matter how diligent and energetic man may be, it is still God who plays the major part. And they point out that there is a question mark hanging over every tomorrow. All plans are provisional.

1 Planning that is pleasing to God

We plan in the knowledge that we serve a God who plans. He is a God of purpose and order. He does not simply respond to events, but plans in anticipation or, more accurately, in foreknowledge of developments. He had far-ranging plans for Abram (Gen. 12:3), but although Abram had certain knowledge about some things, it was none the less partial. It is only in the New Testament that the full ramifications are revealed. '. . . the promise was based on faith . . . – not just to those who obey the law, but also to those who believe as Abraham did. For Abraham is the spiritual father of us all; as the scripture says, "I have made you father of many nations" ' (Rom. 4:16–17, see also Gal. 4:22–27). God's entire plan of salvation was formulated before the foundation of the world. Little by little it was revealed to his people in the course of history. God did not keep his people entirely in the dark concerning his purposes. 'I have not spoken in secret or kept my purpose hidden' (Is. 45:19). Through Isaiah and Jeremiah he informs Israel that he is in control of the future; they are therefore warned of the consequences of their disobedience (Is. 48:3–8) and reminded of the good things that he has in store for them (Jer. 29:10).

God's plans for man's salvation are fully implemented in Jesus Christ. The opening chapter of Ephesians is a classic statement of God's cosmic purpose expressed in the mission of his Son. 'Because of his love God had already decided that through Jesus Christ he would make us his sons – this was his pleasure and purpose . . . In all his wisdom and insight God did what he had purposed, and made known to us the secret plan he had already decided to complete by means of Christ. This plan, which God will complete when the time is right, is to bring all creation together, everything in heaven and on earth, with Christ as head . . . All things are done according to God's plan and decision; and God chose us to be his own people in union with Christ because of his own purpose, based on what he had decided from the very beginning' (Eph. 1:5, 8–10, 11).

Secondly, *we engage in planning in recognition that we are responsible co-workers with God*. Paul describes himself and his colleagues as working together with God (2 Cor. 6:1). God has created us as intelligent beings and works through our thought processes. He expects us to use our judgement and discernment in deciding issues rather than looking for sign-posts at every turning. We are encouraged to use our intelligence and whatever means are at our disposal. God promised Abraham and his descendants that they would be given a territory for their inheritance, yet they still had to fight to take possession of their promised land. God inspired planners for the building of the Temple, but craftsmen had to do the designing and building. This delicate balance between divine guidance and dependence on him on the one hand, and human responsibility and resourcefulness on the other, is expressed in Psalm 32:8, 9. 'The Lord says, "I will teach you the way you should go; I will instruct you and advise you. Don't be stupid like a horse or a mule, which must be controlled with a bit and bridle to make it submit." ' God does not treat us like animals, demanding mindless obedience. Rather, he relates to us as rational and responsible human beings with whom he communicates via our thought processes. He guides us through consultation, not conditioning.

Two personalities in the Old Testament, Joseph and Nehemiah, illustrate the need to draw up and implement plans. Joseph was given the gift of interpretation to unlock the meaning of Pharaoh's dream. Having alerted the Egyptian ruler that seven years of famine would follow the seven of plenty, he then steps beyond his brief by outlining a job description and offering a plan of action to deal with the emergency (Gen. 41:33–36). He made such a favourable impression on Pharaoh that he himself got the job of organising the famine measures for the entire nation.

We see similar initiative and strategic thinking in the case of Nehemiah. On hearing the reports brought by his brothers of the ruined state of Jerusalem, he seeks an audience with Emperor Artaxerxes to ask permission to leave Babylonia to take charge of the rebuilding of his ancestral home. His bold request is granted and the subsequent account demonstrates the planning and leadership gifts of Nehemiah. He makes a thorough inspection to ascertain the size of the task and what must be given priority consideration. He allocates responsibilities so that each group knows the area in which it is to operate. He identifies the opposition and protects his work force from attack by arranging them in a shift system with half of them performing guard duty at any one time. By skilful planning, motivation and coordination he is able to complete the project, which had eluded his predecessors, in fifty-two days (Neh. 6:15). If the art of management is the ability to get things done through other people, then Nehemiah belongs to the top bracket of senior management!

Thirdly, *as co-workers with God, Christians are held accountable for their actions*. This is emphasised in the parable of the three servants (Matt. 25:14–30). When their master was about to leave on his journey he 'put them in charge of his property'. They were expected to shoulder responsibilities and show initiative in the management of substantial resources. One was given five thousand silver coins, another two thousand and the third one thousand. When we realise that the silver coin represented a day's wage for a manual worker we can appreciate the degree of trust that this hand-out represented. The fact that different amounts were given to the three individuals was in recognition of their varying levels of ability or motivation. Their master was not prepared to give them more than he knew they could handle. Having trained and appointed them he knew the extent of their capabilities, and the servants, for their part, understood what was expected of them. He does not leave them with lists of detailed instructions for them to follow during his long absence. He expects them to use their initiative in working to further his interests. They are to work with the capital entrusted to them to obtain a good return for their investment.

When the master eventually returns 'after a long time', he calls the three servants 'to settle accounts' with them. The servant entrusted with five thousand silver coins and the one with two thousand each report a hundred per cent capital gain. To which the master responds, 'Well done, you good and faithful servant!' By their skilful trading they had shown their profitability. Having proved themselves at that level they are rewarded with increased responsibilities.

When the master calls to account the servant with the one thousand silver coins, the outcome is very different. This man reacts instantly with anger and bitterness. He falsely accuses his master of not providing the necessary resources. 'Sir, I know you are a hard man; you reap harvests where you did not sow, and you gather crops where you did not scatter seed.' He had appeared as a man without any resources at his disposal not because he had been deprived by his master, but because he had deprived himself by burying his capital. He had no one but himself to blame. The money was more of a burden than an asset. He demonstrated his inadequacy in his attitude of fear and by his failure to shoulder responsibilities. He played for safety by burying the resources so that he could hand them back intact. Because he had achieved nothing his master describes him as a 'useless servant' and deprives him of the resources which he had failed to utilise. He was castigated not for theft – his honesty was never in question – but for inactivity. He had failed to exercise initiative.

When God appoints us as co-workers he expects us to use the resources which he supplies, using our intelligence and endeavouring to be effective. We cannot 'pass the buck', for each will be held responsible, for to whom much is given from him much is expected.

Fourthly, *we engage in planning in the understanding that in the final analysis we are utterly dependent on God's providence*. For planning to be pleasing to God it must be directed to the achievement of the objectives that he requires to be obtained, using methods which are worthy and effective to those ends. As we have already stressed, planning comes through our thought processes. These must be consciously placed under the control of Christ, who is the head directing the body which is his Church. He guides us not by providing a celestial print-out, but by gifts of knowledge, discernment and faith which enable us to grapple with the issues. We begin by praying for guidance, and then plan, believing that he has answered our prayers. From time to time we may pause for further help in understanding and, when decisions cannot be postponed, be prepared to come down one side or the other confessing our confusion and asking for his overruling. In many instances a wrong decision is preferable to no decision at all.

We acknowledge our dependence on God not simply at the planning stage, but at every level of implementation. Spiritual results cannot be obtained apart from spiritual means. While planting and cultivating are man's responsibility, the provision of the harvest is God's. In response to the Lord's command to witness to all peoples everywhere, the Church may make thoroughgoing plans to ensure that people know how to tell their story and are strategically located to do so, but not one individual will become a child of God as a result of all this activity unless the Spirit of God convicts of sin and imparts spiritual life. Regeneration is entirely and exclusively a work of God. While our planning needs to be thorough, we may have to recognise that we can only achieve a part. There are always imponderables involved. Results cannot be determined, they can only be estimated and anticipated, on the basis of assumptions which should be clearly stated.

Our planning is also inevitably provisional. We see through a glass darkly. Even on the clearest of days our vision is blurred and restricted. Although Paul planned to go to Spain the Acts record ends without his having achieved his objective. God is never limited or conditioned by our planning. He may surpass our expectations and surprise us by acting totally outside and independent of our planning framework. Planning which is pleasing to God is therefore flexible and open-ended.

2 Generating a sense of expectancy

A congregation's level of expectation tends to be influenced more by past performance than by future prospects. In situations where there has been little or no substantial growth within living memory the leadership is infected by a 'failure syndrome' which instantly attaches a lead weight to every kite which is flown. People have resigned themselves to the fact that apparently 'nothing works here'.

In its most extreme form, this attitude leads to 'remnantitis' or a 'General Custer's last stand' mentality. The Christian community has given up hope that they will ever succeed in breaking through the surrounding hostility or cold wall of indifference, so they have resigned themselves to maintaining their isolated positions until their ultimate rescue, with the Lord's return. Sometimes their attitude is one of detachment rather than defensiveness. It is as though they have their bags already packed and are in the departure lounge for Heaven!

Until there is a sense of expectation among the people of God it is unlikely (though not impossible) that anything will happen. In Nazareth Mark reports that our Lord could do no mighty work because of their unbelief (Mark 6:5). There are a number of factors which may contribute to a sense of expectancy arising among the church members:

2.1 *We need an appreciation of the biblical emphasis on the growth of the people of God through the preaching of the Good News.* Both Old and New Testament contain many references to God's intention that his people should be numerous and widespread. This is clear from the promise to Abraham that he would have countless offspring, the vision of the prophets and the psalms of the nation spontaneously converging on Jerusalem, and the blessing resulting from the mission of the servant of the Lord. In the gospel our Lord prepares his disciples for their global commission with the sending out of the twelve, followed by the mission of the seventy-two. This great commission is spelled out with varying emphases at the conclusion of each of the four Gospels and in the opening of the Acts of the Apostles. The early Christians responded to the intention of our Lord and turned it into a practical programme. Within the space of thirty years tens of thousands of individuals had become Christians (Acts 21:20) and churches had been established in many cities and outlying areas throughout the Middle East, Asia Minor and Europe. The New Testament concludes with a vision of heaven filled with enormous crowds that no one can number (Rev. 7:9).

2.2 *We need an experience of the power of God to enable God's people to be effective witnesses*. The rapid expansion of the early Church would have been impossible without the experience of Pentecost. It was the coming of the Holy Spirit in power upon the disciples which motivated them for mission. He replaced their timidity with boldness. He turned frightened scurrying rabbits into bold exploring ferrets! He gave them their message and provided essential first-hand experience about which they rejoiced to speak. He confirmed their witness and proclamation by miraculous signs demonstrating that the gospel was about power and not simply a matter of words. He guided them through internal prompting, and the external pressures of persecution and circumstances, to move at the right time, in the right direction, to the most receptive people. In the subsequent history of the Church fresh advances have come despite seemingly unpromising prospects, through the renewal of the people of God as they have waited upon him conscious of their inadequacy and seeking fresh power from on high.

2.3 *We need an awareness of how the Church is growing in the world today*. Contrary to popular belief this century has witnessed some of the most rapid growth of the Church around the world in all of the long history of the Church. This is especially so in Africa, South of the Sahara, Latin America and in areas of Asia such as Indonesia and South Korea. News of what God is doing elsewhere brings encouragement. 'Hearing good news from a distant land is like a drink of cold water when you are dry and thirsty' (Prov. 25:25). The success of the Church elsewhere communicating its message and creating growth-enabling structures has prompted churches which have become bogged down to ask some radical questions about their traditional ways of doing things, which have long ceased to be effective. It is no coincidence that many of the growing churches in the traditional missionary-sending area of the world are in close contact through their missionary links with other parts of the world so that they are mutually enriched by their experiences in different situations. While there are few models of church growth which are readily transferable, there are a number of principles which are widely applicable, many of which have been pursued in the preceding chapters of this book.

When examples of growth come to our attention from our own country and from situations comparable to our own, then we have even greater cause for encouragement. One way to heighten expectations is to arrange to visit growing churches with which you can identify to experience the exhilaration of their vitality and growth. For people who have been encased in one church all their lives such a visit can be a real eye-opener and lead them to say, 'If it can happen there, it can happen here too.'

2.4 *We need the presence of a confidence-building and enabling leader*. In the previous chapter we dealt in some detail with the significant role played by the leadership for initiating and sustaining growth. Here we briefly emphasise the point that incompetent leadership increases the sense of frustration while effective leadership releases the leadership initiative and creative energies of the congregation, harnessing a diversity of activity in a unity of purpose, thus raising expectation.

2.5 *We need to exercise the gift of faith*. Some Christians are sometimes given a clear vision of what God intends through a 'gift of faith' (1 Cor 12:9). This is defined by Donald Bridge and David Phypers: 'The gift of faith is the outstanding faith given to some Christians enabling them to rely on God in a special way for the accomplishment of some specific task, or for the provision of their daily needs, or for some special demonstration of his nature and power' (Bridge and Phypers 1973:54). This gift of faith enables them to fly in the face of the seemingly insurmountable. The exercise of such a gift by individuals in the church has sometimes lifted the spiritual horizon of the entire congregation, enabling them to rise above circumstances and to formulate God-sized and God-shaped plans.

It is a far healthier and more promising strategy to seek to motivate people by raising their expectations rather than by imposing a sense of guilt. The latter approach is frequently adopted in churches by leaders acting out of a sense of personal frustration. Rather than constantly scolding people for what has not been done, we should be inspiring them with the anticipation of future possibilities, and encourage them by drawing attention to achievements, even though they be small ones.

2.6 *Last, by way of climax and not tail-end, we need to appreciate the strategic importance of corporate prayer*. Prayer has a vital part to play in the identifying of objectives (see next section). James assures the Church, 'if any of you lacks wisdom, he should pray to God, who will give it to him; because God gives generously and graciously to all. But when you pray, you must believe and not doubt at all. Whoever doubts is like a wave in the sea that is driven and blown by the wind. A person like that, unable to make up his mind and undecided in all he does, must not think that he will receive anything from the Lord' (James 1:5–8).

In many churches the planners are divorced from the prayers. To separate decision-making from intercession is to court disaster. Prayer gives us the divine perspective on things, even though if frequently dimly and partially perceived, yet sufficiently clear to set us on course with a consistent sense of direction. Prayer clarifies vision and stimulates faith, saving us from many time and money-wasting exercises in triviality and futility. Prayer helps to safeguard us from attempting ambitious schemes which are wrongly motivated. They have arisen out of a need for self-perpetuation, or a desire for self-glorification, rather than to advance the Kingdom of God. From the outset of our planning we need to cultivate the rare art of corporate listening to God. Praying brings shape and generates faith in our planning, and planning brings precision, urgency and sense of adventure into our praying. It ensures that our prayers grow arms and legs to facilitate their implementation.

3 Establishing general objectives

In many organisations activity tends to crowd out purpose. We become so engrossed in doing things that we do not pause to ask why we are so engaged. Do we have a clear objective in view? Is the objective strategic? Is our method of achieving it the best way, given that conditions may have changed drastically? Like any other institution the Church should sit down from time to time in order to redefine its mission. The committed membership needs to ask itself: Why has God put us here? What kind of people does he want us to become? What should be distinctive about our motivation, goals and life-style? What does God want to get done through us? What are our inbuilt strengths and limitations? What other churches and groups are also serving the area? What are their distinctive contributions and how can we complement one another?

Many of our church planning meetings are disunited, inconclusive and prolonged through lack of any agreed statement of purpose and priorities. Consequently, all decisions are taken in isolation, with the result that a decision taken in one area is later found to be at variance with a decision taken in another. Opinions are moulded by tradition, the minister's views, influential cliques, financial limitations, frustration with interminable discussion, or a desire to find the easiest way out rather than to achieve mutually agreed objectives. If there is no eye to the future and no sense of destiny then in dealing with the items on a crowded agenda we will succumb to the temptation 'to fill in the background with so many details that the foreground goes underground'! A house which is divided against itself cannot even stand never mind about grow.

The driver of a parked car was disturbed by a man tapping on the near-side window. As he wound down the window the pedestrian asked, 'Excuse me, but is this the second turning on the right?' It was an impossible question to answer because the pedestrian had stated neither his starting-point nor his intended destination. Any road will do until we have decided where we are wanting to go.

Some churches in North America refer to their statement of objectives as their 'philosophy of ministry'. In Britain we can perhaps more easily identify with some such title as our Church or Parish Profile. This is a concise, crisp and clear statement which attempts to set out the kind of church we believe God wants us to become as we currently perceive his mind. It should be kept short, succinct and as non-controversial as possible. During World War Two Winston Churchill insisted on report summaries being confined to one side of a sheet of foolscap. Anything longer was not easily assimilated. The following considerations will all have a bearing on the formulation of a Parish Profile:

1 *Biblical priorities* as we understand them, covering

the areas of worship, life-style, evangelism and service.

2 *Situational demands*. How can we relate meaningfully to our area of ministry or constituency? What special emphases are required? What cultural adaptation is necessary?
3 *Denominational emphases*. Which are most appropriate to the area? Do any need modification or reinterpretation?
4 *Membership characteristics and resources*. What do we have to contribute recognising who and what we are? How would we define the potential church member from among our personal contacts and the community? Are we likely to attract them? Are we open to change?
5 *Leadership insights*. Inevitably these will both give direction and blinker our vision. As we respond to God's will so our perspective changes causing us to re-examine our general objectives. They may need to be clarified, enlarged or modified.

In drawing up the Church Profile do not be afraid of stating the obvious. What is clear cut and non-negotiable to one person may on discussion prove to be obscure or open to debate in the views of others.

Here is an example of how a Church Profile might be stated.

> St Silas is situated in a residential area with a high proportion of young families, 90 per cent of whom have at the most only a tenuous link with the Church.
>
> In our worship we therefore recognise the need to adapt our cherished traditional heritage to enable new members to worship with their heart and their understanding. We try to live with the tension of winning the new without alienating the old. We therefore retain a familiar liturgical structure while welcoming informal and spontaneous contributions.

> We aim for extensive congregational participation in making music and sharing testimony.
>
> Our fellowship is geared to meet the needs of the age and interest groups of the existing congregation. It is structured to help individuals to come to a personal relationship with Christ and to encourage one another in the Christian faith.
>
> We are concerned to be part of our community and to demonstrate our faith by our presence and, wherever appropriate, to communicate by proclamation and persuasion. In so doing we recognise that we have a great deal to learn as well as to share. We seek to be sensitive to the felt needs of the community and to respond appropriately to those needs wherever possible.

Aldridge Parish Church near Walsall has drawn up the following definition of its primary objective:

> To create a Christian community that by its lifestyle and loving concern commends Christ to the neighbourhood in such a way that people have to come to terms with his claims on their allegiance.

Once the general objectives have been defined, they can then be expressed in the areas of pastoral care, worship, evangelism, community service and overseas missions. (see Fig. 21).

4 Working for consensus

How should the statement of general objectives be arrived at? Is it introduced from above by the appointed leader? Are the objectives formulated by the church's management committee or crystallised through a process of congregational debate? There is no simple answer to this question. Much will depend on the leadership style of the minister, the effectiveness of the executive and the spiritual maturity and commitment of the bulk of the

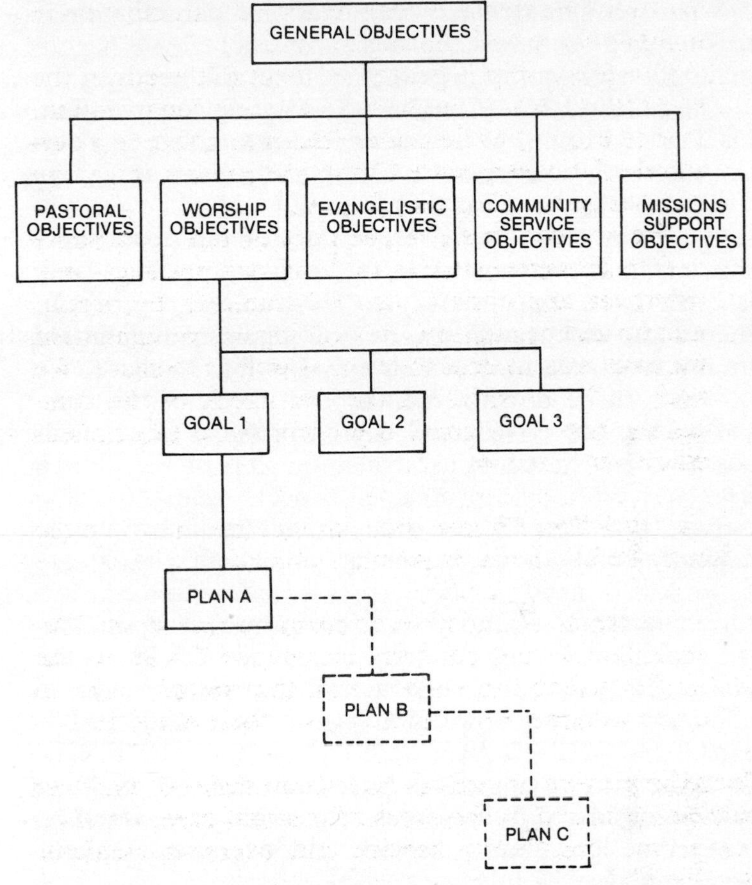

Fig. 21
A strategic planning model

congregation. As the statement of general objectives will ultimately need to be owned by the congregation if it is to be implemented, they need to share in the formulation.

The congregation however will expect guidance from its leader in this exercise. Although they may rightly resent being treated as a rubber stamp, they will expect starting-points to provide a basis for further discussion.

Where congregational cohesion and commitment is lacking then the minister and church council will have to make the running, in drawing up general objectives.

The minister may need to go away privately to write his Parish Profile. When he has done this to his own satisfaction he will need to ask himself if this is a vision with which he can personally identify. Could he see himself working effectively and feeling fulfilled operating in that imaginary framework? If he could, then his next step is bring back the summary to his leadership group for them to comb through, suggesting possible amendments until it reaches a form which is acceptable to all.

When the leadership is in substantial agreement then the overall objective – the church profile – needs to be accepted by the committed membership of the church. This may often be a protracted process taking a year or more to complete. The various areas outlined in the document, which should be circulated among the congregation, will need to be explained at length through sermons, seminars and discussion groups. The status of the statement is that of a discussion document during this phase. Congregational response may introduce suggested additions or changes of emphasis. These will then be considered by the appropriate church body, be that the parochial church council, deacons' court or Church Meeting. To ensure that the discussions don't go on interminably a time-limit should be set for this exercise of agreeing on a statement of purpose.

When the statement is presented for the vote either with the church committee or at a congregational meeting the following cautions outlined by the North American church consultant Lyle Schaller should be borne in mind.

1 '*Do not ask people to vote prematurely*'. They need to become thoroughly aquainted with all relevant facts, and the various facets of each issue explored. Make sure that people understand what they are voting for, otherwise they will vote 'NO' to be on the safe side or to conceal their ignorance.

2 '*Present only one issue at a time*'. Take things step by step. Seek agreement in one specific area before moving on to the next. Otherwise, people will be tempted to veto the whole package for the sake of one controversial element. Suspicion raised in one area is likely to spread into the others. Secure the undisputed territory. Progress and improvement in this area will generate confidence to tackle areas where there is less unanimity of viewpoint.

3 '*Whenever possible avoid the use of 'YES' or 'NO' type of questions in a ballot*'. These will tend to draw a dividing line between positive and negative thinkers, rather than indicate true levels of support. Furthermore, they drive the opponents into a purely negative stance when they might want to follow a more positive, alternative line. The 'YES/NO' vote can polarise the situation and paralyse the group, preventing them from further action. People don't want to hear the issue raised again, for each time merely stokes their feelings of anger and frustration. Often there is more than one route to achieve a goal, so keep the options open as long as possible, and confront people with two affirmative choices. If people have to say 'YES' one way or the other, then they cannot avoid facing the issue by sheltering behind a 'NO' vote. For instance, in balloting the congregation for their views on the newly introduced Family Service, don't do this:

> I like the new form of family service – YES/NO

but do this:

> What are your views on the new family service?
> I like it in its present form.
> It could be improved in the following ways:

4 '*It is unwise to let an issue come to a formal vote until most of the leadership are reasonably sure of the outcome of the balloting.*' When leaders lose contact with the followers they cease to be leaders and become loners. To

allow an issue to be put to the vote when you have a strong inclination that it will be defeated, is to put yourself out on a limb and saw yourself off. Discernment and timing are of the essence of successful leadership. Schaller draws attention to the frequently overlooked fact that the formal vote is not the most decisive point in the implementation process. It is merely the legitimatising of a decision that has already been arrived at informally. (Schaller 1978a:149). If the most active part that people are going to play towards the implementation of an idea is to raise their hands or place a cross on a piece of paper, then little has been achieved. While the 'YES' vote may turn the traffic light to green it may not serve to take the brake off the waiting vehicle or engage the clutch.

5 '*Education is alienation from the rest of the congregation*'. 'Whenever a few people in a congregation share an educational experience that enlarges their vision, alters their definition of the purpose and mission of the Church, or changes their system of values, this experience tends to alienate those few persons from the rest of the congregation'. It is all too easy to open up a communication gap between the front runners and the rest of the field. This occurs in churches which have over-secretive committees and poor internal communications, or may arise when thinking moves ahead quickly during a parish residential conference, causing resentments among those who were unable or unwilling to attend. The pace must be set at a rate which enables the main body to keep together (Schaller 1978a:147–149).

When an individual or small group become enthusiastic about an idea, the temptation is for them to seek out other likely supporters at the earliest possible moment to enlist them for the cause. Such a move, however, can be counterproductive in the long term. As soon as the opposition sense that the enthusiasts are on the move they will begin to exert a counter-pressure to maintain the congregation's equilibrium (or inertia, according to your point of view!). This in turn leads the innovators to exert still more pressure, which then has to be countered by the other side. If the pressure continues to mount, without either side giving ground, then the tension will become so great that the congregation will be in great danger of being torn apart into warring factions.

According to Kurt Lewin's 'force field theory' a better strategy is to go at an early stage to those who are likely to be most opposed or entertain the strongest reservations. Talking the issues through with them before plans have been detailed, or momentum allowed to gather, will give the leadership an indication of how far they are likely to carry people with them and where are the sticking points. In these initial consultations they may also discover that God has something to say through the 'opposition'!

Another important factor in attitude change is involvement. When people are encouraged to contribute their ideas and their opinions are actively sought and sympathetically listened to, a climate of trust and openness to innovation is created. As they get involved and become positive contributors to the change process so they become more flexible and adventurous.

In the previous section we emphasised the need to establish 'an overall objective'. While this is something which will need to be agreed eventually, in a seriously divided congregation it might be wiser to arrive at this statement in stages, rather than try to introduce the whole thing in one exercise. At the same time great care must be taken that by doing this the overall objective is not diluted or left to evaporate. The important point is that the leadership should at least know where they are going as they pick up the individual pieces and try to fit them together in a meaningful way.

5 *Achieving specific goals*

While an objective is a general statement of purpose, a goal is a specific result to be accomplished by a certain date. Many churches think they have goals, but in reality they are only vague intentions. A goal must be specific enough to eventually be able to measure whether or not you have attained it! To say that we want to increase the level of participation in the music of our church services is an objective. It is a statement of intent. To know to what extent we are successful in achieving it depends on goal setting. We might therefore decide:

1 To appoint a director of music.
2 To increase the choir membership from 12 to 25 in the next two years.
3 To teach the congregation one new hymn a month.
4 To begin the evening service once a month with a fifteen-minute congregational hymn practice.
5 To have a four-member singing group with guitars etc. to introduce modern music once a month.

Having clarified the distinction between an objective and a goal we proceed to examine goal setting from a Christian perspective in greater detail.

5.1 A goal is a statement of faith

It represents what we believe God wants done, and what he will provide the resources to enable us to achieve. Goals are not grasped out of the air. They must be set prayerfully and responsibly. On the one hand they help to release us from timidity. On the other, they must not lead us into arrogant presumption.

As a statement of *faith* it is not simply a projection based on calculations from past performance. It is the product of the gift of faith, which we have noted is given to some Christians. However, a word of caution is necessary at this point. Our congregational goals should not be uncritically adopted. They must represent a corporate level of faith, with which the leadership can identify and by which the congregation are inspired. 'To have faith is to be sure of the things we hope for, to be certain of the things we cannot see' (Heb. 11:1). If assurance and confidence are lacking then the goal may be a statement of folly rather than of faith! Our faith is in order to achieve something which is over the horizon, not on the far side of the moon.

5.2 Our goals pin-point our priorities

The range of goals should express the extent of our concerns. They should be in line with our objectives. Their achievement will bring about detectable changes for the better. Goals should be set to reflect a balance of concerns in each area of the church's life. They might be conveniently listed under the following headings:

(a) Worship – styles, events, range of congregational participation.
(b) Relational – knowing groups and individuals and relating to their felt needs.
(c) Organisational – overall policy formulation, performance monitoring.
(d) Educational – themes, methods, feed-back (i.e. opportunities to respond to the teaching).
(e) Evangelistic – numbers trained, events held, response measured.
(f) Missions Support – home and overseas
(g) Social concerns – in the community served by the church; further afield.
(h) Resources – use of buildings; involvement of people; financial commitment.

5.3 A goal is a target for achievement

It is stated so as to define the point of aim, and to enable the degree of achievement to be assessed. McGavran and Arn caution that 'a goal is not a tyrant but a target' (McGavran and Arn 1977:108). It is something to aim at, not to be bound by. Some people are reluctant to set goals due to the fear of failure. However, failure can be itself a valuable part of the learning process. Failure, regarded positively, represents the elimination of possibilities. It contributes to the funnelling of effort towards eventual accomplishment. When we set a goal and aim for it, we are then in a position to measure how close we came to scoring a bull's eye. On the basis of our performance we can then take steps to improve our aim and increase our fire-power. We may even decide to move the target: nearer to us, if we even failed to register one hit, or further away, if we score a bull's eye every time. A goal should be seen as a moveable target and not as a fixture. The quantities or timing may need to be adjusted in the light of experience.

Goal-setting challenges us to earth our fantasies. During the First World War, Will Rogers, the celebrated American raconteur, volunteered an idea for ridding the Atlantic Ocean of German U-boats. His novel answer to the problem was to bring the ocean to boiling-point, so that all the U-boats were forced to surface before their crews were pressure-cooked. Then waiting patrol boats could force them to surrender. When asked how he would go about heating the ocean, he replied, 'Oh! I'm just the ideas man. You work out the details!' Goal-setting provides the necessary discipline to ascertain to what extent ideas are achievable.

In addition to being measurable it must have a time-frame-indicating what needs to be done by when. For some people time is an eschatological concept! They live in a never-never land. In the case of many projects the biggest waste of time is in getting started.

5.4 A goal provides a test of commitment

Goals spell out the practical implications of embarking on a course of action. As we describe our goals in precise terms we place a price tag on each item in terms of time, effort and financial outlay. We can then decide whether or not we are prepared to proceed.

From experience in the business world, it is clear that people are most prepared to accept goals which they themselves have had a hand in formulating. Imposed goals are regarded as a threat rather than a challenge. Goals must be accepted by the individuals or group responsible for their implementation. Larger congregational goals may therefore need to be broken down into sub-goals with which individuals and groups (i.e. organisations and home groups) can more easily identify. Alternatively, the agreed congregational objective can be taken into appropriate groups for them to draw up their own goals representing their particular organisation's contribution towards meeting the stated objective.

5.5 A goal should be established on the basis of research

Our goals will be in danger of being nothing more than castles in the air, unless in shaping them we have gathered as much relevant information as possible. Faith is not belief in spite of evidence, but living in scorn of consequences. Thus a church setting worship attendance goals will look carefully at trends during the past ten years. They will also take note of community developments. Is there any evidence of increased receptivity? What are the population trends likely to be? How many existing properties are scheduled for demolition? Are any new estates likely to be developed? Are new industries bringing families into the area, or is it a static and ageing community? What proportion of residents from our catchment area are we likely to attract, bearing in mind the kind of people we are and the activities in which we engage?

All these factors must be taken into consideration when formulating goals. But having done our homework, we do not simply let the facts determine the goals, else we may react as did ten of the twelve spies who reconnoitred the Promised Land and decided that the giants and walled cities presented too great an obstacle. We must take care to balance the positive alongside the negative factors.

Many people find it helpful to draw up a 'for and against' list to help in decision-making.

St Thomas's, Crookes, an inner city parish in Sheffield, provides an impressive illustration of faith-inspired goal-setting. Twenty years ago their Sunday worship attendance was under a hundred. Today it stands at between five and six hundred (seventy per cent of whom live within one mile of the church). Their goal is to double their congregation between 1977 and 1982, and they are on target. Robert Warren, the vicar, now leads a full-time staff of six. Their premises are no longer adequate to cope with their greater numbers and range of activities, so they have agreed upon a £564,000 building scheme, which they aim to have paid for by the time the work is completed in September 1980. By the end of 1979 £300,000 had been contributed (£34,000 on their gift day), and in January 1980 the rate of giving was £1,000 a day!

6 Formulating workable plans

Plans are designed to convert intention into achievement. 'Planning is trying to discover how to accomplish goals *before* you commit yourself. Planning is moving from the *now* to the *then*, from the "way things are" to the "way we want things to be". Planning is trying to imagine the future as we would like it to be, and explaining how it could be. For the Christian, planning is trying to understand God's will and respond to that understanding by our actions' (Dayton 1974:125). Decisions commit us to a course of action. As someone has commented, 'Having fired a bullet it is very difficult then to catch up in order to move the target!'

We do well to remember that there is almost always more than one route to achieve a goal. Sometimes leaders conclude mistakenly that a goal has been rejected because a particular plan was turned down. First agree on the goal and then you are free to examine all the alternative routes which are open to you. If we are not clear about the goal, the plan will inevitably be confused. Albert Einstein once commented that 'few things characterise our day so much as perfection of means and confusion of goals.'

Therefore write up the goal for everyone to see, and keep looking at it during the planning session. Then invite ideas by means of a brain-storming session. List the suggestions on an overhead projector or blackboard without interrupting the flow of ideas by stopping to discuss them. If the planning group is too inhibited to participate freely, then divide them into buzz groups of four to six people for them to share suggestions among themselves before voicing them to the rest of the meeting. Once the list is complete, examine each idea in the light of the agreed goal. Delete those which will lead in other directions; they are the red herrings. Grade the remainder in order of likely probability. Take the 'A's' which represent the most promising and consider the pros and cons of each. If necessary follow with the 'B's' and 'C's'. In the light of your more careful considerations do you wish to revise the grading of any situation? Sometimes the least obvious suggestion proves on closer inspection to be the most ingenious. You may then want to take a break to allow the ideas to 'incubate' before you make your choice.

A plan by definition must be workable. It consists of a series of logical steps to convert aims into achievement. Each step must be within reach from the one before. Some plans are so ambitious that they result in pigmies struggling on a giants' causeway. The steps need to be attainable as well as logical.

7 Drawing up an organisational framework

An organisational framework shows the various steps in the achievement of a goal and indicates the relationship between them. Such diagrams are called 'PERT' in management circles – *P*rogramme *E*valuation and *R*eview *T*echnique. A simple PERT diagram for the parish concert might appear as follows. (See Fig. 22.) This provides a detailed breakdown and scheduling of all the steps involved. While at first glance this may to some look unnecessarily complex, it only takes a few minutes to draw up. As you undertake the planning exercise you will then become aware of the things you might otherwise have overlooked and you will see who will need to relate to whom and at what stage in the operation they should each begin to act. It also provides an invaluable record to help someone else to take over responsibility for its achievement on a subsequent occasion.

Such planning also entails the acceptance of mutual responsibility. We must move on from *what* needs to be done, to consider *who* is to do it and by *when*. This aspect of planning may be clearly represented on a 'Responsibilities Chart' (see Fig. 23.) Once this has been agreed by all those involved it is distributed to everyone with a calendar of pre-arranged check-points to ensure that progress is being made. The establishing of clear areas of responsibility at the outset can help to save heartaches, embarrassment and frustration later on. The greater the complexity of the operation and the more people involved, the greater the chances of misunderstanding and organisational breakdown.

8 Allocating adequate resources

The following cry from the heart appears on a partition in a certain open-plan London office:

> We, the willing,
> led by the unknowing
> are doing the impossible
> for the ungrateful.
> We have done so much
>   with so little
>   for so long,
> We are now qualified
>   to do anything
>   with nothing.

People are more important than plans. In Christian en-

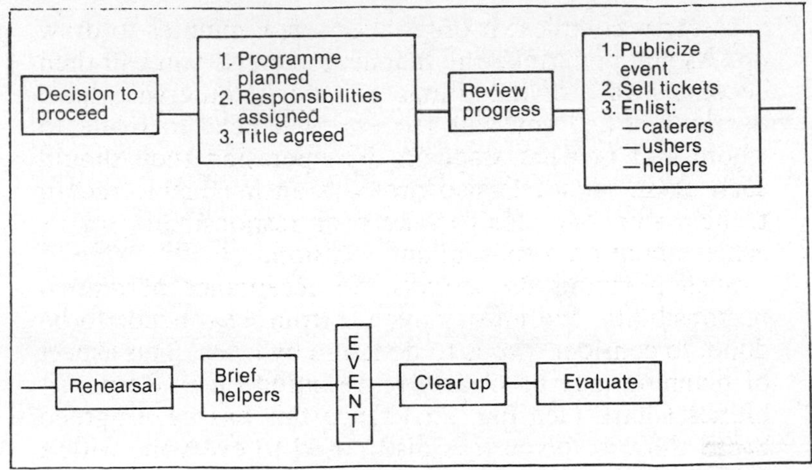

Fig. 22
PERT diagram: parish concert

Fig. 23
Responsibilities chart

PARISH CONCERT June 15th								
Task	*Date*		*Person Responsible*					
	Start	*Finish*	*MARY*	*BILL*	*JACK*	*JOAN*	*JOHN*	*FRED*
1. Programme	*Mar 1*	*Mar 25*		×				
2. Tickets	Apr 6	May 20	×					
3. Advertising	Apr 6	Jun 1			×			
4. Refreshments	Jun 10	Jun 15				×		
5. Lighting	Jun 10	Jun 15					×	
6. Caretaking	Jun 10	Jun 15		×				
7. Equipment	Apr 20	Jun 15						×

terprises people should not be ruthlessly driven to breaking-point. Plans are formulated to inspire, not manipulate. Individuals and groups must therefore be convinced of the worthwhileness of the job they are being invited to undertake, and that they will be given adequate support and encouragement to enable them to perform to the best of their ability. In a previous chapter we have already discussed the principles involved in enlisting and handling volunteers. It is an irresponsible stewardship of human resources to give a person a job without the essential decision-making authority or basic resources to fulfil the task. This is an all-too-common occurrence in Christian work.

Every goal carries a price tag and each constituent item must be carefully costed. How many people will it need? What gifts, insights and skills are essential? What level of commitment will it demand in terms of hours per week (including preparation as well as performance)? How long should the appointment be expected to run for? What space will be required? What amenities? What expenditure for capital equipment and on-going expenses? These issues need to be faced *before* personnel are enthused and committed, otherwise they will become quickly frustrated and ultimately disillusioned. That is one of the reasons we have more vacancies than applicants in so much church work.

8.1 The church's budget

One of the major problem areas is a failure to bring budgeting into line with planning. In many churches the statement of accounts reflects precedents which have been established during the course of many years. The budget is drawn up on the basis of past performance rather than to achieve anticipated goals. Its bias is to ensure the maintenance of the status quo rather than responding to new challenges. Established items take precedent over new suggestions, which may only be added if there is surplus capital, or if ear-marked new money can be raised.

If a church is to adapt to new situations or gear itself for growth it must often revise drastically its budgeting procedures. The power of precedent needs to be broken. The budgeting exercise should be undertaken as part of the church's total programme planning. The budget must be structured to become more of an irrigation channel and less of a dam wall! Its purpose is not conservation but facilitation. Lyle Schaller, with penetrating insight, describes a church's budget as:

> 1 A theological document, identifying the gods that are worshipped, and ranking them in a hierarchy.
> 2 A statement of purpose – the priorities are reflected by the allocation of resources.
> 3 A political manifesto. Resources are scarce, and the budget is a result of bargaining. It reflects how the conflicts have been resolved.
> 4 A declaration of expectations. It shows what the organisation expects to achieve, and the sources from which it expects to receive them.
> 5 A precedent. Once adopted, a budget becomes a precedent for future decisions. It is more difficult to subtract existing items than add new ones. (Schaller 1978a:38–46).

Review the current budget to ascertain to what extent its fails to reflect the church's policy and plans. If it is at serious variance, then isolate the points where there is an obvious divergence.

It is common for a budget, once established, to become a god to be served without question. We should not lose sight of the original budget objectives but operate on a flexible basis within a changing situation. If the need for major changes becomes apparent we should not be afraid to face up to this.

Schaller has two practical recommendations to help

break the precedents created by the budget. One is to look at each of the areas in your statement of overall objectives and give each a percentage rating by which to apportion expenditure. Then allocate anticipated receipts for next year according to these percentages. Under each overall objective place a list of specific goals in order of priority with a price tag against each one. Distribute the allocated amounts as far as they will stretch down the list of items. This will reveal what you are likely to be able to afford. Items for which no funds are available then become part of an opportunity budget. They present a challenge to overall increased giving. Some you may wish to take up as special projects.

The suburban Anglican parish of St Andrew's, Chorleywood, Herts., has a clear financial policy which was stated to the author by Mr Fred Evans, churchwarden and one-time treasurer in these terms. 'We say our policy is firstly, to provide the means for an effective Christian ministry from our church to the local community. To do this we provide funds sufficient, but not more than reasonably required to,

1 Pay the diocesan quota, which effectively pays for our clergy.
2 Pay all reasonable clergy working expenses.
3 Pay all necessary church running expenses.
4 Enable all key church organisations (youth, choir etc.) to operate effectively.
5 Maintain the church plant in good working order.
6 Set aside sums to equate the cost year by year of major expenditures, such as car replacement, major building repairs, replacement of key items of equipment.

This in turn protects our second policy aim which is to maintain a broad based support of mission both at home and overseas within a list of priorities laid down by the church council and reviewed annually so that each of the object of our support can rely on the level of support (whilst the need continues) being maintained as far as possible in real terms. For this objective we have an unwritten target that we would in any one year aim to give away not less than £1 for each £1 allocated under policy one.'

Another useful way to break the power of precedent and to prune items is to undertake a 'zero base budgeting' exercise. Instead of basing next year's budget on this year's itemising and expenditure level, place a zero against each item as an initial response. Then justify to your own satisfaction each allocation of amounts.

9 Stimulating enthusiastic participation

In the chapters dealing with every-member ministry and enabling leadership we considered at length a number of important issues relating to the identification, activation, deployment and developing of gifts. Under this heading we will confine ourselves to the following points:

1 The church's programme must be sufficiently relevant, imaginative and attractive to motivate people to want to be party to its implementation. Simply stated, people must a) understand it, b) believe in it and c) relate to it.

2 They must have confidence in and access to the leadership.

3 The overall programme should be broken down into manageable parts so that it does not appear too daunting.

4 Do not rely on broadcast announcements to enlist support. Get people involved at the planning stage. When they have had a share in their formulation they are more likely to get involved in their implementation. Hand pick the key people, and enlist the bulk of the support through the small and intermediate groups.

5 Allow opportunity for the groups involved in each project to exercise their initiative and creativity within general guidelines.

6 Set a time limit so that volunteers know from the outset that they have not committed themselves indefinitely.

Often people are reluctant to get involved for fear of not being able to extricate themselves without a great deal of 'hassle' and embarrassment.
7 Affirm and encourage people in their jobs. The bouquets should outnumber the brickbats.
8 If any part obviously is not working don't leave it to limp along indefinitely. Locate the source of the trouble and deal with it.
9 Don't dwell on the difficulties – emphasise opportunities and achievements. Foster a positive attitude and a buoyant spirit.

10 Ensuring good internal communications

In many churches the congregations suffer from 'mushroom management'. They are kept completely in the dark except for brief moments when the door is opened for manure to be thrown over them! This is not a style of management conducive to church growth! People must be kept informed and not left in the dark until their help is required or blame apportioned. Few churches pay sufficient attention to their internal communications. There may be a great deal of planning activity at committee level but few of their concerns percolate through to the people in the pew. Churches tend to operate on the mystery tour principle. The coach-driver is the only one aware of the route. It is assumed that as far as the passengers are concerned, the attraction in making the journey is not knowing where they are going or blind faith in the driver's ability. Adopting such a style of operation means that the congregation will never be other than passengers, or more likely, that before long many will cease to turn up at all.

The church has a number of channels for regularly communicating with its membership.

10.1 A popularised budget summary

This should be a communication vehicle, not a confusion of mystery items. It is the church's action plan for a stated period in financial terms. It should clearly state in a readily assimilable form what the church intends to do. All figures should be rounded up to include only two significant digits, because this is apparently all people can take in at a glance. It should be structured according to overall objectives, with charts and pictorial diagrams used wherever possible.

In churches where it is the practice to invite members to reconsider their financial support each year, the appeal letter and covenant forms should be accompanied by the budget summary so that people can see clearly what they are being asked to contribute towards. Furthermore it is helpful to indicate the percentage increase in giving, needed to achieve the budget and support this with a simple example. They are then in a better position to make an informed and responsible decision, in the light of the competing claims on their financial commitments. Many churches receive a low level of support from their members because they have not taken sufficient care in communicating the relevance of their programme. 'To plead for money is to advertise failure' (Perry 1977:160). The single most important factor is the commitment of the individual member. This will only flow from a personal commitment to Christ and the gospel. The church may provide the plan – but the Holy Spirit opens the heart and the pocket.

As an experiment to measure the power of your budget to communicate, send out your annual stewardship letter with one batch accompanied by the budget summary and other without. Have the response forms coded in such a way that you can measure the response rate between those who received the budget statement and those who did not.

10.2 The noticeboard

Some churches display their budget, for instance, in an attractive diagrammatic form on a notice board, and indicate month by month the progress being made as funds become available. People will give when they know what they are giving for with some hope that something will be done about it.

10.3 The magazine or news-sheet

This should also reflect the progress made in the achievement of objectives. The knowledge that you are succeeding in getting things done will encourage and generate more faith. The news-sheet can have more of a personal focus than the noticeboard, highlighting the various departments and their activities.

10.4 The notices

These should be more than a diary of events and should never be allowed to degenerate into a tale of woe. If the minister's instinct tells him that people are unlikely to support a particular event, no matter what he says, then he should not indulge in unproductive exhortations. They merely destroy credibility. Such items should be given the briefest mention, or relegated to the news-sheet.

People find it incredibly difficult to take notice of notices. From time to time it is good to highlight a particular activity by inviting an enthusiast to share his enthusiasm. While enthusiasm is contagious, it also tends to be protracted, so the enthusiast will have to be held on a short rein. He will need a strictly enforced time limit. Alternatively, he can be invited to speak in an interview situation, which enables the interviewer to exercise control over the situation.

The larger the congregation the more formalised the communication system needs to become. It is usually safe to assume that the message has not got through, or if it has, then it has probably become garbled in the process (Schaller 1978:134–140). Therefore, to avoid communication bottle-necks and 'static interference' use all the channels available to you. People need to hear the same things said in different ways, on a number of occasions, through different media, to be sure of getting the message. And even when every route has been exploited it can be assumed that some people will not have heard!

Two-way communication is preferable to one-way. The fact that people have assented does not mean that they will necessarily do anything about it. Therefore, whenever possible, build in opportunities for response by allowing for reactions and asking for specific commitments of time and talents.

A church with more than 150 members needs established procedures to encourage and handle suggestions and hear grievances. If not, people will vote in the only other ways open to them – with their pocket or with their feet. The quality of the commitment depends to a large extent on the quality of the communication.

11 Coping with change

The one thing certain about tomorrow is that it won't be like yesterday. Change is an indispensable ingredient of life, but in many areas the pace of change has increased unnervingly. Lloyd Perry maintains, 'Change in the local church is no longer an option, it is a necessity. Modern man feels a gap between the world of the church and the outside world. The world is changing rapidly and the present-day church, with its rigidity of form, cannot cope with that changing world. We must be ready to face a changing world with a changing church' (Perry 1977:119).

The Church, like many other institutions, has to find ways of adapting to remain in contact with its potential membership, while at the same time avoiding alienating its long-term members. Most senior citizens, not to mention some younger churchgoers, cannot cope emotionally with too great a change inflicted upon them without due warning and preparation. If the changes proposed do not achieve their desired ends, they may alienate the existing membership without attracting the new constituency for which they were devised. It is all too easy to break eggs without succeeding in making omelettes.

In the chapter on leadership and relationships we

argued the case for innovative leadership, which introduces the new without threatening the inherited patterns. By so doing the leaders are free to be creative without gaining the reputation of being subversive. As we have seen, people often resist change because they lack confidence in the one desiring it.

The innovative change agent needs to be open to suggestions. If he presents an inflexible image, insisting that his way is the only way, he will tend to generate the same attitude in those around him. Discussion has been described as 'seeking a meeting of minds without the knocking together of heads'. A flexible leader who is constantly inviting participation and encouraging suggestions generates a positive, creative attitude around him. People want leaders who know where they are going (or at least appear to), but who at the same time are open to explore alternative routes.

Change generates uncertainty. Therefore, focus attention on increasing the level of trust by highlighting the points of assurance rather than the dramatic nature of the change. The pace of change may suddenly increase as people become excited by the attractiveness of the goal, or as it comes within their grasp, or a sudden crisis galvanises them into action.

The change agent must be realistic enough to recognise that for many people any proposal for change constitutes bad news. He must therefore prepare himself for an initial adverse response. Many good ideas are thrown out first time. He may have to keep the idea simmering gently, choosing his moment wisely to reintroduce it. He must be prepared to rejoice if someone else subsequently produces it, claiming it as his own. The ideas of a successful leader carry no copyright. They are left for anyone to adopt. The goal is that the idea be implemented, not that the ideas-man be acclaimed. Many ideas are relegated to glass cases through the proud possessiveness of their inventors.

12 Resolving to act

A depressing postscript can be added to many church projects, 'When all is said and done, too much is said and too little is done.' We need to guard against our conversations becoming a substitute rather than a preparation for action. In order to avoid action, churches either live in a nostalgic past or a fantasy future. We have to learn to live in the present, for now is the acceptable time, now is the day of salvation. What is our attitude to the present? Today is not an empty concept. I believe that we must become excited about today, for there are increasing indications that it is a day of opportunity for church growth.

Frequently we are more skilled in formulating plans than in implementing them. Most churches have a poor track record in the area of numerical growth, especially in attracting those who have had little or no previous contact with the Christian Church. As a consequence we lack both experience and confidence. We have to remind ourselves that plans are made to be implemented. No matter how enthusiastic the planning, if they are then carried out in a hesitant and half-hearted manner the most promising of plans will fall to the ground. Their execution must be equal to the inspiration.

13 Evaluating and reformulating

One of the greatest impediments to planning is the fear of failure. Win Arn responds to one of McGavran's comments regarding the psychological problem of goal-setting. 'True! If you have no goals you need not fear failure. Fear frustrates faith. I'm convinced that freedom to fail is a most important freedom and one that pastor and people must recognise as inherent in any significant effort' (McGavran and Arn 1977:160).

Goal setting is not carried out on the basis of 'direct revelation'. It represents an estimation of results. We therefore need to review our goals critically in the light of further reflection and more extensive experience, to see whether they are still the right goals. Not all plans work well. Many need to be modified in the light of experience, otherwise the goal may either contribute to despondency or complacency.

Sometimes the problem lies not so much with the plans as with an inadequate organisational structure to secure their implementation. David Wasdell highlights the need for flexible structures to facilitate 'continuous organic evolution of the organisation within a rapidly changing and unstable environment, while retaining a clear grasp of the institutional purpose' (Wasdell 1979:1).

A further factor which underlines the need for periodic evaluation and reformulation of goals is the appearance of unscheduled developments. It is common experience among churches which have implemented goal-setting, then to find that God has introduced a few surprises! This may be to keep us on our toes or drive us to our knees. It also seems that when God sees that we are emerging from inertia and demonstrating that we are prepared to move in a given direction, he can then move us into other areas.

Our planning model is therefore not linear and climactic but cyclic. We must ever remain open and responsive to the revolutionary newness of the gospel. God's purposes will continue to unfold until he takes the stage in person once again.

14 Conclusion

Having concentrated so much on the practical aspects of church growth we must now return to the place where we started, namely the reason for church growth and the kind of growth we are concerned to nurture. God has declared his unswerving purpose for the world, namely that Christ should reign supreme over the whole creation. We humbly, and thankfully, acknowledge that it is he who brings into being his kingdom. In our day this is partly realised in a provisional form through his Church. We are acutely aware of our weakness and imperfections.

We confess our negativism and apathy. But thank God in many places today where once such attitudes prevailed there are an increasing number of churches which are becoming bored with their complacency! The Spirit is stirring dry bones into life. He is calling us to live adventurously and dangerously. We are emerging from our culs-de-sac to walk the Jesus Way. May this volume serve as a slight contribution to that end. To God be the glory both for what he has done, for what he is even now doing through his people apart from them and despite them (!), and for what he is yet to do, the splendour and magnitude of which will stagger us all.

APPENDIX A
CHURCH OF ENGLAND

Year	Easter Day			
	Communicants (Thousands)	Total Communicants (Thousands)	Electoral Rolls (Thousands	Sunday Attendance (Thousands)
1900	1,902			
01	1,945			
02	2,012			
03	2,037			
04	2,084			
05	1,939			
06	1,988			
07	2,023			
08	2,108			
09	2,158			
10	2,212			
11	2,293			
12	2,195			
13	2,304			
14	2,226			
15	2,203			
16	2,097			
17	2,095			
18	2,122			
19	2,153			
20	2,172			
21	2,214			
22	2,171			
23	2,291			
24	2,315		2,537	
25	2,388		3,602	
26	2,373		3,621	
27	2,391		3,636	
28	2,339		3,642	
29	2,304		3,627	
30	2,261		3,656	
31	2,288		3,649	
32	2,280		3,652	

Year	Easter Day			
	Communicants (Thousands)	Total Communicants (Thousands)	Electoral Rolls (Thousands	Sunday Attendance (Thousands)
33	2,328		3,634	
34	2,319		3,568	
35	2,300		3,599	
36	2,242		3,550	
37	2,226		3,508	
38	2,250		3,464	
39	2,245		3,390	
40	1,998		3,389	
47	1,729		2,990	
50	1,848		2,959	
53	1,941		2,923	
56	2,168		2,895	
58	2,073	2,245	2,944	
60	2,159	2,339	2,862	
62	2,159	2,347	2,793	
64	1,957	2,142	2,739	
66	1,899	2,075	2,682	
68	1,795	1,975	2,636	1,606
70	1,632	1,814	2,559	1,535
73	1,510	1,684	2,021	1,410
74			1,986	
76	1,503	1,681	2,033	1,247
77		1,672	1,998	1,267
78		1,698	1,755	1,247
79		1,715	1,796	1,254

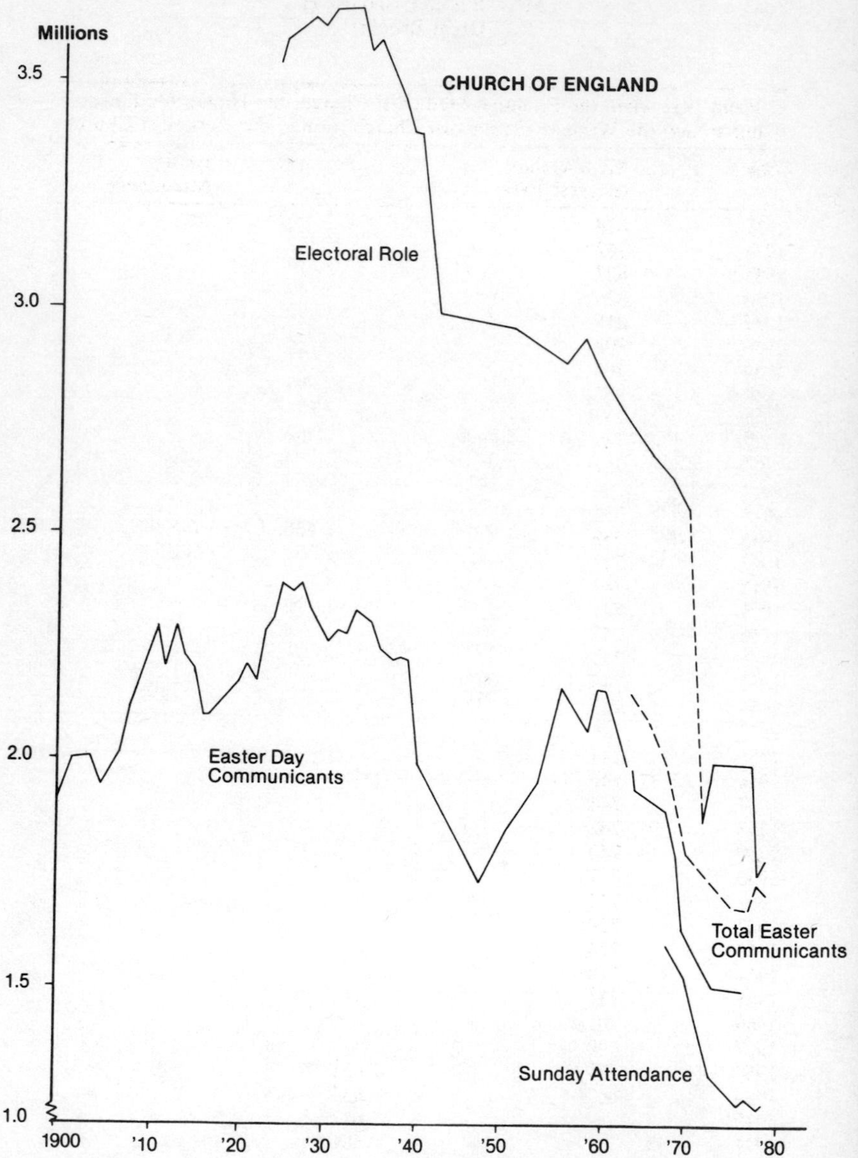
Millions
3.5
3.0
2.5
2.0
1.5
1.0
CHURCH OF ENGLAND
Electoral Role
Easter Day
Communicants
Total Easter
Communicants
Sunday Attendance
1900
'10
'20
'30
'40
'50
'60
'70
'80

APPENDIX B
METHODIST CHURCH
(Great Britain)

From 1932 when the Primitive Methodist Church, the United Methodist Church, and the Wesleyan Methodist Church formed the Methodist Church

Year	Membership (nearest 1000)	Total Attendance
1933	838	
1934	852	
1935	827	
1936	825	
1937	818	
1938	808	
1939	805	
1940	802	
1941	792	
1942	778	
1943	767	
1944	760	
1945	756	
1946	753	
1947	747	
1948	743	
1949	741	
1950	743	
1951	744	
1952	745	
1953	742	
1954	744	
1955	744	
1956	745	
1957	744	
1958	742	
1959	740	
1960	737	
1961	734	
1962	729	
1963	724	
1964	719	
1965	711	
1966	701	
1967	690	
1968	679	651(1)
1969	667	635
1970		617
1971		601
1972		585

Year	Membership (nearest 1000)	Total Attendance
1973	570	
1974	557	
1975	545	476
1976	528	
1977	517	463

(1) Method of gathering statistic changed

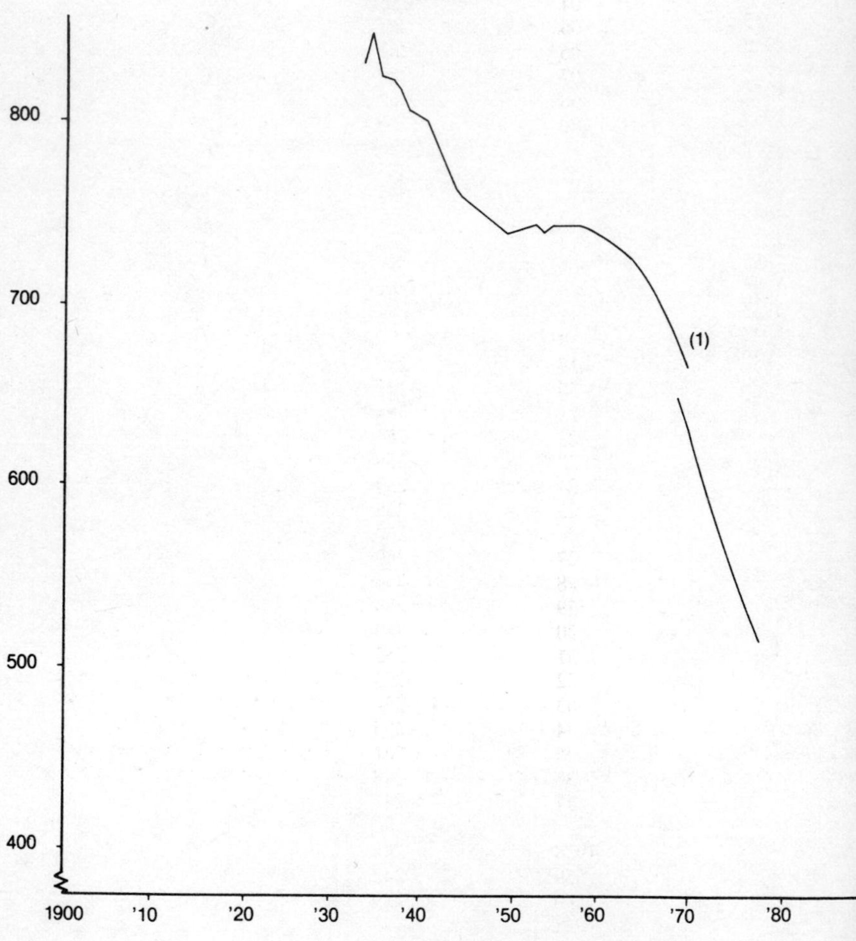

APPENDIX C
BAPTISTS
(England)

Year	Members (1000s)
1900	239
01	244
02	246
03	253
04	256
05	262
06	267
07	268
08	267
09	267
10	266
11	267
12	266
13	266
14	265
15	236
16	261
17	
18	
19	255
20	255
21	254
22	255
23	258
24	259
25	258
26	260
27	259
28	256
29	254
30	254
31	255
32	255
33	254
34	253
35	251
36	248
37	247
1938	244
39	242
40	239
41	

Year	Members (1000s)
42	
43	
44	226
45	
46	219
47	215
48	210
49	209
50	207
51	206
52	205
53	203
54	201
55	202
56	204
57	204
58	203
59	200
60	199
61	197
62	195
63	187
64	189
65	186
66	183
67	181
68	180
69	176
70	173
71	
72	168(1)
73	149
74	149
75	146 168(2)
1976	147
77	145
78	142
79	142 162(3)
80	

(1) Until 1972 Baptist Churches not in the Union were included
(2) 'Signs of Hope' report
(3) 'Prospects for the Eighties'

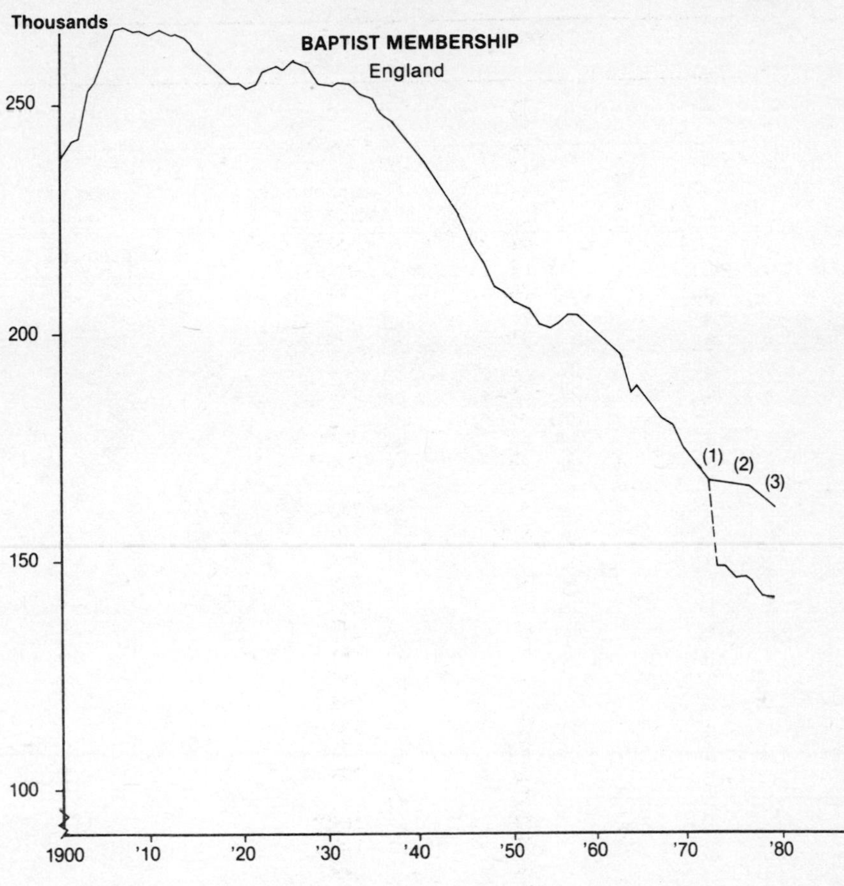
Thousands
BAPTIST MEMBERSHIP
England
250
200
150
100
1900
'10
'20
'30
'40
'50
'60
'70
'80
(1)
(2)
(3)

APPENDIX D
CONGREGATIONALIST, PRESBYTERIAN, UNITED REFORMED
(England)

Year	Cong (Thousands)	Pres (Communicants) (Thousands)	URC (Thousands)
			England and Wales
1900	257	76	
01	258	78	
02	269	80	
03	272	82	
04	277	83	
05	279	85	
06	285	86	
07	288	86	
08	291	86	
09	291	87	
10	288	87	
11	288	87	
12	287	87	
13	288	88	
14	290	88	
15	291	87	
16	289	87	
17		86	
18		86	
19		84	
20		84	
21		84	
22		84	
23		85	
24		85	
25		85	
26		85	
27	291	85	
28	290	85	
29	288	84	
30	287	84	
31	286	84	
32	285	83	
33	283	83	
34	280	82	
35	275	82	
36	273	80	
37	268	80	
38	263	80	
39	260	78	

Year	Cong (Thousands)	Pres (Communicants) (Thousands)	URC (Thousands)
40		77	
1941		75	
42		71	
43		70	
44		69	
45	230	68	
46	224	67	
47	221	67	
48	215	70	
49	212	71	
50	210	70	
51	207	69	
52	203	69	
53	203	69	
54	202	70	
55	201	70	
56	200	71	
57	200	71	
58	196	71	
59	194	71	
60	193	71	
61	192	71	
62	190	70	
63	187	70	
64	185	69	
65	182	68	
66	180	66	
67	175	65	
68	165	63	
69	154	61	
70	151	59	
71			
72			
73			192
74			187
75			181
76			175
77			166
78			162
79			157
80			

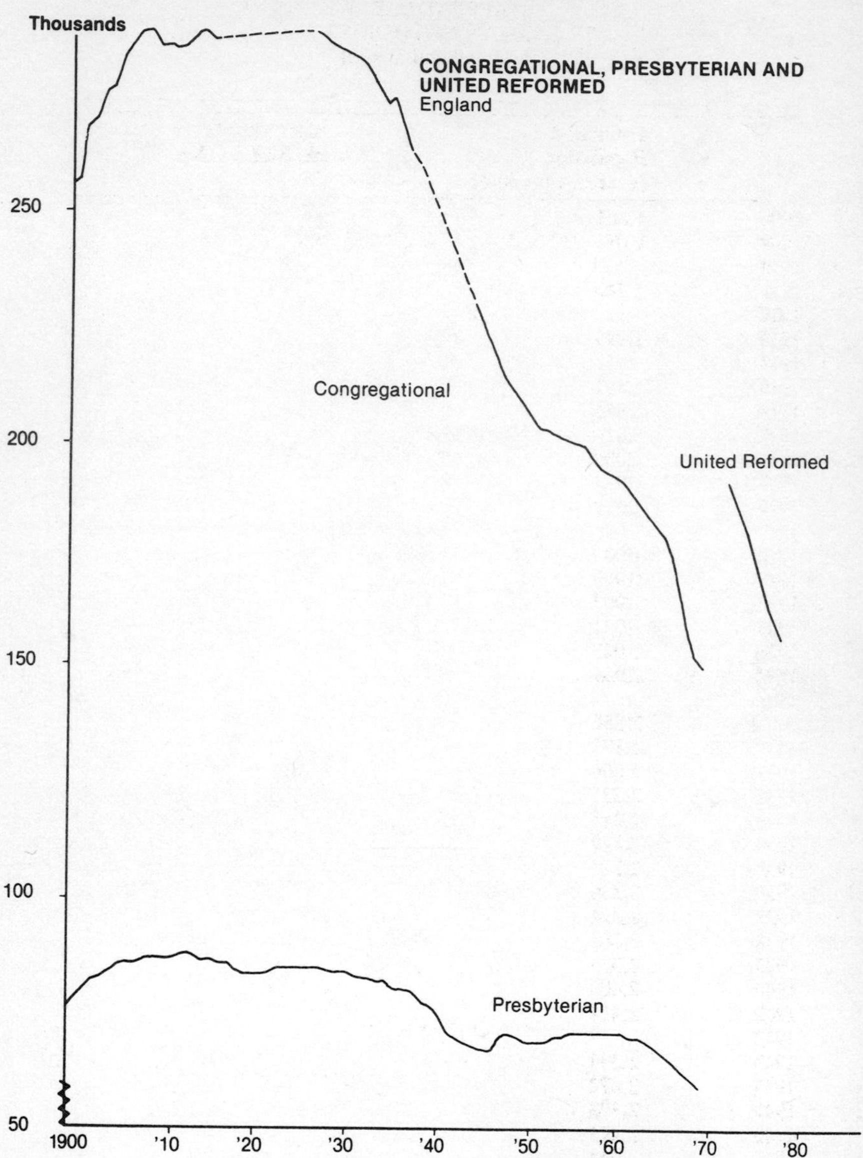
Thousands
CONGREGATIONAL, PRESBYTERIAN AND UNITED REFORMED
England
Congregational
United Reformed
Presbyterian
250
200
150
100
50
1900
'10
'20
'30
'40
'50
'60
'70
'80

APPENDIX E
ROMAN CATHOLICS
(England and Wales)

	Estimated Population (nearest thousand)	Mass attendance last Sun. in Oct.
1908	1,661	
1909	1,671	
1910		
1911	1,710	
1912		
1913	1,799	
1914		
1915	1,891	
1916	1,886	
1917	1,894	
1918	1,890	
1919	1,904	
1920	1,899	
1921	1,915	
1922	1,932	
1923	1,966	
1924	1,997	
1925	2,031	
1926	2,043	
1927	2,056	
1928		
1929	2,156	
1930	2,175	
1931	2,206	
1932	2,335	
1933	2,245	
1934	2,279	
1935	2,321	
1936	2,336	
1937	2,354	
1938	2,362	
1939	2,375	
1940	2,406	
1941	2,414	
1942		
1943	2,334	
1944	2,372	
1945	2,393	
1946	2,415	
1947	2,444	
1948	2,528	
1949	2,649	

	Estimated Population (nearest thousand)	Mass attendance last Sun. in Oct.
1950	2,754	
1951	2,809	
1952	2,838	
1953	2,878	
1954	2,939	
1955	3,032	
1956	3,170	
1957	3,292	
1958	3,343	
1959	3,422	
1960[1]	3,553	
1961[2]	3,803	
1962	3,905	2,093
1963	4,017	
1964	4,001	
1965	4,048	
1966	4,088	2,114
1967	4,144	2,092
1968	4,090	2,055
1969	4,085	1,988
1970	4,114	1,935
1971	4,071	1,900
1972	4,142	1,886
1973	4,177	1,832
1974	4,174	1,752
1975	4,182	1,791
1976	4,191	1,722
1977	4,190	1,699
1978	4,221	1,694

(1) Figures prior to 1960 are based on Bishops' estimates
(2) Figures after 1960 are based on parish returns to Catholic Education Council.

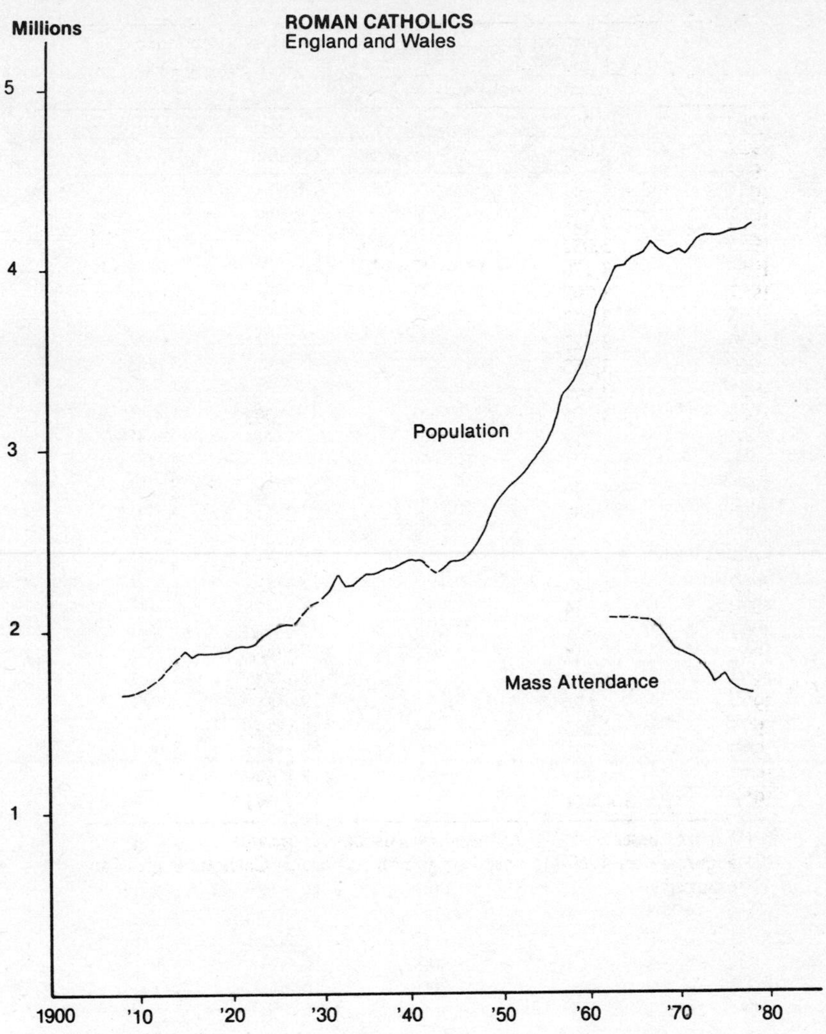
Millions
ROMAN CATHOLICS
England and Wales
5
4
3
2
1
Population
Mass Attendance
1900
'10
'20
'30
'40
'50
'60
'70
'80

APPENDIX F
OTHER CHURCHES (To nearest hundred)
(United Kingdom)

Year	Christ	Nazarenes	Moravians	Quakers	Adventists
1900	11,800			17,300	
1901	12,200		5,900	17,500	
1902	12,500		6,000		
1903	12,800		6,200	17,700	1,200
1904	13,000		6,200	17,800	1,400
1905	14,000		6,200	18,500	1,500
1906	14,300	100	6,300	18,700	1,700
1907	14,300		6,300	18,900	1,800
1908	14,500		6,500	19,000	1,700
1909	14,400		6,500	19,300	1,800
1910	14,800		6,500	19,500	1,900
1911	14,700		6,500	19,600	2,000
1912	14,800		6,500	19,800	2,400
1913	15,300		6,600		2,400
1914	15,200		6,600	19,900	2,700
1915	15,200	700	6,600	19,100	2,800
1916	15,200		6,100	19,200	2,900
1917	15,100		5,900	19,200	3,000
1918	16,400		5,600	19,100	3,300
1919	16,200		5,500	19,100	3,300
1920	16,000		5,300	19,000	3,500
1921	16,100		5,100	19,100	3,600
1922	16,300		5,000	19,000	3,700
1923	16,500		4,200	19,100	3,800
1924	16,400		4,100	19,000	4,100
1925	16,300		4,100	19,100	4,200
1926	16,300		4,000	19,100	4,400
1927	16,400		4,000	19,000	4,500
1928	16,600		4,000	19,100	4,500
1929	16,600		3,900	19,100	4,500
1930	16,600		3,800	19,100	4,800
1931	16,000		3,800	19,200	4,700
1932	16,100		3,800	19,100	4,900
1933	16,000		3,800	19,200	5,000
1934	15,500		3,700	19,300	5,200
1935	15,300		3,600	19,300	5,400
1936	15,800		3,700	19,300	5,500
1937	15,800		3,600	19,300	5,500
1938	15,500		3,600	19,400	5,900
1939	15,200		3,600	19,700	6,000
1940	14,900	1,000	3,600	19,800	5,900
1941	14,300		3,600	20,200	6,000
1942	13,500		3,500	20,300	6,100
1943	13,100		3,500	20,400	6,200

Year	Christ	Nazarenes	Moravians	Quakers	Adventists
1944	12,800		3,500	20,500	6,400
1945	12,100		3,500	20,500	6,400
1946	11,700		3,500	20,700	6,300
1947	10,600	1,000	3,400	20,700	6,200
1948	10,400		3,400	20,700	6,400
1949	10,000		3,400	20,800	6,500
1950	9,800	1,100	3,4000	20,800	6,700
1951	9,600	1,200	3,300	20,800	6,800
1952	9,500	1,300	3,300	21,000	6,900
1953	9,300	2,300	3,200	21,100	7,300
1954	8,900	1,200	3,300	21,200	7,500
1955	8,800	1,300	3,200	21,300	7,800
1956	8,700	2,000	3,300	21,500	8,100
1957	8,500	2,000	3,200	21,500	8,300
1958	8,200	2,000	3,100	21,600	8,700
1959	7,900	2,100	3,100	21,600	8,900
1960	7,800	2,100	3,100	21,200	9,300
1961	7,600	2,100	3,300	21,200	9,600
1962	7,500	2,000	3,300	21,200	9,900
1963	7,300	3,500	3,200	21,100	10,100
1964	6,800	3,500	3,000	21,100	10,300
1965	6,600	3,600	3,000	21,100	10,500
1966	6,400	3,600	3,000	21,100	10,900
1967	6,100	3,600	2,900	21,100	11,200
1968	5,600	3,600	2,900	20,900	11,700
1969	5,400	3,500	2,800	20,900	11,900
1970	5,100	3,500	2,700	20,800	12,100
1971	4,900	3,600	2,700	20,700	12,300
1972	4,600	3,600	2,800	20,600	12,400
1973	4,400	3,600	2,800	20,400	12,500
1974	4,200	3,600	2,700	20,300	12,500
1975	4,000	3,600	2,800	20,100	12,700
1976	3,900	3,600	2,800	19,800	12,800
1977	3,700	3,700	2,800	19,600	13,200
1978	3,600	3,700	2,700	19,200	13,600
1979	3,600	3,800	2,800	18,800[1]	14,000
1980		3,900			

(1) Covers England, Scotland and Wales

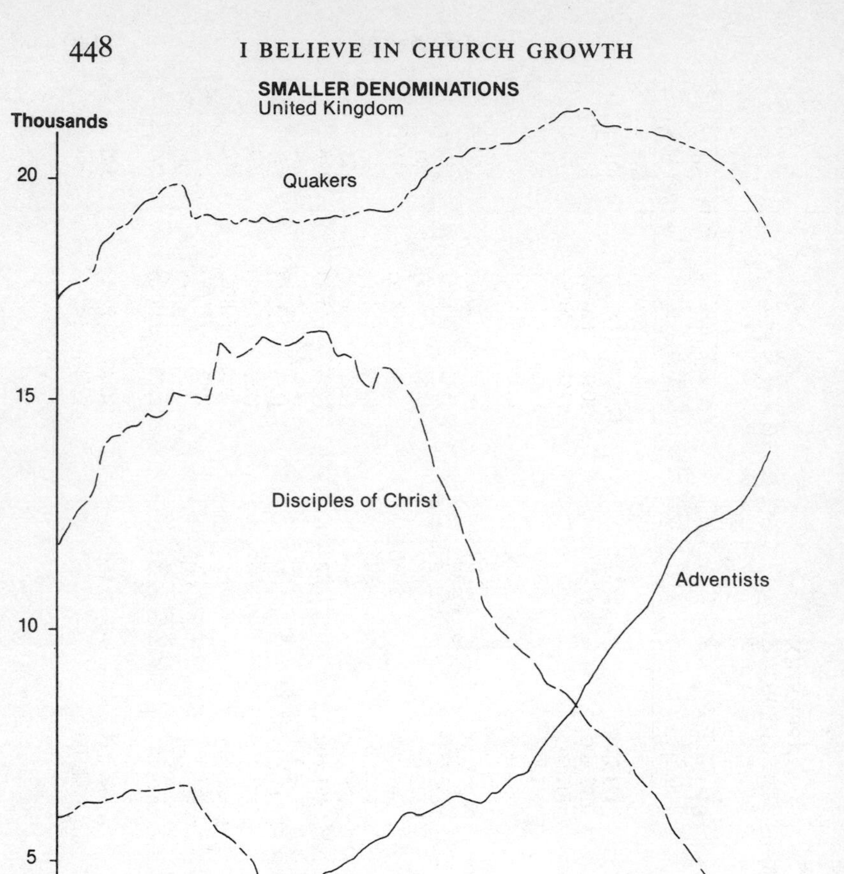
SMALLER DENOMINATIONS
United Kingdom
Thousands
20
15
10
5
Quakers
Disciples of Christ
Adventists
Nazarines
Moravians
1900
'10
'20
'30
'40
'50
'60
'70
'80

APPENDIX G
CHURCHES AND CHURCHGOING IN ENGLAND

County	Churches[1]	Population[2] – adult	Persons[1][5] per church	Adult[1][3] Attendance		Persons[2] per sq km
Avon	823	726,700	883	11%	(16%)	685
Bedfordshire	425	373,700	879	12%	(21%)	401
Berkshire	401	517,400	1,290	10%	(16%)	534
Buckinghamshire	559	401,000	717	12%	(20%)	279
Cambridgeshire	784	441,800	564	11%	(18%)	167
Channel Islands	129	105,000	814	12%	(26%)	
Cheshire	719	706,000	982	14%	(29%)	395
Cleveland	278	427,800	1,539	9%	(20%)	975
Cornwall & Isles of Scilly	856	332,700	389	13%	(15%)	117[4]
Cumbria	771	372,000	482	15%	(28%)	69
Derbyshire	854	698,000	817	8%	(13%)	341
Devon	1,283	762,300	594	12%	(18%)	141
Dorset	744	478,800	644	13%	(19%)	221
Durham	601	471,600	785	12%	(23%)	248
East Sussex	660	538,500	816	14%	(21%)	364
Essex	1,103	1,111,600	1,008	10%	(18%)	391
Gloucestershire	668	386,000	578	13%	(18%)	187
Greater London	3,350	5,561,900	1,660	9%	(18%)	4,381
Greater Manchester	1,477	2,057,300	1,393	10%	(21%)	2,070
Hampshire	1,140	1,131,600	993	9%	(16%)	385
Herefordshire & Worcestershire	856	474,100	554	11%	(17%)	156
Hertfordshire	634	734,600	1,159	10%	(17%)	580
Humberside	630	650,300	1,032	7%	(9%)	241

Isle of Man	136	48,100	354	15%	(22%)	
Isle of Wight	127	92,900	731	10%	(16%)	300
Kent	1,148	1,127,100	982	10%	(18%)	388
Lancashire	1,139	1,071,300	941	16%	(32%)	447
Leicestershire	816	646,000	792	9%	(14%)	326
Lincolnshire	1,076	417,000	387	13%	(19%)	90
Merseyside	785	1,198,600	1,527	14%	(35%)	2,370
Norfolk	1,272	536,500	422	10%	(15%)	127
Northamptonshire	574	393,300	685	11%	(18%)	218
Northumberland	379	228,100	602	11%	(19%)	58
N. Yorkshire	1,128	526,500	467	12%	(20%)	80
Nottinghamshire	752	755,500	1,005	8%	(11%)	450
Oxfordshire	668	423,000	633	10%	(16%)	207
Shropshire	599	284.100	474	10%	(17%)	105
Somerset	790	323,900	410	14%	(18%)	119
S. Yorkshire	755	1,008,900	1,336	7%	(12%)	836
Staffordshire	813	770,000	947	9%	(15%)	367
Suffolk	886	462,300	522	12%	(15%)	156
Surrey	639	790,200	1,237	12%	(19%)	593
Tyne and Wear	629	914,300	1,453	9%	(18%)	2,158
Warwickshire	480	359,700	749	12%	(16%)	237
W. Midlands	1,306	2,090,400	1,601	9%	(15%)	3,016
W. Sussex	462	511,800	1,108	12%	(17%)	319
W. Yorkshire	1,463	1,595,700	1,091	10%	(17%)	1,014
Wiltshire	702	377,200	537	12%	(17%)	148

(1) Nationwide Initiative on Evangelism Survey 1979
(2) 1978 National Census
(3) Percentage in brackets = Church Membership
(4) Population density figure excludes the Isles of Scilly
(5) This has been obtained by adult population/churches

APPENDIX H
SPIRITUAL GIFTS

From Romans 12.

Gift		HAVE	NOT SURE	HAVE NOT
1. Prophecy (inspired utterance of a word from God).	1.			
2. Service	2.			
3. Teaching.	3.			
4.. Exhortation (encouraging, stimulating faith)	4.			
5. Generosity (quickness to give or share)	5.			
6. Leadership.	6.			
7. Mercy (compassion, sympathy, showing kindness)	7.			

From I Cor. 12 (in addition to above)

Gift		HAVE	NOT SURE	HAVE NOT
8. Wisdom (particular insight or understanding)	8.			
9. Knowledge (ability to learn or study)	9.			
10. Faith (to do great or unusual things)	10.			
11. Healing.	11.			
12. Miracles.	12.			
13. Discerning of spirits (insight to know when God is speaking or at work and when not)	13.			
14. Tongues (ecstatic utterance in languages not learned).	14.			
15. Interpretation of tongues.	15.			
16. Apostles.	16.			
17. Helpers.	17.			
18. Administration (practical organising and doing)	18.			

From Ephesians 4 (in addition to above)

Gift		HAVE	NOT SURE	HAVE NOT
19. Evangelist	19.			
20. Pastor (caring for God's people)	20.			

From other New Testament passages

Gift		HAVE	NOT SURE	HAVE NOT
21. Celibacy (I Cor. 7.7.)	21.			
22. Voluntary poverty (I Cor. 13.3.)	22.			
23. Martyrdom (I Cor. 13.3.)	23.			
24. Hospitality (I Peter 4. 9–11.)	24.			
25. Missionary (Ephesians 3. 1–9.)	25.			

*The New Testament lists are in no sense meant to be 'complete' lists. God gives spiritual gifts as he wills for the fulfilment of His purpose and the up-building and ministry of his Church. Many other gifts (e.g. the gift of intercession in a special degree) might be added.

SPIRITUAL GIFTS DISCOVERY EXERCISE

Read the following points and mark yourself out of 5 for each. If you give yourself 5 it will be one of your very strong points. If you give yourself 0 or 1 it will be one of your very weak points. Fill how many you give yourself in the square with the number of the point on the next page.

1. I am good at listening.
2. I enjoy explaining things to others from the Bible..
3. I love preaching or talking about Jesus to a congregation or group.
4. I am often used to bring others to Christ.
5. I enjoy administrative work.
6. I feel a deep, caring love for those ill and a call to help them get well.
7. I am handy at most things and adaptable.
8. I am deeply concerned about the world and social affairs.
9. I am usually looked to for a lead.
10. I make helpful relationships with others easily.
11. Others are helped when I teach them things.
12. I love the study and work in preparing a message.
13. God has given me a great love for others and a longing to win them for him.
14. I can organise well, clearly and efficiently.
15. Others find my presence soothing and healing.
16. I like helping other people.
17. I am active in service in the community.
18. In a group I am often elected chairman or leader.
19. I can encourage others and help bear burdens.
20. I love study and finding the facts.
21. My sermons have been clearly blessed to others.
22. I find my life is full of opportunities to witness to Christ.
23. I love doing office work and do it thoroughly.
24. I have sometimes laid hands on the sick and they have been helped.
25. I am a practical type.
26. I am very aware of the needs of society today and feel called to do something about it.
27. When leading something I put a lot of preparation into it.
28. I really care about other people.
29. I have patience in helping others understand Christian things.
30. I feel a clear call to preach.
31. I love to talk to others about Jesus.
32. I am painstaking about details in organisation.
33. I spend time praying with and for sick people.
34. I spend much time helping others in practical ways.
35. I feel God is at work in the world today and I must work along with Him there.
36. I am good at delegating work to others in a team setting.

p.t.o.

1	10	19	28	A
2	11	20	29	B
3	12	21	30	C
4	13	22	31	D
5	14	23	32	E
6	15	24	33	F
7	16	25	34	G
8	17	26	35	H
9	18	27	36	I

Add up the totals along each line and place them in the end of the column.

If your highest total is in column	A your gift is	Pastoral
,, ,, ,, ,, ,, ,, ,,	B ,, ,, ,,	Teaching
,, ,, ,, ,, ,, ,, ,,	C ,, ,, ,,	Preaching
,, ,, ,, ,, ,, ,, ,,	D ,, ,, ,,	Evangelism
,, ,, ,, ,, ,, ,, ,,	E ,, ,, ,,	Administration
,, ,, ,, ,, ,, ,, ,,	F ,, ,, ,,	Healing
,, ,, ,, ,, ,, ,, ,,	G ,, ,, ,,	Practical help
,, ,, ,, ,, ,, ,, ,,	H ,, ,, ,,	Service to Society
,, ,, ,, ,, ,, ,, ,,	I ,, ,, ,,	Leadership

It is easy to mislead yourself and it may therefore be helpful to give a copy of this form to 4 of your closest friends and ask them to fill it in for you (i.e. changing each of the statements to 'he', 'he is' etc.) as honestly as possible. Don't show them your marks until after you have theirs.

This form can be rewritten to include other fields of gifts.

Bibliography

ABERCROMBIE, D. 'Paralanguage', *British Journal of Disorders of Communication*, Vol. 3, pp. 55–59. Reprinted in *Communication in Face to Face Interaction*, ed. John Laver and Sandy Hutcheson. London: Penguin Books, 1972.

ALLMAN, J-J von. *Vocabulary of the Bible*. London: Lutterworth, 1958.

ARGYLE and KENDON. *Communication in Face to Face Interaction*. London: Penguin Books, 1972.

BARCLAY, William. *Commentary on Colossians* (Revised Edition). Edinburgh: Saint Andrew Press, 1975.

BARRETT, C. K. *The Gospel According to St. John*. London: SPCK, 1960.

BAVINCK, J. H. *An Introduction to the Science of Missions* Philadelphia: The Presbyterian and Reformed Publishing Company, 1961.

BEASLEY-MURRAY, Paul. *Turning the Tide*. London: The Bible Society, 1981.

BITTLINGER Arnold. *Gifts and Graces*. London: Hodder and Stoughton, 1967.

——, *Gifts and Ministries*. London: Hodder and Stoughton, 1974.

BONINO, Jose Miguez. *Revolutionary Theology Comes of Age*. London: SPCK, 1975.

BRIDGE, Donald and PHYPERS, David. *Spiritual Gifts and the Church*. Leicester: Inter-Varsity Press, 1973.

BRIGHT, John. *The Kingdom of God*. New York: Abingdon, 1953.

BUCKLE, E. G. *Paroikia The House Alongside*. Diocese of Auckland, New Zealand, 1978.

CLEMMONS, William and HESTER, Harvey. *Growth Through Groups*. Nashville, Tenn.: Broadman.

CONGAR, Yves M. J. *Lay People in the Church*. London: Geoffrey Chapman, 1959.

COLEMAN, Lyman. *Serendipity*. Waco, Texas: Creative Resources, 1972.

COLEMAN, Robert E. *The Master Plan of Evangelism*. Westwood, N.J.: Revell, 1963.

CONN, Harvey M. ed. *Theological Perspectives on Church Growth*. Nutley, N.J.: Presbyterian and Reformed, 1976.

COOK, Harold R. 'Who Really Sent the Missionaries?' *Evangelical Missions Quarterly*, October 1975, pp. 233–239.

COSTAS, Orlando. *The Church and Its Mission*. Wheaton, Ill.: Tyndale House, 1974.

CULLMAN, Oscar. *The Early Church*. London: SCM, 1956.

CURRIE, R., GILBERT, A. and HORSLEY, L. *Churches and Churchgoers: Patterns of Church Growth in the British Isles Since 1700*. London: Oxford University Press, 1977.

CURRY, Mavis W. *Advancing the Smaller Church*. Grand Rapids, Mich.: Baker, 1968 (first printed 1957).

DAVIDSON, Leslie. *Sender and Sent*. Guildford and London: Lutterworth, 1969.

DAYTON, Edward R. *Tools For Time Management*. Grand Rapids, Mich.: Zondervan, 1974.

DOUGLAS, Tom. *Basic Groupwork*. London: Tavistock Publications, 1978.

DUBOSE, Francis M. *How Churches Grow In The Urban World*. Nashville, Tenn.: Broadman, 1978.

ENGEL, James F. and WILBERT NORTON, H. *What's Gone Wrong With The Harvest?* Grand Rapids, Mich.: Zondervan. 1975.

——, *How Can I Get Them to Listen*? Grand Rapids, Mich.: Zondervan, 1977.

GAY, John D. *The Geography of Religion in England*. London: Duckworth, 1971.

GETZ, Gene A. *Sharpening the Focus of the Church*. Chicago: Moody Press, 1974.

GIBBS, Eddie. *Urban Church Growth: Clues from South America and Britain*. Nottingham: Grove Books, 1977.

——, *Grow Through Groups*. Nottingham: Grove Books, 1979a.

——, *Body Building Exercises for the Local Church*. London: Falcon, 1979b.

GOLDINGAY, John. *History, Culture, Mission and the People of God in The Old Testament*. Evangelical Fellowship for Missionary Studies Bulletin No. 5, 1975.

GREEN, Michael. *Evangelism in the Early Church*. London: Hodder and Stoughton, 1970.

——, *Evangelism – I Believe in The Holy Spirit*. London: Hodder and Stoughton, 1974.

——, *Now and Then*. Leicester: Inter-Varsity Press, 1979.

GRIFFITHS, Michael. *Cinderella's Betrothal Gifts*. London: Overseas Missionary Fellowship, 1978.

——, *Shaking the Sleeping Beauty*. Leicester: Inter-Varsity Press, 1980.

HARPER, Michael. *Let My People Grow*. London: Hodder and Stoughton, 1977.

HARRIS, Jeffrey and HARVIS, Peter. *Counting to Some Purpose*. London: Methodist Home Missions Dept., 1979.

HESSELGRAVE, David J. *Communicating Christ Cross-Culturally*. Grand Rapids, Mich.: Zondervan, 1978.

HIEBERT, Paul G. *Cultural Anthropology*. Philadelphia: J. B. Lippincott Co., 1976.

HOUSTON, Tom. *Communicating The Good News In a Television Age*. London: The Bible Society, 1978.

HUNTER, George G. *The Contagious Congregation*. New York: Abingdon, 1979.

JEREMIAS, Joachim. *New Testament Theology*, Vol. 1, *The Proclamation of Jesus*. London: SCM, 1971.

KELLEY, Dean M. *Why Conservative Churches Are Growing*. New York: Harper and Row, 1972.

KIDNER, Derek. *Genesis*. Leicester: Inter-Varsity Press, 1967.

KLAPPERT, B. Article in *Dictionary of New Testament Theology*, Vol. II, pp. 372–389, *King and Kingdom*. Exeter: Paternoster Press, 1976.

KRAEMER, Hendrik. *A Theology of the Laity*. Guildford and London: Lutterworth, 1958.

KRAFT, Charles H. *Christianity in Culture*. Maryknoll, Orbis Books, 1979.

LADD, George Eldon. *The Gospel of the Kingdom*. Grand Rapids, Mich.: Eerdmans, 1959.

——, *A Theology of the New Testament*. Guildford and London: Lutterworth, 1974.

LALIVE, Christian D'Epinay. *Haven of the Masses*. Guildford and London: Lutterworth, 1969.

LILLEY, J. P. U. Article in *The New Bible Dictionary*, 'Justification'. London: Inter-Varsity Press, 1962.

LUM, Ada and SIEEMENS, Ruth. *Creative Bible Studies*. Bombay: Jyoti, 1973.

McGAVRAN, Donald A. *Bridges of God*. London: World Dominion, 1955.

——, *How Churches Grow*. New York: Friendship Press, 1959.

——, *Church Growth and Christian Mission*. Pasadena, Calif.: William Carey Library, 1965.

——, *Understanding Church Growth*. Grand Rapids, Mich.: Eerdmans, 1970.

McGAVRAN, Donald A. and ARN, Winfield C. *Ten Steps for Church Growth*. New York: Harper and Row, 1977.

McGAVRAN, Donald A. and HUNTER, George G. III. *Church Growth: Strategies That Work*. New York: Abingdon, 1980.

McQUILKIN, J. Robertson. *Measuring the Church Growth Movement* (originally entitled *How Biblical is the Church Growth Movement*?) Chicago: Moody Press, 1973, 74.

MENOUD, PH-H. *Article in Vocabulary of the Bible*, pp. 259–266, 'Ministry'. ed. J-J. von ALLMAN. Guildford and London: Lutterworth, 1958.

MEYER, Ben F. *The Aims of Jesus*. London: SCM. 1979.

MILLER, Keith. *The Taste of New Wine*. London: Word Books, 1965.

MURRAY, Iain. *The Puritan Hope*. Edinburgh: Banner of Truth, 1971.

NEILL, Bishop Stephen. *Call to Mission*. Berkeley, Calif.: Frontier, 1970.

NEWBIGIN, Lesslie. *The Open Secret*. London: SPCK, 1978.

NIDA, Eugene A. *God's Word in Man's Language*. New York: Harper and Row, 1952.

——, *Customs, Culture and Christianity*. London: Tyndale Press, 1954.

NIEBUHR, H. Richard. *Christ and Culture*. New York: Harber and Row, 1951.

NOLAN, Albert. *Jesus Before Christianity*. London: Darton, Longman and Todd, 1976.

O'CONNOR, Elizabeth. *Journey Inward, Journey Outward*. New York: Harper and Row, 1968.

OLSON, C. Gordon. 'What About People-Movement Conversion?' *Evangelical Missions Quarterly*, July 1979, pp. 133–142.

ORTIZ, Juan Carlos. *Disciple*. London: Marshall, Morgan and Scott, Ltd. Lakelard Books, 1976.

OSMASTON, Amiel. *Sharing the Life: Using Small Groups in the Church*. Nottingham: Grove Books.

PACKER, James I. *Knowing God*. London: Hodder and Stoughton, 1973.

PADILLA, C. Rene ed. *El Reino de Dios y America Latina*. Buenos Aires: Casa Bautista de Publicaciones, 1975.

PANNENBERG, Wolfhart. *Theology and The Kingdom of God*. Philadelphia: Westminster, 1975.

PERRY, Lloyd. *Getting the Church on Target*. Chicago: Moody Press, 1977.

PETERS, George W. *A Biblical Theology of Missions*. Chicago: Moody Press, 1972.

PIPPERT, Rebecca Manley. *Out of the Saltshaker*. Leicester: Inter-Varsity Press, 1980.

REID, Gavin. *Good News to Share*. London: Falcon, 1979.

RICHARDSON, Don. *The Peace Child*. Glendale, Calif.: Regal Books.

RICE, A. K. *Learning for Leadership*. London: Tavistock Publications, 1965.

ROOT, John. *Encountering West Indian Pentecostalism*: Nottingham: Grove, 1979.

ROBERTS, Ted. *Partners and Ministers*. London: Falcon, 1972.

ROBERTSON and PLUMMER. *International Critical Commentary – 1 Corinthians* Edinburgh: T. and T. Clark, 1911.

ROWLEY, H. H. *The Biblical Doctrine of Election*. Guildford: Lutterworth, 1950.

SCHALLER, Lyle E. *The Pastor and the People*. Nashville, Tenn.: Abingdon, 1973.

——, *Parish Planning*. Nashville, Tenn.: Abingdon, 1978a.

——, *Assimilating New Members*. Nashville, Tenn.: Abingdon, 1978b.

SCHILLEBEECKX, Edward. *The Mission of the Church*. London: Sheed and Ward, 1973.

SCHULLER, Robert H. *Your Church Has Real Possibilities*. Glensdale, Calif.: Regal, 1974.

SHENK, Wilbert R. ed. *The Challenge of Church Growth*. Elkhart, Indiana: Institute of Mennonite Studies, Herald Press, 1973.

SHEPPARD, David. *Built as a City*. London: Hodder and Stoughton, 1974.

SIMON, Ulrich E. *A Theology of Salvation*. London: SCM Press, 1953.

SMAIL, Tom. *Reflected Glory*. London: Hodder and Stoughton, 1975.

SNYDER, Howard A. *The Problem of Wineskins*. Downes Grove, Ill.: Inter-Varsity Press, 1975.

——, *The Community of the King*. Downes Grove, Ill.: Inter-Varsity Press, 1977.

STAUFFER, Ethelbert. *New Testament Theology*. London: SCM Press, 1975.

STOTT, J. R. W. *Baptism and Fullness*. Leicester: Inter-Varsity Press, 1975a.

——, *Christian Mission in the Modern World*. London: Falcon, 1975b.

TIPPETT, Alan R. *Church Growth and the Word of God*. Grand Rapids, Mich.: Eerdmans, 1970.

TOZER, A. W. *The Root of the Righteous*. Harrisburg, Pa.: Christian Publications, Inc., 1955.

TRUDINGER, Ron. *Cells for Life*. Basingstoke: Olive Tree Publications, 1979.

TRUEBLOOD, Elton. *The Company of the Committed*. New York: Harper and Row, 1961.

Von RAD, Gerhard. *Genesis*. London: SCM Press, 1961.

WAGNER C. Peter. *Frontiers in Missionary Strategy* Chicago: Moody Press, 1971.
——, *Look Out The Pentecostals Are Coming*. London and Eastbourne: Coverdale, 1973.
——, *Your Church Can Grow*. Glendale, Calif.: Regal Books, 1976.
——, 'How Ethical Is The Homogeneous Principle?' *Occasional Bulletin*, Vol. 2, No. 1. Fuller Seminary, 1978.
——, *Your Church Can Be Healthy*. Nashville: Abingdon, 1979a.
——, *Your Spiritual Gifts Can Help Your Church Grow*. Glendale, Calif.: Regal Books, 1979b.
——, *Our Kind of People*. Atlanta: John Knox Press, 1979c.
WARREN, Max. *I Believe In The Great Commission*. London: Hodder and Stoughton, 1979.
WASDELL, David. *Let My People Grow*. A workpaper presented to the General Synod of the Church of England, November 1974.
——, *Divide and Conquer*. AGM of the Archbishop's Council on Evangelism, November 1975.
——, *Long Range Planning and the Church*. Urban Church Project, 1979.
WAYMORE, Bob and WAGNER, C. Peter. *The Global Church Growth Bulletin*. Santa Clara, Calif, 1980.
WINTER, Ralph D. *The Decade Past and the Decade To Come: Seeing The Task Graphically*. Evangelical Missions Quarterly, Jan. 1974.
——, *The Two Structures of God's Redemptive Mission*. Missiology, January 1974.
YOHN, Rick. *Discover Your Spiritual Gift and Use It*. Wheaton, Ill., Tyndale, 1974.

Reports and Periodicals

BRITISH COUNCIL OF CHURCHES. *Stand Up and Be Counted*. Report of the Committee on Mission, 1972.
EVANGELICAL MISSIONS QUARTERLY. January 1974.
H.M.S.O. *Annual Abstract of Statistics*. 1979 Edition.
INFORMATION SERVICE, Lausanne Committee for World Evangelization, June 1979, May 1980.

INTERNATIONAL REVIEW OF MISSIONS, October 1965. July 1968.

NATIONWIDE INITIATIVE IN EVANGELISM. *Prespect for the Eighties* – a 1979 Census of Churches in England.

PASADENA CONSULTATION – *Homogeneous Unit*. Lausanne Committee for World Evangelization.

SIGNS OF HOPE. London; the Baptist Union, 1979.

THE WILLOWBANK REPORT. *Gospel and Culture*. Sponsored by the Lausanne Theology and Education Group, 6–13 June, 1978.